THE GREAT DIVIDE

Also by Alex Fynn (with Lynton Guest)

The Secret Life of Football
Heroes and Villains
Out of Time
For Love or Money

Dream On (with H. Davidson)

Cantona on Cantona (with Eric Cantona)

THE GREAT DIVIDE

The inside story of the 1999–2000 season at
Arsenal and Tottenham Hotspur

Alex Fynn and Olivia Blair

André Deutsch

Dedication

To my father, who encouraged me to play
up in the first place.

Olivia Blair

To George Robb, who performed the same
task for me.

Alex Fynn

First published in Great Britain in 2000
by André Deutsch Ltd
76 Dean Street
London W1V 5HA
www.vci.co.uk

10 9 8 7 6 5 4 3 2 1

A catalogue record for this book is available from the British Library

ISBN 0 233 99786 5

Jacket Design Slatter Anderson
All photographs © NI Syndication

Typeset by Derek Doyle & Associates, Liverpool
Printed and bound in the Great Britain by
Mackays of Chatham

ACKNOWLEDGEMENTS

It will be apparent that this book could not have been produced without the help of many people, prominent amongst them the key personalities who reoccur throughout the pages. So a huge debt of gratitude is owed to Messrs Dein, Wenger, Graham and Pleat, and of course the players. Among the people directly quoted in this book special mention must be made of Danny Fiszman, Liam Brady, John Sedgwick, Daniel Sugar, Douglas Alexiou, Peter Barnes, Peter Suddaby and Les Reed for their invaluable contributions. The consideration of the press officers – John Fennelly, Jay Bigwood and Jennifer Warner at Tottenham, and Amanda Docherty, Dan Tolhurst and Angela Taylor at Arsenal – and also the match day assistance of Jim Skinner and Gerry Warwick at Tottenham, was especially important.

Many representatives of the media are deliberately kept at arm's length by the authorities yet they have much to contribute. It is our good fortune that we were the recipients of friendly and expert advice from Philippe Auclair, Patrick Barclay, Denis Campbell, Malcolm Folley, Norman Fox, Simon Kuper, David Lacey, the irrepressible Amy Lawrence, Callum Murray, Ed Newman, Gary O'Reilly, Myles Palmer, Bill Pierce, Xavier Rivoire, Dr Robert, Adam Smith, Kevin McCarra, John Sadler, Steve Stammers, Martin Thorpe and Brian Woolnough.

Alex Phillips, Bernie Kingsley, Kevin Witcher and Mark Whitford read and suggested significant improvements to the manuscript. Philip Cornwall, Geoff Dobson, Liam Doyle, Mel Goldberg, John Simmons, John Sinnott, Gerrard Tyrrell and Greville Waterman performed a similar task on a selected basis. The Deloitte & Touche Football Industry Team, and Interbrand, Newell and Sorrell, provided key background information, while Stephanie Noble and Marci Rigg-Samuel expedited matters when the need arose. We are very grateful to all them.

Fans come in many forms, and most are worth listening to. So in addition to those quoted in the book we would like to give a second thank you to Steven Greenblatt, Morris Keston, John Harris, Danny Peters, Mark Perryman and Matt Tench for the insights provided on the object of their affections. Similarly, the *Gooner, Highbury High, Cock-a-Doodle-Doo* (CaDD), *One Flew Over Seaman's Head*, and *My Eyes Have Seen the Glory*, and the web sites *www.arsenal-world.net*, anr.uk.com and the Spurs Interactive site.

Friends and colleagues who gave vital support include Jason Tomas, David and Paul Stern, Jane Duke, Simon and Emmy Jones, Peter Suchet, Chris Howman, Pat Barker, David Forrester, Cliff Francis, Edward Freeman and Stuart Mutler. The book would certainly have been a taller order without the common love and rare friendship provided by Hazel Shaw, the invaluable support network afforded by Angela Hames and the thoughtfulness of the staff at Noah's Ark nursery, who altered the fixture list when the going got tough. Special thanks go to Brian, for braving the inclement weather, and to Ruby, a cradle-to-grave affair of a different kind.

Over at *The Times*, Keith Blackmore, Andy Moger, Dominic Young and especially Richard Bonfield were helpful and generous with regard to the use of the photographs, while Richard Lewis, Rob Bagchi, David Luxton, Carwyn Pipe, Matt Mankelow and Chris Bradshaw at John Gaustad's Sportspages performed over and above the call of duty, as did Rhoda and Danielle Fynn over the last year.

Lastly thanks are due to the André Deutsch personnel: Tim Forrester and Alasdair Ogilvie for their backing, and Nicky Paris and Kerrin Edwards for their considerate and skilful editing.

CONTENTS

Preface		ix
Prologue	Mind The Gap	1
Chapter One	Money! That's What I Want	15
Chapter Two	The Way It Is	45
Chapter Three	After The Lord Mayor's Show	70
Chapter Four	Give Me Joy, Don't Give Me Pain	89
Chapter Five	The Man In Black	129
Chapter Six	Le Technician Alsacien	165
Chapter Seven	The Great Divide	206
Chapter Eight	Believe In Me	242
Chapter Nine	The Bitter Sweet Years	281
Chapter Ten	Show Me The Money	312
Chapter Eleven	The Way We Are	337
Postscript	The Best Is Yet To Come?	370

PREFACE

Before *Heroes and Villains*, which covered the 1990–91 season at Arsenal and Tottenham, was written, the author, though he has absolutely no recollection, apparently told a number of fans that he thought Arsenal would win the League and Tottenham the FA Cup. No such clairvoyance was behind this book. Quite the opposite, in fact, as although it was felt Arsenal and Tottenham would do well in the Champions' League and the UEFA Cup respectively in 1999–2000, that would have been a bonus. The main point of the exercise was to use the compare-and-contrast formula of *Heroes and Villains* but to endeavour to take it to another level.

So this is not a match by match account of the 1999–2000 season. Rather, by capitalizing on the privileged access to players, directors and fans, it is an odyssey that uses the chronology of the season to examine the personalities, policies and events that shape the life of these two great rivals. And inevitably, as neither club plays in a vacuum, there have been digressions into the wider world of the Premier League, European football and of course television, linked by the all-pervasive common denominator of money.

The temptation to be hindsight experts has been resisted, so sometimes events have overtaken us, leaving us looking mistaken or occasionally prescient. The book should therefore be viewed as an unfolding chronicle of how two great institutions fared during yet another momentous season, and hopefully shed some light on the way in which each, in its own way, attempts to realize its goals.

Alex Fynn and Olivia Blair   June 2000

MIND THE GAP

There are just five minutes left on the clock when the referee blows for a free-kick. It's about five yards inside the opposition half and roughly the same distance in from the touchline, not exactly what you might call a threatening position, certainly nothing worth altering the script for. The right-back's made a probing run and he's been fouled, simple as that. Happens all the time. His side are winning anyway, so best to run the ball down the line and waste a bit of time holding it up by the corner flag.

Instead, the ball is given a little dink twenty-five yards or so upfield towards a team-mate who's jostling for space on the edge of the box, trying to shake off the unwelcome attentions of the centre-back breathing down his neck. Clearly, there's not much on for the forward. He's got options, but with his back to goal, they're hardly clear-cut scoring chances. He could, perhaps, turn on the proverbial sixpence, swing a right boot in the general direction of the goal and hope to win at least a corner from a deflection off an opposition defender's backside. He could shift the ball to his left into the path of a (hopefully) onrushing colleague. Or he could play it safe and simple by passing the ball back towards his supporting cast in midfield.

Wrong. On all three counts, just like the 36,019 fans present in the ground that night, none of whom could possibly have predicted what was to happen in the few seconds between the ball leaving the player in question's foot and it hitting the back of the net. Which was that, with a nugget of skill that in football parlance would be described as 'right out of the top drawer', the forward watched the ball bounce once, controlled it on his chest before it bounced again and, quicker than you could say 'See you', flicked it over the defender's head, turned and walloped it right-footed on the half-volley between the goalkeeper and his left-hand post. Bingo. Eighty-five minutes gone. 3–1. Game over.

Quite how such a quality goal failed even to make the top ten goals of season 1998–99 will remain a mystery. Perhaps those 'experts' who judge these things took pity on the then nineteen-year-old defender who was left rooted to the spot by the speed of thought and touch of the scorer. Or perhaps – and this is surely the more likely reason – they had simply become accustomed to the scorer's skill, been spoilt by the apparent ease and regularity at which he pulled off the unexpected. He'd done it the previous week, for heaven's sake, outrageously back-heeling the ball into the goal and coaxing even the opposition fans out of their seats to applaud. 'He's done it again,' screamed the commentator, as if to back up the theory.

The goal scored by Paul Gascoigne for England against Scotland at Wembley during Euro 96 is one that fans will always remember: how Gazza cheekily lobbed the ball over Colin Hendry and dispatched it emphatically past Andy Goram. It's an ironic comparison, given that this later goal was scored at White Hart Lane, the ground where Gazza 'matured' into one of Europe's best, and in front of a set of fans used to watching players with the seemingly God-given ability to transform football into an art form. The list of Tottenham players with enough skill and audacity to have scored that goal stretches back over the years: among them David Ginola, Gazza, Chris Waddle, Glenn Hoddle, Alan Gilzean, Jimmy Greaves and Alfie Conn, not to mention any member of the 1961 Double-winning side.

But there was something inimitable about this goal ... and that is, that it was scored by a player who was not wearing lilywhite, or blue and white, or purple and blue or yellow and blue (or any of the other colour combinations that have masqueraded as a Tottenham strip in the recent past). In fact, it was not even scored by a Tottenham player. It was scored by someone wearing red and white, an Arsenal man, namely the Nigerian Nwankwo Kanu, then Arsenal's newest recruit to a squad containing several stars – among them Dennis Bergkamp and Marc Overmars – who could have scored a goal of that quality.

It was proof that things are not what they used to be in north London, that the footballing tables have turned, that Tottenham are no longer the entertainers they once were, and that Arsenal are anything but the dour, dogged, defensive diggers-in whose 'boring, boring' tag has been one of the most enduring labels of the last twenty years. Until now, that is.

We know that football is not the game it once was, but some things never change. Do they? It was always one of football's unwritten rules that Tottenham would play with style and flair, but that they perennially lacked the stomach for a fight. Lily-livered, if you like. For Arsenal, read the opposite. Never pretty, but always pretty effective. It's a legacy that stretches back to the first meeting between the two sides when the story goes that Arsenal turned up late, scored early against an adventurous, attacking Tottenham side and battened down the hatches for the rest of the match before losing 2–1. And that's the way it's always been (except that Tottenham have not always won).

That set the scene for almost a century of rivalry, although things got particularly bad for those of a red and white persuasion when the Tottenham side of the 1960s, managed by Bill Nicholson and captained by Danny Blanchflower, carried all before them, along the way becoming the first British side to win a European trophy. As far as the media were concerned, that Tottenham side was the bee's knees. They positively drooled over the men from White Hart Lane who could not put a boot wrong, which was particularly irksome to the Arsenal fans considering their side had established itself as arguably the most famous club side in the world in winning five Championships in the 1930s.

But it was the manner in which Tottenham accomplished their achievements that won them so many plaudits. Tottenham played with style and a swagger that was to define their character over the years to come. In stark contrast their north London neighbours received grudging praise when they re-established themselves as the kingpins in north London with their own Double-winning exploits in 1971. Why? Because while Tottenham played with panache, Arsenal were defiant and functional, their success the consequence of diligence, consistency and team spirit, qualities which were never going to stand comparison with Tottenham's more exhilarating brand of football. 'We played as we wanted to play, didn't bother about the other team,' was how Dave Mackay explained the Tottenham philosophy. 'We wanted to entertain and if we won but hadn't played particularly well, if you saw Bill Nic afterwards you'd have thought we'd lost because he was so disappointed in the way that we'd played.' And Arsenal? Well, according to Charlie George, the one Arsenal player in that 1971 side who was deemed skilful enough to have graced White Hart Lane: 'We had a great rapport – all for one and one for all.'

The post-war records of Tottenham and Arsenal set in stone the personalities of the two rivals: Arsenal were expected to win while Tottenham were expected to entertain. The two teams have carried those tags around with them over the years: in football, reputation tends to categorize you, however deserved it may or may not be. Thus Watford will always be a 'long-ball' side; Leeds will forever be 'cynical', while mention is continuously made of the West Ham 'academy' because of one-time contemporaries like Malcolm Allison, John Bond, Noel Cantwell and Frank O'Farrell, who graduated to top managerial posts thirty years ago.

Given those comparative images, it's easy to understand why Arsenal fans still feel aggrieved that their club was not afforded the respect their accomplishments warranted – and why Tottenham fans are now seething that Arsenal appear to have turned the tables and assumed their mantle as the style side of north London. But the character change had been on the cards for some time. You can probably trace the start of the metamorphosis back to July 1995 when Arsenal splashed out £7.5 million in order to bring Dutch striker Dennis Bergkamp to Highbury, at a time when then Tottenham manager Gerry Francis was still shopping for 'bargains' yet shelled out a total of £8.5 million on the likes of Ruel Fox and Chris Armstrong. It was all the more galling for Tottenham fans that the young Bergkamp's idol was Glenn Hoddle. As far as they were concerned there was no question about it: Bergkamp was a Tottenham kind-of-a-player, and he had gone to Arsenal. It was a defining moment.

If anyone doubted it, they had only to listen to Tottenham chairman Alan Sugar sounding off in the *Sun* about the Bergkamp transfer. 'Arsenal have taken an almighty risk,' Sugar said. 'There's no way he is going to have the same impact as [Jürgen] Klinsmann. If Bergkamp thinks he is going to set the world alight he can forget it. There is no way it is going to happen. Arsenal got him because they needed a bit of cosmetic marketing.'

'I don't think Tottenham could ever sign a superstar like a Klinsmann or a Bergkamp again,' Sugar had bullishly predicted. 'These guys are floaters. They'll go anywhere, play for anyone who pays them the most . . . If Bergkamp doesn't start popping them in . . . he will be under immediate pressure. As the season progresses and the fog, ice, and cold arrive, his approach could change – especially when someone gives him a good kicking, an elbow in the ribs or a whack in the earhole. I'm shocked how much Arsenal have spent. I even think it's somewhat irresponsible. It will be interesting to see whether their new manager Bruce Rioch has the qualities and capabilities of George Graham. That must be a concern for the club.'

Fast forward three-and-a-half years to the night of 5 May 1999 when it would have been no surprise to have seen someone trying to stuff those ill-advised words down Alan Sugar's throat. Two slide-rule passes by Bergkamp to set up Nicolas Anelka and Emmanuel Petit, and that wonder-goal by Kanu, had given Arsenal a comprehensive 3–1 victory in the north London derby at White Hart Lane. The scoreline had been flattering to Tottenham thanks to a Darren Anderton free-kick which had somehow squirmed under David Seaman's dive just before half-time, but frankly, it failed to tell the whole story. It was the manner in which the Gunners achieved their victory that emphasized the gulf in class between the two sides. Arsenal didn't just beat their rivals; they thrashed them. They beat them at what used to be Tottenham's own game, with a display of incisive, exhilarating, counter-attacking football, the like of which had been conspicuous by its absence at White Hart Lane since the days when David Pleat's five-man midfield, including Hoddle, Waddle and Ossie Ardiles, habitually laid goals on a plate for Clive Allen.

Yet the fact is that Arsenal have been the better side in an overwhelming number of the north London derbies in recent memory.

No wonder, then, that Arsenal fans will tell you this victory had been coming for a while. No wonder it rankled with them that their side had failed to exit enemy territory with three points to show for their superiority on all but one occasion in a decade prior to this match (in August 1993, when a solitary goal from Ian Wright separated the teams). No wonder, then, that among the emotions of the visiting fans was relief, first when Kanu's goal hit the back of the net, then when the final whistle blew. Arsenal fan Alan Birch summed it up: 'Kanu's goal was sheer, unadulterated bliss. What was so great about it was that it was a moment of skill detached from any perspective, a beautiful thing, and then when you give it its layers it becomes something almost surreal. First, we had to win to keep our title hopes alive [with only two further games after the trip to White Hart Lane anything less than a victory could have handed the title to Manchester United, who had a game in hand over Arsenal]. Then it was the derby. And we hadn't won at White Hart Lane for ages, yet under George Graham we had won there loads, and that was so frustrating. It was like a key moment when you could say: "That's where we are, up here, and that's where Tottenham are, down there." '

Mind the gap. Arsenal were still in contention to retain the Championship they had won the previous season, while Tottenham were simply playing for pride, for the thousands of pounds per place that would come with the Premiership's end-of-season pay-out, and for the parochial pleasure of knowing that if they helped Manchester United win the title they would finish the season with one more piece of silverware (the Worthington Cup) in their trophy cabinet than Arsenal. But appearances can be deceptive, as Arsène Wenger emphasized in his pre-match press conference when he put Tottenham firmly in their place. 'They've done well in the Worthington Cup,' the Arsenal manager admitted, 'but for us the Championship is the most important thing and that's where we have to show them we are the better side.' That aside, Wenger was relaxed enough to joke about the rivalry. 'No, really?' he asked, feigning surprise on being told that Tottenham really would prefer it if Arsenal didn't reclaim the title. However, underpinning his comments, and those of his Tottenham counterpart George Graham, was the reality that this was a derby game and therefore unpredictable to say the least. Frankly, the last thing Arsenal needed at this late stage of the season was to meet their greatest rivals on their own ground with their former manager in charge.

No one connected with Arsenal could have failed to be aware of the presence of Graham looming large between the Gunners and the Championship finishing line, like a giant centre-half towering in front of a seemingly open goal. As the title race neared its climax, it became obvious this particular derby was to take on an even greater significance than usual.

The Tottenham fans had clearly taken great heart from their team's 0–0 draw at Highbury back in November. Perhaps, however, the action on the pitch that day had been overshadowed by events off it – it was Graham's first return to Highbury with Tottenham – and that masked the reality that Arsenal had been the better side but had failed to make their supremacy count. Still, you could hardly blame the Tottenham fans for having dreamt that this was to be the night when they would deal a huge body-blow to their rival's title aspirations. After all, they would rather see Teddy Sheringham – once a White Hart Lane hero – win a Championship medal with Manchester United than see the title go to Highbury for the second season in succession; even if it did mean revising the words to north London's favourite chant of the season: 'Ooh Teddy Teddy, went to Man United and he won f*** all'. (As well as reverberating regularly around White Hart Lane, the chant was belted out of various pubs in the Islington area with gusto as Arsenal fans celebrated winning the Double and putting one over on the former Tottenham star.)

In the end the form book, usually redundant on derby days, told. Aside from the opening five minutes, when Ginola appeared to be in the mood to torment, Arsenal dominated the first half to such a degree that the Tottenham supporters were reduced to taunting the vociferous Arsenal fans with the news of Dwight Yorke's opening goal for Manchester United at Anfield. Lee Dixon, aided by Ray Parlour, continued to hold sway over his old adversary, David Ginola. Tim Sherwood, described by Graham as 'a winner', was doing anything but win the midfield battles with Emmanuel Petit and Patrick Vieira, while his midfield partner Steffen Freund, whose demeanour had been likened to 'a Dobermann pinscher patrolling in front of his back four', seemed to have lost his bark as well as his bite. And to round off Tottenham's inadequacies, Nicolas Anelka's movement was bemusing the usually immovable Sol Campbell and his sidekick, Luke Young.

So Kanu's goal, swiftly followed by the final whistle, was blessed relief for the Arsenal fans, many of whom had spent the evening listening to the radio for news of events 200 miles north, and who were to raise the biggest cheer of the night three minutes later when news of Paul Ince's equalizer at Anfield filtered through the airwaves. Manchester United's failure to take three points off Liverpool propelled Arsenal to the top of the table with a three-point lead, but they had still played one game more than their northern rivals. One Arsenal fan who was watching the game on the big screen at Highbury summed up the mood. 'We were all getting nervous. It was really in the balance because Tottenham were putting us under pressure and I found myself thinking that it would be a travesty of justice if they scored, and that we were going to regret not converting our chances. But then Kanu scored – we knew it was going in and soon as he hit it, he belted it so hard. Until recently, we would never have expected a goal like that from an Arsenal player.'

You do now. Nothing was going to spoil the rejoicing for the Arsenal fans, although the media, somewhat predictably, focused on the antics of Nigel Winterburn, whose excessive celebrations in front of his side's dug-out could easily have been interpreted as taunting the home crowd. Winterburn's behaviour was bound to attract controversy, and he was reported by the fourth official Graham Poll for 'inciting behaviour'. 'It is safe to say I was very happy and when there are opposition fans on four sides of the ground, the safest place to celebrate is in front of your own bench,' was Winterburn's explanation. It would have done little, however, to appease the Tottenham fans. There has never been any love lost between them and the Arsenal defender, ever since he publicized his anti-Tottenham feelings from the top of Islington Town Hall steps during one of many celebratory occasions. Moreover, he is the kind of combative left-back that Tottenham have lacked for so long. When he was sent off during their 1996 New Year derby match at White Hart Lane, they said it couldn't have happened to a nicer chap. Or words to that effect.

Vieira also had to be restrained by his team-mates as he went down the tunnel, furious that the only outcome of a tackle on him from behind by Freund, that was compounded by Sherwood trampling all over him, had been a yellow card for dissent for Petit. But the fact that Tottenham had had to resort to huffing and puffing and trying to knock Arsenal down said it all: the Gunners had ripped to shreds whatever carefully laid defensive plans George Graham had made, and had rubbed salt in Tottenham wounds by winning back the initiative in the title race.

Graham knew it, although he refused to be drawn afterwards on the destination of the Championship. 'I would rather talk about my own team,' he said. 'I am totally focused on getting it right here, and that's going to be hard work. The teams at the top are a long way ahead of the rest of us. There is a lot of hard work to be done and I anticipate a lot of changes.' You could almost hear the Tottenham fans muttering something about a glimpse of the bleeding obvious as they beat a hasty retreat down Tottenham High Road, trying to drown out the all-too familiar chant of 'We beat the Scum 3–1'. You could hardly blame the Arsenal fans for rubbing it in for they had been forced to tolerate chants of 'Yid Army' from their counterparts as the tension rose prior to the game. Par for the course, but it never ceases to raise the hackles.

Besides, as former Gunner Paul Merson once said, this is 'the fans' game'. In football lingo that means of course it's a big game for the players, but in the modern game when big games come thick and fast, every game is a cup final, the next game is the most important blah blah blah, there is less riding on derby games than for the fans, for whom derby day defeat can bring on a deep depression. Back in the sanctuary of the Arsenal dressing room, Martin Keown summed up the mood. 'There was a lot of euphoria in our dressing room,' said the Arsenal defender, 'but part of that was due to the fact that we had beaten Tottenham and part was a feeling of "Can you imagine what it would have been like if we had lost?" It was a good night for us, but only that.'

And therein lies the rub. While for most of the Tottenham following, beating the Arsenal would have been the highlight of the season, Arsenal were looking beyond parochial pride at a far bigger picture: one that encompassed not only the Championship but the

Champions' League the following season, and the season after that, and the season after that as well. Sure, if they could teach Tottenham a lesson or two along the way, then so much the better, but that is all it was: one step along the way rather than the be-all-and-end-all.

The humbling reality for Tottenham is that Arsenal no longer even compare themselves to their near-neighbours from what each other terms 'the wrong end of the Seven Sisters Road'. And this is no new phenomenon. Four years ago, at the time when Arsenal were negotiating the signing of David Platt from Sampdoria, it was suggested to their vice-chairman David Dein that the likes of Sampdoria were now the benchmark for his cosmopolitan side. Dein looked surprised. 'Not Sampdoria,' he corrected, 'but Milan and Madrid' – and this at a time when Sampdoria were realistic Serie A challengers with a side featuring the talents of Attilio Lombardo and Roberto Mancini and a manager with the pedigree of Sven Goran Eriksson.

Dein, of course, is one of the architects of the revamped Champions' League and has long been an advocate of reducing domestic fixtures in favour of more European games. His primary objective for 1998–9 was for his club to secure guaranteed entry to the first group stage of the Champions' League with the knowledge that, were they to qualify for the second group stage, Arsenal's share of the pot would rise to at least £15 million. Not a bad little earner and one that would help set the strategy for future transfer market activity. No wonder Dein could afford to smile when asked, on the final Sunday of the season when Arsenal were still in with a realistic chance of retaining their title – while they had crucially lost to Leeds, Manchester United had overtaken them and went into the final game one point clear at the top of the table – whether he could enjoy the day whatever the outcome. 'Of course,' he replied. For Arsenal the Championship these days is a means to an end as well as an end in itself.

Arsenal, like Manchester United and Chelsea, are now spending for the future, spending to strengthen a squad that is already among the major forces in European football. Arsenal had the foresight to spend big at a time when £7.5 million for Bergkamp and £4.5 million for Marc Overmars seemed a small fortune; both signings look like comparative bargains when you consider how much both are now worth. As for the £500,000 they paid for Nicolas Anelka (and even that was a sop to Paris St Germain, who had failed to renew his contract) . . . well, that could work out as one of the best, albeit one of the most protracted, pieces of business in the history of the English game.

The likes of Tottenham, meanwhile, were simply spending to catch up with the rest of the also-rans, to prevent the gap from gaping wider. At least, however, they now had a manager who had already won them one cup in his first season, and who had made it clear that he had no intention of tiptoeing around when it came to upholding the Tottenham tradition; the one that defines Tottenham as the team that does everything in style, that plays with panache and pizzazz, that would rather entertain than bore and win. 'I believe,' Graham has said, 'that Tottenham use that myth as a crutch. I think they've had enough of the idea that they'd rather entertain and lose.'

Alan Sugar must have been fed up with carrying that tag like a millstone around his neck. What else could explain his choice of Graham? OK, so Graham was renowned as one of the game's great winners, but a winner at what cost? Style, certainly, was never high up on his list of priorities. As *Observer* journalist Amy Lawrence, whose life was changed at the age of six when a Liam Brady goal distracted her from the toy Wombles she had brought along to Highbury to keep her entertained, admits: 'There's this notion about George's teams, that they play boring football. It's like, "Don't bother with the Valium, just stick on the video of George Graham's Arsenal. They might have won a bit of silverware but we're only going to give them grudging praise because their football never won our hearts." '

But in essence, that derby game exemplified Graham's 'style', as personified by the 'new Arsenal' and the 'new Tottenham'. For just as it's fair to say that George Graham's Arsenal would have probably shut up shop and defended their lead after scoring a second goal, so Arsène Wenger's Arsenal continued to attack in search of further goals. On the other hand Christian Gross's Tottenham (and for Gross substitute whosoever you please from a list that includes Gerry Francis, Ossie Ardiles and even, arguably, Terry Venables) may have folded after conceding a second goal. But George Graham's Tottenham are made of sterner stuff.

You can just imagine Sugar muttering 'Lovely jubbly' to himself as he – or rather his chauffeur – cranked his Rolls Royce (with the number plate AMS 1) up a gear and drove away from Wembley after the Worthington Cup final. After all, he could now look forward to next season and the prospect of European football, which would net Tottenham £15 million if they went all the way to the UEFA Cup final. He had got the taste for success, as anyone who saw his reaction after Allan Nielsen's late, late goal that won the game, will testify. It's hard to begrudge him his taste of glory. In fact, anyone with a thinner skin might well have cashed in when the going got as tough as it did. Instead, Sugar rode the crisis and put his neck on the line by hiring, of all people, the former Arsenal manager. It was a huge risk given Graham's background (oh, to have been a fly on the wall of the Tottenham boardroom on the day Sugar announced that particular plan) and undoubtedly the Tottenham chairman's last throw of the dice after the misguided appointment of Gross. But it has – so far – paid off. 'We've got the right manager,' Sugar told a Tottenham fan at the Football Writers' dinner while watching a familiar scene – the 1999 player of the year David Ginola being confronted by a queue of autograph hunters as long as the banqueting hall at the Royal Lancaster Hotel. 'Now we've got to make sure we spend enough money to make us real contenders.'

He knows it, Graham knows it, and the Tottenham fans know it too. They all know that it will take more than the odd flash of brilliance from 'Gee-no-la' for Tottenham to make an impact either at home or abroad, even if he remains the star attraction in N17 (after the derby game he was frog-marched out of the ground by security men, seemingly under instruction not to sign any autographs, although he did veer off to sign for a few young fans who yelled at him from the assembled masses). What was rather more definitive was that both Tottenham's fans and their management, in affording Arsenal the kind of grudging admiration that comes with knowing you have been fairly and squarely beaten by the better team, had finally realized that season 1999–2000 was going to be a crucial one if Tottenham were to avoid repeating the patterns of the past when they have promised so much, only to deliver so little.

The core of the team would surely remain: goalkeeper Ian Walker, Campbell, Sherwood and the Norwegian striker Steffen

Iversen, for whom Graham had high hopes. Ginola too, despite the misconception that he was not 'a Graham player', would not be on his bike back to France before the 1999–2000 season was out. But a number of questions, as always, remained hanging over White Hart Lane as season 1998–99 drew to a close. Would Alan Sugar put his money where his mouth was? Could George Graham entice the right players at the right price? And could Graham add the requisite artistry and flair inherent to the competitive mentality that he had instilled in his players and so mount a serious Championship challenge into the millennium?

At Arsenal, the situation was clearer. There was to be no disbanding of a team that had so nearly succeeded in retaining their Premiership crown, a failure which Wenger attributed to dropping too many points in the first half of the season with too many of his players still suffering from World Cup hangovers. His aim, he said, was to 'keep the players I have and bring in three new ones'; in other words, to strengthen an already strong squad to challenge both domestically and internationally the following season. There was not even to be a dramatic break-up of the legendary Arsenal defensive stalwarts – Winterburn, Adams, Dixon, Keown and Bould – although Bould was deemed expendable, but only because, as the eldest statesman, he opted to take up Sunderland's offer of a longer contract. 'I think our defence can go on for another season. They may be the oldest back four but they are also the best. To concede only seventeen league goals in a season is a remarkable record,' was Wenger's opinion (only Liverpool have ever conceded fewer goals in a season). But he was well aware that the demands placed on his side by the fixture list the following season would necessitate a larger pool of players and some expert squad rotation. 'Just to reach the quarter-finals of the Champions' League we will have played twelve games in Europe by March. Then you have to add the Premiership and the domestic cups. Nobody can play in every game because we will be playing all the time and will need two teams to do so.'

So while Tottenham fans enacted some measure of retribution on the night by chanting 'You're gonna win f*** all', their Arsenal counterparts weren't unduly bothered. They were already in Europe, so although they eventually lost out on the Premiership – despite amassing the same number of points as the previous season (seventy-eight) and conceding fewer goals – the only blow was to their pride. Coming second rather than first was certainly no great financial loss, since they received £3.5 million as compared with the £3.7 million that went into the Old Trafford coffers. Bluntly, the view shared by the majority of Arsenal fans was that expressed by Amy Lawrence, who admitted: 'We were a bit piqued to see Tottenham dancing about at Wembley with the Worthington Cup, but it was only the Worthington Cup. If it had been the FA Cup it would have been a bit different. But we were a point off winning the title, and a penalty-kick away from reaching the FA Cup final . . . most of us look back on last season and see progress; an improving squad; and great football, perhaps the best quality football played by Arsenal since the 1950s or even the 1960s.'

Still, nobody likes to lose, and the fact that Arsenal fans at Highbury for the final game of the season were prepared to hold banners proclaiming 'C'mon you Tottenham scum', in the hope that Tottenham would do the business against Manchester United and so hand the title to Arsenal, spoke volumes for their ambition. But as George Graham said after the 2-1 defeat that confirmed United as champions: 'The best team always wins the title.' And he should know.

CHAPTER ONE

MONEY! THAT'S WHAT I WANT

The FA Premier League is an outstanding success, no doubt about it. It certainly isn't the best technical league in the world, and it may not even be – for all the hype – the most entertaining, but it is undoubtedly the best marketed league in the world. That the media feels it need make no apology for interrupting news of eclipses, Royal cruises and millennium fever in order to herald the start of The New Football Season, bigger and more bloated than ever before, is confirmation of the fact that football nowadays touches so many people's lives. Frankly, no other business of comparable size would get anything like the attention from radio, press and television. It really is media hype gone crazy.

Yet is football really big business, or is that just one of the most clichéd of the decade's catchphrases? How can you justify football being big business when the turnover of most Premier League clubs is less than the turnover of a large supermarket – and that's just one outlet (say, Marks & Spencer in Camden High Street), not the whole chain; and when outside the Premier League the turnover of most Second and Third Division clubs is no more than that of a large car dealership? So not only is football not big business, it looks to be a poorly run business as well. What's more, as many as half the Premiership clubs make a pre-tax loss; for some, like Everton and Liverpool, it's a loss that runs into millions of pounds.

Football clubs are sales exploiters able to lever their monopolistic powers because fans are different from customers. OK, so most of us tend to patronize a particular brand given the choice, but not to the total exclusion of the rest. Just because you normally put Persil in your shopping trolley doesn't preclude you from favouring Ariel when it's on special offer. But that's just not the case with football clubs. It's unusual for a fan to swap allegiance. Supporting a club is a birthright, a cradle-to-grave habit. You don't just bale out as soon as the going gets tough (if you do then frankly, you don't fit the definition of a fan). From Macclesfield Town to Manchester United, brand loyalty is endemic in football. Clubs are brands which, even when they perform abysmally, can count on the continuing support of their fans. (Manchester City still attracted an average of over 25,000 to Maine Road even when their visitors included the likes of Bournemouth and Gillingham rather than Liverpool or Arsenal.) With demand exceeding supply in the Premiership, no wonder club directors and shareholders rub their hands together gleefully at the thought of a handsome return from their captive audience, whether it be through season tickets, match-day tickets or merchandise. It's box office bonanza time, folks. Roll up, roll up to the greatest show on earth, but mind you show us your money first. The fairground has come to town.

Also, businesses have strategies. Three-year, four-year, five-year business plans. It's called forward planning. Projection. But in football there is no long-term strategy. There is hardly any research – questionnaires in match-day programmes being football's version of trying to establish the facts. When a club like Leicester is perennially lauded for being unusually fan-friendly, then it's time to listen for the sound of a barrel being scraped. Frankly, no one in football can be bothered to ask the question: 'What is it that we can do that our customers want?' They know that the customer will still be there on Saturday (or, for that matter, on Monday, Tuesday, Wednesday, Thursday, Friday and Sunday). It's Hobson's choice. Take-it-or-leave-it time. But fans won't leave, so the clubs simply cash in on their fidelity.

In the clubs' defence, football's current economic climate dictates that there is simply no time for long-term strategies. Short-termism reigns. The brutal fact is that there is no life outside the Premier League. The name of the game is the price of success or the avoidance of failure. To Arsenal this means winning trophies and qualifying for the Champions' League. For Coventry it means avoiding relegation. For Tottenham it means playing catch-up. And by any of these criteria the tactics are the same: throw money – and lots of it – at players' wages and transfers.

Thus begins the vicious circle of wages and transfer fees. In fact, Premiership clubs have invested billions over the past seven years, with over £650 million in the 1998–99 season alone, and most clubs in both the Premiership and the Football League are spending an unhealthily large proportion of their turnover on players' wages. Frightening. Yet ask yourself this: who, apart from Manchester United – and arguably Arsenal (who have yet to make an impact in the Champions' League) and Chelsea (who have not won a Championship for nearly half a century) – is really, truly satisfied? Certainly not Liverpool and Everton, or Blackburn and Bolton, whose grandiose spending has led to debts of millions, no trophies on the one hand and relegation on the other.

The problem is that money goes out of the clubs' bank balances even before it has gone in. Sugar, in inimitable fashion, calls it the 'prune factor'. Coventry chairman Bryan Richardson refers to it as 'financial diarrhoea'. And yet both these chairmen have been major perpetrators of the plight that is crippling football. Coventry were the fourth-highest spenders of all the Premiership clubs in the five years up to 1998, and where did they end up? On average, fourteenth in the Premiership but at least they stayed up – and that's the bottom line. There is such an extortionately high price to pay for relegation from the Premiership that Coventry now have no choice but to spend heavily each close season to retain their top-flight status – around 70 per cent of their income goes on wages. To emphasize the predicament, Richardson was prepared to offer the club's then major asset, Dion Dublin, a salary it couldn't afford before his transfer to Aston Villa in November 1998, despite the fact Coventry's spending on transfers and wages had put the club £10 million in debt the previous year. When asked whether there was a method to his madness Richardson replied: 'You draw the line first and foremost that you have to stay in the Premier League.' So in Coventry's case, whether they make a profit or not is immaterial.

Of course, it's not only the balance sheets of the Premiership clubs that suffer. Lower-league football is being strangled by the ever-decreasing amount of money flowing by way of transfer fees from clubs at the top to those at the bottom. Of the record £140 million splashed out by Premiership clubs in the summer of 1999, more than half the money went abroad while just over a million went to the bottom two divisions; a measly one per cent. As Gerry Boon of the Football Industry Team at consultants Deloitte & Touche put it: 'Money that previously supported smaller English clubs is now backing Italian football.' The Serie A players, or rather their agents, get out their calculators, check the rate of exchange and realize due to the strength of the pound how much more bang for their buck they and their clients will get from the Premiership. By contrast, most of the £390 million spent by Italian clubs in the summer, a figure that was inflated by Christian Vieri's word-record £31.3 million move from Lazio to Inter Milan, stayed at home. Unlike the Premier League, where star players seldom move internally (when was the last time a player moved between Liverpool and Manchester United?), Serie A clubs do a great deal of internal buying and selling, as well as many loan deals.

Serie A, of course, is still where it's at in terms of financial clout; the fact that Vieri's transfer fee to Internazionale was the same as West Ham's total turnover tells its own story. Italian clubs have always enjoyed the benefit of loads of lire thanks to the importance of TV rights. In 1987–88, for example, while English clubs were still struggling under the BBC/ITV duopoly that depressed the free-market value of TV rights before competition came along in the shape of BSkyB, Serie A clubs received £40 million from State broadcaster RAI, despite there being no live transmissions for the domestic audience (only highlights packages). Meanwhile the old English Division One clubs banked a measly £3.1 million. In addition to that, Serie A clubs were benefiting from the investment of millionaire sugar-daddies, such as Silvio Berlusconi at AC Milan; all of which makes it easier to understand (along with the post-Heysel five-year ban on English clubs) how Italian clubs came to dominate European football from the late 1980s onwards (they won nearly 50 per cent of the European trophies on offer). Even now, thanks to Italian and Spanish clubs owning the TV rights to their home games, the likes of Juventus and Real Madrid are guaranteed the equivalent of over £30 million before a ball is even kicked, whereas Manchester United's share of the BSkyB TV money pot is a modest £10 million, and that will only be achieved in part by the merit payment for winning the Premiership.

And as television money is pure profit – there are no comparable overheads to the labour costs in merchandising and corporate hospitality – it's no wonder that most of it goes towards paying for players' transfers and their wages. The Premiership clubs may have more revenue streams and generate more income through their ownership of all-seater stadia and the development of commercial activity than either Serie A or La Liga, but the Italian and Spanish giants spend more money on players. It is no coincidence that the world's record transfer fee, for Christian Vieri, and the game's highest earner, Alessandro Del Piero of Juventus, both ply their trade in Serie A. Manchester United's turnover is double that of Lazio, but they are still out-spent by the Roman club. And this pattern is set to continue – recent TV accords in Italy, France and Spain have overtaken the current BSkyB/BBC Premiership deal and the next one will have to rise to about £500 million a year if the top English clubs are to keep pace with their continental rivals.

1992 was the watershed in English football. The purists don't like it (how often do you hear them lamenting that 'it's not the game I used to know and love'?), but there is no denying that Sky has changed the way football is structured (the Premiership would not have come about without television interest), financed, watched and even played – the Premier League is now the only competition that matters (even the FA Cup is clearly not sacrosanct any more). And the brutal truth is that it is played for the benefit of television. Do managers and players really enjoy playing on a Saturday morning, or a Monday night? Do the fans really enjoy watching four or five matches in a row, with none of them being a traditional Saturday afternoon kick-off?

Clearly Sky has become the major player in football, although initially it was not Sky's money that changed things – the Premier League only got £30 million from the first year of the contract, which wasn't a huge hike-up from the £18 million that was forthcoming in the last year of the ITV contract. No, it was Sky's presentation. A four-hour football programme with replays, statistics and debate ad infinitum replaced the live ITV broadcast shoehorned into a two-hour period, a format whose restrictions were never more clearly highlighted than on the occasion when presenter Elton Welsby asked then Leeds manager Howard Wilkinson what it felt like to have won the Championship – but was unable to wait for the answer because the ad break was due. For punters brought up on a meagre diet of hour-long *Match of the Day* highlights programmes and that worthy ITV stalwart, *The Big Match*, Sky's presentation – together with repeats, previews and discussion programmes – was nirvana. It may not have been 'a whole new ball game', but what Sky did was to force a quantum response from all other parts of the media. They forced other broadcasters to reassess their commitment to football. Furthermore, Sky's presentation created the platform for the commercial revolution with massive increases in merchandising and gate receipts and, subsequently, sponsorship and television rights.

The 1999–2000 season would see the second revolution marked by the onset of digital television and pay-per-view. The OFT ruling, that the contract which constitutes the Sky/BBC four-year deal with the Premier League is not anti-competitive, was heralded by all and sundry in the game as a triumph: open up the market to the highest bidders paying for the best teams, they reasoned, and it would fragment TV rights, leaving the Premiership fat cats to get fatter while the rest wasted away. But the OFT built their case on an 'unsatisfied consumer demand' for live games. They argued that only sixty live games were being shown and that the public had a right to see more. They also argued that the supremacy of BSkyB was impeding 'the development of competition in the pay TV market'. What's wrong with opening up the market so the smaller clubs could sell the rights to screen matches not televised by Sky so that they could be seen more often by their fans?

The reality is that the OFT case was thrown out because it was felt that there was no better alternative arrangement. However, the ruling just reinforced the positions of both Sky and the Premier League. The important factors as far as Sky was concerned was not just that they retained the rights to show sixty Premiership matches each season, but that no one else won the right to screen the remaining 320 games. It meant that BSkyB remained undisputed ringmaster and paymaster. However, television should be the servant not the master of a game which is about far more than just the Premier League and Sky. No one suggests those two acts shouldn't get top billing, but let's have some worthwhile supporting acts and some fluidity to the system that makes money less paramount and achievement more important. There will always be a gap between the top two divisions but Premiership money has made it an unbridgeable chasm.

However, it's hard to see much bridge-building going on until something is done to redress the balance and so curb the amount of money lining the players' pockets. In the meantime fans have to put up with an ever-decreasing rapport between themselves and the players whose wages they help to pay through match-day and commercial income. Gone are the days when a footballer was a true working-class hero. These days, the top footballers are akin to supermodels, refusing – not to get out of bed, but to get on to the pitch – for less money per week than the average Briton earns each year. Frankly, the lunatics have taken over the asylum and are holding the staff to ransom. The game, and those that play it, have risen so far above their roots that the only glimpse a young fan may have of his hero away from the pitch is through the darkened window of a Ferrari, Jaguar or top-of-the-range BMW. The transformation was summed up by the chair of the Football Supporters' Association, Alison Pilling, who commented: 'Football used to be a game for the people. Now it's a game for people with money.'

To be fair, it is hard to ask the likes of Roy Keane to be circumspect in their demands when city analysts predict Manchester United could soon be worth around £1 billion. Gordon Taylor, chief executive of the Professional Footballers' Association and a man who over the years has stood up for his members maintains that no one 'should have to justify their wages these days. It's what the business of football is all about: supply and demand, with every labourer worth the price of his hire.' Supply and demand, of course, is the economic basis of any good industry, but in football's case, for how long will demand continue to outpace supply? Are crazy contracts creating chaos, or are the players worth it? Should their huge salaries match their often huge egos, or should these prima donna players be taken down a peg or two?

Are their demands outrageous, or should they be entitled to cash in on what is after all a relatively short career? Will football's bubble burst? 'Have your say,' as one radio phone-in urged. 'It won't cost you £22 million, because your call is free.'

Ah. £22 million. Or was it £23 million, or even £25 million? The true figure may never be revealed, since that is the way Arsenal like to conduct their business, but what is certain is that no one connected with football will ever forget the transfer tango of summer 1999 that culminated – eventually – with Arsenal's *enfant terrible*, Nicolas Anelka, moving from Highbury to Real Madrid for £18 million plus Real's Croatian striker Davor Suker, plus (according to vice-chairman David Dein) 'a lot more'.

The Anelka saga, or 'Anelkagate' as it was inevitably dubbed, was the clearest and most portentous example yet of player power in the modern game. Pierre van Hooijdonk may have started the rot in England with his 'contract-busting industrial action', but the actions of Anelka, and more significantly, of his two elder brothers Claude and Didier, left a bitter taste in the mouth of everyone at Arsenal.

You could have forgiven Arsène Wenger were he to roll his eyes at the mere mention of his former protégé's name. But Wenger is far too much of a gentleman to display any sense of bitterness; besides, he has admitted that the role of a football manager and his players is like that of a father and son: 'You do your best to help them and don't expect any reward.' Still, it must have been hard for the Arsenal manager to stomach Anelka's anarchic behaviour. When the stalemate between Arsenal, Anelka's coterie and the striker's would-be employees (who included Lazio, Juventus and Real Madrid) was at its height, David Dein and Wenger attended a meeting at Arsenal's Hertfordshire retreat, Sopwell House. Dein recalled how Anelka seemed to snub Wenger's overtures to stay at Highbury before refusing to credit his manager for his progress. 'It was mid-June,' Dein remembers, 'when we still thought there was an outside chance Anelka would stay. But he made it quite clear he wanted to go to Lazio. So Arsène looked at Anelka, who hadn't said a word but had obviously heard everything [the meeting was conducted in French] and said: "I hope when you look at yourself closely, at what you have become and at what you may become in the future, you may just think that I have helped you a little bit." Anelka said absolutely nothing. So Arsène continued: "Do you want to stay at Arsenal?" Anelka replied simply: "I want to go." ' *Merci*, for nothing.

Nicolas Anelka arrived at Highbury in early 1997, an unknown teenager who initially stood out for his inability to get to grips with the offside rule, and left, according to Real Madrid president Lorenzo Sanz, as 'one of the best footballers in Europe, if not the world' (well, he would say that, having paid a small fortune for him). It was Arsène Wenger who engineered that transformation, converting the then raw seventeen year old into the international striker whose two goals and all-round play so comprehensively destroyed England at Wembley in February 1999 during France's 2–0 victory. Anelka came of age that night, and it wasn't his father he had to thank. As Wenger was to recall later: 'After the first train-ing session I said to myself: "There is really something special. Straight away I was impressed by the attributes which you see in him today: startling speed off the mark and something which is very, very rare – *une alliance de force et de souplesse* [a combination of strength and flexibility]." '

Although he had been in the French side that won the European junior Championship (with Thierry Henry), Anelka had played just a handful of League games for Paris St-Germain – the highlight of which was a stunning goal against Lens, his only goal in the French First Division – yet Wenger had no hesitation in exploiting a loop-hole in the French regulations that allowed him to swoop for the teenager before his club had been able to renew his contract. Wenger had obviously seen enough in Anelka's repertoire, and was, as he put it, 'convinced by his intense desire to leave France and PSG'. PSG were furious, even though Arsenal paid them £500,000 by way of 'compensation', a fee which Dein admitted 'we needn't really have paid'.

The fans' initial reaction to Arsenal's newest recruit was 'Nicolas who?' As far as they were concerned he was just another French player following compatriots Patrick Vieira and Rémi Garde to Highbury, and perhaps one for the future. Wenger had other ideas. Anelka made his first appearance in an Arsenal shirt as a substitute in a 3–0 win at Stamford Bridge a few weeks later. Then, in 1997–98 his impact was immediate and dramatic. His speed, strength and stamina were instrumental in helping Arsenal win the Double in a season when many people doubted they would be able to cope with the loss – both in terms of goals on the pitch and personality off it – of Ian Wright, who was absent through injury during much of the second half of the season.

No one who watched Anelka's quantum leap at Arsenal could have doubted that he had the qualities to become a great striker. There was certainly no suggestion that he would suffer from comparison to Wright. From the outset he appeared more skilful on the ball and adept at linking the play, but clearly lacked Wright's penalty-box predatory instincts. What he did possess, in abundance, was speed, and as Arsenal fan Alex Phillips added: 'Many other attributes way above the average striker: strength, close control, an extremely powerful shot, good in the air (when he tries) and what nobody ever seems to mention – he's a team player. Very unselfish but selfish enough to be an excellent striker.' However, according to journalist and Arsenal season-ticket holder Matt Tench, 'He didn't make a great impression at first, but he started to do things during the Double-winning season that took your breath away. Spectacular things. Like switching on the after-burners. He'd leave a quick defender for dead and you'd think, "Jesus, he's fast." And he scored against Manchester United (his first Arsenal goal) at Highbury that season, which is when the tide of opinion started turning. We thought, "If he can score against this lot then he has to have something." '

Doubts concerning Anelka's commitment, his disinterested air and his occasional petulance were overlooked because most acknowledged they were watching a precocious talent. 'Put it this way,' Tench continues, 'he had his own song – "Super, Super Nic . . . Super Nic Anelka" [after his departure he still had his own song but the words had changed a mite, to 'F*** off, F*** Nic, F*** off Nic Anelka'] – but he was way short of cult-hero status. He had this air that suggested he thought he was carrying the team, when the reality was he had the likes of Bergkamp, Petit, Vieira and Overmars around him. But as far as we were concerned, if Arsène thought he was the boy then he was the boy. I think a less tolerant set of fans would have given him a far harder time than we did.'

Speak to a cross-section of Arsenal fans and it becomes evident that as far as Anelka is concerned, there are a hundred different shades of grey. Some will claim they feel privileged to have witnessed the development of a phenomenal talent; at the other end of the spectrum there are others who would warn Anelka to stay away from Highbury if he cares for his health. One prominent Arsenal fan has simply said that every time he looks at the record of the Double-winning season he feels sad that Anelka's goal clinched the FA Cup final.

Following another successful season with seventeen goals from thirty-four starts, which was instrumental in securing Arsenal's runner-up spot in the Premiership and subsequent Champions' League place, Anelka's disenchantment with his club and English football came to the surface. Not that the club itself was any the wiser. Sure, there had been problems. Anelka's sulks were widely reported, and much had been made by the media of his public falling out with Marc Overmars, whom he claimed either ignored him completely during games or gave him balls that were impossible to reach. He was reported to be a loner, a solitary figure who preferred to spend time by himself in his room playing computer games rather than join in the typical dressing room banter. It was rumoured that he was unhappy in London, that he was missing Paris; Wenger was concerned enough to encourage him to find a girlfriend.

But all of this was overlooked while Anelka was doing the business on the pitch, and few people suspected that *terminé* was already scribbled on his Arsenal career. After all, he signed a new contract that Christmas that was supposed to tie him to the club for the next four years. But then, at PSG he'd also signed a contract for Atlético Madrid before it was annulled, his brother Claude admitting that the money on offer '*ça fait tourner la tête*' [turned (Nicolas's) head] and probably ingrained the thought of using his clubs as stepping stones.

For David Dein, the alarm bells started to ring when Marseille made overtures in May 1999 which were immediately rejected. 'We said, categorically, that he was not for sale,' recalls Dein. But that was just the start of it. Claude Anelka, the eldest of the brothers, later admitted that they had offered Nicolas's services to a number of clubs – Marseille in October 1998, Parma in January 1999, Real Madrid in April then Lazio in June – but that 'Arsenal knew nothing about it'.

It appeared that most clubs in Europe knew that Anelka wanted out of Highbury – except Arsenal themselves. 'We eventually got wind of the fact that the brothers were touting him around Europe,' says Dein. 'You can imagine the scenario: "Hello, Barcelona, this is Claude Anelka. Would you like our brother next season?" Then again: "Hello, Inter Milan, this is Claude Anelka" . . . and so on.'

It was when the call came through to Dein's office in June, from Real Madrid vice-president Juan Onieva, that those alarm bells became more strident. 'He made us an offer and said that he'd had a meeting with Anelka's advisors and that they had even given him their brother's terms and conditions [a signing-on fee of £1.5 million and a monthly salary of £200,000, which most of the potential purchasers agreed to in principle]. I said we were not interested, end of story.' But Arsenal were furious that the Anelka brothers had gone behind their backs and unfortunately, unlike the other clubs, Real Madrid appeared to be genuinely interested. Arsenal attempted to head off the discussions by reporting the Spanish club to FIFA for making an illegal approach to their player.

By this time, however, the writing was on the wall. Anelka had publicly stated that he wanted to leave Arsenal; according to Didier, 'the club of his heart is Real Madrid' (his original first choice, Marseille, had been priced out of the race by Arsenal's initial £18 million valuation). Wenger had responded by claiming that 'there were no footballing reasons for Anelka to go, that by leaving Highbury he would be making an enormous strategic error. He was a *titulaire* [first choice] at Arsenal and for the national team, there was a risk in moving.' Surprisingly, Claude agreed and advised his brother to stay put 'as he had only been a professional for a year'. His advice seemed to fall on deaf ears. 'It was impossible to get him to change his mind,' said Claude. 'He was *têtu* [obstinate]. Nicolas was quoted as saying that he would be "upset and embarrassed" if he had to return to Arsenal. "*Je ne veux plus continuer,*" he told the French newspaper *l'Équipe*. "*J'en ai marre d'Arsenal*" [I don't want to carry on. I'm fed up with Arsenal].'

Although Anelka had earlier claimed that Italy held no attraction for him, in mid-June, with Real Madrid seemingly losing interest maintaining that £18 million was too much, (they had offered £11.4 million plus Predrag Mijatovic, the Yugoslav striker whose goal had won them the European Cup the previous year), Lazio entered the race. The Roman club had already spent £19 million on the Argentinian midfielder Juan Sebastian Veron from Parma but had money and a striking berth to fill after the sale of Italian international Vieri to Internazionale for that world record £31.3 million. The fee they reputedly offered – eventually £22 million – must have ranked pretty close to heresy in the Eternal City, given that the *Vatican Daily* had two weeks earlier denounced football trading as 'an offence against poor people'. Still, Lazio were so keen to get their man that they were prepared to include one from Alen Boksic, Pavel Nedved, Fernando Couto or even recent signing Kennet Andersson, as part of the deal.

According to David Dein, however, Arsenal were neither interested in human or cash trading (despite suggestions they might have negotiated had the Chilean striker Marcelo Salas been available). 'We wanted Anelka to stay,' Dein claims. 'The money was secondary. Money comes and goes with great regularity in this business. That's why we tried to outprice him at £30 million.' Wenger, talking to *l'Équipe*, echoed Dein's sentiments when he appeared to imply that Anelka and his agents, by contrast, were only interested in money and an eventual transfer. 'Why should we lose a player for a price that doesn't suit us?'

On 20 June, the Lazio president Sergio Cragnotti imposed a midweek deadline on the deal, which passed with no deal having been done. *Quelle surprise*. Cragnotti, like the rest of the Arsenal fans – whose opinions ranged from 'let him rot in the reserves' to 'take Lazio's money and get rid of him' – was becoming increasingly frustrated with the reluctance of Anelka's brothers to conclude the transfer, despite the generous terms on offer (Lazio, after all, are not generally associated with having tight purse strings; they had spent extravagantly in the previous year assembling a squad capable of wresting the balance of power in Italy away from Turin and Milan and had narrowly failed to land the Scudetto for the first time in over twenty-five years). When Real pulled out of the race on 28 June, Cragnotti must have thought he was finally going to get his man. However, his good mood was short-lived since it was then revealed that Juventus had allegedly offered £22 million for Anelka, with Thierry Henry moving to Highbury as part of the deal.

This latest twist in the tale shifted the goalposts. It was common knowledge that Wenger was an admirer of Henry's: Monaco, his former club, had even rejected an Arsenal offer before selling Henry to Juve. Wenger had watched the player's progress since nurturing him at Monaco, and admired his versatility and his pace and power: the very qualities, ironically, that had attracted him to Anelka. But the word on the street was that Juventus were playing spoiling tactics; that their plan was to turn up at the party uninvited and hang around long enough to prevent their rivals Lazio from drinking all the champagne.

Lazio responded by immediately offering £18 million, which was rebuffed by Arsenal, who were holding out for £20 million-plus. By this time Cragnotti, who Dein later acknowledged had behaved honourably throughout the entire proceedings, must have felt like throwing in the towel; indeed, he said as much when he admitted he was 'sick of the story. We are walking away.' Two days later, however, he was back – and had increased his offer by £2 million.

One wonders what Anelka must have thought of proceedings, holed up with his computer games somewhere in Paris but still picking up five-figure weekly pay cheques as an Arsenal employee while waiting for his brothers to resolve his future. It is tempting to paint a picture of him as some twenty-year-old malcontent whose only crime was to have been born with enough talent to rise above his roots and so enable those less gifted members of his family to profit handsomely from his worth. A sure-fire recipe for avarice, if ever there was one. It happened, after all, to Ronaldo, who apparently reneged on his eight-year contract at Barcelona to sign for Internazionale on the say-so of his advisors. Bobby Robson, who watched Ronaldo progress under him when he was the coach at PSV, and then in a similar capacity at the Nou Camp, could have empathized with Wenger, who said that he had 'explained the risks of moving to him [Anelka] but he doesn't listen. He has had his head turned.' Robson remembers asking Ronaldo at the end of his first year whether he really wanted to leave Barcelona. 'He said to me: "No I don't",' recalls Robson. 'I told him: "Listen, I don't want to lose you either. You're the king of the city, the whole of Catalonia's in your pocket, you're a fantastic player and a lovely kid. Go and tell your agents you don't want to move."' But Ronaldo's agents appeared to be working to a different agenda. So they took him to Internazionale. Wrong time, wrong place. Ronaldo's career has been stop-start ever since.

It is hard, however, to look beyond the notion that Anelka's career path was already mapped out for him when he arrived in London, that he knew – even if Arsenal were in the dark – that two years was about as good as the club were going to get from him. There was no chance that he would learn from Ronaldo's mistakes. Following Arsenal's vital final match of the 1998–99 season against Aston Villa, a match in which Anelka looked nothing more than a peripheral player, his body language – head bowed, boots off, socks rolled down around his ankles – suggested that this was so long then, and thanks for the memories. As Claude Anelka admitted in an astonishing interview for Radio 5 Live a few days after Anelka's transfer to Real Madrid was finally concluded: 'When we came here [to London] we decided to stay two or three years and at the end of the first year I asked Nicolas if he wanted to stay and he said he had problems with the press and wanted to leave.' Pressed on why, then, Anelka had put pen to paper on a new contract, Claude replied: 'Contracts in football mean nothing. They might mean something on paper yes, but if a player isn't happy he has to leave. In the beginning you are happy and want to stay but then you want to leave. In football it's like that. It's a shame.'

It was that total disregard for the written agreement that led to Anelka threatening to take the unprecedented step of buying himself out of his contract at Arsenal, effectively leaving him a free agent. At one point he ominously stated that he had asked his lawyers, Marguerite Fauconnet and the Belgian lawyer Jean-Marie Dupont (who famously acted for Jean-Marc Bosman in his landmark case) to 'look into the legal aspects of this issue'. Didier took up the theme, claiming that unless 'we can resolve the contract with Arsenal we will regard Nicolas as a free agent. If he doesn't have a club, how can he represent France, who have an important match against the Ukraine in September?' (a key qualifying fixture for Euro 2000).

Fauconnet and Dupont argued that Anelka had a good case in law in that his contract didn't reflect his change of circumstances – his rise from fringe player to major star. They were preparing an argument that would allow their client to rip up his four-year contract with Arsenal and pay the club just three months' wages in compensation, around £150,000, at a stroke making contracts and transfer fees obsolete. Dupont claimed: 'We want the same rights for Mr Anelka as for normal workers.' Understandably, there was an immediate outcry. The *Sun*, under the banner headline 'Anarchy in the UK', carried interviews with the likes of Leicester manager Martin O'Neill, who claimed that it would be a 'total disaster for football if this [case] were to go through. Are the rules not suited to the players' needs enough as it is? It could send clubs to the wall. There are already spiralling wage demands. The idea that someone can sign a five-year contract then buy himself out of it at the drop of a hat is incredible.'

What always appeared a somewhat unlikely scenario never happened. Nevertheless, it brought the subject of the contract right to the top of football's agenda. Dupont, in an interview given to Radio 5 Live, admitted that in his opinion the way ahead in terms of contracts and transfers could only be smoothed by standardizing contracts across Europe to two/three years' maximum, eliminating any reason for players or clubs to break a contract since a player's circumstances would not have radically changed in that timespan. 'When you sign a player [on a two-/three-year contract] you don't overpay him by thinking, "Oh well, he has a seven-year contract but we'll sell him after three years",' Dupont explained. 'You pay exactly what he is currently worth on the pitch so as to avoid any speculation.'

Dupont's argument made perfect sense. Unlike commercial operations, he reasoned, football competes across national frontiers. Lloyds TSB, for example, are not in competition for bank employees with the Banque National de Paris (BNP), but the likes of Manchester United and Arsenal frequently come head to head with Marseille and Monaco. Footballers are free to ply their trade all over Europe, so why not standardize contracts – a move which would put the brakes on transfer fees, since no club is going to pay £30 million for a player who signs up for three years?

Nice idea in theory; in practice, it's a non-starter – because of player power. Every one of Europe's top clubs craves success above all else, and to get that success they need to sign the best players, who will in turn demand top-whack wages. No player is going to accept a two- or three-year contract when he knows that by signing a seven-year contract he'll be set up financially for life. Conversely, he won't sign any contract at all when he knows that he will be a free agent within the year under the Bosman ruling. The clubs are in hock to the players and, frankly, there is no way out.

It's the same conclusion with the idea of capping salaries, which happens in the NBA. But since playing basketball anywhere other than the NBA is a downward step, the players simply have to accept it because there is nowhere else for them to go. If there were a salary cap in England, however, all the best English players would simply move abroad to earn more money and the foreigners would go elsewhere, too. Therefore, the cap would have to be applied Europe-wide, which just isn't going to happen. Can you see the likes of Real Madrid, who despite being in debt to the tune of millions still go on spending small fortunes on players and their wages in their desperate quest to be the best, accepting a salary cap? With the clubs literally falling over each other in the mad scramble for glory and untold riches, the only currency that matters is players. They call the shots.

Anelka's threat, while it was never carried out, had the immediate effect of prompting Lazio to up their offer to £22 million on the condition that Anelka's entourage lowered their demands. It was this proviso that was the key to the protracted negotiations. Anelka and his brothers were reportedly holding out for around £9 million, a significant part of the transfer fee, which was just not acceptable to Arsenal. 'We had lengthy negotiations with Lazio and Juventus,' explains Dein. 'The problem was that we wanted money, the group [the Anelka entourage] wanted money and the player wanted an annual salary – the entire package came to too much. We wanted to reduce the group's commission so our fee could go up. Theirs was weighing ours down. There had to be a balancing act, which is why we fought long and hard until the end. We were quite prepared to let him sweat in the reserves but there came a time when we wanted shot of him because it was getting more and more acrimonious. The crunch came when they took a substantial, and I mean substantial, reduction to their demands and that meant that a club could pay us what we wanted. Otherwise it would have meant a stand-off going into the season and we didn't want that.'

Wenger reminded everyone of his priorities after Arsenal had played a pre-season friendly in France against Saint-Étienne when he commented: 'Nicolas is available for transfer and if he doesn't find a club within the next forty-eight hours he will return to us. The affair has gone on long enough. We can't leave the situation to continue indefinitely. We have a season to prepare for.' On Friday 30 July, two days before the Charity Shield, he was still sticking to his guns. 'The player will go for our price or he will go nowhere. Even if he doesn't play. That's for sure. It's already a bank robbery for me if we have to be punished twice. We drop the price and we lose a player we wanted to keep. If we still have to drop the price it is better that he doesn't play any more.'

The reality is, however, that the scenario of letting Anelka 'rot in the reserves' would have had significant ramifications for both club and player. For a start, Arsenal would have been left with a diminishing – not to mention, disenchanted – asset on their books; the last thing they wanted at this stage, after holding out for so long, was for Anelka's value to start falling. Secondly, with football being a 'people business' there is no room for a bad apple in the barrel (as Nottingham Forest would probably confirm). Lastly, Arsenal would have run the risk of being accused of acting in spite by confining Anelka to reserve-team football.

Thankfully for all concerned such an impasse was avoided, not least Dein, who commented: 'Anelka and his brothers have taken over my life for the last six weeks. I've become a bad husband and father. We went to France for two weeks and I think I saw my family for two hours.' Suffice to say the feelings were mutual. Claude admitted: 'I don't like David Dein. He wanted to push Nicolas into Juventus to make a lot of money . . . Nicolas liked London and Arsenal but he only had a problem with David Dein. He liked everyone else. Just not David Dein and the press. Everything he did on the pitch the press were very bad with him. He had all the time to prove something. [They were on his back] after he said something about Overmars and Bergkamp, after he didn't come to the awards ceremony [to pick up his Young Player of the Year Award].' (Nicolas preferred a night out *en famille*, although the trophy has pride of place in the house in Edgware he shared with his brothers and where Claude still resides while he attempts to establish his credentials as a DJ, his role as his brother's agent temporarily on hold.)

Quel dommage! How tough life must have been for Anelka during his two years in London. After all, he was so far from home (the Eurostar got him from London to Paris *tout de suite*); he had no one to talk to (seven of Arsenal's first team squad were French); he had a manager who didn't understand him (Wenger's handling of both Anelka's talent and his moods was above reproach; when Anelka fell out with Overmars, Wenger brought the pair together and asked Anelka in French what he thought of the Dutchman. The reply was less than flattering. Wenger looked at Overmars, paused, and told him Anelka thought he was a terrific player); and of course, the players around him weren't up to scratch: what a chore to have to play alongside Dennis Bergkamp and in front of Emmanuel Petit. And as regards the press, there is evidence to suggest that Anelka exaggerated the problems somewhat. The *Daily Telegraph*'s Henry Winter recalls how the striker came up into the press box when Arsenal were playing Dynamo Kiev in the Champions' League and was 'really quite sweet. He was offered a drink and he stayed and chatted a bit. There wasn't any problem there at all. I think the Anelka brothers stirred that particular pot up a bit.' Someone who ran into him at a nightclub used the same description, contrasting his demeanour with those of his two companions, who were acting the image of the spoilt, arrogant football superstar.

So, you have to ask: what more could Anelka have wanted? The answer one suspects is money, even if Claude Anelka claims that 'for Nicolas, money is nothing. He just wants to be number one and he will if he continues [to play] like that.' Anelka's monthly salary at Real Madrid is reputedly £200,000 a month, a king's ransom compared to the £12,000 a week he was on at Arsenal. Could money really have nothing to do with it? After all it was the Anelkas' wage demands that was the sticking point of the deal.

Anelka himself, speaking to *France Football* after signing for Real, passes the buck fairly and squarely on to Arsenal and to David Dein in particular, saying the reason for moving was a desire to play in Spain rather than improve his bank balance: "If I had been attracted by money I would have signed for Juve. Turin made me a huge offer: £30 million. But money is not my obsession . . . it wasn't me who dragged this saga out for two months. Real's offer didn't vary . . . Dein bought me for £500,000, realizing a wonderful increase in value, and yet he has thrown obstacles in the way. A bigger club than Arsenal, Real, asked me to come. Naturally I accepted without knowing how much money I would earn . . . He forgets that when he took me from PSG I was still under contract. He did what Real did but he won't accept it.'

So, according to Anelka, Arsenal are not the paragons of virtue they pretend to be. However, if both parties were guilty of brinkmanship, if anyone tries to tell Dein that the actions of 'le clan Anelka' – a term the brothers disapprove of because it has Mafia connotations – were anything other than hubris of grand proportions they will get short shrift. He claims the saga was 'one of the most unpleasant experiences of my life. There was a lot of intrigue and duplicity involved regarding the role of the agents, who have shown disrespect for the club, for Arsène and the fans. I feel sorry for the fans who bought shirts with "Anelka" on their backs, and for Arsène, who brought him out of obscurity in Paris.' Oh for the days, eh, David, when Ian Wright would breeze into your office when his contract was up for renewal and say: 'Where do I sign?' Wright didn't even want to know how much he was getting. He simply said: 'I just want to play for Arsenal.'

All Anelka wanted to do, apparently (after Marseille failed to come up with the entry price) was play for Real Madrid, although it's an indication of just how much moving of the goalposts was going on that when Real originally pulled out of the chase and Lazio appeared to be the only bidders, Didier was reported as saying that Nicolas 'wants to go to Italy and has chosen Lazio. Nicolas wants the best and today, the best is Lazio.'

And tomorrow, and next month, and in two years' time . . . who will be the best then? There may have been a hint of sour grapes from Dein when he claimed that Anelka would do the same to Real as he did to Arsenal, but Claude Anelka betrayed his agenda when he said, on being asked how long his brother would stay at the Bernabéu: 'I don't know. Anything can happen in football.' So it seems, but the game may as well just hang up its boots here and now if every jumped-up millionaire player, too immature or unwilling to comprehend the notion of commitment, suddenly decides that his contract is worthless and that he is off to seek infamy and fortune elsewhere and sod the consequences.

Anelka claims that Dein is wrong to suggest that his loyalty to Real Madrid will be short-lived. 'Certainly,' he admits, 'I am often uptight after a defeat but I have never changed my character. I worked hard at Arsenal. I gave of my best.' Those who witnessed the lacklustre display against Aston Villa in particular might argue with that and be tempted to say 'more fool Real Madrid'. Time will tell, however, whether their investment will pay dividends, and whether Lazio and Juventus will be left to rue their loss. But then Lazio never really considered Anelka to be worth £22 million; and besides, they were priced out of it by the clan's refusal to lower their demands. Juventus, on the other hand, were not really a serious proposition since their game-plan, using Henry as bait, was to 'park' Anelka for a year – farm him out to a smaller club – until the Old Lady was ready for him; a bit like a millionaire buying another property for his portfolio just to spite a rival. If the move worked out Juve would add him to the roster; if it didn't then they'd get most of their money back by selling him, someone else having picked up the tab in the interim. A deal with that sort of risk attached to it was never going to appeal to the Anelkas.

So Real came back onto the scene, financially empowered by the annulment by royal decree of a large chunk of a £50 million debt, not to mention the tying up of a television deal that was to be worth £260 million over five years from 2001. Having signed Steve McManaman and the Bosnian forward Elvir Balic from Fenerbahce, and renegotiated Roberto Carlos's contract, the club wanted to give their fans one more pre-season present . . . and what could be better that one of the most exciting strikers in the world who, better still, was only twenty? So, on the eve of the Charity Shield between Arsenal and Manchester United, Real president Lorenzo Sanz announced that a deal had been agreed between Real and Arsenal. 'Anelka is a great champion whose play will brighten football in the next ten years,' the Real president said, adding, 'Real seeks only great champions.'

Of course, one of the drawbacks of being considered a 'great champion' is that great things are expected of you. If Anelka didn't know that already, he would doubtless have found that out when he first stepped out into the melting pot which is the Santiago Bernabéu stadium, which at twice the size of his old club makes Highbury seem like the Dell. He must surely have felt the weight of expectation that hung in the sultry Spanish air at 10.30 p.m. on Tuesday 3 August, the time when his plane touched down at Madrid airport and Nicolas Anelka, *un petit ingénu* from Trappes, near Paris, became the hottest property in (Real) Madrid.

Imagine how it must have looked to the innocent bystander. One minute you are happily passing through passport control on your way to baggage reclaim, looking forward to that plate of paella and a cold San Miguel, when suddenly there is a commotion. People scurrying, hundreds of cameras clicking, a multitude of voices barking orders. Aisles are cleared and cordoned off to prevent 'José' Public from getting close to, or even (God forbid) touching the chosen one. Police escorts, minders, all shepherding the centre of the attention along, protecting him from the fans who have gathered to welcome him. The crowd is enormous, massive, frightening even. A sea of people – men and women, young and old – many of them clad in the distinctive white shirt of *Los Meringues*. Anyone would have thought that a world-famous pop star had just landed, not simply a reclusive twenty-year-old footballer with just two professional seasons under his belt. Pressure, what pressure? Goodbye London, *buenos días* Madrid.

Anelka used the word 'surprised' to describe how he felt on seeing the size of his welcoming party. Understatement, or what? His initial expression bore the startled look of a rabbit caught in the glare of onrushing headlights, although at least he appeared more composed – and had recovered some of his characteristic spikiness – by the time of the press conference arranged by his new club to formally announce his signing. So yes, he was surprised that so many people were waiting for him. 'I hope,' he said, 'that I won't disappoint them. I am used to pressure. There is as much pressure at Arsenal as at Real. I will do the best I can. When I think something, I speak the truth that's all ... what happened to me in England couldn't be worse ... I'm here to play at Real Madrid, one of the greatest clubs, that's all.'

What did happen to him in England, he claimed, was that he was constantly harangued by the English media who, apparently, were forever comparing him to Ian Wright and had written off his chances of ever succeeding in England before he had even done the customary pose in an Arsenal shirt. 'They were criticizing me before I had even arrived,' he insisted in a later interview. 'They were jealous because I was young and I had taken the place of Ian Wright, or something. It wasn't like that. They pointed out that I didn't smile during a match. Neither does Bergkamp [which of course is absolutely true]. But they said nothing about him. They were constantly looking for things, pointing out that I didn't like London because I went home occasionally to see my parents at the weekend.'

The reality is that Anelka has only himself to blame for his bad PR. Everyone – members of the press included – warms to a footballer who plays the game with a smile on his face; the likes of Gianfranco Zola and Dwight Yorke come to mind. Anelka's constant sullenness simply gave his critics sticks with which to beat him. Then, of course, there might just have been a touch of xenophobia, which would explain why Anelka was never going to be extolled by the British media in the same way that they lavished praise on the comparably precocious talent of Michael Owen.

At this point, however, it was tempting to say: you ain't seen nothing yet. For if it's fair and balanced treatment by the press you're looking for then Spain is not the ideal place to play your football. There are four dedicated Spanish sports dailies, one of which – *Marca* – is predominantly Real Madrid-oriented and has the highest readership (nearly two and a half million every day) of any sports paper in Europe; footballers, particularly those carrying a conspicuously high price tag around their necks, are bound to live in the proverbial goldfish bowl.

The Spanish media lost no time in homing in on the most expensive player in Spanish history. Anelka's first training session on the Thursday night was transmitted live on Real Madrid TV; even the goal he scored during practice was heralded the following morning in the Madrid-based *AS* with the headline 'Anelka's goal'. *Marca* simply carried the banner headline 'He is in our league'. The intensity led Anelka's compatriot in the French national team, Christian Karembeu, to offer some words of advice to his new club team-mate: 'I told him not to worry if the crowds chanted his name or wanted to touch him. That's the way it is in Madrid.' Whether Anelka copes with Madrid's way remains to be seen, but there are more than a few people who will have their doubts. Unlike Arsenal, where he arrived unknown and could benefit at his own pace from Arsène Wenger's private tuition, at Real most of the training sessions are conducted in front of a critical paying public of literally thousands. Moreover, Anelka didn't have the pre-season opportunity of tuning in to his team-mates' needs. He was the big foreign star who would be judged by higher standards than his striking partners: the two young and gifted Spanish internationals, Raul and Morientes. You didn't need to be a clairvoyant to foresee there would be trouble ahead unless he delivered immediately.

Back at Highbury, meanwhile, Arsenal had been left without both the previous season's leading goalscorer and a replacement in time for the Charity Shield against Manchester United or, more critically, in time for the start of the season. Technically Anelka was still an Arsenal player on the day, but if his spirit was anywhere near Wembley it would not have enjoyed the experience. The Arsenal fans made no secret of their feelings towards him as they watched their side win the first of the new season's silverware, chanting 'Let him rot' periodically throughout the game. Wenger, however, was characteristically more charitable. 'Nicolas is not a bad boy,' he maintained. 'He's twenty years of age and maybe he has been pulled into that situation without really wanting it. But I think FIFA have to control the transfer market much more than they do at the moment. I wouldn't say it's a question of controlling player-power in football but of controlling business power. I don't think players control the game. People who have no responsibilities in the game, control the game.'

It was a dig at the role of so-called agents, namely the Anelka brothers and their associate, Marc Roger. Both Wenger and Dein, who had lodged a complaint against the Anelka entourage with FIFA (which was conveniently sidelined when the transfer went through), believe that both FIFA and UEFA must look very closely at the role of the agent. Dein goes so far as to call his viewpoint a 'crusade' against the unscrupulous working practices of these characters. In fact, he felt so strongly about the repercussions of the Anelka affair that he agreed to give an hour-long interview to the television journalist Martin Bashir on the subject, which was subsequently screened on Trevor MacDonald's *Tonight* programme and billed, in rather dramatic fashion, as 'The Anelka Tapes'. But to Dein's chagrin, just a few minutes of his interview were used, and the programme failed to air what he described as his 'four-point plan' for dealing with agents, which he regarded as the most import-ant part of what he wanted to say. 'I strongly believe,' he says, 'that the way forward on this matter would be helped if (1) a club can only deal with FIFA-registered agents; (2) at the time of the transfer the agent undertakes to sign a legally binding contract with the buying club agreeing not to directly or indirectly influence the player to move during the time of his contract, and accepting that if he does the buying club can take legal retribution against him; (3) there is to be a scale of remuneration to the agent; and (4) any commission to the agent is paid during the course of the contract rather than upfront.' (Madrid appear to have taken the lesson on board as half of Anelka's signing-on fee of £4 million will only be activated during the latter years of his seven-year contract.) Otherwise, Dein believes: 'We are going to be killing each other. There will be no loyalty, no stability and players will be moving on every one or two years. If there's a legally binding document that agents must sign then we have a chance.'

Of course it's unfair to tar all agents with the same brush; there are some honourable, above-board agents out there whose prime objective is to secure good deals between club and player. Besides, as Dennis Roach, a one-time poacher turned gamekeeper who is now president of the International Association of Football Agents says: 'If every club only dealt with licensed agents then there wouldn't be a problem. But they all dive in when a top player becomes available and will deal with everyone. Marc Roger is not a licensed agent yet they all wined and dined him. If Anelka had turned up at Real Madrid with his brothers and Roger, and the Real president had turned round and said that he wasn't interested because Anelka was still under contract then this situation wouldn't have arisen. But who is going to punish those at the top end? Nobody, because they run football.' Roach is being a touch disingenuous as Roger works with the former French international Jean-François Larios who, as a licensed agent, is a member of Roach's association.

The game had to go on, of course, and the season kicked off with that traditional curtain raiser at Wembley in which it was immediately apparent that Arsenal *sans* Anelka lacked their usual cutting edge upfront. Not even the most objective of Arsenal fans would have admitted to missing the errant striker on the day, but how they missed his lightning runs on to Emmanuel Petit's clever through-balls, his strength when holding the ball up with his back to goal. True, they won 2–1, but their goals came from a midfielder, Ray Parlour, and from Kanu, who was playing upfront with Swede Freddie Ljungberg, chosen for that role despite the availability of strikers Christopher Wreh and Luis Boa Morte (which suggested that Wenger had little faith in the duo as long-term striking options).

It was clear, then, that Arsenal would have to spend some of those millions promised from the Anelka deal. And quickly. Which they did, immediately returning £1 million to Real Madrid in order that Davor Suker could implement his escape clause and buy out his contract. The contrast between the two transfers could not have been greater. While Anelka's brothers were still negotiating the extortionately high demands of their brother's contract with Real Madrid, Suker's agent managed to tie up a deal within twenty-four hours that saw the thirty-one-year-old Croatian star board a plane at Madrid airport to fly back the way Anelka had come. No welcoming party to speak of, but a breath of fresh air none the less considering that the leading scorer at France '98 had reportedly taken a 'substantial' pay-cut (in the region of £15,000 per week) to fit into Highbury's wage structure; a move that Wenger agreed was 'very unusual'. Dein, who Wenger claimed had 'aged a year in two months' over the summer's saga, told the press that he wanted the next morning's headlines to read: 'Arsenal go from a Sulker to a Suker'. At least he could now joke about it.

A positive move then, given Suker's pedigree, but the feeling within Highbury was that Suker was more of a half-measure than a straight swap; that Wenger must still be on the look-out for a quick, young striker to give the squad strength in depth. His options had been limited by the unavailability of long-term targets Chris Sutton (who had gone to Chelsea), Robbie Fowler (who was staying at Liverpool) and Emile Heskey (not considered quite the finished article). The player he did choose . . . well, you could have forgiven the Arsenal fans for having a sense of *déjà vu*. A young Parisian with two brothers. A pacy, attacking player who had been nurtured at the French national football academy and thrust reluctantly into the spotlight before maturity had really had a chance to kick in. A player, moreover, who admits to having a penchant for computer games, and who prefers rap, and the rapport of home-grown mates, to the traditional trappings that come with stardom. Oh, and Wenger gave him his head (at Monaco), too. But that is where the similarities between Thierry Henry and Nicolas Anelka end.

For a start, Wenger described the player for whom he finally paid Juventus in the region of £10 million on the day after Suker's arrival as a 'happy' boy; furthermore, Wenger admitted Henry was more a wide player than a target man, although the Arsenal manager said he hoped his new recruit would eventually move into the centre.

Henry's pace and power, combined with the versatility to play either wide left or right, have long made Wenger one of his greatest admirers. But he's not been the only one. Henry had been at the forefront of transfer rumours ever since he broke into the Monaco first team at seventeen; his potential represented the possibility for agents to make a killing on him. Which, of course, they did, but not before falling foul of FIFA, who fined Henry and declared his agent, Michel Basilevitch *persona non grata*, for signing a *protocol d'accord* (pre-contract) in 1996 with Real Madrid at a time when Henry was still a trainee pro with Monaco and under contract until 1998. The agreement was totally irregular, all the more so since Basilevitch was not a FIFA licensed agent and Monaco were never contacted by Real. The 'crime' was compounded when Real claimed that the pre-contract was a full contract.

In 1997, after signing his first professional contract with Monaco, Henry again found himself in trouble with FIFA after signing with two different agents (one of whom was Jean-François Larios, Marc Roger's boss), both of whom then tried to tout him to the likes of Barcelona. Monaco, however, refused advances as they were entitled to do since Henry was now under contract until 2002. But Europe's top clubs were alerted again after Henry gained a place in the French squad at France '98. First Arsenal's £10 million offer was rejected by the French club despite Henry's insistence that they consider it. The Monaco president Jean-Luis Campora was perhaps reluctant to sell to his former coach, who he had summarily dismissed after seven successful years, particularly since Wenger had already taken Petit, Grimandi and Wreh from Monaco to Highbury.

Then, in January 1999, Juventus intervened. Their bid, of £7 million, was accepted, since Monaco told Henry that he had either to take this offer or honour his contract, to which Henry replied: 'You don't turn down Juve.'

So what of Tottenham while all this wheeling and dealing at the top table was going on? One fondly imagined, given Sugar's pre-season assurances, that they had been busy tying up deals of their own to strengthen a squad that, although it had somewhat surprisingly won the Worthington Cup, had again spectacularly under-achieved in the league. For a club with Tottenham's past standards, a record of Won 11, Drawn 14, Lost 13, and a final placing of eleventh behind such powerhouses as Middlesbrough, Leicester and Derby County, was pretty poor. Everybody knew that Sugar had to put his hand in his pocket and dig deep, certainly deeper than in the previous close-season, when having been linked with the likes of Patrick Kluivert, Ariel Ortega and the De Boer twins, Tottenham signed an unknown Italian left-back (Paolo Tramezzani) and an ageing keeper (Hans Segers) who would double up as a specialist coach.

He did. Just. Willem Korsten, a relatively unknown left-sided winger, arrived from Vitesse Arnhem via Leeds, where he had been on loan, for £1.5 million. It was not a signing to warm the hearts of the Tottenham fans, since the club already had a left-sided winger who was quite a good player as it happened; after all, he'd won both the Players' and Writers' Footballer of the Year awards for the previous season and was the most popular player at the club. Then, in July, Tottenham paid Wimbledon £4 million for centre-half Chris Perry, a defender who had been Mr Consistency over the past few seasons for the Dons but who had lately fallen down the popularity charts among the Selhurst Park faithful. But then George Graham had bought Martin Keown (after first selling him to Aston Villa) and also Steve Bould, and really, you couldn't argue with their

Highbury records. Besides, Perry looked good enough alongside Sol Campbell in the pre-season friendly against Queens Park Rangers and the club had lacked a decent centre-half pairing since the days of Richard Gough and Gary Mabbutt, so at least Perry's arrival augured well.

The flurry of inactivity in N17 couldn't have been more of a contrast with the goings-on on the other side of north London. Arsenal, for goodness sake, had even found time amidst all the furore over Anelka to sign the Brazilian, Silvinho, from Corinthians (£4 million), Oleg Luzhny from Dynamo Kiev (£1.8 million) and Stefan Malz from TSV 1860 Munich (£600,000). OK, so they wouldn't have wished the debilitating Anelka saga on their worst enemy but at least they had made significant additions to their squad and their coffers were still full, even after the purchases of Henry and Suker. To make matters worse for Tottenham supporters, they regarded many of Arsenal's signings – in particular Suker, who will always be remembered for his exquisite chip over Peter Schmeichel in Euro 96 – as very much Tottenham type of players. In fact, Suker had a predilection for Tottenham and a guaranteed striker's role at a London Premier League club but the come-and-get-me request was never followed up and Arsenal stepped in with alacrity.

George Graham, talking after the 2–2 pre-season draw with QPR, admitted that 'even the big clubs are finding it hard to sign players, so we're finding it even harder'. His inference was clear: that Tottenham were no longer a big club; and that despite his and Sugar's ambitions, they were just not prepared to pay the requisite money – in transfer fees or wages – to bring the top players to White Hart Lane. Yet Suker was a veritable snip by today's standards, so why didn't Tottenham want him? Why didn't they pursue the likes of Mustapha Hadji, the Moroccan World Cup star who went to Coventry for £4 million? Why not Eyal Berkovic, the type of play-maker Tottenham have lacked for so long, offloaded by West Ham to Celtic for £5.5 million; or Christian Ziege, the German left-back bought from AC Milan for £4 million by Middlesbrough, despite the fact that Tottenham fans have being crying out for a competent full-back since Chris Hughton a decade earlier? And upfront? OK, so Chris Sutton admittedly wasn't cheap at £10 million, but Robbie

Keane was young, groomed in England and gifted – not a bad package for £6 million by today's standards. If Coventry could afford him, then surely Tottenham could?

It seemed not. So once again the start of the season was something of an anti-climax. Tottenham often signed a star attacking player at the start of a season. The tradition goes back as far as Bill Nicholson. Moreover, Jimmy Greaves was a few pounds short of being the first £100,000 player, Martin Peters was the first £200,000 transfer, while Paul Gascoigne was the first footballer to cost £2 million. Keith Burkinshaw had astonished the football world with the ground-breaking signings of Argentinian World Cup stars Ossie Ardiles and Ricardo Villa in 1978. Then there was Conn and Crookes and Archibald and Waddle and Allen and Lineker and Klinsmann. Like most other traditions at Tottenham, however, this one seemed to have flown out of the window and was last seen heading for Highbury.

One thing was for sure, though: it was going to be a long hard season. The Premiership itself is undoubtedly one of the most competitive leagues in the world given the intensity of matches, the quality of the teams and the pace of the football. And then there was the Holy Grail of Europe. Alluring, but was it going to prove unattainable? Could the new-look Arsenal finally make an impact in the competition that mattered? Could the old-look Tottenham regain some lost pride and get back up among the big boys?

Voire c'est croire (seeing is believing), as Wenger might say. But Arsenal's manager was sure of just one thing on the eve of the new season. When asked whom he wanted to avoid in the Champions' League draw, he had no hesitation in replying: 'Real Madrid.'

CHAPTER TWO
THE WAY IT IS

There is no doubt that the money that has poured into European football over the last decade has had a far too pervasive influence. It has overstayed its welcome to such an extent that it has become the root of many of the evils in the modern game, as personified by rapacious wages, over-the-top transfer fees, exorbitant television income, omnipotent media moguls, extortionate ticket prices, widespread merchandise rip-offs, excessive corporate hospitality and disproportionate player power. As the average fan probably views it, football at the highest level is now all about the best players playing for the wealthiest clubs and earning most of the cash. It's about a game in which David can seldom triumph over Goliath because Goliath has become too powerful and too rich, and the rules have been bent in his favour.

The revamped UEFA Champions' League is the epitome of this imbalance. As the juggernaut rolls back out weekly onto the streets of Europe – Berlin, Zagreb, Florence, Munich et al. – one cannot help but fondly recall the old European Cup, a simple knock-out tournament based on sporting merit and involving the champions of the various UEFA member countries. designed to be an exhilarating diversion from the week-in, week-out diet of domestic league football. But this new Champions' League format has turned UEFA's premier competition into a monstrous, bloated tournament for the European élite (i.e. the biggest teams from the richest countries) in which the criteria appear simple: play more games and earn more money. By the time the winners lift the trophy on

24 May 2000, they will have played seventeen matches and earned at least £30 million. With so much money at stake, is it any wonder that greed appears to have become the overriding principle?

And yet. Despite the fact that money so obviously matters, there is evidence to suggest that winning trophies is actually quite important too. Former Tottenham striker Steve Archibald said as much when he admitted to Sir Alex Ferguson that the worst thing about Barcelona losing the European Cup final on penalties to Steaua Bucharest in 1986 – apart from losing the match itself – was having to stand so agonizingly close to the trophy without actually being able to touch it. That, confessed Archibald, really hurt. Ferguson never forgot that sentiment; thirteen years later he used it to vitalize his jaded troops during his half-time team talk in the 1999 Champions' League Cup final against Bayern Munich at the Nou Camp. According to Teddy Sheringham, Ferguson told his players that if they lost, 'you'll have to go up and get your losers' medals and you won't be able to touch it. And for many of you that will be the closest you will ever get. Don't you dare come back in here without giving your all.' Of course, they did give their all, all in the last minute – which just goes to show that never mind being the biggest and the richest, the players who actually do the business out there on the pitch are also motivated by being the best.

Despite not living up to its star billing, Manchester United's late, late show (as it has become known) was certainly a tasty appetizer for the new and revised Champions' League competition that UEFA was planning to serve up in 1999–2000. It was also a welcome fillip for UEFA themselves, whose premier competition had been threatened by the Media Partners (an Italian sports marketing company obsessed with the idea of creating a European Super League) proposition based on money and pre-selection according to tradition and size, which in reality was nothing more than a glorified arrangement to ensure the biggest clubs would be performing in front of the largest television audiences.

That, frankly, would have made a mockery of the *raison d'être* of the Champions' League; namely, to answer the question: 'Which is the best team in Europe?' It was that question the former French player and later editor of the French sports daily *l'Équipe*, Gabriel Hanot, sought to answer when he initiated the European Cup competition in the 1950s. Hanot was piqued by English press claims that Stan Cullis's Wolverhampton Wanderers were the 'champions of Europe' purely on the basis of victories against two of the top continental sides of the time, Honved of Hungary and Spartak Moscow. Ridiculous, he responded, and the European Cup was conceived. Ironically, the inaugural competition did not insist on league champions; *l'Équipe* simply invited the newly formed UEFA to send representatives – and the first ever 'European Cup' was won, in 1956, by Real Madrid.

It was the Spanish side's five consecutive victories (in particular their thrilling 7–3 triumph over Eintracht Frankfurt in the 1960 final) that underpinned the popularity of the competition. Since then, winning the European Cup has always been considered the pinnacle of success in club football, and the list of those who have grasped football's most distinguished club prize includes many of the world's most talented footballers – Di Stefano and Puskas (Real Madrid); Johann Cruyff (Ajax); Franz Beckenbauer (Bayern Munich); Ruud Gullit, Marco van Basten and Frank Rijkaard (AC Milan); Kevin Keegan and Kenny Dalglish (Liverpool). However, while not wanting to detract from the achievement it's a fact that to prove they were the best they only had to play a maximum of nine games in the course of the competition, since the European Cup embraced a knock-out format as opposed to a league template, which meant that there was always the chance that David, on his day, could overcome Goliath.

Now that money has become top priority, such a format would, of course, be far too risky; the possibility that small fry could end up in the final would give the mega clubs sleepless nights at the thought of the prospective loss of revenue. AC Milan president Silvio Berlusconi realized this when he commented that this old-style European Cup was not based on 'modern thinking', and his opposition effectively signalled its deathknell. Changes – and more importantly, expansion – were inevitable. The turning point came in the early 1990s when the format was extended to include a group phase followed by the traditional knockout mode. It was soon expanded to encompass sixteen teams, and then twenty-four – which now seems positively conservative considering the thirty-two teams who went into the hat for the 1999 draw. As the portentous blurb in UEFA's weighty Official Guide puts it, 'Europe's premier club competition had developed at an astonishing pace, to the extent that, had we been manufacturers of a new product, one could truthfully have stated that we were having problems matching supply to demand.'

Not any more. On the contrary, the matches have been coming so thick and fast since the first group match-day on 14 September 1999 (not forgetting the three qualifying rounds in the height of summer) that the Champions' League is already in danger of becoming too much of a good thing. What's more, the players – not to mention the fans, for whom the midweek European clash used to be an eagerly awaited treat – are starting to feel the pace before the domestic league season has even cranked into gear. Frequent midweek European trips – airport, hotel, match, airport, home – followed by a return to a gruelling league schedule appear to have taken their toll to such an extent that on the weekend of 25–26 September, Arsenal struggled to beat Watford, Chelsea made hard work of beating Middlesbrough, while Manchester United could only draw with Southampton; games which under normal circumstances would have represented a probable three points in the bag for the big boys. (Cynics might argue that it has had a beneficial effect as it's made the domestic Championship more competitive.) The debilitating effects of the Champions' League programme were manifest across the continent as Barcelona, Real Madrid, Bayern Munich, Milan and Marseille were all unusually off the pace in their domestic leagues.

What's more, there were already signs that the clubs involved were making the Champions' League a priority over and above their own national championship. As far as Manchester United, Arsenal and Chelsea were concerned, resting key players for Premiership matches – to say nothing of the Worthington Cup ties – they might expect to win in preparation for the big midweek encounters might make perfect sense in the heat of the battle, but it's a dangerous game to play. After all, you only get one of those coveted invites to the Champions' League party if you are successful in your own backyard.

George Graham underlined the dilemma when he was unable to answer the question of whether he would rather win a cup or finish second or third in the league – and this from a man whose *raison d'être* is winning trophies. The inference was clear: the Champions' League is the only competition that really matters in terms of both kudos and cash. Yet since when did coming second or third in the league ever signify success? What, in fact, did Arsenal and Chelsea win that gave them the right to take part in this League for 'Champions'? The short answer is nothing. (It is possible that a club like Parma, which has never won its domestic league in its entire history, could now win the ultimate European prize.) So why call it the Champions' League? Why not describe it as a European League, or even revert back to the 'European Cup', the name some traditionalists still insist on using? Why, indeed, allow second- and third-place teams to participate in a competition for which the champions of smaller, less successful nations – such as the Ukrainian champions Dynamo Kiev, semi-finalists in 1999 – are forced to pre-qualify? In essence, the designation 'Champions' League' is a misnomer (although some of those who call radio phone-ins to complain might do well to remember that they support clubs in the First Division, which is really the Second).

However, the reality is that UEFA have actually devised a competition that at least has its roots in merit and sporting contest. Furthermore, it will – eventually – determine which is the best team in Europe (after all, few would argue that Manchester United weren't the rightful winners in 1998–99, even if they weren't the champions of England). UEFA had to include more than one representative from, at least, the top ten countries to avoid a scenario whereby the champions of, say, Malta, appeared in the Champions' League to the exclusion of a team that finished just one point behind Manchester United. UEFA conceded the clubs' argument that the top-placed teams in the best leagues (which are decided on a ranking basis dependent on the European performances of each country's representatives over the last five years) had just as much right as the champions of the lesser countries to appear in the premier competition.

Consequently, UEFA upgraded the Champions' Cup to the Champions' League, with central marketing guaranteeing television and sponsorship revenue for the pre-qualified champions in the top-ranked markets (coincidentally also the ones with the biggest television audiences). That done, they downgraded the UEFA Cup and did away with the thirty-nine-year-old Cup-Winners' Cup – yet one more battle lost by the federations and won by the clubs – so that, rather like the Premier League nationally, the Champions' League became the only competition that mattered. The UEFA Cup was marginalized, shoe horned into Thursdays so as not to distract from the top-of-the-bill Champions' League, a nomenclature that was retained for marketing purposes only. Considering that UEFA have spent millions on establishing their top-selling brand, they were hardly going to change it and run the risk of undermining the event. OK, so the champions of their respective leagues did not contest the last final . . . but that hardly mattered when so much time, effort and money had been employed to establish the brand equity of the Champions' League as *the* competition. So, short of revolutionary restructuring, like Nike, Sega, Vodafone and Lloyds TSB the 'Champions' League' is a brand that is here to stay. Like it or lump it, and regardless of whether the champions are competing or not.

By and large UEFA have, for the moment, succeeded in producing a competition that meets the needs of the big clubs, the major television networks and international sponsors, but one which – more importantly – embraces the notion of merit. In other words, the Champions' League stands for quality as well as quantity, even if the likes of Dynamo Kiev might feel they've drawn the short straw. However, where UEFA have blotted their copybook is in endeavouring to beef up the UEFA Cup with the clubs which fall by the Champions' League wayside: with the losers from the qualifying rounds and, worse still, with the third-placed teams from the first group stage of the Champions' League. Whoever heard of teams being knocked out of one competition and going into another that is taking place concurrently? The idea that heads you win, tails you don't lose has no place in any sporting contest, and does much to undermine the value of the UEFA Cup, particularly for the likes of West Ham, who had to toil through three rounds in the InterToto Cup to get into the UEFA Cup in the first place (although the fact remains that the InterTwo-Bob Cup, as the *Sun* memorably christened it, is in itself a competition for failures). According to George Graham, 'It's typical of the people who make up these competitions. How can they lay down ground rules whereby failure in one competition can promote you to another? We [Tottenham] could do well to reach the third round [of the UEFA Cup] then end up facing Manchester United, Chelsea or even Milan, so the thing is farcical really. When you enter a competition you don't expect to get some new runners and riders half-way through. It's just symptomatic of caving in to the big clubs' unceasing and changing needs and wants.'

But having loaded the dice heavily in favour of the big clubs, UEFA then had to put its money where its mouth was and apportion the money on offer. It had its hand forced by the Media Partners' proposal which had guaranteed at least £20 million per club in the opening season. UEFA had to at least match that offer to make its plan viable. Thanks to the fact that TEAM, UEFA's media agency, had quadrupled its annual television income to a whopping £400 million, UEFA was able to announce that each of the thirty-two clubs involved in the Champions' League was to get a participation bonus of £600,000, plus bonuses per match played (£200,000), won (£200,000) and drawn (£100,000). In the second round there is no participation bonus but the payout for a draw or win is the same. Points certainly mean prizes in this game show, because the stakes rise considerably for the quarter-finalists, who get £1.6 million, while the semi-finalists pocket £2 million and the losing finalists £3.2 million. The fee for the triumphant finalists is £4 million – which means that in total the 1999–2000 UEFA Champions' League winners would be better off to the tune of £30 million when receipts from home matches and television shares were added in.

It is the change in television strategy that so transformed the spectacle of the 1999–2000 Champions' League campaign. Hitherto, ITV had brought us one match live – Bob Wilson, Terry Venables and co. – on the Wednesday evening of a European week (which in the words of one football analyst contained only the odd perceptive comment from Terry Venables.) But now, with thirty-two clubs involved and UEFA's requirement that every match should be screened live, the key terrestrial networks in the five top television countries of Germany, England, Spain, France and Italy have had to take a pay television partner because as general entertainment channels they couldn't find the necessary slots on their schedules.

However, this is where it has all started to go awry for the UK viewer who has not yet got to grips with the machinations of pay-per-view (ppv) and doesn't understand why the Champions' League has to be run on a totally different system. In the major continental countries the Champions' League has embraced the pattern of the domestic programme. Although the number of pay-television viewers is currently minute in comparison to free-to-air, they are a vital component of any television package. In the equivalent UK scenario, the established pay sports network, Sky Sports, would have been the terrestrial station's natural partner but with ITV companies Granada and Carlton owning ONdigital, they naturally voted to keep it in the family.

Thus the average UK viewer has a midweek minefield to negotiate in front of the box, a pot mess of a programming schedule. As *Daily Telegraph* columnist Giles Smith wrote, with not a little sarcasm, all you need to watch your full complement of football is 'a set-top box, a second set-top box and/or a supplementary cable or satellite connection, perhaps a third set-top box for luck, some string, a typical household washing-up detergent bottle and a roll of sticky-backed plastic ... thus goes the contemporary predicament of the sports viewer: spoilt for choice, and at the same time – as the market-leaders play out their war games – strangely choiceless.'

Choiceless maybe, depending on your preferred choice of equipment. Bemused and out of pocket, certainly, given that the total annual cost to ensure complete coverage (including the BBC licence fee) is now around £700. Of course, when Sky first signed their deal with the Premier League at least you knew you could see all the live matches if you owned a dish or cable, and that failing that you could at least watch Sky's live broadcasts in a pub. Now that's off the cards too since ITV's pay partner, ONdigital, who have the rights to show the Tuesday night Champions' League matches, don't allow their matches to be shown in pubs. To make matters worse the home legs of the UEFA Cup matches involving Tottenham and West Ham were only available to Sky Digital viewers.

So, with fewer than two million digital homes as the UEFA competitions got under way, many of the choice encounters were off-limits to the majority of English fans. Nevertheless, with ITV audiences of nearly ten million, the Champions' League was already doing comparable business to the soaps and quiz shows. It was the same story around Europe. Television audiences of eight and nine million in Italy and France respectively watched Chelsea's impressive performance against AC Milan and Andy Cole's spectacular overhead kick against Marseille. As for the advertisers, for whom the typical football couch potato perfectly suits their conception of an ideal target audience for certain product categories such as cars, alcohol, mobile phones and financial services, no other programme provides such a cost-effective return. Moreover, in this age of niche channels the Champions' League, like the NFL in the States, provides an increasingly rare opportunity for the shared viewing experience (going back to the days when one could only watch the most popular sport on free-to-air television), allowing the network to put a premium on the ad rates. Both broadcasters and advertisers must be high-fiving all the way to the bank, particularly since only eight of the thirty-two teams involved would fall by the wayside after the first group stage.

The current Champions' League trophy is actually the second of its kind; the first was awarded outright to Real Madrid after their sixth triumph in the competition in 1966. When the then general secretary of UEFA, Hans Bangerter, decided to create a new design, settling on one that would appeal to all those taking part proved a problem. Its creator, Jürg Stadelman, recalls going to Bangerter's office and 'covering the floor with drawings. He made comments like, "The Bulgarians would like the bottom of that. The Spaniards would like that but the Italians would prefer that and the Germans would go for that bit." We put the design together like a jigsaw puzzle. It was a "bastardized" design. It may not be an artistic masterpiece, but everyone in football is keen to get their hands on it.' Too right. The former ITV commentator Brian Moore hit the nail on the head when he once described it as 'almost seventeen pounds of silver that's worth its weight in gold'.

As far as Arsenal were concerned, however, their 1999–2000 Champions' League campaign had more than just monetary value. For Arsène Wenger and his players the competition represented a chance to salvage some of the pride lost following the previous season's disastrous results when, despite having twice beaten Panathinaikos, they failed to beat Dynamo Kiev at their adopted

European home of Wembley or in the Ukraine and then, most crucially, lost at Wembley to Lens having only managed a 1–1 draw in the away leg in France. It was not a campaign anyone connected with Arsenal wanted to remember – or repeat – in a hurry. Least of all Wenger. 'Going out of the competition in the first stage hurt me,' he confessed. 'We had the quality to go through but paid the price for not having enough players.' Arsenal also paid the price – unlike Manchester United and Chelsea, whose recent European exploits guaranteed them preferential treatment (even though Chelsea had to pre-qualify) – of not being seeded.

So Wenger's high hopes for the 1999–2000 campaign must have been somewhat dented when Arsenal came out of the hat in Champions' League Group B along with the Swedish champions AIK Solna (so far so good)... then Fiorentina and Barcelona. There is always one so-called Group of Death in tournament football, and this was most definitely it. The Italian side boasted a renowned three-pronged attack of Gabriel Batistuta, Enrico Chiesa and Predrag Mijatovic, with Argentine international Abel Balbo in reserve. Barcelona were most people's favourites to win the tournament with a side jam-packed with stars: among them Josep Guardiola, Luis Figo, Luis Enrique, Patrick Kluivert and the De Boer brothers. Oh, and some bloke called Rivaldo, too. AIK Solna were more of an unknown entity, but given that they were managed by a Scot and combined the traditional Swedish characteristics of skill allied to stamina, they were clearly not just along for the ride.

Arsenal, however, were a very different proposition from the side which had so underachieved during the 1998–99 European campaign. The likes of Christopher Wreh, Luis Boa Morte, Remi Garde and Stephen Hughes, all of whom started vital fixtures, had been replaced by players with the calibre and experience of Davor Suker, Thierry Henry, Silvinho, Nwankwo Kanu and Oleg Luzhny. Clearly Arsenal had decided to add both brain and brawn to their ranks in their quest to be considered a significant European side. The upshot was that, on paper, they had no need to be frightened of anyone. The big question was: did this new-look squad now have the requisite self-belief to succeed where its predecessors had failed?

It was a question that no one could answer until Arsenal had come through the confrontation with Barcelona in the Nou Camp on 29 September. Before that, there was the small matter of seven Premiership matches, as well as the Champions' League fixtures against Fiorentina and AIK Solna to address. Somewhat prophetically, Arsenal started their 1999–2000 season in shirts bearing the product name – Dreamcast – of its new sponsor Sega; looking at the quality of the players they had on the field and on the bench, one could be forgiven for thinking that Wenger was very close to assembling exactly that. Yet despite the fact that he had at least £20 million worth of talent at his disposal on the Arsenal bench in Marc Overmars, Silvinho and Henry (with Suker still fine-tuning on the training ground) Arsenal had to rely on an injury-time own goal by Frank Sinclair to beat Leicester in their opening game of the season at Highbury. 'Everybody can lose everywhere,' was Wenger's thought afterwards, suggesting that he had accepted that domestically he was in for a hard slog.

By the time Arsenal's Champions' League campaign kicked off in Florence on 14 September Wenger had been deprived of the services of the influential Emmanuel Petit thanks to a knee ligament injury sustained in a bruising encounter with Sunderland, and learnt that Dennis Bergkamp and Kanu would need time to evolve into a potent striking partnership. Both players were clearly more comfortable and at their most effective playing behind a pivotal target man and lacked the pace to capitalize on some often sublime approach play. 'We miss Anelka,' reflected David Dein. 'For all the attacking players we've got, he would add something.' Thierry Henry was clearly not the answer; not yet at least. His profligacy in his first few appearances in an Arsenal shirt suggested that his shooting boots had not been in his baggage when he arrived from Turin, and gave those watching cause to wonder at Wenger's prediction that his £10 million man's best position, long-term, was as a central striker.

Arsenal's errant former striker had scored in both the League clashes with Manchester United the previous season. Yet in the first confrontation of the season between the two heavyweights on 22 August the man who made all the difference in an enthralling exhibition of free-flowing, classic counter-attacking football, was Roy Keane. The United captain's two goals inflicted on Arsenal their first home defeat in twenty months. 'The defeat is not only a psychological blow to us,' admitted Wenger afterwards, 'but a mathematical blow as well as we dropped points against one of the teams who will fight for the Championship. How we respond is the most important thing now.' The only consolation to the Arsenal fans was that United's win knocked Tottenham off the top of the table. 'At least we could laugh about the fact that they were only up there for twenty-three hours,' sniggered one fan.

However, those willing to face the truth would have admitted that Arsenal's start to the season had an uncharacteristically topsy-turvy look about it. Indifferent against Leicester yet inspired against Derby. Ponderous against Sunderland yet penetrating against Manchester United (despite the defeat). Enervated against Liverpool yet energetic against Aston Villa. Consistency, clearly, had not been achieved.

Nor, it seems, had self-restraint. Arsenal – and you have to say this is unsurprising – had once again courted controversy. The streak of ill-discipline that Wenger's side appears to have in common with many of its predecessors reared its ugly head again when Patrick Vieira tangled with Roy Keane (although it clearly did little to put Keane off his game), and the problem was compounded when Gilles Grimandi attempted to rearrange Josep Guardiola's facial features in the key Champions' League fixture at the Nou Camp, an offence for which he was sent off. However, to dwell on that incident would be to detract from what was arguably Arsenal's greatest performance on a European stage – and that's including the 1994 Cup-Winners' Cup final against Parma when an Alan Smith goal won the match at the expense of the much-fancied Italians. On that night in Copenhagen a vintage Arsenal display full of grit and tenacity – it could not be much else given the spirited but somewhat workaday midfield pairing of Steve Morrow and Ian Selley – famously snuffed out the threat of Gianfranco Zola, Faustino Asprilla and co. Yet despite that victory there has always been a suspicion hovering over Highbury that Arsenal carried a chip on their shoulders into Europe. If you really want to stir the hornet's nest, it's a fact that Arsenal haven't even enjoyed as much success in Europe as Tottenham, who were the first British club to win a trophy (the Cup-Winners' Cup in 1962–63) and have twice won the UEFA Cup.

So the result – and, more significantly, the performance – on that balmy night of Wednesday 29 September 1999 in the cauldron that is the Nou Camp stadium, meant everything. It was, as one fan commented afterwards, 'a turning point. It was as if suddenly Arsenal had the right to stand up and be counted in Europe, as if we had at last earned the respect of the rest of Europe.' It seemed that this encounter, for all the Florentines' style, was always going to be the decisive one in Group B and the fans were, as it goes in football parlance, well up for it. Despite the 118,000 capacity just 1,400 Arsenal fans had tickets, yet thousands more descended on Spain, and hundreds welcomed the Arsenal side at the airport wearing T-shirts with 'Arselona 99' on them. Tom Watt, the Talk Radio (soon to be relaunched as Talk Sport) presenter who wears his heart prominently on his sleeve when it comes to supporting the Arsenal, opened his late afternoon show – broadcast live from the Nou Camp – with a rousing rendition of the Freddie Mercury and Montserrat Caballé hit 'Barcelona', and the chat on the airwaves concerned little else bar the game. *The* game, as far as Arsenal fans were concerned. It was stirring stuff if you were of the red and white persuasion. Everyone else just wondered how many Arsenal were going to get stuffed by.

The problem was that Arsenal's Champions' League campaign, like their domestic one, had yet to get well and truly off the ground. Sure, the 0–0 draw in Florence showed a level of endeavour combined with no little skill that must have encouraged those who doubted Arsenal's affinity for the European stage. And on the evidence of the result Arsenal had certainly learnt from their past mistakes against Lens and Dynamo Kiev. The outcome was the same as it had been in France – a draw, albeit a scoreless one – but you could hardly say it was a voice from the past. Yes, Arsenal were profligate in front of goal, but in reality, the only similarity between the two matches was that they had dropped two points in their opening Champions' League fixture. After conceding a late equalizer in the ninetieth minute in Lens Wenger and his disconsolate troops had slunk home with their heads down. This time they positively strutted out of Italy, knowing that had Freddie Ljungberg not shot wide from six yards when it looked easier to score, and Kanu not missed from the penalty spot in the eightieth minute, their baggage back home would have contained a precious three points and a nice little win bonus of £200,000.

For that, Wenger should take a great deal of the acclaim. Fiorentina's Giovanni Trapattoni is Italy's most successful coach, yet he was out-thought and out-manoeuvred by his counterpart, who later maintained that his side gave 'the most mature display we've had in the Champions' League'. No wonder the Arsenal fans expected their side to walk all over AIK Solna at Wembley the following Wednesday. That AIK narrowly failed to upset the apple-cart on the night was in the main down to Wenger's decision to make a double substitution after sixty-eight minutes, replacing Ljungberg and Overmars with Henry and Kanu, and play with four strikers in an attempt to break down the stubborn Swedish resistance. It smacked of desperation, but then desperate times call for desperate measures. Besides, the gamble paid off when first Henry and then Suker struck deep into injury time to secure the three points. The relief washed over Wembley like the rain that had fallen in torrents before the match.

It was a stark reminder of how quickly footballing fortunes can turn. The late double strike had every journalist present frantically rewriting copy, and left the crowd, which had grown increasingly irritated with Arsenal's inability to kill the game off, unable to contain their delight. True, they had greeted the double substitution with one of the loudest cheers of the night, but the renewed hope it had given them turned to despair when Henry dragged an easy chance wide with nine minutes left on the clock. Yet they should now know that it is never over until the thin man makes his substitutions. Nevertheless, sitting calmly in the bowels of Wembley afterwards, Wenger admitted he had been rattled. 'It was a big gamble for me to play four strikers at the end,' he said, 'but I wanted to keep AIK under pressure. If we did not win here it would have been very, very difficult for us to qualify for the next stage. Leaving it that late is not very good for the heart. The quality of the players I was able to send on was the deciding point in the game. Henry and Kanu are just the type of players you need in these tight situations. If you look at the statistics for the Champions' League games, more and more are being decided in the last five minutes when players are tired. Yet I was really scared we could lose the game because we had everybody upfront and AIK were always dangerous.' Lucky old Arsenal, then? 'Yes, we were a bit lucky tonight,' Wenger conceded, 'but I still say it's down to the quality of my substitutes who had such a big impact on the outcome. We kept trying until the last minute and got what we needed.' At that point someone informed Wenger that Barcelona had beaten Fiorentina 4–2 in the Nou Camp, and at last he could afford a wry smile. 'That's shows how difficult it will be for us next week. A lot depends on how well we do out there. It will take nine or ten points to go through, and that's what we are aiming for.'

And so to Barcelona. Arsenal's party, which comprised the team, staff, club officials and a number of executive box holders as well as the media, flew out the day before the match and checked in at the Barcelona Plaza. (The plan was for the players to train in the morning, as customary, at the Nou Camp itself in order to get their body clocks adjusted.) The size and fervour of the 'welcoming' party at the airport, where Suker (because of his Real Madrid past), Seaman (who broke Spanish hearts with his penalty save at Euro 96) and Kanu and Overmars (who both worked under Barcelona coach Louis van Gaal) were in demand for interviews, was an indication – as if any were needed – of just how huge this game was. 'It is a big test because everyone says Barcelona are the biggest side in Europe,' Wenger said. 'I like their front six: Luis Enrique, Guardiola, Rivaldo, Figo, Kluivert and Cocu, who are all good. Because of the size of the pitch and the quality of their technique and passing Barcelona can destroy any defence. If they run after the ball they can slowly kill you. It's like drowning; you cannot do anything against it.'

Wenger went on to identify Guardiola ('a rare player who knows when to give the ball and when to keep it') as the key; part of his game-plan was to pressurize the Spanish international whenever he had the ball and then unsettle Barça's defence, which in his opinion was the weak link. Overmars concurred, saying: 'They are weak defensively. If you hit Barça on the break you can create chances.' The hundreds of Arsenal fans who had discussed all possible outcomes via the internet before the match were doubtless tempted to believe one Gooner, whose view was that Barça 'defended like an Ossie Ardiles team'.

That was by no means the only insult flying around prior to the match. Louis van Gaal, Barcelona's coach, who had equalled Wenger's feat at Arsenal in 1998 by leading Barcelona to the Spanish League and Cup Double in his first season, and followed that by retaining the title in 1998–99, is no shrinking violet. He had turned a deaf ear to the accusations that he was trying to create a 'Little Amsterdam' in Catalonia by signing the De Boer brothers, goalkeeper Ruud Hesp, Michael Reiziger, Boudewijn Zenden, Philip Cocu, Patrick Kluivert and Winston Bogarde, and then survived the ordeal of having a sea of white handkerchiefs waved at him after his side had tumbled out of the 1998–99 Champions' League at the group stage. So, it was hardly a surprise that van Gaal decided to put his oar in and cause a few ripples as the match approached.

Responding to Wenger's observation that Barcelona had a team of imported stars, he stated that Wenger 'has been busier in the transfer market than me'; maintained that 'no other club anywhere' could match Barça's outstanding number of youngsters in the first-team squad; and boasted that Barça were now stronger than when they faced Manchester United in the previous competition. However, there was one final sting in van Gaal's tail. When asked what he liked best about Arsenal, van Gaal replied: 'Above all, I like the characteristics of the players Wenger has bought. But I would. I started the best of them off myself.' No wonder Overmars described his former manager as a man who 'has a certain attitude about him . . .'

All that simply added spice to a game which few Arsenal fans back home could see, thanks to Carlton TV's controversial decision to screen Manchester United's match against Marseille, despite the huge demand to see Arsenal. Carlton defended their decision thus: '. . . audience research has repeatedly shown that in the London region more viewers want to see Man Utd. We are obviously sorry if this upsets Arsenal fans but the whole match will be available on ITV2 and there will be extended highlights on ITV between 2330 and 0035. The decision about which matches we will screen in the future will be based on the same criteria.' Judging by that statement it was tempting to draw the conclusion that Arsenal were never going to get the nod from Carlton. The decision exposes ITV's claim that it is the UK's regional broadcaster within a national framework, and makes a mockery of the positioning of Carlton and its much-vaunted slogan: 'Carlton For London'. Granada would surely have opted out of the network game if it had been Arsenal, and shown United in their area.

Had the game finished after the first half, however, those Arsenal fans who missed out might not have felt so deprived. Barcelona's performance was so sublime, Arsenal's so pedestrian, that it was almost painful to watch. Arsenal were frequently cut to ribbons by Barcelona's passing movement, most of it emanating from the sweet and sorcerous left foot of Rivaldo and the vision of Guardiola, once a ball-boy at the Nou Camp. Guardiola spent the first half relentlessly sweeping the ball out to Rivaldo and Sergi on the left, Luis Figo and Reiziger on the right, or just down the middle to the industrious Luis Enrique. It was Luis Enrique who was the beneficiary of Patrick Vieira's aborted attempt to juggle the ball out of danger in his own six-yard box, the little Spaniard nipping in to prod the ball home for the opening goal. *Gracias*.

Arsenal looked down and out of it at half-time, reduced to a bit-part role by a team who, as Wenger admitted afterwards, were 'technically perfect in the first half. We couldn't stop them so I said to the players to be more audacious. In the first half we tried to stop Guardiola; in the second half we tried to stop their defenders getting the ball to Guardiola so I pushed Dennis Bergkamp further upfield.' Wenger's tactical re-think started to trouble Barcelona, who found their supply lines to their midfield playmaker severed, first by Bergkamp and then by his replacement, Suker, whose reception was predictably hostile.

Wenger was right when he said afterwards that it was 'a great result from a great Arsenal team', that 'once again we've seen the spirit of Arsenal', recalling other memorable examples such as the FA Cup finals of 1979 and 1993, Anfield 1989 and Juventus in the semi-final of the Cup-Winners' Cup in 1980. It was no surprise that Arsenal fought back; as Barcelona tired, Wenger threw caution to the wind again and introduced Henry and Suker with seventeen minutes left on the clock. It was the defining moment. Suker's Real Madrid past visibly upset Barcelona's present; it was he who struck the eighty-first-minute shot which Hesp failed to hold, and Kanu drove home the rebound. 'When they saw Suker coming on Barcelona's defenders became insecure because they knew he had so much success in Spain,' Wenger said. He made it sound as if he'd planned it that way, but he must have been getting twitchy as the clock ran down. 'I was nervous in the last minutes when we were down to ten men,' he divulged. 'That's when Kanu dropped back to midfield to emphasize what we are all about. We have the spirit and the quality. That's five points for us now. Our fate is in our hands.'

At the back, Tony Adams once again answered Arsenal's call. It was indicative of Adams's towering performance in the heart of the defence that he should be the player who, at the death, blocked a certain Dani goal and prevented a Catalan victory. Adams was simply outstanding, and it came as no surprise to learn after the match of how he had stood in the Arsenal dressing room at half-time and told his team-mates: 'You have to give me more.' As his sometime England team-mate, Gary Neville, concurred: 'He is passionate about the game and he will walk around saying motivational things, telling you to make sure you have no regrets at the end of the match. I think it probably helps his own concentration but he is an inspiration to the rest of the team as well.'

Adams, more than anyone, realized how much the Barcelona game meant to Arsenal – he had been at the club for nearly sixteen years and become its youngest-ever captain aged twenty-one – and he wasn't about to give up the fight so easily. Of course, he had done this sort of thing before. As his beleaguered team-mates lay down and out on a Parisian pitch after former Tottenham midfielder Nayim's sensational last-minute winner for Real Zaragoza in the 1995 European Cup-Winners' Cup final, it was Adams who had dragged himself off the turf to console them, before delivering a rousing speech back in the dressing room. Typical. George Graham dubbed Adams a colossus, and it was probably never more true than in the Nou Camp that September night.

How must Adams relish nights like these? These days, of course, he is clear-headed enough to appreciate them, but it goes deeper than that. He has always used defeat as motivation, which means that such exploits taste particularly sweet. Moreover, Adams' meta-morphosis as both person and player since he admitted his alco-holism in 1996 has altered his outlook on life. Whereas before he would eyeball defeat and failure as if they were his sworn enemies, he is now able to see the bigger picture – in which they are merely blips on a much larger landscape. He has taken off the blinkers. 'You lose, you feel bad. It's natural,' he acknowledges. 'But it does not ruin my life today.' Paradoxically, the fear of ruining his life was what inspired him to give up alcohol and remains a constant motivation to perform at his best.

This change of perspective has meant that the late 1990s version of Tony Adams is poles apart from the earlier model, the one who spent his days – some of which he can remember, many more of which will for ever remain a blur – waging war on his mind and his body. These days he has about him a candour that is positively refreshing in a society which is sceptical of anyone who expresses emotion and admits vulnerability. And while he still possesses in abundance those characteristics which always earmarked him as the archetypal British bulldog – balls, bottle, pride and passion – he now channels them in a very different direction. You still see him cajoling, urging and occasionally admonishing, but the battle which he wages daily against his 'illness' (alcoholics are never 'recovered' but always 'recovering') is far more serious than anything he is likely to encounter on the football pitch, so he knows where and when to draw the line.

His need to distance himself from other people's problems whilst he is still on a voyage of self-discovery might explain why, in the words of a colleague, Adams 'went missing' during Patrick Vieira's misadventure at Upton Park (Vieira was dismissed for a second bookable offence, then spat at Neil Ruddock as he was on his way off the pitch, adding insult to injury). Recall the incident, and you won't remember Adams racing in with eyes blazing and fists clenched, intent on sorting it all out as the Adams of old would almost certainly have done. He might be the Arsenal captain who still wants to win every game as much as he ever did, but these days putting other people's wrongs to rights with a rush of blood is no longer his style. 'I may have been a little impetuous as a younger player. Maybe now I'm too slow to get there,' he jokes, before continuing in a more serious vein. 'But I'm not too slow to say something. If something needs to be said I'll say it.' But obviously not in the heat of battle, when he now knows that acting in haste might mean repenting at leisure.

The Arsenal management, apparently, were 'disappointed' that Adams kept out of it, but 'understood' his perspective. Too right. After all, does any Arsenal player epitomize the club more than Adams? Has any other player done more for the Arsenal cause? Probably not, which is why you'd expect the club to cut him whatever slack he might need. However, Adams's preoccupation with his own self as an antidote to the depths of despair and shame that forced him to renounce alcohol might well cloud his judgement on issues concerning his nearest and dearest. For example, he has compared Vieira being racially abused to him (Adams) being labelled 'donkey' or 'big nose', describing them both as a form of racism. However hurtful the insults might have been, it clearly isn't, as they were not calling into question his race or religion. Perhaps just as wide of the mark is his claim that racism in football is 'very isolated'. It's not. Less noticeable, perhaps, as the explosion of overseas imports (nearly 200 at the last count) has provided an alternative target. However, like crowd violence, racism is a latent and omnipresent boil waiting to burst.

Still, no one should begrudge Adams his standpoint. His admission that he was an alcoholic who needed help took more courage, more guts, than any of the hundreds of last-ditch tackles or goal-line clearances that he has made during his career, and it would be a small-minded person who resented him his new lease of life. Which is not to say some don't. Tabloid journalists no doubt preferred the previous incarnation. He was better copy then. They roll their eyes when he comes out with comments such as 'I love today, I'm enjoying today', can't fathom his equanimity and dismiss him as 'being on another planet'. Football is notorious for taking perverse pleasure in watching its heroes fall, for putting players up on pedestals and then pushing them off again, and Adams has had to deal with such hypocrisy throughout his career. He carried around for years the baggage of that 1988 European Championship defeat to Holland, when Marco van Basten ran him ragged. He was just twenty-one, and it hurt his pride. If it happened to him now, he could deal with it. 'I've got enough self-esteem and self-worth about me,' he declares, 'so I can go out there and say, "Well, Tone, what are you? Are you going to let that affect you?" I know I can go to the mirror now and say, "No, you're OK." The element of fear has gone.'

Ten years on and Marco van Basten again touched his life. Prematurely forced out of football through degenerative ankle problems caused by tackles from behind, which was the impetus behind the FIFA law change banning them, the former European Footballer of the Year and Adams happened to meet in a restaurant in the South of France when Adams was recuperating. At the crossroads of yet another debilitating injury and with the landmark of his thirtieth birthday behind him, Adams could easily empathize with van Basten's unfulfilled career. He felt that he owed it to himself to continue doing what he was best at as long as he was able to. It was back to work with a vengeance.

He now eschews the limelight, cringes at his erstwhile popular image of bellicose, chest-pounding leader. Simplistic it might sound, but he just wants to get on with his life, on and off the pitch, which in no way means his passion for football has diminished. On the contrary, he claims it's 'as important as ever, but it is in the right place in my life. I take my job very seriously. I love the self-respect that it gives me after I have done a good day's work.' His ambition remains undimmed. He wants to win more trophies with Arsenal and captain England again (he captained the side before Alan Shearer usurped his position) but if it's not to be then that's OK as well. The inference is clear: football is just a part of Adams's life now, not his whole life and nothing but. These days he does other things, things he never had time for when life was just a series of Wednesdays and Saturdays and nothing very much in between; at least, nothing that he can remember. He is helping RAPT (Rehabilitation for Addicted Prisoners) in Pentonville Prison. He is learning the piano. He reads. He does stuff that normal people do, stuff that brings him serenity. And if people condemn his refurbished image of esoteric Essex boy as a contradiction in terms ... that's tough. As Lee Dixon observes: 'The difference is unbelievable. If you knew him before and you know him now he's a nice person to be around, whereas a few years ago he wasn't particularly nice to be around all of the time. Although he was still a mate he had problems but we really didn't know how to help him. He changed himself. It just shows the character of the man.'

This remarkable transformation is perfectly encapsulated in a story told by a neighbour of Adams's in south London, an undergraduate student whose younger brother shares the same piano teacher as Adams and who, along with a friend, first ignited Adams's interest in literature. She invited Adams to a party, where he blended in so unobtrusively with the other guests that few people realized who the tall, unshaven character standing chatting in the garden was until one young boy rushed in and breathlessly said to the hostess: 'There's a man in the garden who looks just like Tony Adams', to which she replied: 'It is Tony Adams.' Adams forged such a friendship with the girls that he arranged for them to travel to Saint-Etienne to watch England play Argentina in the World Cup. After England's traumatic defeat, in a bizarre case of role reversal, it was Adams who comforted the distraught girls with the advice: remember, it's only a game.

As far as the Arsenal fans are concerned, Adams is perhaps even more the embodiment of the club than he was when George Graham was manager, when his status was such that the players dubbed him 'Son of George'. Many fans believe that the club simply won't be the same when he retires, although exactly when that will be is anybody's guess. Arsenal fan Alex Phillips even goes so far as to say: 'I often think I'll stop going when he retires, and go and watch Enfield or someone else instead.'

Now thirty-three, Adams has been the central cog in a defence which, according to its critics, has been on its last legs for at least four seasons now. It is geriatric on paper, young at heart, and it's surely not just fluke that the renewed vigour which was so evident during Arsenal's triumphant Double-winning season – not to mention during the subsequent campaign when the Gunners' defence conceded just seventeen goals – coincided with Adams's renaissance. It was as if his revitalization had galvanized his team-mates, driving them collectively to greater heights. 'He is a big influence. It's nice to have him out there,' says Lee Dixon, stating the obvious. 'When all the senior players are together we do rely on each other and when one of us isn't there it seems different.' Arsène Wenger elaborates: 'Adams takes over from the manager on the field. I've always liked rugby and those half-times when the players stay on the pitch. That's the proof that the captain is both the leader and the inspiration on the pitch, and that's Adams.'

However, while Adams's personal reformation is purely down to him, he is indebted to Arsène Wenger for his renaissance as a footballer. It is incredible to think that Adams very nearly jumped ship when Wenger was appointed manager. 'Oh no, bloody hell, I've got to play for a Frenchman? You must be joking. I'm definitely off this time,' he reportedly said. But as he later admitted, gut reactions are not always the right ones – Wenger encouraged Adams, gave him a licence to go forward which culminated in a new chant at Highbury during that Double-winning season: 'Tony, Tony Adams, Tony Adams on the wing'. The goal he scored at Highbury in the 4–0 victory against Everton on 3 May 1998 that effectively sealed the Championship, just summed it all up. Steve Bould chipped the ball forward and there was Adams, steaming through the middle to slam the ball home decisively with his left foot (in Graham's era he hardly got beyond the half-way line, save for setpieces). Then, instead of haring away like a mad thing he stood quite still, arms aloft, chest proudly puffed out, lapping up the applause. After all the trials and tribulations he was going to make damn sure he enjoyed that moment to the full.

Of course, his attributes are still most evident in the heart of the defence. Wenger has called him a 'doctor of defence', and it's easy to see why. He is not as dogged as Martin Keown, but his positional play is so smart that he is more often than not the player who makes the crucial interception or saving tackle. He more frequently brings the ball out from the back now too, which never used to be a feature of his game. He's no Beckenbauer, no Baresi, not even a Leboeuf, but then he doesn't pretend to be. Nowadays, though, he now reads the game probably as well as anyone else in his position in Europe. 'I'm never going to be an Alan Shearer or a Paul Gascoigne, but my particular job I feel I do very well.'

All of which goes some way towards explaining why Adams had once again proved to be the key on the European stage. It was evident from their display against Barcelona that Arsenal had finally come to terms with adapting, when necessary, to a more methodical, patient, continental-style pattern of play – solid in defence and sharp on the break – as opposed to domestically, where the focus is more often on the midfield and attack and the likes of Petit, Vieira and Bergkamp dictate the tactics. Those who believed that the loss of Petit would hamper Arsenal's progress in Europe were no doubt surprised by the side's ability to cope without him, in particular against Fiorentina and Barcelona. Moreover, those Arsenal fans who had been breaking out in a sweat at the thought of Lee Dixon coming up against the mighty Rivaldo in the Nou Camp – and there were plenty who felt that Oleg Luzhny should be given the nod ahead of the veteran after Luzhny's promising debut against Fiorentina – probably ordered a huge slice of humble pie on the flight home from Barcelona. True, Rivaldo showed enough of his repertoire of tricks and treats – including one mesmerizing piece of skill when he left Dixon for dead in the centre circle and headed for goal, only to be crowded out by a veritable cohort of Gunners (he showed a little too much of his less palatable side, too, going down far too easily in some observers' estimation) – but overall Arsenal's defence frustrated Rivaldo's constant probings, and as their former team-mate Alan Smith noted after the game, Rivaldo ended up as 'another notch on the bedpost for Arsenal's wily back four'.

Nobody connected with Arsenal football club that night cared that the superlative football had been played by the team wearing blue-and-grenadine striped shirts. All they cared about was that Arsenal had gone to Spain and plundered a precious point – the press had a field day with references to the Gunners and the Spanish Armada – despite the odds being stacked against them after Grimandi got his marching orders. David Dein, no less, admitted that he was so mesmerized by the quality of Barcelona's football that it wasn't until he watched a re-run of the game on his video in the early hours of the following morning that he realized the enormity of Arsenal's achievement. Having flown back with the Arsenal entourage after the match, Dein arrived home at 4 a.m. and immediately rewound his video. 'It was the only thing to do,' he said. 'The adrenalin was still pumping, the mind was racing, there was no way I was going to sleep. It's the same after every Arsenal game I get back from. Besides, you miss so much, invariably things your own players do, especially when you're playing Barcelona and during the game you can't take your eyes off Rivaldo or Luis Figo or Luis Enrique . . .' He could have gone on, but there was no need. The inference was clear: Barcelona's current crop of players may have been feted as the heirs to Ronald Koeman and co., clear favourites to lift the trophy for the first time since 1992, but the Gunners had turned up in Spain and spoilt their party and there was now a real possibility that Arsenal could beat Barcelona in the return leg. It was, though, only an away point, not an away-goal advantage. To qualify Arsenal simply had to win their home matches.

Amidst all the euphoria, however, Dein was circumspect, perhaps keen to allay the widespread concern that the Champions' League was too much of a priority, and that the Premiership was in danger of becoming an after-thought. 'I personally believe,' he said, 'that the domestic Championship comes first and foremost, that our next game is equally as important as playing Fiorentina and Barcelona, even if those games do have a certain charm and charisma. Europe is another kind of test of the club's ability, not to mention an extra excitement for the fans. We went to Barcelona, to that magnificent stadium with our fans stuck up there in the gods, and we held them on their own territory. So that was a great experience. But winning the League is the ultimate test of how good you are domestically and we want to be better than everyone else. That is the priority. But they are both important in their own ways.'

Being the best domestically these days, of course, means being better than Manchester United, who on the night Arsenal drew in Spain had staged another late show at Old Trafford, scoring in the seventy-ninth and eighty-third minutes to beat Marseille 2–1 and go top of their Champions' League group. In the Premiership, meanwhile, United had the edge on Arsenal, who lay two places behind Alex Ferguson's side, in fifth. However, United had developed the odd chink in their armour, particularly at the back where they were unable to decide on the rightful heir to Peter Schmeichel's goalkeeping mantle despite being spoilt for choice with three keepers. Moreover, with Ronny Johnsen, Wes Brown and Gary Neville injured, and Roy Keane stalling on signing a new contract, United were in dire need of a commanding central defender to play alongside Jaap Stam. They needed someone who was good in the air (Gary Neville's height was always going to count against him when he played in that position), who knew when to play it long and keep it short, and who was confident enough to bring the ball out from the back when necessary. If he were English, then so much the better. In short, they needed Sol Campbell.

CHAPTER THREE

AFTER THE LORD MAYOR'S SHOW

There had been more than just a few sceptics prepared to question Alex Ferguson's judgement when he paid PSV Eindhoven £10.5 million to make Jaap Stam a Manchester United player in 1998. The towering Dutch defender had suffered a disappointing World Cup and looked shaky and static during his first few months in English football (although he has silenced the doubters comprehensively since). By contrast, there were few dissenting voices when the rumour surfaced that it was only a matter of time before Sol Campbell became a Manchester United player. Campbell's steady rate of progress had continued throughout the World Cup, so much so that he was now undeniably one of the top centre-halves in Europe. Besides, trying to buy Campbell to play alongside Stam was like attempting to add Park Lane to Mayfair in your Monopoly portfolio. The prospect of such a formidable double-act made the millions it would inevitably take to buy him look cheap.

United's interest had been ignited by the fact that Campbell, who had come through the ranks at Tottenham, was stalling on signing a new contract (his present contract still had eighteen months left to run). But their bid was no sooner made than rejected. Despite Tottenham's acute need for a striker – they had dismissed rumours of a swap deal involving United striker Ole Gunnar Solskjaer, who would have made a perfect foil for his Norwegian international colleague Steffen Iversen – it was hard to see George Graham sanctioning the sale of a central defender, particularly one as irreplaceable as Campbell. It was common knowledge that Graham wanted to build his side around Campbell, and besides, the Tottenham captain was considered by many fans as a symbol of the club, certainly the key player in their bid to hang on to the coat-tails of the Premiership's élite. There was surely no way Alan Sugar would risk the wrath of the fans by letting him go.

However – and it is a big however – with Tottenham either unwilling or unable to pay top money for top players, it was also highly unlikely that Sugar would risk the prospect of Campbell nearing the end of his contract without having signed a new one. Otherwise he could depart as a free agent under the Bosman ruling once his contract had expired – and that would mean Tottenham getting no recompense for an asset worth millions.

It is quite difficult to conceive of a player whose early progress as a footballer was so hampered by growth spurts that he waddled when he ran, as being worth millions – but only for those who have not been privileged to watch Campbell play regularly over the past few seasons. Long gone are the days when the Tottenham fans derided him with the sobriquet 'Mitchell Two' (an allusion to the former Tottenham defender Mitchell Thomas, who in his latter days had a propensity for calamitous errors); Campbell is now – both inside and outside White Hart Lane – considered to be one of the world's finest defenders who should be a permanent fixture in the heart of England's defence for the next decade, a latter-day Tony Adams, if you like.

There are flaws in Campbell's game. His left foot lacks the precision of his right but his distribution has improved beyond measure; now, when he goes on one of those characteristic surges from the back – according to David Ginola, 'Sol likes to go on one at least once every match' – he now invariably finds a team-mate where before he used to find an opponent. His positional play is not yet as astute as, say, Adams, but he has obviously learnt from his mistake in the World Cup qualifier in February 1997 against Italy at Wembley that allowed Gianfranco Zola to ghost past him and score the only goal of the game (he says Glenn Hoddle helped him by making him compare his defending to that of the Italians on video), and put behind him the clumsy challenge on Marcelo Salas that gave away a penalty for the Chilean's second goal in the Wembley friendly a year later. You will seldom see Campbell lunge in with an imprecise tackle these days.

Campbell is as much a winner as Tony Adams, as confident in his own ability as the Arsenal captain, although he will not thank anyone who attempts to talk him up – he was incensed when the media, who love to make such comparisons, dared to liken him to a young Ruud Gullit. However, that does not preclude the odd blow on his own trumpet in weaker moments: Campbell once predicted that he was going to become the best defender in the world, and in a later interview maintained he was about 'half-way there'. It's a telling testimony to his defensive prowess that he seems to be respected by the Arsenal fans, brought up as they are to appreciate the art of the defender. Arsenal fan Amy Lawrence concurs, adding: 'Despite the fact that he embodies Spurs, Arsenal fans don't hate Campbell because he just gets on with playing the game, and he's such a cool defender.' He has the same unflappable and authoritative air as Marcel Desailly. He's almost as quick over twenty or thirty yards as Des Walker was in his prime. And he is as rock-solid, as much of a man-mountain, as Stam. Quite frankly, very little gets past him and it's a collector's item to see him muscled off the ball. According to David Pleat, Campbell has 'gained massively, physically over a few years. If you go back in history to the story about Bill Shankly making people walk around Ron Yeats to make him impressive, that's how people feel about Sol at times. I would imagine that knowledge gives him great heart'.

Off the pitch, however, Campbell is the antithesis of his imposing, on-the-field persona. The problem – although it is only a problem for those who consider today's top footballers to be public property – is that you don't hear much talk about him, simply because he doesn't talk very much about himself. In fact, he says very little, preferring to keep his private life and his emotions closely under wraps. Sure, he will talk to the press, but only when really necessary; and even then he refuses to be side-tracked from football topics with a steadfastness that is sometimes misconstrued as mundanity. Someone once rather cruelly commented that talking to Campbell can be like peeling an onion: peel away the skin, they wrote, rip off the outer layer, search for the heart . . . and you're left with emptiness. Not so. The reality is that self-proclamation and gratuitous soundbites are simply not his style. It may be a tedious cliché to say that he lets his football do his talking, but that is exactly how it is. 'I don't need to tell them everything,' he has said of the media. 'They think you're obliged to talk to them but I'm not like that. If I don't want to talk to you I don't want to talk to you. It's as simple as that. If it's a football thing I have to talk to you, but if it's not a football thing what are you coming to me for? I didn't ask you to come here.'

A thumbnail sketch exists, however, which depicts Campbell as a man who places great store by staying close to his roots. He may have moved away from Newham to Hertford, but he has kept up with his boyhood friends and vehemently eschews the lifestyles favoured by many of his contemporaries as much as he avoids the trappings of stardom. In fact, almost his only nod to extravagance comes in the form of a portfolio of flash cars, including a Porsche, and as a music lover the sound systems installed in each car are almost as important to him as the cars themselves – they say at Tottenham that you can always hear Campbell coming because his volume is pumped up so loud. However, he clearly has eclectic musical tastes for like Tony Adams, he has bought a piano and has recently started taking lessons.

So Campbell could be described as somewhat enigmatic, yet his taciturn manner has not surprisingly given rise to the thought that he is not extrovert enough to warrant the captain's armband. He's more your Gary Mabbutt than your Dave Mackay – although surely none the worse for that. You don't have to berate your colleagues to demonstrate your leadership qualities. Besides, never let it be said that Campbell is a reluctant skipper. Les Reed, formerly the FA's director of coaching for the south-east region, remembers the first time he met the fourteen-year-old Campbell during a spell deputizing for Dave Sexton as technical director at Lilleshall. 'Dave used to let the boys take it in turns to be captain during the games,' Reed recalls. 'Of course I had no idea this was the case and I was about to announce the teams for that day when Sol sidled up to me and quietly asked whether Mr Sexton had told me he was to be captain that day. He hadn't, and I had Sol earmarked as substitute. He wanted his chance to be captain and he took it. But that's just the type of player he is. He concentrates fully on his game and anything that will improve it. What's more, he's got a wonderful temperament.' In fact, from a very early age Campbell had an enquiring mind. As club secretary Peter Barnes recalls: 'When he was younger Sol asked a lot of questions. On away trips we had good chats, not only about the game but also about investing his money and things like that. He was a sensible boy right from the off.'

Doubters might well ask how come he's been around for so long, yet has only truly come to prominence in the last eighteen months (when his performances for his country have been as impressive as those for his club). For the answer ask Terry Venables, who first included Campbell in the England set-up in the build-up to Euro 96. Venables maintains that Campbell was held back because he was 'exceptionally shy and it took him a long time to settle down for club and country. But I was always convinced of his ability. The quieter players need patience – I dipped him in and out – but they do come good.' That prophecy was fulfilled when Kevin Keegan recently described Campbell as 'a young man, but a man'.

Campbell has been fortunate to have learnt his trade under three of the most tactically aware managers in the English game – Venables, Glenn Hoddle and now George Graham. However, there are those who query whether he has actually improved significantly under George Graham, who is supposed to know his defensive onions. Season-ticket holder Paul Stern appreciates that Graham 'is trying to establish a pattern so he doesn't have to rely on one super defender' but in doing so he fears that 'some of Campbell's instinctive qualities are being coached out of him in the interests, God forbid, of offside tactics'.

It was Graham who fashioned that famously parsimonious Arsenal defence, and the likes of Lucas Radebe and David Wetherall clearly benefited from his tutelage at Leeds. But it was actually Arsène Wenger's alchemy that reinvigorated Tony Adams – which rather begs the question: does Sol Campbell need George Graham as much as George Graham needs Sol Campbell? Moreover, to regard Campbell as some sort of shrinking violet who is happy to let the White Hart Lane grass grow under his feet would be way off the mark. True, he is fiercely loyal, having been at Tottenham so long he remembers David Beckham at the club before Beckham signed for Manchester United. But he gave a glimpse into his thinking – trying to draw him further on his future is as fruitless a task as trying to get past him on a football field – when he commented during Christian Gross's ill-fated reign: 'It's not up to me if and when I leave Tottenham. It's up to Alan Sugar or the manager to build a team. I want to be winning things but it has been allowed to fall apart for some reason.' A day later, Christian Gross was dismissed as Tottenham manager and the tide turned with Graham's arrival, but one suspects that Campbell would be alarmed at the idea of spending yet another season treading water, and therefore might feel a move away from the bosom of his Tottenham 'family' – for that is how he views the club – might be best, in the interests of ambition. If it should come to that then expect him to play the ball calmly into the Tottenham hierarchy's court by putting pressure on them to match his ambition and make it difficult for him to leave – in his own quiet way.

Campbell tasted some success when he lifted the 1998–99 season League Cup, and it would be an atypical player who was not ravenous for more. Now, his worth to a Tottenham team which, Sherwood and Freund apart, lacks a certain steeliness is implicit. Everyone connected with Tottenham is aware of this, not least his team-mates, as illustrated by a recent training ground incident. Having been at Tottenham for the past fifteen years press officer John Fennelly knows Campbell well; well enough to attract Campbell's attention by shouting: 'Come here, you wanker.' He was overheard by a shocked Steffen Freund, who had clearly not yet grown accustomed to the informality of the Tottenham set-up, for he rebuked Fennelly at once. 'You can't call Sol a "vanka",' he said. 'He is our most important player and we want him to stay. You must show him respect.' Campbell, by the way, found the incident highly amusing.

It was not the first time that Fennelly had been on the wrong end of a reprimand relating to the Tottenham captain. He remembers asking for 'Sulzeer Campbell' when it came to writing a profile on the player who was then just breaking onto the Tottenham scene. 'That's me, man,' came the reply, 'but please call me Sul.' Fennelly agreed, but maintained he would have to write it not as 'Sul' but as 'Sol'. (Campbell was never called 'Sulzeer', always 'Sul', although he'd never written it down.) When Fennelly's profile was eventually seen in print by the player's mother, the Tottenham press officer was subjected to a verbal ear-bashing from a very irate Mrs Campbell who demanded to know exactly who it was who thought they had the authority to muck around with her son's name.

What remains to be seen, however, is whether Tottenham's ambition matches that of their captain. This is the era of financial prudence at White Hart Lane, which basically means that Tottenham have to raise money before they can spend it, and they can raise most money by selling their biggest asset: Sol Campbell.

There would be no shortage of takers if they did decide to cash in. Manchester United were not the only ones who fancied Campbell. Juventus, Internazionale and Lazio had all courted him but none had followed up their interest with a firm bid. However, Campbell was particularly attractive to United as injury had ruled him out of Tottenham's team since the opening day defeat at West Ham, which meant – ominously – that he had played no part in the club's UEFA Cup campaign and would therefore be eligible to play in all United's Champions' League second-round group matches. The Tottenham fans, who had come to rely on Campbell as a constant throughout several abject seasons of upheaval and underachievement, were only too well aware of the situation. They knew that so far Tottenham had failed to match Campbell's aspirations by bringing big-name players to the club, and they needed no reminding, either, of the last White Hart Lane blue-eyed boy to eschew Tottenham's offer of a new contract and up sticks to Old Trafford, fed up at having won sweet FA at White Hart Lane. Oh, Teddy, Teddy . . . went to Man United and he won the Treble.

Contracts are something of a dirty word in modern football. For the most part, the days when a player and his advisors were able to agree terms and sign for a new club within twenty-four hours are long gone (Davor Suker's transfer to Arsenal being a notable exception); the whole process can take weeks, sometimes months, and even then is prone to falling through at the last moment, usually because the player cannot agree terms (which is football-speak for 'the money's not enough'). At White Hart Lane the C-word has a worse connotation than elsewhere – ever since Alan Sugar, in a fit of pique, declared that Jürgen Klinsmann's shirt was only fit for washing his car. It may have been four years ago that Sugar was caught out by the terms of Klinsmann's contract, but now it looked as if history might repeat itself.

According to one Tottenham director, though, the key to the club's future lay in 'how they deal with "the Campbell situation"'. One leading agent, talking at the beginning of the season, maintained that Campbell's transfer to Manchester United was a 'done deal'. It was merely a question of when and how much. This was vehemently denied by financial director John Sedgwick, who said: 'There has been no official approach from Manchester United to us – absolutely none. So if Sol has done a deal then it's a deal in somebody's drawer who's got an option on Sol to go to Manchester United. If that's the case then all we can do is to try and get as much money for him this summer as we can. I think he will be put under pressure to re-sign with us and fingers crossed he will. But if he doesn't, we've got to make an effort to get rid of him.'

Unlike Manchester United, who allowed the will-he-go or will-he-stay Roy Keane saga to drag on interminably so they were left with the difficult choice of succumbing to his exorbitant wage demands or recognizing that he would be a free agent at the end of the season, Tottenham were determined that if Campbell was going to go they would be handsomely rewarded. 'One of the diseases of modern football,' Graham has admitted, 'is that now players are on big contracts, if it doesn't suit them they will not move. They can even sit in the stands and watch a game and not worry. Or the other way, even if you want a player to stay he can see out his contract and go. It's made the job harder. It won't be long, for example, before we have to make up our minds [about Campbell]. We have offered him the top salary at this club. He says he'll wait until the end of the season. Now the club, as a business, has got a problem. They have got an asset worth X. That X is devaluing as time goes on. If he saw his contract through that would be zero. I would want him to commit himself because I would like to build the team around him. But Sol needs to make the decision or we will have to make it for him. It's sad for the fans but we are going to see players moving around more and more.'

John Segdwick goes further. 'If you ask a fan, would he pay £12 million [this is the fee that Tottenham would expect to receive if they sold him before the 2000–01 season] for Sol Campbell for one year, the fan might well acknowledge that he is one of the best defenders in the world but he's not worth that for one season.' On the other hand, if Tottenham were serious candidates for a Champions' League place, the whole issue would be academic. The idea of Tottenham selling their best asset (notwithstanding Ginola, whose age means that he is hardly a long-term prospect) in order to make any sort of progress would appear to be a blatant contradiction in terms, not to mention a rather depressing scenario considering that hiring Graham, winning the Worthington Cup and getting back into Europe after a gap of eight years was supposed to be the launchpad for an exciting new era at White Hart Lane. But then, exciting new eras are always just around the corner for Tottenham. Granted, the club had made noises about signing players (Robbie Keane, Emile Heskey, Ole Gunnar Solskjaer) but nothing had materialized, and the infamous Media Monitor, a clubcall service set up by the club to answer transfer speculation, had been a spectacular non-starter given that every time Tottenham were linked with a new player the stock response seemed to be for Tottenham's director of football David Pleat to issue a statement along the lines of: 'There is no truth in this rumour whatsoever.'

Tottenham had been so markedly inactive in the transfer market that questions had to be asked. Did Graham have the cash to spend, but was unable to secure the players he wanted, or was he being characteristically cautious about a big-name signing? Or was Alan Sugar the problem? Was Sugar sticking to what appeared to be his no-risk strategy, content to see the punters pouring in, the tills ringing and the club stable among the also-rans of the Premiership? Perhaps it was a combination of all three, given Graham's comment pre-season that, just as the big clubs were finding it hard to get the right players for the right money, so the 'smaller' clubs were finding it even harder. David Pleat revealed a glimpse of the player-purchasing mentality at the club in a pre-season discussion with Alan Green on Radio 5 Live. 'I can tell you right now,' Pleat declared, 'that Tottenham Hotspur won't get involved in any stupid, spiralling salaries that we can't afford in the pursuit of glory. We want glory, but in a way that we can cope with. Otherwise it's almost too simplistic. You buy glory, the manager clears off and the players all want to leave and where to from there? You have to keep looking one, two and three years ahead and try and budget accordingly. You have to protect your club.' It's a sound enough principle, but you can hardly describe buying at least one decent striker and one play-maker with an eye for goal (admittedly a rare breed of player in Britain today) as 'buying glory'. It is simply buying a couple of decent players to bolster a squad that is visibly skinny in compari-son to the fat felines at the top of the Premiership.

Pleat can preach sound book-keeping until the cows come home, but to the average Tottenham fan, the club's inactivity in the trans-fer market – and Sugar's perennial refusal to speculate to accumu-late – smacks of lack of ambition. So Sugar boldly went where few Tottenham men would have dared to go when he hired George Graham, and the League Cup was a huge and most unexpected boost to a club for whom avoiding relegation had come to represent a successful season, but a club with Tottenham's history should be looking to build on that progress, not sit back and accept second best. Even Graham himself has hinted at his frustration at the lack of new faces at the club; you can only say 'I need at least four, if not five, new players' so many times before somebody somewhere starts wondering whether there is a hidden agenda to the oft-repeated declaration. Everyone knows Graham's almost unrivalled reputa-tion for making silk purses out of sow's ears, but any manager worth his salt wants to work with decent players; in today's game you don't come first unless you use first-class tools.

His lack of resources had prompted him to write off Tottenham as Championship contenders before the season was a month old, despite knowing that Manchester United, Arsenal and Chelsea might all be there for the taking as they would no doubt be hampered by their Champions' League commitments. 'I don't think we are strong enough. We are a long way from being a Championship team,' Graham confessed.

Yet it was hard not to agree with his assessment. The new sign-ings did not set the pulse racing – Perry and Leonhardsen promised consistency and commitment not necessarily thrills and skills – and the arrival of the left-winger Willem Korsten only served to put in doubt David Ginola's long-term Tottenham future. Ginola had signed a new three-year contract in the summer but frankly that was no surprise considering that there would have been anarchy had the club failed to offer him one. Yet the signs remained that Graham was not as convinced as everyone else that Ginola was worth it. When he removed the Double player of the year from the fray at half-time at Upton Park in the opening game of the season, revealing only that he was 'not injured', it was *déjà vu* time; the previous season Graham had substituted Ginola twenty-three times.

So surprise surprise, Tottenham started the season with much the same side as they had finished the last – and lost 1–0 to West Ham on the opening day. The match was dominated by the performance of West Ham debutant Stuart Pearce, whom Harry Redknapp likened to George Graham's favourite player Dave Mackay, and the all-action display – which he capped by scoring the winning goal – of one-time Tottenham target Frank Lampard. The West Ham midfielder kissed the badge on his shirt in front of the Tottenham fans when he scored as if to say, 'See what you're missing.' Not that they needed telling. A player with Lampard's energy, vision and eye for goal had been conspicuous by his absence in the Tottenham midfield since . . . well, since Gazza. But as one West Ham fan wryly commented: 'Why would Lampard want to go to Tottenham? We finished above them in the Premiership and we're in Europe too. They're no bigger than us any more.' The sentiment was echoed by a *Guardian* editor and disgruntled Tottenham fan Ben Clissett, who muttered: 'Arsenal are Tottenham now. We're just not up there any more. I mean, look at West Ham. Even their ground is not really up to scratch but it's the kind of second-rate stage our performances merit these days.'

Given this damning assessment it was fair to say that dawns don't come much more false than the one which saw Tottenham sitting astride the Premiership for the first time since its inception (cue the irksome clichés about dizzy heights and nosebleeds) after their victory against Sheffield Wednesday on 21 August. Having scored five goals in two games, Graham was prompted to say, with a smirk: 'Come and see a George Graham side if you want entertaining football.' As Ian Ridley wrote at the time in the *Observer*: 'Canny man – play up the entertainment, play down the expectation.'

But subsequent comments by Graham gave substance to the suspicion that his apparent joviality at his team's position masked his concern over his defence – or rather his lack of a defence. He may well have been inwardly fuming when Luke Young was easily turned by Alan Smith when Leeds visited White Hart Lane and ran off with all three points thanks to a half-time re-organization by their manager David O'Leary, who showed tactical nous reminiscent of his former mentor. Graham kept his frustration under control in the immediate post-match press conference, but in an unguarded moment minutes later someone made a general observation that 'Leeds were better organized', inferring that Leeds's second-half tactical reshuffle had changed the game. Graham evidently took the comment to mean that Leeds were better organized than Tottenham, which is like showing a red rag to a bull. 'What do you expect if I have no defence?' he smarted.

You do wonder if the worry of 'having no defence' is something that keeps George Graham awake at night. After all, he is the man who created one of the best English defences of all time at Arsenal, the most famous five since Enid Blyton. You think it must irk him to have to make-do-and-mend. Still, at least he had the increasingly reliable Chris Perry, whose performances thus far suggested he would be a permanent fixture at the back, alongside Campbell or A.N. Other. However, Graham was surely not amused to see a certain Robbie Keane roll off Perry to score Coventry's first goal at White Hart Lane in mid-September. It was almost an identical situation to the one involving Young and Smith, yet Graham chose not to refer to the mistake, and far be it from any journalist present at the post-match press conference to suggest that, God forbid, perhaps he was not-so-perfect Perry after all. Instead, two weeks later, after Tottenham had held Zimbru Chisinau to a goalless draw in Moldova to secure their passage into the UEFA Cup second round, Graham was loudly proclaiming 'Perry for England'.

Mind you, Graham had something else on his mind after that 3–2 victory against Coventry, something that caused him to trudge down the tunnel at the end of the game shaking his head. Judging by the scoreline alone, there wasn't much for him to complain about. So Tottenham had let Coventry back into the match, but they had still escaped with all three points against a team who had so often proved to be a banana skin in the past. However, the scoreline failed to tell the whole story, which was that Tottenham, just like the previous week when they had gone to Bradford and created a multitude of goalscoring chances yet converted only one of them (and were then made to pay for their profligacy when a late goal salvaged a 1–1 draw for the home side), had once again failed to turn their supremacy into goals. Put simply, they lacked the killer instinct. They needed a predator, a Jimmy Greaves, a Clive Allen, a Gary Lineker, a Steve Archibald, a Garth Crooks. Any one of those strikers would have put away more than just three of the fifteen chances Tottenham created in the first forty-five minutes, particularly against a side that had conceded twelve goals in their last three matches, including five in midweek against First Division Tranmere. Yet they allowed Coventry to score twice and almost rescue a point. It brought to mind Graham's pre-season declaration, after Hearts had fought back to 2–2 in a pre-season friendly at Tynecastle, that 'my teams never lose a two-goal lead'. This was a pretty close call.

The reason for that was both Tottenham's wastefulness in front of goal and the zest and zeal of Robbie Keane, who threatened to unhinge Tottenham's defence throughout the second half. Gordon Strachan was right when he claimed that Keane's goal was 'as good as you will see from any striker this season', and contradicted Graham's assessment of Keane as a player who 'might be really good in 18 months'. Keane might not yet be the finished article but if so, he is certainly not far off it. He is an instinctive finisher who, given the service, should score the goals to keep Coventry up. Graham may have regretted not investing £6 million in Keane but all he would say on the matter was: 'I need another two strikers. Most clubs these days have five. I have three. That is not enough.' According to Graham, spending millions on a lower division forward is a pure gamble. By publicly citing the case of Kevin Davies, whose £7 million transfer to Blackburn ended in tears, the unspoken inference was that Robbie Keane was also a risk best avoided. However it could be inferred from subsequent comments that not signing Keane was a mistake.

On the following Monday, the *Sun*'s match report on the game said it all. 'Get the cheque book out, George – or a season that is full of promise will produce nothing,' it read. It's a fact of life that to succeed on the big stage these days a manager needs more than one player upfront who will guarantee him goals. It's no good relying on goalscoring midfielders like Sherwood and Leonhardsen; their goals should be a bonus, not a banker. Look at Manchester United, who can replace Cole and Yorke with those Champions' League goalscoring heroes Sheringham and Solskjaer; at Arsenal, who can rotate between Bergkamp, Henry, Suker and Kanu; at Chelsea, who have Flo, Sutton, Zola, Ambrosetti and Pierluigi Casiraghi (if he returns from injury), as well as the admittedly young Mikael Forssell; and Leeds, who boast four of the best young strikers in the game in Alan Smith, Darren Huckerby, Harry Kewell and Michael Bridges, the former Sunderland striker whom Tottenham courted but failed to entice.

Tottenham . . . well, Tottenham had Iversen (who after three years at the club was still being described as 'promising'), the injury-prone Les Ferdinand and Chris Armstrong, who in the eyes of the fans still had much to prove in a Tottenham shirt despite a satisfactory first season under Gerry Francis. The last time Tottenham had such a paucity of strikers was in the late 1970s when Chris Jones, Ian Moores, Gerry Armstrong and Colin Lee vied for the striking roles. Rory Allen had been sold to Portsmouth for £1 million, even though he showed some promise during his twenty-one appearances, and the rest were clearly considered not old or experienced enough.

The upshot of it all is that on the eve of Tottenham's first European adventure for eight years, Graham acknowledged that he had drawn a blank in his attempts to strengthen his hand. 'We have never been close to signing anyone since the summer,' he said. 'We talked about a few players and there was a chance one or two might join us but they never came to fruition. Since then there has been nothing doing. I probably know every striker in England and they come in three categories. There are the top strikers, of which there are not many, and who are either not available or they are already with big clubs. The second category are those who are just not available and those in the third category are probably not going to be any improvement on what we already have. There is not the quality available that I would like. There is no point in buying someone and regretting it within days, never mind weeks and months.'

Fortunately, Tottenham's lack of striking options didn't matter against opposition as lightweight as the Moldovan champions Zimbru Chisinau. There may be few easy games in Europe these days, but with all due respect to a side who only narrowly lost to PSV Eindhoven in the Champions' League qualifiers after beating

St Patrick's Athletic and Dinamo Tbilisi in previous rounds, it would have been a major shock had Tottenham lost to a team whose players earned a wage of £40 a week, top whack.

Anyway, that kind of upset was never going to happen, not with Graham at the helm. Having been involved in European triumphs as both an Arsenal player (the 1970 Inter-Cities Fairs Cup) and manager (1994 Cup-Winners' Cup) he was not about to let Tottenham's first foray into Europe since 1991–92 – when they defeated SV Stockerau, Hajduk Split and FC Porto before going out on aggregate to Feyenoord in the Cup-Winners' Cup – be a short-lived one. 'I want the big European glamour ties back at White Hart Lane, it's so different from domestic football,' he said. 'I love playing in Europe. As a manager I've learnt so much from previous excursions and my team will go right out there and have a go.' It was taken as read that Tottenham would be well prepared. Graham is a stickler for detail. He prides himself on his organization and his tactics are invariably spot-on. Chief scout Charlie Woods had been sent on a spying mission to Chisinau, while Graham had locked his players in the video room at Tottenham's training ground in the week before the game and made them watch the Moldovans' game against PSV so they would know exactly what to expect. So although Chisinau were something of an unknown quantity, Graham had enough gen on them to know that as long as Tottenham practised what he referred to as 'the two Ps: be patient, be positive' – they should go through.

In the event, a capacity crowd at White Hart Lane, which owed more to the novelty of the European experience than to the appeal of the opposition, watched the home side stroll through a match which at times resembled a training session. The admittedly pacy Chisinau attack lacked guile and initiative, their midfield never got to grips with Sherwood and Nielsen – who made one of his rare starts under Graham despite the fact that many fans preferred him to Steffen Freund – while their vulnerable defence would surely have been exploited on more than just three occasions had Tottenham used the space afforded them more effectively. As it was, Ginola was almost superfluous on a stage which was tailor-made for his skills, and the fans leaving the ground were left wondering whether the killer instinct of the side had got stuck on the murderous North Circular (the kick-off was delayed by fifteen minutes due to traffic congestion). Typical Tottenham. Like their manager they are seldom pleased, although after so much underachievement it would not take much to lift them. It speaks volumes about their general dissatisfaction that instead of welcoming what was, on paper, a sound enough victory, their post-match analysis that night went something like: 'How many would the Arse have put past this lot?' and 'How much longer before Iversen gets a complementary strike partner?' One simply summed it all up by saying: 'I think we'll get hammered by a proper European team.'

The away leg was, for George Graham and his players at least, a lesson in containment. For all that European fixtures against relatively unfamiliar opposition occasionally throw up the odd unpleasant surprise, they knew that all they really had to do was to concentrate, and a place in the UEFA Cup second-round draw would be theirs. Zimbru had offered just enough in the first leg to suggest they might be capable of scoring a goal at home, but that Tottenham would let them score three, let alone four, was about as likely as Chris Armstrong finishing the season with the Golden Boot.

In the event, a goal or two might have at least livened up a game that was as entertaining as Scotland's match in Estonia that never was. Basically, Tottenham did enough to avoid defeat, but that was about it. They offered very little in the way of attacking enterprise and seemed content to get men behind the ball and keep possession, negative tactics that a better side would have punished. As it was, the Moldovans were unable to take advantage of Tottenham's lethargy, although Ian Walker was the busier of the two keepers and in the final ten minutes the Tottenham defence even had to make a goal-line clearance.

For the fans who had made the effort to support the side, the game – notwithstanding the fact that Tottenham progressed into the second round – was an anti-climax. Having had a disastrous journey out to Moldova courtesy of a package put together by Tottenham's travel agents (they flew Air Moldova in a plane that Bruce Lewis, a Tottenham fan recounting the 'adventure' in the Tottenham fanzine *One Flew Over Seaman's Head*, described as 'the pokiest aircraft I have seen outside a museum'), the least they could have hoped for was a stirring display from their side, one that emphasized the class gap. Far from it. In fact, Lewis continued by describing the team's performance as 'awful, downright disgraceful. It was so bad that it would have been unfair on some individual players to say they were that bad, although ... Freund's throw-ins never reached a Tottenham player, Clemence bottled challenges and never took the adventurous options and Armstrong was utterly clueless upfront. To think we came all this way for a performance that was worse than a bad night at the reserves.' The only saving grace, according to Lewis, was Steve Carr who is 'fast becoming the player who has saved Tottenham about £10 million in the transfer market'. To compound the ignominy of it all, only Perry, Freund, Walker and Iversen bothered to applaud the fans at the end of the match, which left a bad taste in the mouth. 'We'd had a shitty flight over in an old bucket of an aircraft,' Lewis wrote, 'spent well over £300 each, all to see a crappy game of football and then not even be recognized by the team. Does [earning] stupid amounts of money each week corrupt [players] that badly?'

Yet the same fans – plus, one suspects, several thousand more – started planning to make the slightly more straightforward trip to Kaiserslautern, situated about 100 miles south west of Frankfurt, when the German club were paired with Tottenham in the second round draw on 1 October. Tottenham may have been the last British club to win the UEFA Cup when they defeated Anderlecht on penalties in the 1984 final, but they were going to have their work cut out if they were to reach the third round. Kaiserslautern, who won the Bundesliga in 1998 and reached the quarter-finals of the previous season's Champions' League, had trounced Scottish side Kilmarnock 5–0 on aggregate in the first round, and boasted quality players like French international Youri Djorkaeff and Swiss playmaker Ciriaco Sforza. With West Ham, Leeds, Newcastle and Celtic having come out of the hat with Steaua Bucharest, Lokomotiv Moscow, FC Zurich and Lyon respectively, the general consensus was that Tottenham had come off worst of all the British clubs. Kaiserslautern were German, for heaven's sake, which just about said it all. 'I think we've got the toughest draw of all the English teams,' was Graham's reaction. 'German sides are similar to the British. They're well organized and it will be a very close game.' He didn't add that Tottenham would need a proverbial rocket up their arses if they were to shake off the lethargy that was prevalent in Moldova and entertain any idea of beating the Germans, but he didn't really need to. Those who saw the first leg knew it. Kaiserslautern, if you like, were that 'proper European team' the fans feared.

As games go, the defeat against Leicester at the start of October perfectly illustrated the shortcomings that had made Tottenham's season thus far such a disjointed one. Fact: Tottenham created some great chances with some laudable approach play but were unable to take them. Conclusion: they need at least a couple of strikers to compete with the best. Fact: David Ginola put in some lovely crosses but faded and didn't complete the game. Conclusion: in the continued absence of Anderton Ginola remained Tottenham's most creative player but was too often sacrificed in the latter stages of games that Tottenham were chasing. Why, for example, after Leicester scored their equalizer, did Graham replace Ginola with Nielsen when a Ginola cross was the most likely source of a Tottenham goal? Fact: Leicester's equalizer came from the head of the diminutive Muzzy Izzet. Conclusion: Tottenham lack height in defence without Campbell. Fact: Tottenham allowed Leicester back into the game and then gifted them three points. Graham says 'all good teams have a mixture of technical players and people who are very strong mentally and physically. Leicester had that.' Conclusion: evidently, Tottenham did not.

The brutal truth, if any Tottenham fan dared face it, was that teams such as Leicester had now risen to Tottenham's level (or perhaps that should read that Tottenham had now sunk to the same level as teams such as Leicester). It was a sobering thought for those who had been privileged to watch the likes of Hoddle, Waddle, Lineker and Gascoigne that the England squad announced the day before the Leicester game for the friendly against Belgium included Leicester winger Steve Guppy (on current form there should have been a call-up for Muzzy Izzet too, which might have subsequently persuaded him not to declare himself for his father's homeland of Turkey), but not one Tottenham player. OK, so Campbell would definitely have been included had he been fit, and Anderton, too, would have been in contention, but Sherwood was overlooked in favour of Paul Ince and really, who else was there? Walker had been consistent but not commanding, and besides, he was still paying the price for conceding that goal against Italy at Wembley; Keegan obviously didn't concur with Graham's view that Chris Perry was an England player in the making; Ferdinand had had his England chances (and really hadn't taken them); while Armstrong ... suffice it to say that there were those who thought it had been an illusion when he appeared on the bench at Wembley for the friendly against the Czech Republic.

The all-too-familiar shortcomings of the side supported the suspicion that Tottenham were content to be in the 'second division' of the Premiership alongside the likes of Leicester, Everton and West Ham. Tottenham had gone from being a club who were a force at home and abroad in the 1960s and 1970s to one which now regarded eighth in the Premiership and a return to Europe after eight years as a successful season and which had to suffer being turned down by a player – Michael Bridges – who didn't even have a century of games in the First Division to his name.

There was, though, a more optimistic view doing the rounds which suggested that Tottenham were playing more like a unit now than at any time in the last decade; that the defensive partnership of Campbell and Perry was potentially the strongest since Gough and Mabbutt; that Carr and Taricco were the best pair of full-backs since ... well how long do you go back? that the signing of Leonhardsen was already looking like one of the bargains of the season; and that the youth policy was finally coming to fruition with the production of promising kids such as John Piercy and Ledley King. However, if the club really wanted what Graham wanted – to win Championships, to succeed in Europe, to be considered as one of the Premiership's élite – then they were going to have to start proving their credentials against the best teams, both at home and abroad.

The fixture list, which had gone gently on Tottenham in the opening weeks of the season, was beginning to look rather more daunting. As October moved into November Tottenham faced Manchester United, still the yardstick by which every other side must measure its progress, followed by the UEFA Cup second-round clash with Kaiserslautern at White Hart Lane. Tottenham then had to visit the Stadium of Light to take on the early season dark horses Sunderland before flying out to Germany for the return leg against Kaiserslautern. After that, it was bring on the Arsenal. And then Tottenham would really know where they were at.

CHAPTER FOUR

GIVE ME JOY, DON'T GIVE ME PAIN

Compared to American stadia, or to many of the great European footballing venues such as the Nou Camp, the San Siro, the Amsterdam Arena or the Stade de France, Wembley appears archaic. It suffers from representing a legacy of past glories at a time when English football should be addressing its future. Yet somehow it has managed to retain a certain charm and renown – the French refer to it as *le temple du football* – which goes some way towards explaining why the atmosphere before Arsenal's first 'home' European clash of the season against AIK Solna was more akin to a carnival than a vital Champions' League fixture.

Frankly, the Arsenal fans could have been forgiven for not whole-heartedly embracing the idea of the club using Wembley once again as their European base; after all, Arsenal's inadequate 'home' results were the reason why they failed to get beyond the Champions' League first group phase in the 1998–99 season, which led to the stadium being dubbed as their 'graveyard'. Still, this was the Champions' League. The big one. The only competition that really mattered. 'Who needs the Premiership when we've got the Champions' League?' would have been an appropriate chant; a satisfactory way of sticking two fingers up at the rest of the Premiership (Chelsea and Manchester United apart) who could only sit back and admire the extravaganza on show.

Bizarrely, a very different message came over loud and clear from the Arsenal fans in the opening minutes of that match against AIK

Solna. Local rivalry may be the sideshow to the main event for those who look at the bigger picture – you can hardly blame Arsenal for considering the crack European sides to be their benchmark, for wanting to see the club progress in the Champions' League and so secure themselves an ever-increasing share of the kudos and prize money on offer – but when it comes down to brass tacks, parochial pride is still paramount to the fans. Thus, just three minutes were on Wembley's clock when the majority of the 70,000-odd Arsenal fans inside the stadium rose, as one, to the chant: 'Stand up if you hate Tottenham.' They belted it out, arms aloft and outstretched. It was never mind these Swedes . . . what about that lot from down the Seven Sisters Road? Arsenal may have risen above their roots, but that didn't mean they were going to sever them completely.

To prove the point, exactly the same thing happened at White Hart Lane on the night Tottenham played Kaiserslautern in the second round of the UEFA Cup. Minutes into the match – and remember that, the first round against Zimbru Chisinau notwithstanding, this was Tottenham's first European fixture of conse- quence since 1992 – the majority of Tottenham fans also got to their feet to shout out: 'Stand up if you hate Arsenal.' Yes, so they wanted to see the Germans off, but beating the Gooners at White Hart Lane in ten days' time seemed to be at the forefront of their minds.

The primacy of the local derby should never be underestimated. It matters not one jot that at the time of the game one team is flying and the other is struggling. The local derby pays no heed to the form book. What's more, it is one of football's maxims that whatever else happens during the course of a season, fans will take great satisfac- tion from having 'done' their local rivals at least once, if not twice; and achieving such a feat will even compensate for having a disas- trous season, as long as it doesn't end in relegation. It's the same in London and Liverpool, on Tyneside and Wearside, in Birmingham and Bristol, in Stoke and Sheffield, in Glasgow and East Anglia – and there are certainly more than just a few Manchester United fans secretly hoping Manchester City would get promoted simply so that they could thrash them next season.

As far as Tottenham and Arsenal go . . . well, they don't go. Simple as that. Tottenham and Arsenal 'hate' each other. The reason for this intensity of feeling dates back to 1913 when south London

Arsenal uprooted from their Woolwich base to Highbury, which in those days was traditional Tottenham territory. Six years later, in 1919, when the League progamme resumed after the First World War, Arsenal were elected to the First Division, no doubt giving Tottenham, who had finished bottom of the First Division, a cursory wave on their way up. Fair enough on the face of it, but hard on Tottenham when you consider that they were to be given a stay of execution thanks to the Football League's decision to expand the top division from twenty to twenty-two clubs by promoting the top two clubs from Division Two, without relegating any from the First Division. But instead, someone at Arsenal – who had finished outside the top two in Division Two – must have been owed a few favours because they were upgraded and Tottenham were relegated.

The events of the last couple of seasons, during which Arsenal have metamorphosed under Wenger into a potent attacking force while Tottenham under Graham have become dogged and defiant, have simply served to spice up the intense antipathy between the two sets of fans, which for the most part is kept under control, but which is given licence to erupt twice a year: on the occasion of the north London derby.

As derbies go, north London's offering is often high in passion, short on style. Thankfully, it lacks the undertones of religious bigotry that characterize the Glasgow clash, and it provokes none of the internecine strife that can threaten family ties on Merseyside. Instead, it is fuelled by acrimony that has worsened now that Tottenham are now managed by a man who featured in that 1971 Arsenal Double-winning side, collected Arsenal memorabilia, and won six trophies – including two Championships – while he was Arsenal manager. When asked before the season where his true loyalties lay, Graham answered ambiguously: 'I've got red blood in me.'

As far as London is concerned it is the needle match. There is little point in saying, as one Radio 5 Live commentator misguidedly did on the afternoon of the first north London derby of the 1999–2000 season, that 'there is another London derby taking place this afternoon at Stamford Bridge where Chelsea take on West Ham.' Chelsea against West Ham is nothing but a contest between two London teams, however much the media try to dress it up. West Ham's bitterest rivals are Millwall, currently languishing in the Second Division; Chelsea against Fulham is the traditional west London derby even though the two sides seldom meet nowadays. Interestingly, both Chelsea and West Ham fans have developed a loathing for Tottenham, which is to do with the north London side's insistence that they are a big club with a style all of their own – when in reality that applies more to Chelsea and West Ham these days.

Ironically, however, there was another hugely significant derby taking place that afternoon. Four hundred miles north at Ibrox, Rangers were 'entertaining' Celtic and a certain Ian Wright, the man who was so often the scourge of Tottenham during his years as Arsenal's prolific front man. Wright was preparing for the first Old Firm encounter of his career and Scotland manager Craig Brown, the Radio 5 Live summarizer for the day, claimed that the player would never have experienced anything quite like the confrontational atmosphere at Ibrox that afternoon. He was probably right. However, there is a common thread that links Arsenal and Rangers over the last couple of years, both clubs being regulars engaged in a perennial battle to assert themselves in Europe.

Celtic, meanwhile, like Tottenham, have had to play second fiddle. The contrast is manifest in the fact that Rangers and Arsenal have both hired cosmopolitan, European managers; both have won a hatful of domestic trophies during the 1990s; and both have the money and the box office appeal to attract Europe's top stars. And that is why the derbies in north London and Glasgow cannot now truly be compared with those between AC Milan and Internazionale, and between Lazio and Roma (and until recently Atlético and Real Madrid), because while Milan, Internazionale, Lazio and Roma are all major players in Europe, Tottenham and Celtic are not, despite Celtic being amongst the top half-dozen best-supported clubs in Europe.

Nevertheless, the appointment of George Graham has given Tottenham a much-needed kick up the backside and caused Arsenal, for the first time in a long while, to cast a cautious glance over their shoulders. There was a nastier edge to Graham's first derby in charge of Tottenham – a 0–0 draw on 14 November 1998 at

Highbury – than there had been during previous seasons when Tottenham were in such chaos under Christian Gross that Arsenal almost laughed them off the park (it's easy to speculate that, had Gross stayed in charge, a gap as large as the one which separates Manchesters United and City could have appeared between Tottenham and Arsenal). Graham's second derby – Arsenal's emphatic 3–1 win at White Hart Lane which so clearly underlined the gulf in class between the two sides – was dominated by Arsène Wenger's side's desperate need to keep pace with Manchester United at the top of the Premiership. This derby – Sunday 7 November 1999 – was a different proposition altogether.

Graham, who had promised there would be no quick-fix panic purchases before he had had a chance to assess the current playing staff, had methodically fashioned a serviceable midfield – and the general consensus was that given an injury-free run and two decent strikers Tottenham would be in a position to challenge for a European place. Lee Dixon suggested as much when he admitted in the build-up that he had had no doubt Graham would make an immediate impact. 'Having been through six or seven years under George's regime,' Dixon said, 'I know what the Spurs players are going through. Lots and lots of hard work. They will basically be learning to defend, learning how to close teams down. It's paying off. I think Tottenham will be a force to be reckoned with in two or three years' time.'

It was some consolation that Dixon's prediction was certainly not what the Arsenal fans wanted to hear. As one said before the match: 'What we want most is for Graham's time in charge at Tottenham to be as bland as possible, and then when he goes we can all get back to things being normal again, when derbies were just derbies, taken at face value.' Ominously, there was a feeling that their erstwhile manager was trying to revive Tottenham in the same way as he had galvanized Arsenal when he first took over in 1986. Then, he had bought in Dixon and Steve Bould from Stoke, Nigel Winterburn from Wimbledon, Brian Marwood from Sheffield Wednesday, Kevin Richardson from Watford, Alan Smith from Leicester and Perry Groves from Colchester, all for just over a couple of million pounds. Those purchases were typical of the transfer market Arsenal plundered at the time – journeymen whom Graham transformed into the nucleus of one of the most effective sides of their generation. Now, for Winterburn read Taricco, for Bould read Perry, for Richardson read Leonhardsen and for Marwood read Korsten. Hard-working, 100-per-cent players. They suited George Graham down to the ground.

In fact, the only discernible difference between then and now was that value-for-money buys were a rarity in English football in the late 1990s. The fact that Oyvind Leonhardsen was already being described as Tottenham's bargain of the season at a cost of £3 million tells its own story. Graham himself admits that he 'couldn't do now what I did at Arsenal because the best players in lower leagues have been in their respective first teams since they were eighteen – the likes of Kieron Dyer and Robbie Keane – and everyone knows about them, which means you have to pay top prices for unproven players.'

To find value for money these days you have to shop abroad, which is what Arsenal have done to great effect. What price Emmanuel Petit and Patrick Vieira now? In this respect Graham admits that 'Arsène Wenger had a head start, knowing the French scene as he does', but then Wenger always had a more cosmopolitan outlook than most British managers. According to Lee Dixon (who, by the way, had an additional incentive for wanting an emphatic win in this particular derby given that it was his testimonial the following day against Real Madrid and 'a win over Tottenham might encourage 20,000 more people to turn up at Highbury on the day'), Arsenal's current prosperity was due both to the manager's astuteness in the transfer market as well as the quality of the side left behind by his predecessors. 'Arsène looked at what George had laid down when he took over,' claimed Dixon, 'and recognized that George had done a good job, so he kept the nucleus of the unit together,' leaning on Pat Rice, who had been at the club boy and man. Wenger was aided by the fact that Arsenal's famous back five was still going strong when he arrived so he had no need to make the kind of wholesale changes Graham had make after he'd got acclimatized at Highbury. According to Dixon, 'the timing of when George took over was significant. There was a lull at the club and he started to build the team on the back of signing me, Nigel and Steve – young, hungry players with a bit of talent. He built that defence himself, almost single-handedly. He saw that we could play together and he worked on that for hours every day of the week. We did it for so long that it got boring at times but he kept plugging away. It's things George taught us then that we've never forgotten; they're second nature to us now.'

However, despite their longevity, the Arsenal defence was not immortal. And in the penultimate match of the Champions' League first group phase they committed a clanger that was costly both in terms of money and morale: they allowed Gabriel Batistuta, whom David Seaman later admitted he was 'quite sick of the sight of' (the Argentinian striker had been his nemesis in the 1998 World Cup as well, when England lost in Saint-Étienne) to escape their strangle-hold for a split second – which was all the time he needed to score the goal that put his side, Fiorentina, through to the second group phase – and dump Arsenal out.

Excuses? None really. Wenger was able to field his strongest side, gambling on the fitness of a predictably subdued Petit, who lasted sixty minutes in his first full game after a lengthy lay-off before being replaced by Nelson Vivas. No, the truth of the matter was that once again Arsenal had shot themselves in the foot by failing to make their superiority count. It mattered not that the Italian side had absorbed wave after wave of incessant pressure culminating in frequent near-misses; it mattered even less that Batistuta, arguably, should not even have been on the pitch after his crude, second-minute lunge at Lee Dixon that signalled Fiorentina's intent. History forgets these events. Instead, the record book will forever show that for the second successive season Arsenal had exited the Champions' League at the first time of asking. They had only won once in Group B – a 3–1 win over AIK Solna secured by two very late goals. Now, instead of looking forward to fixtures against the likes of Lazio, Bayern Munich, Valencia and Manchester United, they were facing the prospect of a third-round UEFA Cup match against – quite possibly – Tottenham. Talk about an anti-climax.

After the match Wenger admitted his players were 'as low as I've ever known them. It is like we have suffered a death in the family and have been in mourning,' said the Arsenal boss, before giving a passable impression of a man desperately trying to take some positives from a season gone seriously awry. 'I know my players have the quality and spirit to come back, but it will take us time to recover. You cannot just jump out of bed the next day and say how beautiful life is. That does not happen unless you are a comedian. What is important is to get on with things and set yourself new targets. Now we have the challenge of the UEFA Cup. It is still a European trophy and something to get excited about . . . even if we do not feel that way at the moment.'

Any further worries he kept to himself, leaving others to voice them. Already there were mutterings about the club's ability to hang onto players like Bergkamp, Petit, Overmars and Kanu, players who were used to playing on bigger stages than they were being afforded at Arsenal, and who needed such motivation to succour their ambition. Arsenal ears must have winced at hearing Bergkamp describe the defeat as 'my biggest disappointment in club football', and Overmars admitting that 'the Champions' League is the best and everything else is below it'. Martin Keown echoed the sentiments in acknowledging that 'part of being a successful club is managing to keep the big players and that requires winning trophies'.

Still, Keown refused to reach for the panic button. 'There isn't too much wrong with Arsenal's personnel or style,' he said. 'The manner in which we play has got us this far over the last three seasons and there is little reason in changing that. Sometimes, however, at this level, we are able to dominate matches but unable to kill off the opposition. They hang on, as Fiorentina did, and then scrape through. We were well prepared . . . essentially we have lost games trying to win them. But that is the way we now play at Arsenal. We don't sit and wait, and try to counter-attack. Perhaps the Arsenal of old might have done so.' Perhaps the Arsenal of old might also have indulged in a little more of the gamesmanship as mastered by the Italian sides of the past. They know well how to mix it at this level, with a mixture of craft and conniving. According to Keown: 'There are so many unwritten rules and factors which are not spoken of, psychological battles.'

There was also, of course, the Wembley factor. Five home points dropped the previous season; this time they'd gone one worse, and most of Arsenal's players alluded to the fact that Wembley, as David Seaman put it, 'had not been kind to us'. All, that is, except Tony

Adams. Writing in his programme notes before the Wembley match against AIK Solna, the Arsenal captain had given short shrift to the notion that Wembley was a hindrance rather than a help. 'There were suggestions last year that by moving from Highbury to Wembley, we lost an advantage in our Champions' League games,' he wrote. 'I cannot go along with that for one minute. When you have 70,000 Arsenal fans screaming for you, Wembley can still be a frightening place, somewhere for the opposition to fear. Believe me, they can be scared when they come up against that kind of atmosphere. The key in this tournament is winning your home games and we failed to do that [last season]. But those results had absolutely nothing to do with playing at Wembley but everything to do with the teams we had out and the injuries and suspensions we picked up.' It was a view endorsed by Wenger, who simply said: 'If you have a good team it plays well everywhere.'

Contrary to popular opinion, money actually had very little to do with the decision according to David Dein. 'It was no easy decision and we agonized over it for days,' Dein revealed, 'but in the end we decided on Wembley, firstly because the demands placed on us by UEFA would have meant moving many of our season-ticket holders at Highbury to accommodate UEFA's needs [in terms of the media, perimeter advertising, sponsors' tickets etc.]; and secondly, because the demand to see games is so great and we need to freshen up the public. We need the young fans. I had one dad come up to me and thank me for choosing Wembley because if we hadn't, then his son would never have got to see Bergkamp play in the flesh. Money was never the issue, particularly since once we'd paid all the overheads at Wembley we hardly covered our costs.' He could have added that had the motive been fiscal then ticket prices could have been doubled for some seats without adversely affecting the gate.

Fine, but the fact remains that Wembley is not Highbury, and in football as in life there is no place like home, however much you try to pretend otherwise. Besides, playing beneath the Twin Towers usually gives the opposition a fillip, more of an edge, not to mention more space; Wembley is a few metres wider and longer than Highbury, although that should have suited Arsène Wenger's attacking strategy just as much as the opposition's. Tellingly, Lee

Dixon echoed the sentiments of the majority of Arsenal fans and players when he admitted after Arsenal had lost 4–2 to Barcelona in the fixture prior to the Fiorentina encounter that 'compared to our ground Wembley is very wide and it affects the way that we play. I definitely think playing there has made us less able to progress in the European Cup.' Wenger concurred: 'Maybe you over-motivate your opponent, and you expose yourself much more because you give more space away. Look how difficult it is for England to win at Wembley. The players didn't really feel at home.' With a wry look at what might have been, Wenger reflected that '[the next group stage] looks very weak compared to the group we were in. We were unlucky to go out. Fiorentina had one shot at goal at Wembley and we missed a penalty away. It is difficult to accept.'

Of course. Arsenal had made it predictably hard for themselves by losing the previous week to Barcelona. Although that game was closer than the 4–2 scoreline suggests, on the night Barcelona – like Fiorentina were to do a week later – proved that when it came to a contest as to who could play the more clinical and the more cynical football, there was only ever going to be one winner. Notwithstanding Philip Cocu's outrageous dive to win the penalty from which Rivaldo scored the Spanish side's first goal, the brutal truth was that Arsenal's back line was cruelly exposed by the movement of Patrick Kluivert and the constant promptings of Luis Enrique, Cocu and Josep Guardiola: Dixon inadvertently laid on Barcelona's third goal on a plate by diverting the ball away from the feet of Kluivert into Luis Figo's path, while Cocu himself split Keown and Adams to score Barcelona's fourth. Their attack, meanwhile, was unable to make better use of some often wonderful approach play reflected in the eighteen chances Arsenal created to Barcelona's eight. In the end, the self-belief that the 1–1 draw in the Nou Camp had given everyone at Highbury gradually evaporated over ninety compelling minutes of full-bloodied Champions' League football, culminating in Arsenal being taught a few home truths. Basically, Barcelona knocked Arsenal down, and Fiorentina finished the job off by rubbing their noses in the Wembley dirt.

The academic victory (both teams were just playing for pride and compensation money) against AIK Solna in Sweden was really only significant in terms of lifting Arsenal morale before meeting

Tottenham. Wenger made a brave attempt to be upbeat when he spoke to the assembled press two days later, on the Friday before the visit to White Hart Lane. 'It is important,' he stressed, 'that when you lose like we did against Fiorentina, you win again quickly, and we did that against AIK Solna. We played well and our attitude was right which shows this team has character and mental strength. We now need some important games to be completely confident again.' Of course there was the UEFA Cup, even if, as Lee Dixon admitted, it 'felt strange to still be in Europe having gone out of Europe'. Still, it would be a fool who looked such a gift horse in the mouth with a third round place and a potential pot of around £15 million to the winners (small fry compared to the Champions' League bumper pay-out but welcome nonetheless).

That morning, the draw had been kind to Arsenal, steering them clear of heavyweight opposition from Italy and Spain and pairing them against French side Nantes. Wenger kept any sense of anti-climax well hidden, and predictably bristled at the suggestion that Arsenal would not be taking the competition seriously. 'This is another chance to do well in Europe and we have the basic quality,' he countered. 'We want to do well in the UEFA Cup without it becoming a handicap in the Championship race.' Besides, he added, 'if you look at the teams in the UEFA Cup it is suddenly a very strong competition.' True, and everyone knows why.

One team who Arsenal would definitely not be facing in that third round were Tottenham, who had been eliminated by Kaiserslautern. There was a suggestion of sour grapes when George Graham pointedly expressed surprise at Arsenal's failure to live up to expectations. Wenger had assembled a 'wonderful team with wonderful players', admitted the Tottenham manager, who then poured oil on troubled waters by saying he was amazed they hadn't gone further in the Champions' League. Mind you, who was Graham to talk? Tottenham's first European campaign for nine years had been cut short when Stephen Carr – arguably Tottenham's player of the season thus far – inadvertently put the ball through his own net to give Kaiserslautern a 2–0 win on the night and a 2–1 aggregate victory. Poor Carr was distraught. Only a few days before he had been a hero when his thunderous, thirty-yard pile-driver had been the crowning glory of a 3–1 win over Manchester United at

White Hart Lane, but fortunes can be fickle in football and what made the own goal all the more cruel – under any circumstances it is a brutal way to go out – was the fact that on ninety minutes the scoreboard showed 0–0 and the Tottenham fans who had travelled to the Fritz-Waller stadium were celebrating their safe passage to the third round. Then, two minutes into stoppage time Andreas Buck hauled Kaiserslautern level on aggregate and almost immediately came the 'Carr-Lamity', as the tabloids inevitably dubbed it.

Carr could do little about the own goal; the ball simply rebounded off his shins and drifted agonizingly over the line. However, given his rapid emergence as one of Tottenham's most consistent performers, it had to go down as one of those maddening ironies that are intrinsically woven into the fabric of football. Naturally nobody blamed him, and it would be a novice pro who was not able, after the initial distress, to put the error behind him. Besides, Tottenham assistant coach Chris Hughton was undoubtedly right when he said that having to focus on the derby so soon after the defeat proved the perfect pick-me-up for Carr (and the rest of the team). 'The games come so thick and fast these days, and Steve had very little time to dwell on the own goal,' admitted Hughton. 'Anyway, he's not the kind of lad to let it get him down.'

Carr, known as 'Freddie' because of an alleged similarity to Fred Flintstone, is already what footballing experts like to describe as a consummate professional – the kind of player every coach dreams of inheriting. Quiet, down-to-earth and 100 per cent focused, he seldom misses training and looks after himself off the pitch too. It shows. In the 1998–99 season he missed just one game (only Sol Campbell showed anything like that level of consistency) while his early-season form of 1999–2000 explained why Tottenham had come, as Hughton puts it, 'to rely on him'.

The most striking aspect of Stephen Carr's emergence is that he has slipped stealthily into the Tottenham right-back berth and made it his own at a time when most Premiership clubs stand guilty of buying established, quick-fix, big-name stars rather than giving callow, home-grown potential the chance to flourish. It wasn't long ago that Carr could be found hanging around the old Tottenham training ground with his youth-team contemporaries watching first-team stars such as Jürgen Klinsmann and Teddy Sheringham hog the limelight. In those days he was a mere boy among men who looked, in his first few appearances for the first team, like a kid invited to a grown-up party. Now he's grown into that number two shirt, and it suits him.

Thank goodness. Tottenham fans have long considered the position of full-back – both right and left – to be a problem. They'd got used to putting up with the whole-hearted if rather pedestrian exertions of Justin Edinburgh, David Kerslake and Dean Austin – even the luckless Stuart Nethercott played full-back on occasions – all the while grudgingly recognizing the consistency of Lee Dixon and Nigel Winterburn still going strong after all those years. No wonder, when Carr made his debut as a raw seventeen year old in September 1993, most of them thought that here was just another poor misguided unfortunate eager to take on the poisoned chalice. Any bets on how long he'd last?

Initially, not long at all. In fact, Carr disappeared off the first-team scene altogether for the next two seasons, although he was a key member of the Tottenham team that reached the 1995 FA Youth Cup final. He re-emerged in 1996–97 under Gerry Francis and the following campaign was a first choice for Christian Gross. According to Hughton, he 'never looked back once he got the nod. We don't normally expect a reserve-team player to push on so quickly as Steve did.' More usually, reserve- and youth-team players are – in football parlance – dipped in and out of the first team for the experience. Carr just threw himself in headlong, made the minimum of splash, and never once looked out of his depth. Now he's such an integral part of the side that the Tottenham fans occasionally have to pinch themselves to make sure that the stocky little full-back with the boundless reserves of energy – the one who never gives up a lost cause – actually plays for Tottenham. With all due respect to the obvious exceptions to the rule like Steve Perryman and Gary Mabbutt, a never-say-die attitude has not been a prerequisite of the traditional Tottenham player.

They will tell you at Tottenham that they always knew Carr had it in him. He was strikingly solid as a teenager, which meant that while most of his peer group were still maturing, he was already more than able to cope with the physical aspects of youth-team football. His strength, coupled with his enthusiasm to get forward and sling in decent crosses initially suggested he could fill a role on the right of midfield. However, it was soon apparent that he was a natural full-back: committed in the tackle, a competent reader of the game, and blessed with something that every successful modern full-back requires – the willingness to bomb endlessly up and down the touchline. According to Hughton, all he lacks is the experience he will get from playing regularly in the Premiership against the likes of Ryan Giggs, Harry Kewell and Marc Overmars, and at international level, now that he has graduated into the full Republic of Ireland squad.

If he continues his current rate of progress he should comfortably eclipse the number of caps won by his opposite number at Arsenal, although of course Carr is Irish and Lee Dixon English, which gives the Tottenham player a distinct advantage. However, at twelve years Dixon's junior he is far from being the complete package, and as one Arsenal fan pointedly reflected: 'If he achieves half of what Dixon's achieved he'll have done well.' Still, it bodes well for Tottenham that Carr resembles Dixon in that both are uncomplicated players who do the business with the least amount of fuss, which means that their efforts tend to go unappreciated by those without a vested interest. That Carr should have been the player to score such a crucial own goal in Germany just amused those who perceive him to be no better than a mediocre squad player; those who knew better just wrote it off as a blip on his learning curve.

Forget the identity of the scorer – the defeat was such a body blow that even the usually undemonstrative Sol Campbell was moved to beat the turf in frustration at the final whistle and had to be hauled up by his manager. As for Graham – it must have knocked the wind right out of his sails, although he seldom reveals any feelings of dejection. He had appeared so supremely confident, after all, that his side would progress into the next round that on being asked immediately after the first-leg victory whether one goal (a Steffen Iversen penalty after David Ginola had been brought down by the Kaiserslautern keeper) would be enough, he bullishly answered: 'Yes,' before adding, 'well you didn't expect me to say no, did you? I've been a manager for a long time and you have to be a super optimist. I've been in this situation many times before, and we'll do it.'

Well, they didn't do it, although no one could doubt their effort on the night or fail to recognize in the performance the hallmarks of a side managed by Graham. Tottenham kept their shape throughout, with Freund steadfast against his midfield compatriots and Ian Walker outstanding in goal. In the final analysis, however, there were two defining factors in the defeat. One was the inclusion in the Kaiserslautern side of the French midfielder Youri Djorkaeff (who had been absent due to injury in the first leg) and the other was the non-inclusion of his Tottenham counterpart and fellow countryman David Ginola.

Djorkaeff is one of those players blessed with the rare ability to both provide and finish, and it was his two defence-splitting passes that led to both Kaiserslautern goals. Ironically, it was later revealed that Tottenham had the chance to sign him during the summer when he was going through an unsettled spell at Internazionale. Ian Anderson, the player's English representative, revealed that 'we went back to David Pleat twice to tell him that Djorkaeff really wanted to go to Tottenham, but they said that although it was flattering, he was not the player for them.' Typical. Of course Tottenham had no need for Djorkaeff's cunning and craft. No way.

As it was, the only man in the Tottenham side with anything like as much ability spent eighty minutes sitting on the bench. Ginola was left out by George Graham, a decision which infuriated the Tottenham fans and caused controversy before the match when the Kaiserslautern coach Otto Rehhagel changed his team just forty-five minutes before kick-off on learning of Ginola's non-selection. Maybe it was 'ungentlemanly' conduct, as an irate Graham described it, but frankly, Rehhagel must have been laughing all the way to the dug-out since Ginola had masterminded Tottenham's first-leg victory at White Hart Lane. Not only had he won the penalty that ultimately decided the game but he'd spent ninety minutes teasing the Germans with his complete repertoire of skills, tormenting them down the left wing and cutting inside to devastating effect. The fact that he had lasted the full match – a rare occurrence this season – told its own story, and the suspicion that the Germans were dreading facing him again in the return leg was backed up by Rehhagel's team change: the German coach replaced Martin Wagner, who had clearly been detailed to man-mark Ginola. For Graham to leave him out – and then compound what in the fans' eyes was a felony by playing his most effective attacker, Iversen, in midfield – was surely a tactical misjudgement, and anyway, would not the smart riposte, on learning of the German side's reaction to his team selection, have been to reinstate Ginola?

But Graham wouldn't have that. Instead, he hinted at his reservations regarding Ginola when he claimed that 'if David had played we'd have lost 3– or 4–0. We'd have been crucified down the right side. See, there are some players whose priority is to get results but others whose priority is to entertain.'

Except that this time there was no favourable result. Tottenham, like Arsenal, were going into the derby match as failures in Europe, even if the luxury of a few days' contemplation enabled Graham to take a more positive view. Speaking on the BBC's *Football Focus* the day before the game he claimed that morale had not really been affected. 'We have come a long way,' he said, 'and in four European ties we only lost to two goals in injury time which isn't so bad. We've done very well with the players we've got; if I could have fielded my strongest team we'd have been in the next round.' Which rather begs the question: would there be no place for Ginola in Graham's strongest team?

Garth Crooks, the interviewer posing the questions, knows a thing or two about north London derbies, and spoke as the Tottenham fan he is when describing the forthcoming match as 'the big one'. Are you, he asked Graham, accepted as a 'Tottenham man' yet? Graham managed a typically ambivalent reply. 'I'm not concerned about that,' he declared. 'All that matters is that the Tottenham fans and I have a common target and that we are after the same thing – success for the team.'

Short-term 'success' meant defeating Arsenal at White Hart Lane the following day, and Graham's involvement was once again according to Lee Dixon the 'key' to the outcome. Under Graham Arsenal became pastmasters at bouncing back after a defeat – the backlash was invariably instant, and pity those who were on the receiving end. Under Wenger, on the other hand, their response has tended to be slower and more measured, and that augured well for Tottenham, who could be forgiven for feeling slightly sore that Arsenal were in the UEFA Cup by default, whereas they had tumbled out in such unfortunate circumstances. Not that there was any sympathy forthcoming from the Arsenal camp. 'They should not show resentment to us but to UEFA,' Arsène Wenger said, 'and anyway, they are not in it any more.'

In fact, given the circumstances, it was tempting to wonder whether this derby match was of less significance than any of its predecessors. Hardly. Wenger had made a vain attempt to dampen the hype by reminding everyone that there were 'just three points' at stake, while Dixon of all people echoed his manager's sentiments when he stated the obvious – which was that 'you only get three points from beating Tottenham'. However, he did add that despite the magnitude of the games that Arsenal had been involved in over the previous couple of months, 'this was still *the* derby game and on the day there's no way we will be allowed to forget that. If you can't get up for this one then it's time to hang your boots up.'

Despite having reached the age of thirty-five and played almost 550 matches in Arsenal's red and white there was no suggestion from Lee Dixon that he was ready to do that just yet. 'My contract expires this summer and the perfect scenario would be for me to sign for another season,' he confessed. 'I do see myself going beyond this season. My wife certainly does – she says I can't give up yet – but whether the manager does is another question. But I don't want to play for another club, so if the club turned round in January and said, "Thanks a lot, see you later," I would seriously think about packing it in.'

He has never considered himself a big star or displayed unbecoming airs and graces. On the contrary, he has seamlessly melded into the community life of Harpenden, a pleasant residential village a few miles north of St Albans, where he has lived since joining Arsenal. A keen supporter of local charities and particularly of his children's sporting endeavours – on a recent freezing autumnal afternoon he was one of only two parents braving the elements to cheer their offspring in a netball game – he can certainly envisage a productive existence for himself and his family after he retires – at the top.

He would not be idle; he has business interests in golf and his investments in Indian restaurants are well-documented. But while he acknowledged that time was obviously not on his side (he would be thirty-six the day before the return fixture at Highbury in

March) when he admitted that Arsenal were still on a learning curve as far as the Champions' League was concerned and that 'we have to learn quickly from my point of view', it would be a safe bet that Dixon was looking forward to facing Tottenham, and David Ginola in particular, more than most.

Over the years he's become a *bête noire* to the Tottenham fans. His sending off at Wembley during the 1993 FA Cup semi-final had been their only consolation of an otherwise miserable encounter, although the fact that Dixon cites Tony Adams's winning goal as his favourite derby moment suggests that the red card didn't take the gloss off his day. (For the record his worst moment was – hardly surprising this – Gazza's free-kick in the 1991 FA Cup semi-final). Moreover, Dixon had a long-standing feud with Ginola stemming from Ginola's time at PSG and carried on at Newcastle (Ginola was sent off at Highbury in January 1996 after being mercilessly provoked by Dixon), which only served to heighten the animosity between the Arsenal full-back and the Tottenham fans.

Mind you, Ginola is not the only French winger to have come off worst in *tête-à-tête* with Dixon. When Arsenal played Lens at Wembley during their crucial Champions' League group match in 1998, the Lens winger Tony Vairelles was sent off after a controversial incident with Dixon who appeared to go down as if hit by a ten-ton truck. Dixon, naturally, saw it differently. 'I was hit in the back which was why I fell,' he claimed. 'I didn't dive, and besides, I was hurt because of the blow.' It earned Vairelles a ban from UEFA and caused a storm in France where the general consensus of opinion was that the winger had left Dixon struggling to cope. To add insult to injury UEFA refused to rescind Vairelles's one-match ban and it still rankles with the player, who was transferred to Lyon in 1999. Recalling the incident, he said: 'It spoilt my joy [Lens had won to eliminate Arsenal],' notwithstanding that Dixon's culpability was acknowledged by both his manager and UEFA.

Ask any Arsenal fan, however, and they will defend their player to the hilt by claiming that at 1–0 down and waving *au revoir* to his Champions' League hopes, Dixon's actions were prompted by frustration and not malevolence. In fairness, it was out of character.

Dixon is no con man. In fact, his most significant shortcoming – if you can call it that – is that he is not a glamorous player. Full-backs seldom are, Dixon less so than most, and unglamorous players tend to miss out when it comes to allotting headlines and determining heroes. You certainly won't find kids in playgrounds fighting over who will play Dixon in the kickabout, nor will you see his name adorning many Arsenal shirts; the phrase 'unsung' could have been coined for him.

At Highbury they acknowledge his worth to the side – quietly. Dixon is invariably the first out to warm up yet the crowd only occasionally sings his name. And while 'Nutty' Nigel Winterburn has a wondrous left peg; Keown can tackle for England; and Adams should patent the word 'colossus', Dixon's worth to the Arsenal back five is less obtrusive. In fact, in a recent Teletext poll to determine who was the most accomplished defender of Arsenal's latter-day rearguard, Dixon came bottom with a measly five per cent (not surprisingly Adams walked it with sixty-six per cent). But strip away any long-standing prejudices and you will discover the perfect example of a player who compensated for what he may have lacked in aptitude through attitude and application. In terms of skill he may lag behind Adams and Keown, yet he never hides, never shirks a challenge, and never gives less than his all. He is a player who does the simple things well, which makes him a pretty fine player if you believe George Graham. In his autobiography, *The Glory and the Grief*, Graham wrote of the player he bought from Stoke in 1988: 'There are more skilful players, better right-backs, better tacklers, more accurate passers and certainly those with better first-time control of the ball. But when it comes to concentration, commitment and maximizing what you've got then Lee takes some beating.'

'I know it's a cliché,' says Dixon, 'but it's the next game that matters,' and in his modest, down-to-earth manner he has always tried to ensure there is a 'next game' to be played. He reveals: 'I've always been philosophical in the way I approach my career – your next match could be your last one as far as an injury is concerned – and it's not really changed as I've got older. I'll just keep going until they tell me not to. Or until I say so.' When John Bond, his manager at Burnley, released him aged nineteen, it instilled in him a desire to succeed which must have seemed like a fanciful, youthful pipe-dream after similar unsuccessful stints at Chester and Bury. But then George Graham plucked him from obscurity at Stoke. 'Even when I went to Stoke, I didn't think that was it [that he had shown Bond the error of his ways]. Stoke were in the Second Division [this was before the Premier League, when the nomenclature meant what it said] and it was my aim to play in the First Division. I wanted somebody to come in and buy me or for me to go up with Stoke. When I got to Arsenal I thought I was at a reasonably high level but I wanted to play for England – and I played for England. I still want to win things. There are always goals to go for. I've never thought, "Oh, I've found my level." I think if you do that, especially at a club this size, if you settle for what you've got and don't drive yourself, then you're on a downward slope.'

Josh Lacey, a North Bank regular, declares that of all the Arsenal players he has the greatest admiration for Dixon. 'He came to Arsenal when his career was seemingly going nowhere,' Lacey recalls, 'and from the day he walked into the club his attitude hasn't changed. He has always been unfailingly constant and his appetite has never wavered, despite everything he's won. After twelve years, you've got to admire that in a player.' Another fan, Damian Hall, claims that Dixon 'represents the remnants of a dying breed of player . . . he is the personification of what an Arsenal player should stand for: commitment, loyalty, conviction and never admitting defeat'.

Dixon's commitment to Arsenal runs so deep that it is easy to forget he is actually a Mancunian who came to Arsenal as a late developer after six fruitless years in the lower divisions. That he is so often a leading protagonist in Tottenham eyes refutes the notion that the passion traditionally engendered by a derby encounter has diminished because of the high number of 'expatriates' playing for both teams these days. If you really care about your team, as the likes of Bergkamp, Petit and Vieira clearly do, and the likes of Jürgen Klinsmann and Erik Thorstvedt did, then you will under-stand just how crucial these games are in the context of north London football and never give less than your best. Besides, how could a player such as Davor Suker, who has played for Real Madrid against Barcelona and for Croatia against Yugoslavia, ever underestimate the importance of Arsenal against Tottenham. 'I like derbies,' Suker said before the game, adding, 'They are the best points in football.' He didn't have to be totally fluent in English to make perfect sense.

Suker would therefore have been disappointed by his exclusion from Arsenal's starting line-up, especially given the goal he had scored against AIK Solna in Sweden – the kind of poacher's goal that Arsenal had been lacking of late. Instead, Wenger opted to start with Kanu and Bergkamp upfront, despite the lack of pace that combination offered and despite the swelling body of opinion among the fans that when Bergkamp was not on his game he should make way for Suker, whatever the occasion. 'Kanu and Suker should have played against Fiorentina,' one fan protested, 'but Wenger doesn't want to drop Bergkamp for the big games.'

A big plus for Arsenal, however, was the return to fitness of Emmanuel Petit, whose re-emergence against AIK Solna had reminded the Arsenal fans of what they had been missing during his enforced lay-off. As for Tottenham ... well, the sight of Stephen Clemence in their line-up would have done nothing to reassure those fans who feared that Petit and Vieira would boss the midfield. Clemence was never regarded as certain to become a regular first-team player; Steffen Freund would surely have proved a more durable midfield barrier alongside Tim Sherwood but his disciplinary record had ensured he was unavailable through suspension. Freund had certainly made his mark in more ways than one when Manchester United had visited White Hart Lane two weeks earlier. His aggressive persona had been on full view and at one point he ran aross the pitch to goad Roy Keane – a somewhat foolhardy thing to do.

Tottenham had beaten Manchester United 3–1 that day, amazing not just their own fans but the rest of football, too. So the first goal definitely got a helping hand (literally) from Iversen and the second Tottenham goal came courtesy of Paul Scholes's head, but then came that belter from Stephen Carr – and out of nothing Tottenham had manufactured one of the shock results of the season. Of course, Graham took it all in his stride. 'We were excellent considering the problems we have had during the week with injuries,' said Graham. 'The fans are certainly getting their money's worth with lots of exciting games and lots of goals. They are probably quite surprised.'

That was quite an understatement. Tottenham's lofty Premiership position (they were fifth after that win) and their surprising 'goals for' record at White Hart Lane (only United had scored more goals at home) flew in the face of popular opinion, which presumed that Graham's sides always played percentage football and that Tottenham lacked firepower. In fact, only on two occasions thus far had Tottenham failed to score three goals at home – not bad for a team so short on forwards. But the paucity of options was well and truly exposed when Ramon Vega was forced to play upfront in the second half at Sunderland after Tottenham had been comprehensively picked off in the first half by former George Graham protégé Niall Quinn, who at thirty-three was playing the best football of his career. Oh what Graham would have given for two front men as effective as Quinn and his prolific striking partner Kevin Phillips.

Arsenal, meanwhile, had played out a 0–0 bore-draw at Highbury against Newcastle the previous day that, safe to say, would not be included in that inevitable end-of-season highlights video. 'Goals: none. Chances: none. Entertainment: none. Things to get excited about: none. That was dire,' said Alan Hansen, characteristically blunt, on *Match of the Day* that evening. And this from a team who had memorably stolen three points off Chelsea at Stamford Bridge in their previous Premiership match thanks to a wonderful Kanu hat-trick.

So the fact that neither club had embraced any semblance of consistency made this particular derby game a tough one to call. Few made any attempt to do so. Not this match. Not with so much pride at stake. However, Graham's involvement was still the foreboding factor, particularly from an Arsenal point of view. 'If Graham manufactures a Tottenham win it will test the loyalties of those Arsenal fans who still have respect for what he achieved at the club,' said one fan on the way into the ground, '. . . particularly if he shows any sign of relishing a victory' (Arsenal fans had felt wounded by David O'Leary's ostentatious show of delight after Leeds' triumph over Arsenal in the 1998–99 season had all but extinguished O'Leary's former club's title aspirations).

Surprisingly, the atmosphere outside White Hart Lane in the hours prior to kick-off was muted. You would hardly have guessed that Arsenal were on their way down (or up, depending on your persuasion) the Seven Sisters Road. Until, that is, the opposition team coach swung into the main entrance at White Hart Lane and prepared to jostle for space amongst the countless Bentleys, Mercedes, Jaguars and BMWs parked bumper-to-bumper on the White Hart Lane forecourt.

Half an hour to kick-off and Tottenham High Road started to buzz as fans spilled out of the pubs and into the ground. *Sport First*, the Sunday sports newspaper, had dedicated its front cover to a 'scoop' claiming that Manchester United wanted David Ginola in exchange for Ole Gunnar Solskjaer. 'Is Alex Gunnar trade Ole for Spurs' Ginola?' ran the headline to the story, which claimed that United were also ready to offer Teddy Sheringham in a player-plus-cash deal for Ginola. The scenario was an unlikely one, and most dismissed the story as nothing but a blatant attempt to sell copies on the day of the game. One thing was for sure though: transferring Ginola to anyone would be akin to treason at White Hart Lane if the amount of Ginola propaganda on sale outside the ground and the endless replica shirts with '14 Ginola' emblazoned on the back were anything to go by.

Also doing good business was a batch of T-shirts commemorating the victory over Manchester United. That a somewhat fortuitous result could be deemed vital enough to warrant being celebrated in this way (aren't commemorative T-shirts usually reserved for special occasions such as Cup finals?) only served to highlight how limited was Tottenham's horizon, how blinkered their vision. Lord knows what commercial opportunities would be seized upon were Tottenham to take the scalp of Arsenal, too.

Ten minutes to kick-off, cue for the hosts to whip up the hype by replaying excerpts from the 1981 FA Cup final on the video screens. The sight of Ricky Villa sashaying through the Manchester City defence to score Tottenham's third goal always guarantees an instant injection of self-belief among the home crowd. Certainly Garth Crooks, who played and scored in that memorable game, appeared as mesmerized now as he watched from his pitch-side seat as he had been on the day, when he stood with his arms aloft so as not to be accused of aiding his colleague from an offside position. The sight of Crooks must surely have served as a painful reminder to the

Tottenham fans of just how much they missed a striker with his balance, control and physical strength. A natural opportunist who scored 75 goals in 176 appearances and who was immortalized by a banner at Wembley that day which read 'Maggie isn't the only one with Crooks at number 11', Crooks formed a potent strikeforce alongside Steve Archibald in the early 1980s. What would Tottenham give for just one half of that double act now?

Bizarrely – and Crooks himself was whispering this in the press room prior to the game – his son is an Arsenal fan. The boy's teacher was so astounded when he found out that he was moved to suggest to Crooks, tongue firmly in cheek, that he should take his parental responsibilities a little more seriously. On a more serious note, however, Crooks's failure to keep Tottenham in the family is not unique; Irving Scholar's son, for instance, is a staunch Liverpool fan, a disclosure that would appal those traditionalists who believe that loyalty to a football club should be passed down through the generations. By contrast, David Dein's children, Gavin, Darren and Sasha, are all die-hard Arsenal fans. So what does that say about Tottenham and their long-term appeal?

The current Tottenham players were not privy to this obvious indulgence in past glories, emerging to a cacophony of noise a few minutes before kick-off – but they might just as well have been, judging by their performance in the first twenty minutes of the match. They literally tore into Arsenal like men possessed. It had obviously been drummed into them that if they failed to make any superiority tell in the opening exchanges then class might eventually tell. And so it proved. On seven minutes a speculative Leonhardsen chip found Iversen totally unmarked – heaven knows where the Arsenal defence was – and he could hardly miss. *One-nil to the Tottenham* came the predictable chant. On twenty minutes, Petit fouled Armstrong and from the resulting free-kick Ginola touched the ball to Sherwood, who curled the ball round Arsenal's wall and beyond Seaman's desperate dive. The perfect execution of the kick momentarily belied Sherwood's reputation as a journeyman midfield merchant. 'It was like Roberto Carlos,' quipped the *Guardian* correspondent David Lacey later, 'except that's where the similarity ends.'

Over the last few years a view has evolved that just as the best way to beat Arsenal is to score late and give them no time to reply, so the best way to beat Tottenham is to let them score early, whereupon they will almost certainly become complacent and vulnerable and will ultimately self-destruct. Thus, when Patrick Vieira's thirty-ninth-minute header gave Arsenal some reprieve, the smart money would probably have been on the Gunners staging a comeback similar to the one they had effected at Stamford Bridge two weeks earlier. That they did not was not due to any footballing prowess on Tottenham's part. Granted, they hung on manfully throughout the second half against a palpably better side but they failed to create any goalscoring opportunity of note. No, the reason for this win was the red mist which seems to descend all too readily whenever Arsène Wenger's Arsenal are playing and which threatens to undermine their quest for success.

Two red cards, for Ljungberg and Keown (not to mention five yellows, for Petit, Bergkamp, Vieira, Dixon and Suker) took Arsenal's toll of red cards under Wenger to a staggering twenty-six. The manager's constant bleats that his players are more sinned against than sinners would appear more dubious than Alex Ferguson's allegation last season that Manchester United's foremost rivals 'liked a scrap'.

However, this was certainly a scrap. Graham must have heeded Ferguson's words for his side methodically drew Arsenal into a war of attrition. 'I think George knows how to wind us up,' said Adams on reflection. That much was obvious. Arsenal wanted to strut their stuff but Tottenham were too streetwise on the day; they seemed to know that once they'd secured the lead the most likely way they were going to hold on to it was to provoke Arsenal into blowing a collective fuse.

As a game-plan it worked to perfection. Arsenal's composure was rattled and they never had the chance to settle into their normally fluid passing game once Ljungberg was sent off for allegedly shoving Justin Edinburgh in the face eight minutes into the second half. The fact that all around people were losing their heads (four Tottenham players went into referee David Elleray's book, too) was emphasized by five cards (one red, four yellow) in one chaotic, twelve-minute spell; one couldn't help wondering who was going to be adjudged the next culprit. The level of persistent, deliberate fouling and the wanton disregard for the rules made a mockery of Wenger's statement that 'everyone was highly committed'. Oh please. This was so bad, you could actually at times forget there was a game going on out there.

It camouflaged the fact that both Sol Campbell and Tony Adams played magnificently (which augured well for England's forthcoming European Championship play-off with Scotland), even if there was one moment during Tottenham's twenty-minute onslaught where Adams's uncharacteristically helpless shrug of the shoulders seemed to suggest he had no answer to Tottenham's domination. It marginalized Ian Walker's outstanding double save from first Overmars and then Suker, which preserved Tottenham's lead fifteen minutes from the end. It took the gloss off the performances of Vieira and Petit, who once again strode through the midfield like proverbial colossuses, notwithstanding the fact that the much-derided Clemence had his best-ever game in a Tottenham shirt. And luckily for Tottenham, it distracted from the reality – which was that the best team lost.

The Tottenham performance hardly surprised the observant Graham watcher. All the signs were that he was keen to encourage his players to adopt a more aggressive approach; he had made that much particularly clear after Tottenham let slip a 2–1 lead at home against Leicester and ended up losing the game 3–2. 'We've got to be more mean, even nasty,' Graham announced. 'We must get this nasty streak in us and be more dominant when we go in the lead. We have got to learn how to see teams off. We are much too nice.' It's safe to say that none of Graham's predecessors had ever uttered a remark like that; Tottenham's managers just did not say that sort of thing. In one short sentence he had rejected the traditional Tottenham way; for Graham's Tottenham it was victory first, entertainment second, and if that meant his players had to put themselves about a bit, then so be it.

That philosophy could have been one reason why this particular head-on collision boiled over in such spectacular manner. The other was the apparent inability of certain Arsenal players not to lose their rags. It is a liability that has dogged Wenger throughout his time in England. His captain, Tony Adams, believes that 'it comes down to the individual and how well he accepts provocation. We have foreign players who are very successful and they get stick. They have to learn how to handle that stick. Some players are on a knife-edge.' Adams might just as well have been giving a succinct match report when he added: 'We try and play football to win games, the opposition try and disrupt it and it can develop into a kicking match. They know how to wind up certain characters. If you have had a bad day and your emotions are flowing there can be resentment and you can be provoked.'

But for all that it is hard not to draw the conclusion that someone at Highbury was not conveying the right message – which was that indiscipline of the sort demonstrated during this match and in previous encounters against West Ham, Barcelona and Manchester United, for example, would not be tolerated. Arsenal chairman Peter Hill-Wood did have his say after Patrick Vieira had clashed with Roy Keane during Arsenal's Premiership match against Manchester United, warning that 'we take a dim view of players who butt their opponents. No Arsenal player should use his head as a weapon. That's not what we're about.' However, the chairman was taken to task by one of his fans, who pointed out: 'There was no head-butt. Why do people just parrot the media instead of actually observing what happened for themselves.'

But doesn't the buck stop with the manager? Nobody in the game denies him the right to stand up for his player should he feel the need, but there is a worrying trend among many of today's managers of offloading blame onto opposing players, managers, referees, linesmen, fourth officials, Uncle Tom Cobbleigh and all; and perhaps Wenger would be fairer to both himself and his players were he to occasionally remove his rose-tinted spectacles. For the fact is that in footballing terms Vieira is a serial offender. He might be 'a nice boy' who 'never goes out to do anyone', but even nice boys can reveal nasty streaks when provoked and the manager must find a way of curbing the over-aggressive tendencies among his players. Their never-say-die spirit is commendable and has undoubtedly contributed to the success story; however, the indiscipline that appears to lurk within remains a blot on Wenger's copy-book that he seems in no hurry to erase, perhaps because he believes his players are adults who should know how to handle themselves. 'Every so often,' admits season-ticket holder Danny Peters, 'I wish he'd come out and say, for example: "Oi, Vieira, you were an idiot." He never bawls them out.'

Yet all Wenger would say after the incident involving Vieira and Keane was: 'Patrick got some severe tackles on him ... Roy Keane is not especially an angel.' The Carling Opta statistics disagreed: although Vieira was at the time the fifth-most-fouled player in the Premiership, he also topped the list of foulers – with Lee Bowyer – with Keane conspicuously absent from both lists, although this really begs the questions about statistics, damned statistics and lies, and the preferential treatment Manchester United get from the referees. And not only referees. Perhaps Arsène Wenger knows that he cannot explicitly make this accusation of favouritism, whatever the justification, for fear of being accused of sour grapes and giving Alex Ferguson a stick to beat him with.

However, not having received – in public at least – a rebuke from his manager, was it any wonder that the question of Vieira's indiscipline raised its ugly head once again at the start of October when the midfielder was sent off for the fourth time in his Arsenal career during a 2–1 defeat to West Ham at Upton Park? This was probably just one bridge too far for Vieira, who had been on the receiving end of numerous unfair fouls and dives throughout the season. Vieira got his marching orders for a tackle on Paolo di Canio but then added insult to injury by clearly spitting at West Ham defender Neil Ruddock as he left the field. It sparked a war of words between Wenger, Ruddock and West Ham manager Harry Redknapp, who claimed that 'Di Canio gets kicked all the time' and refuted accusations that his striker, who made the first and scored the second of West Ham's two goals, also made the most of Vieira's tackle. Ruddock, one of football's most obstreperous defenders who Vieira claimed provoked him by calling him a 'French prat', muddied the waters by alleging that 'all through the game Vieira kept telling me I played for a shit team. He blabbed on about Arsenal being in the Champions' League and said West Ham were crap. All teams have wind-up merchants. It's part and parcel of the game. The difference between me and Patrick is I just laughed it off. The referee didn't have reason to speak to me once during the whole match. Not bad for a cheat and a monster, eh.'

Ruddock was referring to Wenger's comments that Vieira was

being made the scapegoat for the more general malaise in the game which caused 'people in this country to behave like monsters and the next day they say they're not guilty. People cheat and get away with it,' Wenger went on. 'They talk nicely in the papers. Hearing Ruddock say he went over only to see what was happening and claiming to be just a nice guy was shocking. Why is Patrick Vieira being punished? Because of TV evidence. So why not the provokers too? Patrick's response was out of order, we accept that. He knows he was wrong. He has to cope with the situation. He has to master his nerves. It is a part of him that is improving. But he puts his foot in and is genuine.'

There was the predictable post-mortem after the event. Some people thought Vieira should be dispatched back to France *tout de suite*; others claimed he had been as much sinned against as sinning. To give him his due, Vieira was commendably quick to apologize. 'I was completely in the wrong. Nothing can excuse what I did. I saw a television replay of the incident and could not believe I was watching myself. I will accept my punishment and then look forward to playing for Arsenal again as soon as possible.' However, he was planning to present his side of the story to the FA disciplinary commission that had charged him with misconduct, and was in no doubt about the events that led up to the tackle and the spitting incident. 'He [Di Canio] went high from not a big foul and it looked spectacular. I knew what was coming because I had already been booked. I turned back because I felt so frustrated. I promise all I wanted to say to the referee was that he had made a big mistake. Then something was said to me and I reacted how I did. The provocation – a little physical and a little verbal – was going on all through the match. The physical provocation doesn't bother me. It makes me play better. But the verbal went on the whole game and sometimes it gets to you.'

For David Dein, the entire unsavoury incident was a backlash in the wake of the *tour de force* against Barcelona in the Nou Camp four days beforehand. 'Football is a rollercoaster ride on your emotions,' (nice cliché, Mr D) said the Arsenal vice-chairman, 'and I went from being so high coming back from Barcelona to being so low – and it was a low, quite apart from getting beat.' Yet – shades of Wenger here – Dein still chose to defend Vieira and to point an accusatory finger at referee Mike Reed for over-reacting when it would have been easy to take the heat out of the situation. 'Patrick is such a lovely lad, a calm, cool guy, a gentleman,' Dein said, 'and you have to accept that he was really, seriously provoked. It's no excuse as he has to be able to control himself – he's hotheaded but he's talented – but two hours later he made the apology of his own volition. I have to say the referee had a bad day and I'm not usually critical of refs. All it needed was a bit of common sense. All he had to say was, "One more bad tackle like that and you're off." But no . . . and the way he brandished the card as if to say, "Get off." Well I'm sorry but that's not on.'

What both Dein and Vieira declined to make public was the pervasive racist provocation that they believe ignited the incident. The fact that footballers systematically employ brinkmanship and gamesmanship (anything, in fact, they can get away with to gain an advantage and if that means destabilizing an opponent with industrial language and racist taunts, that's fine by them) makes the 'professional' status they are fond of claiming for themselves a contradiction in terms.

Yet the prevailing attitude is that if it's only done for the good of the team it must be fine. The pernicious atmosphere is tolerated on the pitch and allowed to disseminate off it by the half-hearted attempts of the clubs and the authorities to combat it. Laudable though the *Kick Racism out of Football* campaign is, it has no real teeth. A two-line warning in eight-point type in the back of a programme is purely a token gesture when what is required is consistent and salient advertising and PR in the mainstream media.

Other countries can focus the fans' attention by creating antiracist days so why can't the Premier League follow their example? Moreover, indolence by the League is no excuse for a club not to try and control events in its own backyard. Is it beyond the wit of the clubs to run a testimonial campaign to grab people's attention and hammer home the point that racism is wholly unacceptable (although aside from the disgraceful yid chants, racism is not really an issue between Tottenham and Arsenal)? At the very least they could surely run a joint tactical advertisement featuring Sol Campbell and Tony Adams to take the heat out of the derby match, and not just a full-page advertisement in the programme, but using television and press as well. After all, it is not as if the clubs can't afford it.

The Football Association, who in recent years have been accused of being spineless and cowardly in their apparent unwillingness to clamp down on players who have overstepped the mark, bit the bullet on this occasion and levied a record £45,000 fine on Vieira, banning him for four games (he also got an extra two-game ban and £15,000 fine after an incident involving a police officer in the tunnel at Upton Park). Naturally, Arsène Wenger refused to condemn his player. Instead, he fumed: 'I hope Vieira has not been made a scapegoat. That would not be right. It would have meant the FA considered the publicity surrounding this case. They say that spitting is the same as violent conduct yet violent conduct gets three matches. He got four.' However, his retort overlooked Vieira's disciplinary record during his three years at Arsenal; one can hardly reproach the FA for finally deciding to make an example of him. However, the punishment would have been applauded if the FA's approach had been consistent, but one gets the impression that foreign excesses make for soft targets whereas English hard men, particularly if they are in the thoughts of the national selector, get off comparatively lightly – and not only from the authorities. Television and press, too, appear to turn a blind eye to their cheating whilst being seemingly all too quick to expose nefarious imported practices.

Patrick Vieira certainly thought so. As he told French television: 'Viewed from another country, yes the English practise fair play. It is always the image of fair play that emerges, yet when you live in the country itself you know it is further away, it's hypocrisy.' The observation carries all the more weight for being delivered by someone who has a genuine axe to grind but who has chosen instead to take and step back and adopt a broader perspective. 'I adore English football. I adore the atmosphere in the stadia,' he acknowledges, adding that 'since I have been at Arsenal good things have happened to me: I am in the French squad and I played in the World Cup.' But not only on the pitch. 'I am someone,' he claims, 'who when I am content wants to stay [in London]. I want to take advantage of everything I have in England.' It was the mature response of someone facing up to reality, yet it would not be easy to reform, as Vieira reflected after his return to the side. 'I don't want to lose the deter-mination I have on the pitch because if I am a pro it is because I have that quality. I am going to keep it because in the position I play it is really important to have it. I try to keep the same aggression but maybe the things I change are not to accuse the ref or to be upset with other players.'

Canvass a cross-section of fans and you'll probably find that Arsenal are regarded as the most indisciplined Premiership side in the country. However, there is media discrimination at play here. It was only a few years ago, for instance, that similar accusations were being flung at Manchester United, while the successful Leeds team of the 1970s were forever saddled with the prefix 'dirty'. But as Billy Bremner clearly implied, you can be hard without sacrificing skill. 'People are coming to respect us for the way we play the game; we are hard – and courageous. But not dirty,' was Bremner's verdict on Don Revie's Leeds. 'We can match any team in the world for sheer endeavour; and we can match most of them on equal terms when it comes to pure footballing skills.' Arsenal fans would say the same of their current side, and most plead innocent to the charge that their players are dirtier than any of their Premiership contemporaries. 'Arsenal are unfairly portrayed as villains,' believes Eugene Harper, a Clock End regular. 'We are not angels but at the same time we have a fighting spirit others are jealous of.' Danny Peters, meanwhile, maintains that 'Vieira is probably the player everyone would cite as being dirty but having watched him since he made his debut I can honestly say I completely disagree. He never looks for it and nearly always gets into trouble through retaliation. Petit is much the same.'

The statistics certainly support their opinions. On the weekend before that West Ham game Arsenal were a creditable tenth in the Carling Opta disciplinary chart with 197 points (146 fouls, 17 yellow cards, no red cards). So it would appear that when Arsenal get a player sent off – and they had had three dismissed by this time the previous season – the legacy left by incidents such as the infamous 1990 scrap at Old Trafford; Ian Wright's ongoing feud with Peter Schmeichel; and off-the-pitch fracases on overseas trips involving both David Hillier and Ray Parlour to name but two from Highbury's roll-call of dishonour means that Arsenal are often the victims of their own, however erroneous, reputation.

Still, don't be fooled by talk of a record fine: £60,000 is about a month's wages for Vieira. Far more damaging from the club's point of view was the ban: seven matches (the booking at White Hart Lane earned him an automatic one-game ban on top of what he was already due to serve) is a long time to be without the services of a key player, which as one Arsenal fan pointed out, 'was handy for Manchester United. Nudge nudge, wink wink.'

Wenger's acknowledgement in his post-match press conference at White Hart Lane that the suspensions gave him 'a new problem . . . or an old one', suggested that he was well aware of the criticisms that would be coming his way in the following morning's papers. However, he managed to sit on the fence as far as Ljungberg's sending-off was concerned. 'If he head-butted someone then the referee was 200 per cent right and there will be a heavy fine,' said Wenger categorically, 'but it didn't look that way from the bench and it's not right to kill the game for that.' Wenger went on to claim that 'the hardest foul was on Petit. I took him off because sometimes when you are dizzy you never know how a player can react. It was a hard game and you can lose your head a bit. For me it was clear but if you have different glasses on maybe you don't see it.' Wenger was referring to the incident when Tim Sherwood appeared to elbow Petit in the face. The foul went unpunished and Petit showed his obvious displeasure as he stormed off down the tunnel. From the Arsenal perspective, this was not the first time that Sherwood had got away with his indiscretions.

Wenger said that he would be studying video replays of the Ljungberg incident and that he would be upset if it were proven to have been an unjust decision, since the sending-off had forced his hand into bringing on Suker in exchange for Kanu when Arsenal went down to ten men and having to forego the option of taking off a midfielder and leaving Kanu on. Who knows what damage a three-man attack of Bergkamp, Suker and Kanu would have done to a Tottenham side whose resources were by then stretched to the full? But such hypothesis never bothered Graham. During his typically short, straight-to-the-point press conference he revealed that he had 'told the boys it was our ground and our pitch and that we had to dictate the tempo. We were brilliant for half an hour. We gave the ball away too cheaply in the second half which was a bit scrappy but

Ian Walker hardly had a shot to save.' Just the double save, George. 'I didn't see that,' smiled Graham, never one to give his old team too much praise.

He could afford to smile. It was the first time he'd been on the winning side against Arsenal in the Premiership. As for the Tottenham fans, well, they'd waited four long years to celebrate, and they were going to milk it for all it was worth. They had won a battle but the war was still to be resolved, although that was not how they viewed it. 'We beat the Scum 2–1,' was the predictable chant that hung in the air as the fans dispersed, buoyant, into the street. This ubiquitous and small-minded chant seems to be the obligatory chant of the victors. Six months previously, 'we beat the Scum 3–1' was belted out by the Arsenal fans.

Whenever Arsenal meet Tottenham, though, regardless of who the major protagonists are on the pitch and what their behaviour might be at the time, what should be a healthy local rivalry turns into one that is characterized by an animosity that transcends traditional football antagonism. Of course it's acceptable to taunt the 'other lot' – that's all part of the fabric of football. Tottenham fans will for ever more fling jibes at their Arsenal counterparts about Nayim lobbing Seaman from the half-way line, while Tottenham fans are used to the Arsenal fans deriding them with chants of 'You'll never win the League' . . . but smashing up and pissing against cars belonging to opposing fans? Football has long been the means through which society expresses emotions that are otherwise kept under wraps, but that kind of action is extreme. Moreover, it cannot simply be blamed on the increasingly bad behaviour during a game of the players and managers. After all, fisticuffs are common among rugby players and in ice hockey, where it has become a cliché to report that 'a game has broken out', but the crowds who watch these sports are as well behaved as they come. Something does not quite add up.

According to Morris Keston, a Tottenham fan of many years' standing, 'hatred' is not too strong a word to use. Keston revealed how he went after the match into the Centenary Club (an exclusive upmarket section set aside for season-ticket holders in the Upper West Stand offering dining, bar and tea room facilities from £2,000 a year), where he found everyone to be 'on cloud nine. I found it sad – no one dislikes Arsenal as a team more than I do. They are our rivals. If they lost and we lost too it would take the edge off our loss, that sort of thing. But it has become a lot more aggressive today. Guys were actually frothing at the mouth. There was hatred in their eyes.'

It was much the same story at Highbury, where several thousand Arsenal fans congregated to watch the same match, which had been beamed back from White Hart Lane. Arsenal fan Mark Whitford had stood on the North Bank throughout the 1970s and 1980s but had not been to a derby since 1995 when he had been so appalled at the level of personal and physical abuse directed at a few Tottenham 'strangers' who dared to sit among the Arsenal fans that he had decided to boycott the fixture. But on this occasion both he and his family, including ten-year-old Tom, needed an instant pick-me-up after Arsenal's Champions' League exit; having tested the waters at several big games (Manchester United, Liverpool, Chelsea and West Ham) and found no underlying feeling of deep hatred, they decided that 'the credibility of the Gooner was restored', so off they went in good faith to Highbury.

On arrival, Mark Whitford said it reminded him of the 'good old bad days – a pint before kick off, change from £40 and a jovial, good-humoured crowd'. The atmosphere soon soured, however. The first disappointment was that the picture from the main screen in the centre of the pitch was poor, while the two big permanent screens at the corners of the ground were too far away from the North Stand to offer a decent view. 'The players were barely recognizable; I've seen better from my son's Playstation,' was his damning indictment. 'The commentary was barely audible and to top it all, Arsenal were 2–0 down inside twenty minutes.'

It got worse. He actually had to move his family three times to try and find 'a peaceful spot', and on one occasion he was forced to retreat because of the vitriol being hurled at two Tottenham fans who were being bated simply because they were 'strangers'. Quite what they were doing there in the first place, is a mystery, but that's no excuse for the verbal violence they were subjected to, which would have come as a shock for armchair fans who rely on television's glossy veneer to shield them from the increasingly foul-mouthed and laddish displays of exhibitionism that can mar the game for the committed fan. Some would argue that effing and blinding are part and parcel of football, but when the basest elements among the modern English fan threaten to drive out the right-minded, then surely it is time to clean up. 'What staggered me most was the abuse and general bad feeling,' Mark Whitford admitted. 'The game of football was taking second place to the experience of hate. The direction of the fans' abuse was so confused – aimed not just at the opposition, referee and linesmen, but at the Arsenal players too – that no one listening in would have been able to tell which team these fans were supporting. What worries me is that so much vitriolic passion (hard drinking and crowd-watching rather than game-watching) can result in opinions that are less rooted in the quality of the game than the outmoded sentiments of our yesteryears. Once again I left a derby game with a bitter taste in my mouth, this time questioning my own support. Was I really an Arsenal fan? Should I really have to hate Tottenham to be a proper Gooner? Do I really have to stand up to prove my hatred of Tottenham at an Arsenal v Barcelona game? I guess I'll just have to put up with all the rubbish in order to support my team, but should I have to?'

On the other hand, young Tom took a rather more pragmatic view of the whole affair. 'It wasn't a great atmosphere and there was lots of shouting going on,' he admitted. 'But I've been a Gooner since I was born so I was used to it. Whenever Arsenal and Spurs meet blood runs high – you get a buzz that you don't get in a normal league match. But there's always trouble and there's no exception for the live games on the video screens – but do, I have to stand up because I hate Spurs when it's shouted? Of course I do, because I am an Arsenal fan and that's the way it will stay because I hate Spurs.' At a playground level the hatred is tolerable, restricted in the main to teasing and taunting, but how do you demonstrate your loyalty and 'hatred' as you get older?

For the players, many of whom meet regularly on international duty, the depth of feeling does not run so deep. Tony Adams recounted how he had almost tricked Ian Walker into releasing the ball to him after one Arsenal attack. 'I said to him: "Give us the ball. Put it down" and he nearly did. He had to think twice.' For the most part, Adams claims, it is good-natured banter rather than blatant verbal abuse, although Morris Keston admits to being embarrassed by the fans at Lee Dixon's testimonial the day after the derby who called on the Arsenal players to 'wave if you hate Tottenham' and by the number of players who did just that.

As far as the fans were concerned, the bating continued unabashed throughout the following few days. The messages posted onto the respective club's web sites were, predictably, at opposite ends of the spectrum: Tottenham were lauding it and Arsenal were loathing it. 'Man United, Scum, who next? West Ham on the sixth would be nice. Let's finish top of the London league this year,' wrote one Tottenham fan, his judgement clearly clouded by the victory itself rather than the manner of it. 'Beating the Arse is still sweetness unrivalled,' mused another. Amidst the general back-slappers, the occasional realist managed to get his point across: 'We've had one of our best starts in years, and the ball is now in Sugar's court. If he takes these two victories as evidence that we don't need strengthening then he is making a serious error. If he takes it as proof of Graham's prowess and gives him backing then the party could last longer. Please God let Tottenham get something right off the field as well as on it.'

From the Arsenal camp came the expected inquest. Opinions ranged from the back five being 'finished' to 'the title is out of our hands' to severe criticisms of the team as a whole and of individual players. One irate fan protested that he had 'only seen the real Arsenal for fifteen minutes this season – the last fifteen minutes at Stamford Bridge. Where was the pride and the passion?' Many questioned the attitudes of both Dennis Bergkamp and Marc Overmars, whose lack of application suggested their hearts were no longer with Arsenal. Bergkamp had certainly appeared a troubled figure throughout the match, contesting decisions that went against him and grumbling at misplaced passes. Overmars, meanwhile, was more anonymous than his opposite number Ginola (who never imposed himself on the game and spent most of it in Dixon's pocket). Naturally, few Arsenal fans could resist the occasional pop at Tottenham. 'Who can remember the last time they even did the "Single"?' wrote one. If they want Judy Graham as their manager then they'll have to sit through hours of turgid shite,' taunted another. In general, however, they appeared more preoccupied with the shortcomings of their own team than with defending themselves against the anticipated crowings of the Tottenham fans.

But if the fans were low on morale, then imagine how Arsène Wenger must have felt. In the space of ten days Arsenal had been dumped out of the Champions' League and humbled by Tottenham, and Wenger's regular phone call to his parents back home in Duttlenheim in Alsace, eastern France, must have been a pretty low-key one. Alphonse and Louise have the dates of the derby matches circled in red ink on their calendar, although his mother claims that 'we do not talk much about football when he phones. We normally talk about ourselves, the family, anything to take his mind off it.' After Fiorentina had won at Wembley her verdict was that 'he won't be down for long'. Speaking like a true pro she added: 'You win one and you will lose one – he's been in the game long enough to know that.' She also stressed that there was no question of her son throwing in the towel. 'Arsenal have told him they don't want him to go and he is very happy there.'

David Dein called round to visit Wenger later that Sunday night. It was not a totally unexpected visit given that Dein lives just a short walk from his friend in Totteridge, north-west London, and is in the habit of dropping round from time to time. On this occasion, call it intuition. He suspected Wenger was especially down, and the two men simply chatted over the events of the last fortnight. There was certainly no putting of Arsenal's world to rights; that was a longer-term debate.

Immediately after the match itself Dein had gone into the Tottenham boardroom with the two sets of directors. There was no evidence of the camaraderie that had been prevalent when Douglas Alexiou and Tony Berry were on Tottenham's board, and before Graham's appointment. These days the civilities were far more formal, and Dein beat a hasty retreat as soon as Tottenham High Road had cleared. Graham, meanwhile, had gone straight from his post-match press conference to the VIP lounge where his family were waiting for him. It was hardly surprising that he had steered clear of the boardroom, given that there was no love lost between him and the Arsenal directors. Bridge-building was certainly not on the agenda. If anything, the gap that separated them had become a chasm.

By contrast, there was a marked softening of the stance against Graham still adopted by some of the more hardcore Tottenham fans.

No one, least of all Graham himself, expected regular, whole-hearted renditions of 'Georgie Graham's blue and white army' by now – small sections of the crowd at Wembley after the Worthington Cup victory had tried to instigate the chant, which was not taken up – but there was certainly more appreciation now for the job Graham had done on what was clearly a limited budget and with very clear-cut restrictions. Most of the time the fans stuck to chanting about the club itself rather than its manager; when they did sing about Graham, they couldn't bring themselves to chant his name. However, a poll conducted via the Internet suggested that Graham's popularity was at its highest level since he came to the club – about 70 per cent. 'He will never be universally accepted,' countered one fan, which was undoubtedly true. But 70 per cent ain't bad when you're 'one of them'.

So as Graham drove away from White Hart Lane that evening towards his home in Hampstead he could afford to feel pretty pleased with his day's work. The fans were obviously delighted, and as he drove past the pubs on Tottenham High Road, all full to bursting with inebriated fans singing 'Glory Glory Tottenham Hotspur', he may have conjured up a mental picture of Alan Sugar driving home to his Chigwell mansion with a look of contentment on his face like those misguided fans who would doubtless view this victory over 'the Arsenal' as evidence that all was well within the Tottenham camp. Sugar may have shared this view, otherwise the issue of the availability of funds to reinforce the squad would not have been such a controversial subject.

But no. Victories over Arsenal and Manchester United would be remembered long after inept displays against the likes of Sunderland and Leicester had been confined to the past and were the perfect scenario as far as the Tottenham chairman was concerned. They kept the fans happy and they ensured the club remained nicely positioned just behind the chasing pack. Not for Sugar, clearly, the experience of Blackburn. Jack Walker's club, propelled into the Premiership, immediately splashed out on players befitting their elevated status. But before long they were heading back down to the Nationwide, close on £75 million financing the roller-coaster journey from Championship to relegation. For Sugar, it was unthinkable that Tottenham should fall into that trap: no way.

Nice and safe with the odd thrill here and there. That was the way he wanted to play it.

For Graham, too, the victory over Arsenal was hugely satisfying, but for different reasons. He knew that he had been able to motivate his team to beat an obviously classier outfit – he did not need telling that the better team had lost. He was well aware, too, that if the going chose to get tough again at Tottenham then it would be Sugar's blood the fans would be baying for, not his. On that note, George Graham headed off to enjoy dinner at one of his favourite local restaurants. Whatever he ordered from the menu that night, it must have tasted pretty good.

CHAPTER FIVE

THE MAN IN BLACK

It is summer 1994, and the World Cup that will be made memorable by Diana Ross's ludicrous opening skit, Maradona's self-destructive excesses and Roberto Baggio's penalty miss is almost over. July is traditionally a steamy month in Los Angeles, and the Arsenal manager George Graham and his Stateside travelling companion, the club's vice-chairman David Dein, are taking time out from their hectic World Cup schedule. For both men this is a trip designed to mix business with pleasure; with British teams conspicuous by their absence, the idea is to run the rule over any potential foreign transfer targets on the one hand and enjoy a bit of a jolly on the other. Which is exactly what Graham is doing, topping up his tan, when an animated Dein appears, intent on finding his manager to convey what in his opinion is extraordinarily good news.

Dein informs Graham that he's just put the phone down on a call from Jean-François Domergue, the former French international who is now the general manager of Paris St-Germain. Domergue had called to discuss PSG's French international winger David Ginola – or to be more exact, Ginola's availability. He wondered – would Arsenal be interested in doing business? You bet they would. At least, that's what Dein supposed as he eagerly informed his manager of the situation, expecting Graham to be as enthusiastic as he was at the prospect of acquiring one of Europe's most gifted performers. Actually, Dein must have been tempted to say yes on the spot. Arsenal, remember, knew all about Ginola. He had made an indelible impression with his performances in the 1994

European Cup-Winners' Cup semi-final, not least on the biggest fan in the boardroom, Dein himself. Moreover, even the most blinkered Arsenal supporter would surely admit that the team were in need of a fillip. Yes, they were the Cup-Winners' Cup holders, but few would deny that their 1–0 victory over Parma was one occasion on which they could not complain about the 'lucky Arsenal' tag, even allowing for their good organization and greater will to win than their opponents on the day. As Lee Dixon said: 'I remember thinking when the final whistle went, "How in the hell have we won that?"' However, over the course of the long Premiership season their inadequacies had been more clearly exposed, and playing what one pundit described as 'highly organized tedium', they had finished in fourth place behind Manchester United, Blackburn and newly promoted Newcastle, and gone out of both domestic cups at the fourth-round stage.

It was clear that the team had become far too reliant on the goals of Ian Wright and whether or not Paul Merson was in the mood, and was crying out for a more positive approach that might accommodate a big name or two. However, George Graham and stars are seldom of one mind, so Dein should not really have been surprised by a lukewarm response. But when Graham responded with a characteristic twinkle in his eye – he has a nice line in self-deprecating humour – 'We can't have David Ginola at Highbury. He's better looking than I am,' Dein was incredulous that the notion could be dismissed so blithely, and tried in vain to persuade his manager to discuss the matter seriously. But Graham was unmoved. The truth was he simply didn't fancy Ginola – as a player. (Incidentally, after Graham's departure discussions with PSG were reactivated but any deal was stymied by Arsenal's lack of funds after splashing out on David Platt and Dennis Bergkamp.)

Had this particular leopard been prepared to change his spots, the story might have unfolded very differently. David Ginola's arrival at Arsenal might have caused George Graham to adopt a more expansive approach. Ginola, he might have insisted, was exempt from the hard graft, the tackling, tussling and tracking back. Those were the duties of the others; Ginola was in the team simply to attack. Given licence to thrill in this way Ginola might have inspired Arsenal to new heights, Graham might have been rewarded with a salary that he felt was more commensurate with his success and the whole sorry bungs saga might never have happened. And Ginola might have won that Double Footballer of the Year award for his consistently outstanding performances – in a red and white shirt.

But football managers are not renowned for their willingness to change, and Graham was not about to alter his philosophy to accommodate a mercurial winger with a penchant for – as he may well have viewed it – over-elaboration. He'd already tolerated one of those at Highbury for four years, and having just offloaded him (Anders Limpar went to Everton in March 1994 but he was never the same player as the one who shone in Arsenal's Championship team of 1991) he was not prepared to harness another from the same stable. It was Graham's good friend Terry Venables who was famed for his karaoke renditions of the Frank Sinatra classic 'My Way', but as theme tunes go it was ideal for him too. He may have had his tongue in his cheek when he dismissed the idea of signing Ginola but he was deadly serious none the less.

This was not the first occasion Graham had adopted an insouciant attitude. Remember Steve Heighway scoring for Liverpool in the 1971 FA Cup final, and Eddie Kelly equalizing for Arsenal before a Charlie George screamer eight minutes from time secured an Arsenal victory? At least, the record books certainly show that it was Kelly's goal – but you would think otherwise if you watched the footage and saw Graham, the man of the match, wheeling away triumphantly to celebrate what appeared to be his crucial touch for the Arsenal equalizer.

Strikers regularly attempt to claim even the most spurious of deflected goals – it goes with the territory – but this was different. Yet when Graham was later called to account for what might be described as ungentlemanly conduct towards one of his colleagues, he simply replied: 'Well, who do you think my team-mates would rather have hugged: me or Eddie Kelly?' So Kelly was no looker, certainly no match for the sophisticated Stroller, but that was hardly the point.

George Graham has never knowingly undervalued himself, and no wonder. You would expect that from someone who has won the amount of trophies he has, as both a player and a manager. As a result, he's got used to calling the shots. Despite the fact that his only previous coaching experience had been with the youth teams at

Crystal Palace and Queens Park Rangers, he was fortunate at Millwall that, despite the club's precarious financial plight, its reputation for violent fans and its history of under-achievement, there was a willingness by the board to allow this apprentice his head. Their faith was repaid when his motivational and organizational skills swiftly came to the fore and by the time news of his managerial acumen was attracting interest in north London he had taken Millwall into the old Second Division and laid the foundations for promotion to the top division for the first time.

He'd hardly got his feet under the desk at Arsenal before he started to lay down the stringent ground rules which have become synonymous with his style. According to Tony Adams, then a raw and eager-to-please nineteen year old, it was immediately obvious that Graham was going to 'sort out the prima donnas' and from the first day there was no doubt who was in charge. At Highbury he was pretty much untouchable, firmly ensconced at the top of a hierarchy within a club whose core business was football and where the MIP (most important person, the kingpin) was therefore the football manager, unlike at many other clubs where the chairman's ego had to be massaged and business interests pursued.

When Leeds offered George Graham a route back into the game, after the 'bung' scandal – which involved Norwegian agent Rune Hauge and 'gifts' worth £425,000 – had earned him a sacking, a year's worldwide ban and a whole heap of humiliation, he accepted it gratefully. The Yorkshire club were clearly prepared to brush the ignominies of the past under the Elland Road turf; Leeds had just been taken over by Caspian, whose ambitious plans made the appointment of a manager with a proven track record a prerequisite to, as Graham himself put it, 'make a clean sweep'. So they gave him carte blanche, welcoming him back into the game with open arms, if not an open cheque book. A year out of the game and here he was landing a plum managerial post along with a salary worth more than Alex Ferguson was earning at Old Trafford thank you very much.

Fast forward three-and-a-half years, and George Graham finds himself entering the new millennium as manager of Tottenham Hotspur, yet another ailing concern in need of major surgery. His appointment, on 1 October 1998, smacked of a desperate attempt by the Tottenham chairman Alan Sugar to stop the rot at a club which had witnessed a succession of unsuccessful managers throughout seven barren years. Yet on being questioned whether hiring Graham represented a last throw of the dice, Sugar retorted: 'The appointment is to get this football club in shape and get it to start performing in the manner in which it should be, and what it's expected to be, and what its status deserves. [He is] what we consider to be one of, if not the top, manager in British football.' Sugar admitted to feeling sore at the continued 'abuse' he was getting from the disgruntled Tottenham fans but he sure as hell wasn't going to give up without a fight. And in hiring George Graham he had clearly landed a big counter-punch.

So at least Alan Sugar and George Graham were in agreement over the new recruit's remit and reputation. Graham himself defines his 'role in life' as being 'to take over struggling businesses and resurrect them [which of course is how Alan Sugar views the effect he has had on Tottenham Hotspur plc], and then possibly pass them on so someone else can succeed even more'. That was exactly what he did at Millwall, Leeds and Arsenal, and the majority of impartial observers who furiously debated the appointment in print and on air during the ensuing forty-eight hours now considered him to be the perfect solution to Tottenham's problems. Speaking on Sky Sports' discussion programme *Hold the Back Page*, the *Daily Telegraph*'s Henry Winter admitted that 'expediency rules in football, and what Tottenham need is a manager like Graham who will come in and sort out the defence ... it needs a good two months of George Graham drilling on the training ground'.

There are times when Sky television really comes into its own, and the coverage of Graham's appointment was one of them. The cameras tracked his arrival at White Hart Lane every inch of the way. They picked up his limousine as it swung out of Tottenham High Road into the forecourt of the West Stand. They homed in on his grinning countenance as he emerged, impeccably attired as always in a navy blue suit, royal blue shirt and two-tone blue tie. It was like watching a star arrive at the West End premiere of his film. No one could have failed to realize the irony – that what was once enemy territory was now George Graham's perfect stage.

A neutral observer could have been forgiven for thinking that Tottenham's future looked considerably rosier than it had just a few weeks before, when news of the appointment had been pure conjecture. Yet had that person gained access to the press conference he might have come away with a very different impression. Graham, naturally, was upbeat, his soundbites littered with references to 'passion', 'commitment' and 'winning teams'. But sitting next to him, Sugar looked in more sombre than celebratory mood. Significantly, he did not even give the traditional chairman's fulsome welcome. Instead, he simply said: 'Thank you, ladies and gentlemen, for attending this afternoon. The purpose of this press conference is obvious.' And that was it. No lauding, no mutual back-slapping. It was the first indication to the new man that he was not going to be able to waltz into White Hart Lane and assume top-dog status. Because as George Graham was about to learn, top dog was a particularly rare breed at White Hart Lane.

Certainly as far as the fans were concerned there was only one top dog, and he did his business out on the pitch. Yet it was obvious from the outset of the new regime that David Ginola's future at the club was by no means assured. He failed to last the course of the new manager's first match in charge, against Leicester City at Filbert Street, and it was the same story on ten occasions out of the season's remaining twenty-two matches which he started. Most significantly, he was dropped for Graham's first north London derby on 'the other side' when George Graham's Tottenham (who would have ever envisaged those three words tripping so readily off the tongue?) ground out a 0-0 bore-draw against a backdrop of Arsenal fans waving brown paper envelopes and Tottenham fans fearing that they were waving a permanent goodbye to their heritage. Ominously, Graham had declared: 'If I was a Tottenham fan I would be wanting a winning Tottenham team, and I wouldn't care who the manager was' – at which several thousand Tottenham fans must have been left staring apprehensively at the writing on the wall.

On what was a highly charged and nerve-wracking day it was hard to determine which supporters were the more aggrieved. The Arsenal fans, seeing the man they had once worshipped returning to Highbury in charge of a Tottenham team; or the Tottenham fans, who just kept pinching themselves. They could clearly see the Armani suit, but try as they might they just could not come to terms with who was actually sitting in the opposition dug-out in charge of their side. A few years ago, any one daring to predict such a scenario would have been derided. Now, reality was 1–0 up on fantasy, as Mark Jacob acknowledged when he wrote, in *What's the Story, Boring Glory*: 'Tottenham betray their heritage by hiring an Arsenal manager and an Arsenal manager betrays his heritage by joining Spurs.'

Despite the surrealism, it was in many respects a cathartic occasion, an opportunity for emotions to be discharged. It had been six weeks since the appointment and the inquests continued unabated. The front cover of the Arsenal fanzine *One-Nil Down* featured a picture of Graham shaking hands with Sugar under the banner 'Traitor', the copy underneath asking the simple question: 'George, how could you?' Inside, in an obvious attempt to come to terms with the 'betrayal', the editorial column maintained that 'we never really bonded with George emotionally. He was respected for his achievements but never loved, unlike his great protégé, Tony Adams', and issued a 'woe betide' warning to any Arsenal player 'tempted to follow Judas to N17'.

Inside the *Gooner* – the front cover described it as feeling 'Betrayed and Bewildered' – the consensus was that whatever their former manager achieved at Tottenham, and however long he might remain 'in the employ of the enemy, his heart would always remain in N5'. You can take the man out of Arsenal, it reasoned, but you cannot take Arsenal out of the man.

This was the second blow George Graham had dealt the Arsenal fans. It had been painful enough when an acrimonious divorce had brought to an end one of football's most fruitful marriages. Graham's ambition, which had driven him obsessively to chase trophies, had got out of hand and the man who demanded his players lived by the book had sidestepped the rules. Yet many supporters refused to condemn him, preferring to dwell on his footballing achievements rather than his misdemeanours – six trophies in less than nine years and the creation of arguably the greatest back four in the English game was a pretty memorable legacy.

Now, however, he had really blown it by shacking up with the enemy, but that was just part of the story. As the Arsenal fans listened to Graham claim that one of the prime motives for his move was personal, that both his wife and his new grandson lived in

London, they scoffed. They suspected that his move to Tottenham was also about revenge, about settling a few scores with the Arsenal board, and that made them nervous. 'George,' acknowledged the *Gooner*, 'has always been driven by success. He wants to emulate Herbert Chapman and win the League with two different clubs, and that is a very real fear. That he might win them [Tottenham] things. It is a very worrying thought.'

The Tottenham fans did not see it that way. Collectively they were outraged, disgusted and insulted of N17, and as far as they were concerned it was Alan Sugar who had some explaining to do. For not only had he done an abrupt U-turn in appointing the salient personality indicted in the bungs inquiry (which only came into being because of his legal action with Terry Venables highlighting financial malpractice in Teddy Sheringham's transfer from Nottingham Forest to Tottenham in 1992) and a man he felt should have been summarily dismissed by Arsenal, but moreover, he had hired a person whose approach to the game was completely at odds with Tottenham's tradition. 'He bought a lot of mediocre players so I'm happy to see him go,' wrote the former *Loaded* editor and Leeds fan James Brown in the on-line football newspaper *Football 365*, an observation which could also have applied to Graham's latter period at Highbury.

While the supporters were adamant that they would never sing 'Georgie Graham's Blue and White Army'; that according to the former advisor to Chancellor Gordon Brown, Charlie Whelan, writing in the *Observer*, it would take 'a Tottenham win against Arsenal in the real Cup final as well as them returning to the south London suburb where they belong and Arsenal tube station returning to its proper name, Gillespie Road, before Tottenham just might accept an Arsenal man', Graham's immediate impact softened the opposition against him. Hardliners like Whelan would never admit to being prepared to consider that Tottenham had employed the right man for the job, but there were certainly suggestions that resistance was weakening when a few fans tried to chant Graham's name up at Oakwell after Ginola's wonder-goal had knocked out Barnsley in the FA Cup sixth round.

No doubt that brought a wry smile to George Graham's face. For this is a man who is steadfastly sure of his own ability when it comes to reviving the fortunes of jaded football clubs. Ron Atkinson may be able to steady the ships over the short course but it is Graham who has the know-how – firm grasp on the tiller and innate appreciation of the elements – to drive them full steam ahead. Without any sense of conceit he acknowledges that 'I don't have any fear when I walk into a club. Look at all the clubs that I've left: they are all in much better shape than when I took over and that is a testimony to my management.' The cynics would argue that he can only improve matters considering the patchy performances of the clubs he inherited, a fact that is not lost on him. 'The best way to join a business is when it's at the bottom . . . because it's very easy to put things right and get certain principles right; to establish a common target and direction,' he admits, and he's certainly applied the same tried and tested formula to every club he has managed.

At Arsenal, Don Howe's side had been marking time when George Graham strutted in and started to crack his whip. In his first season Arsenal finished fourth in the League and won the League Cup. Graham's oft-repeated mantra – desire plus talent equals success – started to rub off on the home-grown players he had inherited, the likes of Adams, Thomas, Davis, Merson and Rocastle, all of whom respected and admired the single-mindedness of their new manager, even if they did not always warm to his methods.

Despite the flop buys – among whom Eddie McGoldrick, Jimmy Carter, Chris Kiwomya, Glenn Helder and Pal Lydersen stand out – Graham was also a more perceptive player in the transfer market than he is given credit for. 'When I left Millwall to go to Arsenal, no one knew the lower divisions better,' he recalled. 'I was nicking players for a few hundred thousand.' He also raised substantial amounts of cash by selling John Lukic, Kevin Richardson, Charlie Nicholas, Niall Quinn and Martin Hayes. David Dein, no mean operator himself, once admitted that when it came to negotiation, 'George has me beaten into a cocked hat'.

A decade later, and *plus ça change, plus c'est la même chose*, as Arsène Wenger might have remarked on observing the almost immediate impact Tottenham's twenty-third manager made at the opposite end of the Seven Sisters Road. Defence was prioritized: Perry, Taricco and Freund were purchased, and Stephen Carr brought on in leaps and bounds. Moreover the League Cup was displayed in Tottenham's trophy cabinet within five months of his arrival – which is remarkable considering that the only regular sighting of silverware at White Hart Lane in recent years had come in the shape of the sleek metallic Mercedes and BMWs which sat in the forecourt, and that he had inherited a bunch of disaffected players whose confidence had been shot to pieces by the hapless Christian Gross. With Graham it was quite the opposite. 'George has this presence about him,' explained Darren Anderton. 'That is mainly down to respect. A lot of us haven't played in Cup finals. He has, and he's won Championships, so you take in what he says because it makes sense.' Ian Walker, meanwhile, admitted there was also a sense of apprehension. 'We knew George's reputation beforehand,' disclosed Tottenham's keeper. 'There was a bit of fear there. We knew we had to knuckle down otherwise we would not stay at the club.'

There was never any doubt that the new overlord was going to pander to players' sensitivities. 'This is the direction I am going and this is the direction I want you to go and unless you come along with me you will very quickly be shown the door,' they were warned (probably in industrial language that needed no interpretation). Very matter of fact, Graham admits that 'the players knew all about how I worked and that definitely helped. They knew it was going to be tough, and that's good. At the start some players walked in late and I said to them: "I expect everyone to be out on the training pitch at 10.15 a.m. and if you're not there we start without you. And if that happens you'll be disciplined." ' As Les Ferdinand recalled: 'Christian Gross had a reputation for being a disciplinarian. Also, he came with a lot of new ideas – changes to the way we train, our diet, match-day preparation (even staying in a hotel for home games). He made all these changes yet it didn't improve us on the pitch, so you are never going to get any respect. George arrived with the same reputation. His regime was probably harsher than Christian Gross's but he had success with that regime and people respect that.'

Of course, the problem with hard taskmasters is that they can foster rebellious attitudes. That was certainly the case during Graham's tenure at Highbury. His players toed the line while under his jurisdiction, only to veer wildly off the rails when school was out. Problems with drink, drugs and gambling were well publicised, yet he loyally stuck by the miscreants. During working hours George would refer to his charges as 'professionals', categorizing them as he saw himself – on a par with doctors, lawyers and accountants, who by dint of exhaustive study and training had earned a certain status in society. 'I like the standards the professions set,' he explained. But in truth footballers are gifted tradespeople who are the beneficiaries of the dramatic transformation of their sport into show business, and many have proven to be ill-prepared for the fame and fortune that has been suddenly thrust upon them.

This inability of the chief to appreciate that the Indians had changed, and his commitment to the job rather than the individual, may have caused a backlash. Referring to the problems of individual players off the pitch Graham said: 'I disagree 100 per cent that it was my fault,' and cited a comparison that only serves to beg the question. 'Alex Ferguson manages very similarly to me,' he says. The case for the prosecution is explained in part by Tony Adams in his autobiography, *Addicted*. 'Could he have done anything to help me address my drinking?' Adams questions. 'Perhaps there were times when he could have been tougher with me rather than indulging me and enabling me to keep drinking. Perhaps he could have been concerned for my welfare rather than that of the team at times ... but he was a realist. He needed me performing and didn't want to do anything to upset that.' So, when Adams and Ray Parlour got involved in an incident involving a fire extinguisher and some Tottenham fans in a pizza restaurant, it was Parlour who received the dressing-down from his manager. 'He's [Adams] doing it for me week in, week out,' explained Graham to an understandably bemused Parlour, 'and when you are as well I'll back you to the limit.' It was a pragmatic approach, and perhaps a wholly acceptable one considering that Graham was, in essence, simply fulfilling his remit, since nowhere in the job description of a manager does it state that he should look out for his players off the pitch as well as on it. Besides, there was actually a widespread belief in the game that the macho drinking culture would cement team spirit.

In Arsenal's case, therefore, it was always the directors who picked up the pieces. For his part, Graham refutes the suggestion that his tricks of the trade backfired. 'If that is the case, then why are they [the Arsenal players] going off the rails now?' he retorts. 'I think we've gone too far to the left in embracing this idea that if you give a body of people responsibility, they will grow. I think that's balls. I think that when a manager or chairman walks into a club then people should sit up and take notice, because every business needs an element of fear. It's the key word.' Graham's need to command his players' whole-hearted approbation and let them know who's boss is such that he has no qualms in actively seeking to confront a player – if it's a leading figure in the dressing room, then so much the better – just to make sure he gets the message across.

David O'Leary would doubtless endorse that theory. O'Leary, one of Graham's most loyal servants at Highbury (where he played over 600 games before moving to Leeds), was both appalled and piqued by what he considered to be Graham's heavy-handed treatment of him when he returned to Highbury late for pre-season training after being involved with the Republic of Ireland squad during Italia '90. Graham fined O'Leary for unprofessionalism and the player, apparently still livid about the incident eight months later, may well have made a mental note to be more flexible in his approach when he made the step into management. Since taking over the reins at Leeds his man-management skills have shown him to possess enough strength of character to be both boss and buddy to his players, a manager who brings to the job a more human touch than has ever been associated with his mentor. And although it would be wrong to suggest that O'Leary still bears a grudge, he certainly recalled the incident when it was mentioned to him in the Highbury boardroom after Arsenal played Leeds in December. 'I'm still fuming about it now,' he said with a smile. But then, many a true word is spoken in jest.

Yet Graham's methods have brought him success so you would hardly expect him to alter his philosophy. 'I believe that when I took over at Arsenal, the way I managed was what people wanted,' he says. 'In life, 99 per cent of people want to be organized, want to be led, want to know what's expected of them. People say, "Oh, he doesn't let them express themselves", but of course I do – within the framework of the team, not to the detriment of the team. That's why I'm a great admirer of the Liverpool team that was so great over three decades. In every sentence you heard "Liverpool Football

Club", and that was all down to Bill Shankly. They never forgot the club, it was as if they had been brainwashed. That is my managerial philosophy and I can tell you that at every club I've been to, 95 per cent of fans think I'm doing a good job because they can see people who are committed to putting in a good day's work.'

All of which neatly leads on to the subject of those who are perceived by Graham as not putting in quite as hard a day's work as perhaps they might, of dragging their heels along the pitch instead of covering every proverbial blade of grass on it – in other words maverick players with a tendency to drift in and out of games and only turn on the style when they're in the mood. For someone like Graham, that simply appears not to suffice. Charlie Nicholas, for example, was an early victim. If he imagined, on Graham's arrival at Highbury, that the man who had enjoyed his own hedonistic reputation during his playing days would make a welcome drinking partner then he was sadly mistaken. During his first pep talk at Arsenal's London Colney training ground Graham spotted Nicholas and Graham Rix wearing earrings and immediately rebuked them: 'If you want to wear an earring it's compulsory to wear a dress. Wear it socially no problem, but don't come to work in an earring.'

Nicholas was soon discarded, along with the experience of Rix, Kenny Samson and Steve Williams, who Graham felt would not espouse his doctrine as readily as his own new recruits. Nicholas's claim that 'he [Graham] hardly ever spoke to me' did much to forge the view of Graham as a manager who, given the choice between the honest, workaday pro and the enigmatic entertainer, will go for what he believes he will get on a regular basis rather than what he feels he might get only spasmodically. This opinion was underlined by his treatment of Anders Limpar, whom Graham bought from Cremonese in 1990 as a replacement for Brian Marwood on Arsenal's left, even though Limpar had been mainly employed in central midfield by his Italian clubs. However, while Marwood could be relied upon to toil unstintingly for ninety minutes, Limpar was less assiduous. Moreover, Graham became increasingly frustrated by the regularity with which he lost the ball – so creating a gap on the left-side of Arsenal's midfield and an open invitation to the opposition to exploit it – as well as his apparent reluctance to shoot when given the opportunity. The upshot was that Graham froze Limpar out over the course of the next few seasons before offloading him to Everton in 1994.

A left-sided, goal-shy forward who has been criticised for losing the ball too often, Graham must have thought it was *déjà vu* when he inherited David Ginola. Unsurprisingly, the media wrote off the relationship before it had started. It was odds-on, the pundits predicted, that Ginola would be on his way before the season was out, particularly given that he was arguably more prone to giving the ball away than Limpar and scored fewer goals too. (Limpar managed thirteen goals in 1990–91, which wasn't a bad return for a supposedly reluctant striker.)

There was also the problem of Ginola's cult status at White Hart Lane. He was the undisputed idol of the fans and Graham was notoriously suspicious of such celebrity status, citing it as a potentially disruptive influence. 'Football is eleven units, so why should only three or four players enjoy the success?' he has asked, although he maintains that his only gripe is with stars who 'don't perform'. 'Working stars who are prepared to dirty their hands and feet', as he describes them, get the thumbs-up. However, he clearly gave John Barnes the thumbs-down. Arsenal's rejection of then Watford star Barnes in 1987 was because Graham felt that there was 'a big question mark over John's approach to the game, it's very laconic'. Stars, he said, have 'got to do what everyone else does'. So Barnes ended up going to Liverpool where a team of stars was organized to maximize his strengths. 'If you are a star with me the difference is in your contract, not on the training ground where everyone is treated equally,' is Graham's view on the matter.

Based on that assessment, it's no wonder Graham was adamant about not signing Ginola from PSG. Ironically, Graham again uses Liverpool to explain his point of view. 'I am a great admirer of Liverpool because the great players of Liverpool conform to the team ethic. Their target is to win things.' He emphasizes that 'I want value. The money players get today, good luck to them, but I want a return. Working stars are fine, but too many managers don't get the return. I think that's sad. The game would be better if some other managers had a similar attitude.'

Yet he had promised that he would give every player a chance to show his worth and in the event, both Ginola and Graham surprised each other. The player proved to the manager that he was willing to 'work my butt off every training session, which might have been a surprise to George Graham; maybe he thought I was a bit lazy'. Graham in turn conceded that Ginola's attitude and application could not be faulted. 'He has not missed a day's training and has not been on the treatment table since I arrived,' he revealed.

However, a close confidant of Graham's revealed that 'he [Graham] certainly didn't fancy Ginola at first. His opinion was that Ginola just went past players and didn't do anything with the ball.' No wonder, then, that Graham concentrated on improving Ginola's efficiency. 'In training, as soon as he started, head down, beating legs, I'd stop everything and say: "David, oh no, no, no",' Graham revealed. 'I tell David that simplicity is genius and talk to him about Pelé. I bet you that eighty out of every ninety minutes Pelé played was simple. Give it and pass it. For five to ten minutes you'd have genius and that's all people remember.' 'What I asked him to do,' Graham spelled out, 'is to either get outside the full-back for a cross, an early cross, or come inside for a shot or to play a one-two and set other people up. The dribbling across the pitch and losing the ball is not for me. I want him to be a productive entertainer.'

Sound principles, of course, and under Graham's tutelage Ginola's contribution has undoubtedly improved. He regularly topped the Carling Opta charts as the player with the most dribbles and crosses and was rewarded with the accolade of both the players' and writers' Footballer of the Year in 1999. The suspicion remains, however, that Graham is yet to be fully convinced that Ginola is, to plagiarize his L'Oréal advertisement, worth it. The number of times the manager has substituted his star turn continues to astound and in many cases infuriate those who consider Ginola to be the one Tottenham player capable of producing the necessary moment of magic – which can be all it takes to alter the outcome of a game.

Graham tends to justify his standpoint by stressing that effectiveness is what matters above everything else. 'How many goals has he scored?' he questions. 'How many has he made? Then the entertainment value can come into the equation but there is no point in having entertainment value if he is not scoring goals or making goals. When he is going forward he is breathtaking. At White Hart

Lane when he is in possession, it's a fantastic sight.' Agreed, says lifelong Tottenham fan John Harris, who goes on to point out that it is a different story away from home and maintains that 'you must not give George stick [for withdrawing Ginola]'. John would undoubtedly concur with the manager that 'David, for his ability, should score more goals.' Ginola is without question the main source of Tottenham's goal supply – the amount of crosses he puts in, the strikers must think it's Christmas every week – but he does lose the ball more than most. However, according to the law of averages that is only to be expected considering he is on the ball more than most, too.

Graham will also remind his detractors that Ginola is not as young as he was. After comparing him to 'a jewel that you have to look after' to explain his withdrawal during Tottenham's League victory against Watford, on Boxing Day, he pointed out that 'David is thirty-three and we have to use him wisely, preserve him.' Occasionally, his reason will be on tactical grounds, as it was after Tottenham's defeat at Middlesbrough the previous week. Then, the sight of Juninho running the show was a stark reminder to the visitors that their only comparably skilful player had been left sitting in the dressing room when the teams reappeared for the second-half, despite the fact that Ginola had delivered the ball onto Vega's head for the opening goal, and that it was from the same source that Perry almost scored moments later. 'We were getting outrun in midfield. Juninho started running a bit and was the instigator of Middlesbrough's attacks,' was Graham's explanation. 'We needed an extra midfield player in there.' His tactics were painfully clear. Instead of attempting to rescue something from the game he sought to stifle it, hoping for a lucky break by replacing a genuinely creative player with another journeyman.

Graham's apparent ambivalence towards Ginola dents his esteem. 'Do the top players, the best and the brightest, want to play for Graham?' asks Stafford Green in the Tottenham fanzine *Cock-a-Doodle-Doo*. 'Put yourself in their shoes: you know the manager is dour, he's defensive, you know the way he treats Ginola.' How different, for example, is Graham's attitude to that of Alex Ferguson, who constructed a side designed to accommodate Eric Cantona. (Graham defends his position by calling Cantona 'a cry baby when the going gets tough', but then goes on to explain how Ferguson coped with the fact that 'Cantona was lazy in spasms' by doing what he had never considered doing for Ginola – 'a protective shell of Kanchelskis and Giggs was put around him [Cantona] whenever he lost the ball.') How different, too, from Arsène Wenger, who as manager of Monaco allowed Glenn Hoddle scope by instructing him to defend only in his opponent's half.

Certainly, comparing Tottenham with Manchester United is not comparing like for like and perhaps it is unrealistic for a man of his age to change the tried and trusted (and successful) habits of a lifetime. However, you do wonder how Brian Clough in his dotage can see his own solution regarding Ginola, while it apparently remains a blind spot for Graham. 'The young man from France crosses the ball beautifully, George,' Clough is reported to have said to Graham after watching Tottenham's match at Derby in October. 'Yeah, Brian,' Graham replied, 'but the trouble with Ginola is that he wants the ball all the time.' 'Well, in that case, give him the bloody thing,' was Clough's blunt retort.

In fact Graham seems to have taken the opposite track by implying to Ginola's team-mates that he can be a liability. When you listen to Steffen Freund explaining that Ginola 'is a very good player but he gives the ball away too often' you can almost hear his master's voice. Moreover, Graham gives Ginola an inordinately hard time. Watch him when he comes down pitchside in the second-half (he usually spends the first forty-five minutes in the stand) and you'll notice how he spends most of the time racing between the dug-out and the touchline, from where he will frequently berate Ginola – gesticulating wildly – for some perceived inadequacy, which has usually resulted from him being out of position. If Graham's rebukes fall on deaf ears (although Ginola pays Graham more attention than most of the others on the receiving end) then Sherwood will harangue his team-mate. Once, Graham even claimed that José Dominguez 'had come on and shown Ginola how it should be done'.

If Ginola was a weaker character he would probably have buckled under the weight of so much fault-finding. Arsenal players have revealed that Graham would on occasions go too far in his criticisms of them, and it is to Ginola's credit that he has risen above the reproaches, even finding time to insist that 'George Graham says things to me sometimes which are more than praise.' But when you are constantly and inexplicably substituted and replaced by inferior players then you must surely question whether you are with the right club.

Ginola must have despaired at being left on the bench for Tottenham's second leg of the UEFA Cup second-round tie against Kaiserslautern in Germany, and there were few people who didn't sympathize with him. Yet if, as John Sadler maintained in his column in the *Sun*, Graham 'comes from the school where closing down takes priority over opening up' (Graham's glass is probably always half-empty, never half-full) then this was clearly an exercise in damage limitation – Graham will claim that his side was ninety seconds away from qualifying for the next round – not a mission to win the game. It was essentially a perfect example of the contrast between the philosophies of Tottenham Hotspur and of George Graham.

Some observers consider Graham's continued sporadic use of Ginola to be his one sop to the Tottenham tradition that embraces such free-spirited players. Somehow, though, one cannot see Graham pandering to a style that he has already dismissed as effete and obsolete. He has a clear ambivalence towards Ginola that has prevailed since his arrival at White Hart Lane. 'My first job on coming to Tottenham was to get the balance of the team right,' he explains, 'and on certain occasions David will, without question, win us games but on other occasions he will be less effective. Against Arsenal, for example, Lee Dixon had his easiest game for ages. So what do you do if you know that, yet you're a fan of his? Do you do something about it or just accept the inevitable? The problem is that a lot of the fans just see one dimension whereas I have to see the whole picture. And that's why I've been successful because I see the end product – and the end product is the success of the team.'

Of course the problem at Tottenham will always be that the fans are sustained by the memorable cameos provided by players such as Ginola, the latest in a long line of illustrious entertainers, and Graham's apparent unwillingness to comprehend this threatens an uneasy truce between the manager and the fans. Morris Keston, who has known Graham for over thirty years, believes his friend is wrong to alienate Ginola. 'George is not being sensible in the way he's treating him,' Keston warns. 'We know he's not George's type. George would never have signed a Jimmy Greaves or a Glenn Hoddle, we know that, but he still should make an ally of Ginola.' We know, too, that he would probably not have signed Davor Suker, even though Suker apparently wanted to go to Tottenham (where in theory he could be certain of regular first-team football). Given his ball skills and that sublimely gifted left foot Suker is undoubtedly a Tottenham-type of player. However, fifteen months on and Tottenham, with Les Ferdinand injured, still had no regular striking partner for Steffen Iversen, while Davor Suker was Arsenal's top scorer with eleven goals despite the fact that he was not regularly in the starting line-up.

The debate regarding Ginola came to a head in the space of four very traumatic days over the Christmas period. On 22 December Tottenham travelled up to St James's Park to face Newcastle in an FA Cup third-round replay and were humiliated 6–1. It was an inept display, compounded by the fact that it was Tottenham's worst FA Cup defeat since they were beaten by Huddersfield in the 1928 quarter-finals. 'Bobby's crackers stuff George's turkeys' ran the *Sun*'s headline the next morning, with Ian Walker admitting the following day that 'We're c*** and we know we are.'

Frankly, they were. All, that is, except Ginola, who was the only Tottenham player to catch the eye, not just for his skill on the ball but for his determination to haul his side back into the game, for his never-say-die attitude – which is seldom a quality one associates with flamboyant players. He scored Tottenham's only goal and was their only bright spark on the night; that he performed as he did against a backdrop of incessant boos and jeers directed at him from the fans who had once revered him made his performance even more commendable.

Yet with the score at 3–1 Graham hauled off Ginola and replaced him with Dominguez. It was hardly like for like, which made it hard for anyone watching to understand Graham's line of thinking. Sky pundit Neil Warnock, whose Sheffield United side were due to meet the winners of the tie in the fourth round, maintained that Graham was attempting to save Ginola from further humiliation both on and off the pitch. However, although Ginola had started to get frustrated with one or two contestable decisions he was far from downcast. Besides, he has been through much worse. This, remember, is a player who was once accused of a criminal act by his coach Gerard Houllier for a debatable error of judgement in the final qualifying tie for the 1994 World Cup which improbably led to France's elimination. (In the last minute Ginola hit a long centre rather than playing safe, Bulgaria gained possession and scored and went on to the USA in place of France.)

A less charitable interpretation is that Ginola was a sacrificial scapegoat, and his reaction at being taken off suggested he thought as much. He left the field applauding the Tottenham fans and directing a filthy look towards the Tottenham dug-out. You could hardly blame him. He knew, as did everyone watching, that this match represented a defining moment in Tottenham's season. Out of the UEFA Cup, out of the League Cup . . . an early exit from the FA Cup would effectively leave them devoid of any purpose save the scramble for an elusive European place through the League placings.

Four days later, on Boxing Day, Tottenham put four goals past Watford at White Hart Lane, yet the festive atmosphere turned sour when Graham, for the thirty-third time in fifty-nine matches, replaced Ginola fifteen minutes from time. This time, it was not Ginola who showed his displeasure. His reply to the BBC interviewer who informed him that Graham had described him as 'a jewel' was: 'That's nice. But I will continue to do my best whatever the manager thinks of me . . . I was enjoying myself and didn't want to come off. I wanted to carry on playing. The fans love me.' A blinding glimpse of the obvious that, considering almost every occupant in the lower West Stand adjacent to the dug-out and press box at White Hart Lane rose to hurl abuse in Graham's general direction when they saw Ginola's number was up.

It was an unprecedented attack on a manager whose team had just routed the opposition and obviously touched a nerve with Graham, who felt compelled to justify his decision by engaging in a heated exchange with one enraged fan. By the time he had to face the post-match press conference, Graham had regained his composure. 'With David's age and the fact that we have another game next Wednesday I was surprised,' he admitted. 'With a player so talented you have to hone his talents and it sometimes surprises me that some fans can have a lack of foresight and knowledge. If only they thought about it they would see what I'm trying to do.'

Charlie Whelan once claimed in the *Observer* that Graham's 'handling of the media was more impressive than most top politicians', so the manager was not about to let his guard down and give the media a stick with which to beat him. In front of the press he admits he's 'a bit of an actor. I keep myself in check. You mustn't lose it and do something stupid because it makes the media's day.' He has little respect for the press and it shows. It stems from the dark days, when various members of the press got, in his opinion, 'far too brave when the fox was on the run'. These days he keeps his media obligations sweet and very short. Whereas Arsenal stage a briefing before every match and make Wenger and players available for interview, Graham avoids these conferences like the plague. If he doesn't feel he has a point to make he will try to avoid talking at all or just have a chat with Bill Pierce of the Press Association so at least there is a quote to pick up on. It's no wonder, then, that Arsenal get the more favourable PR, which is a pity, because press chief John Fennelly maintains that 'this is probably the nicest bunch of players who have been here during my fifteen years'. Yet taking their cue from their leader they are reluctant to speak to the media and unlike at Arsenal, nobody forces them to do so.

Graham is not much more effusive in his post-match press conferences, when the assembled hacks get about five minutes, tops, of his time. This, admittedly, is more a result of their timidity rather than of any terseness on Graham's part. Frankly, no one dares ask him the awkward questions. In the press room at Upton Park after Tottenham had lost to West Ham in the first game of the season, Graham claimed he had been encouraged by his side's performance, especially in the second half, and maintained that he was (and at this point he lowered his voice for effect) 'soooo excited about the season'. Never mind that Tottenham were woeful in the first half, not much better in the second, and that Steffen Iversen's lone forage upfront and the lack of creativity behind him hardly augured well for the rest of the season. Still nobody took Graham to task, and that surprised even him. 'None of you famous journalists got anything to ask me then?' he questioned with a smirk, before leaving the room with his customary sign-off: 'OK, boys.' He is a canny operator. He reels you in and reels you out again expertly without giving away much of substance in between. However, unlike Gerry Francis, who would often make it a rush to file copy for the first editions by forcing journalists to kick their heels before he deigned to put in an appearance, Graham is never tardy, usually arriving within a few minutes of the end of a match. John Fennelly and Peter Barnes, the club secretary, both testify to similar consideration. They say: 'He is very good to work with. He knows what he wants and is straightforward' which is a direct result of the standards Graham sets himself. He would never, for instance, encroach on John Fennelly's personal life by phoning him on Christmas Eve to check his programme notes, as one of his predecessors did.

Graham may have faults, but lack of passion is not one of them. In fact he claims there is 'no one more passionate in the game' which he attributes to his 'fear of failing'. 'It's just the way I was brought up,' he reveals. 'Nobody could ever accuse me of not trying, of not giving my best. I'm good at my job and the one thing I know is that I will always give it 100 per cent. It's an easy thing to say but I genuinely do.' This work ethic is so deeply ingrained in him that he seriously believes that 'If I take a day off on during the week and we lose on the Saturday, then I think that maybe it was because I took that day off.'

The Newcastle débâcle, then, was a body-blow to his pride. This was not in the original script. George Graham's sides have been accused of many things, but never of throwing in the towel. This was a manager, remember, who talked about desire as 'that lovely word', whose philosophy decrees that 'if you're going down, then go down fighting, scratching, biting, kicking. I love people having a go, even if they're getting beaten. Have a go! Don't give in too easily, fight all the way.' What made it worse was that three weeks previously Tottenham had been humbled by First Division Fulham in the League Cup. 'It was the worst performance since I came here,' Graham fumed. 'What hurt me more than going out of the Cup was the manner of our defeat and our display. Our performance was unacceptable. Fulham had more desire than us and it hurts me to say that.'

The realization that he had been unable to motivate his side for two crucial Cup ties must have hit home hard. Doubtless, it tugged at his conscience and made him feel embarrassed. Angry, too, that his attempts to strengthen his squad had consistently been thwarted. It was almost certainly the moment when he realized the limitations of his resources and accepted that his rebuilding plans at Tottenham had hit a brick wall. It might even have caused him to question whether he had a future at White Hart Lane at all.

Until then one suspects that Graham had made do, making light of the handicap of what was clearly an unrealistic budget. According to John Harris, whose devotion to Tottenham cannot be questioned, 'Graham was absolutely the best man for the job at that time; the only man who could have done it – managing Spurs without any money, giving players who were previously hopeless a sense of direction. He's knows what he's doing but you can only do so much. Whatever you do you are not going to turn Iversen or Armstrong into Jimmy Greaves. These are workaday players.' This assessment mirrors the view inside the club. 'George is really there to run the first team. He's done a remarkable job given the people we've got,' maintains club secretary Peter Barnes. 'We need several players to make up a squad that can go and challenge other clubs.'

Before the Fulham and Newcastle fixtures Graham had ominously presaged the situation he now faced. 'I keep telling people, without knocking my own players, that we need to get a better squad,' he warned. 'I hope we don't hit a brick wall, a halt to the improvement. There comes a stage when you say, now we need the special ones. When that day comes it will not be my decision.' You sense that even then he knew he would still be trying to make bricks out of straw. 'Sadly,' he says, 'my reputation holds me back. People may say, "George, if you did have a lot of money you may blow it, you may not be such a good manager." But I would like the opportunity to have had the cheque book. I know that I will always have a job because of the kind of manager I am – there are managers out there who just don't know what it's like to take over a team of unknown players and get them half-way up the Premiership – but I do wish I'd pushed a bit harder at times. I remember I tried to buy Marc Overmars when I was at Arsenal but his wage demands were ridiculous, and it was never on. Yet within weeks of me leaving, Arsenal bought Bergkamp for £7 million and David Platt for £4 million and I thought: George, don't blame anyone but yourself.'

The counter-view to that, as put forward repeatedly by Richard Littlejohn on his *606* show on Radio 5 Live, is that Graham may be loath to share his stage at Tottenham. 'George is the sort of man who likes to buy a player and develop his potential. He doesn't want to buy in a big-name Charlie.' Graham himself agrees. 'I am still looking for a bargain. It's my Scottish upbringing.' But Littlejohn has speculated on other reasons. 'I think George likes to be the biggest name at the club and doesn't want anybody there who is going to be earning more money than him and is going to be more important than him.' Though this may not always be feasible in today's game long-time season-ticket holder and shareholder David Stern backs this by observing: 'I think Alan Sugar likes George Graham because he is as parsimonious as he is.' Indeed, with no sense of intended irony, Alan Sugar complimented his manager at the Tottenham AGM in December. 'I have to say I'm finding for the first time someone who is treating the club's money as if it was his own,' Sugar remarked. Warmly applauded both before and after his short speech at the AGM, which could be summarized as 'We hope to finish in the top six' and 'We are on the right lines', David Stern felt nevertheless badly let down. 'You go hoping you are going to hear something that is going to inspire you with confidence, but I didn't hear anything new from George Graham and he is the man who is going to make it happen. Oh well,' he concluded resignedly, 'we'll plod on.' But could Graham really afford to take a non-interventionalist line?

The fallout from those two Cup defeats left Graham with a choice to make. Was he going to coast, or was he going to force the issue and take Alan Sugar to task over the subject of money and transfers, and just who was responsible for both? There had already been rumblings in the press that all was not well behind the scenes. David Pleat was obviously unhappy playing the role of piggy-in-the-middle between Sugar and Graham, while the manager was clearly fed up at constantly proposing players he would like to sign, only for there to be a singular lack of any action in that department, despite Pleat's incessant scouting missions both at home and abroad. Pleat himself feels that more should have resulted from these trips and openly voices his frustration. It is obvious to other members of staff that he lacks complete job satisfaction, and that he misses the hands-on activity of a manager. According to Peter Barnes 'he is bursting to get back into a tracksuit'.

Of course, this lack of cohesion among the Tottenham hierarchy is bound to impact – sooner rather than later – upon the players; below-par performances on the pitch are generally symptomatic of a more general malaise off it. As such, someone who knows Graham well feels he will achieve nothing by accepting such a status quo. 'Why doesn't George go to Alan Sugar and ask him: "Who do you want to be the manager of this club?" What Sugar wants, he is entitled to have as he's the boss, but George has to say to him: "If you want David Pleat to be the manager, then tell me".' But his friend Morris Keston remains convinced that Graham won't force the issue suggesting it may be that he's fought shy of the really big decisions. 'And that makes sense when you look at what happened to him at Arsenal,' says Keston. 'He could have got what he wanted. That's what I can't understand. He had his chance of going on the quiz show and knowing all the questions beforehand, because if he'd asked for a £1 million bonus there is no way Arsenal could have refused; they knew that if he went elsewhere he could have doubled his wages.'

Yet Graham eschewed the idea of asking Arsenal for the bonus he clearly felt he deserved. Instead, he chose what appeared to be the easier option and accepted £425,000, which he viewed as an 'unsolicited gift' to thank him for the assistance he had given agent Rune Hauge, in addition to the two Scandinavian players (John Jensen and Pal Lydersen) who were bought by Arsenal through Hauge. While Graham saw it as generous largesse, Arsenal saw it as 'our money' (which begged the question of how and why agents were able to siphon money from transfers into their own pockets, and led directly to FIFA instituting corrective regulation). On the face of it, it was an act completely out of character – one of the most rigid disciplinarians in the game with an innate sense of values suddenly deeming it admissible to profit directly from transfer dealings to which he was not contractually entitled. A manager who exasperated his own players by adhering to a rigorous wage structure appearing to adopt double standards when it came to his own remuneration.

Yet Graham is still loath to divulge his reasons. 'Why [do you want to know]? What is the point of looking back on it?' he asked Amy Raphael when she questioned him about the incident in an article she wrote for *Perfect Pitch*. 'To understand: you loved Arsenal and live in a flat with a shrine to the club [as Graham did at the time],' she replied, which prompted this admission from Graham. 'It was a downright mistake. My career hit rock bottom. I had a decision to make. To walk away with my tail between my legs or to decide to come back. Everyone gets knocks but the winners are the ones who refuse to give up, to give in. I came back with Leeds and I'm proud. And whatever anyone says, I am one of the great Arsenal managers.' Which is true. But had he already reached his apogee? In the fast-changing world of the Premiership, would he have won another Championship?

Besides, that still does not sufficiently explain his motives. In retrospect one suspects that Graham justified his actions by convincing himself that he was somehow entitled to the money. Perhaps, he reasoned, Arsenal were never going to agree to pay him a salary that fairly reflected his achievements and he was therefore entitled not to look a gift horse in the mouth. He definitely felt that managers were underpaid and cites the examples of Graham Taylor at Watford and his friend Alex Ferguson at Manchester United, both of whose success defied expectations. 'If Alex had said to the board, "I am going to win five Championships and a European Cup. How much is that worth? Would you give me £20 million if I can do that?" then he would have been told: "You can have more if you want." ' Certainly, the climate at the time could have fostered this delusion, and the suspicion that Graham was not the only one to have taken a bung, just the poor unfortunate who got caught, was given credence by the reported comment of one Premiership manager, who said: 'We all like a drink, but the trouble with George was that he took the whole brewery.'

While David Dein and Graham had forged a good working rapport, the relationship between the Arsenal chairman Peter Hill-Wood and his manager had always been more distant. On one side there was Hill-Wood, a staunch upholder of establishment principles who had first joined the board when his father was the chairman; on the other, Graham, the son of a Scottish steelworker made good, whose Arsenal team – in Hill-Wood's opinion – had from time to time failed to live up to Arsenal's standards of behaviour. 'We were always told as kids: "Remember who you are, what you are and what you represent",' Tony Adams once disclosed, 'yet David Rocastle and I used to spout it out as a joke; when I used to have to polish the statue in my apprentice days I could never see what Herbert Chapman had to do with me getting in the first team.' However, that was the way it was around Highbury and Hill-Wood must have been mortified by the plethora of unsavoury incidents while Graham was in charge. Speaking after the infamous Old Trafford scuffle in 1990, which involved every player on the pitch apart from David Seaman and led to Arsenal being deducted two points (probably as a result of media overkill setting Arsenal up for the FA to knock them down), he certainly implied that another manager might have been seeking alternative employment. 'If it had been someone other than George in charge,' he conceded, 'then we might have taken a different course of action'.

When the *Mail on Sunday* broke the bung story Arsenal did not act (despite being encouraged by Alan Sugar to fire their manager), probably because the board was divided as to what it should do. When some time later Graham was informed that David Dein had battled for him he retorted: 'So he damn well should have.' Dein later acknowledged that 'we did our best to understand George's position, or what was ultimately his defence. We really left it to the Football Association and their disciplinary report because they were the fact-finders, the police in the case. When the report came to us we had no alternative but to take the route we did.' What actually happened at the crucial meeting was that the Arsenal board met to finalize their decision on how to deal with the incident and were presented with a choice of options by their counsel. He informed them that they could, in the light of what was previously a special relationship, forget the incident altogether. They could dismiss Graham immediately for unprofessional conduct. Or they could call the police.

The first option was clearly out of the question as the directors felt personally let down. Significantly, there were those who felt that there was a case for dialling 999. However, it was decided that the manager should be asked to clear his desk immediately, although

Graham's subsequent criticism of his former employers has unquestionably caused the Arsenal board to reconsider whether they actually made the right decision.

For his part, Graham certainly feels that he was hit below the belt after everything he had accomplished (the job so consumed him that he even cited it as a major reason for his divorce from his first wife). Aware that it was possibly only through the efforts of a minority of the board that a worse fate did not befall him, he felt these efforts were no less than he deserved. 'OK,' he admits, 'I was upset at the time. I was upset at Arsenal. They could have handled things differently.' He then refers, enigmatically, to 'people who were born with silver spoons in their mouths', implying that there was one rule for them and a different, harsher rule for him. The club had, after all, stood by Tony Adams and Paul Merson when their problems with drink and drugs emerged. The realization that he could have suffered a worse fate does not make him any the less incensed at Arsenal's actions.

He maintains now that the past is a closed book, that 'it's [the bung issue] totally out of the way, honestly'. Yet like the jilted lover who claims to be over a relationship but who nevertheless continues to bring the subject up, Graham admits that he will never completely get Arsenal out of his blood. 'Without question there's a little part of me still there,' he stresses. 'How can you spend fifteen years at a club and have the success I had without feeling that's part of you? Of course it is.' Besides, he knows only too well that his legacy will stand the test of time. 'When I am gone,' he reflects, 'and the Arsenal directors are gone, the fans will remember George Graham.'

Of course there will always be a hard core of Tottenham and Arsenal fans to whom Graham will for ever remain an anathema for having made his 'pact with the devil', but don't expect Graham to let that bother him. 'I can understand the fans,' he says, 'but I think this hatred between clubs is sad. Can't you support one team without hating another? When I was a boy I used to support Airdrie. I was never a fan of Rangers or Celtic but I used to go and watch them as well.' He does, however, accept that this hatred is 'just part of football', maintains that he has 'got used to it. If I was that thin-skinned I wouldn't have lasted so long in the game.'

No doubt that pragmatic attitude has served him well, yet the reality is that a part of Graham's heart will always remain in N5. As far as anyone could be described as having found their life's work, then George Graham found his at Highbury. Call it karma, call it destiny, call it whatever you will – Graham and Arsenal were made for each other. Graham put on the Arsenal suit and found it fitted him perfectly. More's the pity that he grew out of it, not because the suit itself became threadbare but because the man who prides himself on his appearance had temporarily let himself go. His residency down the road, on the contrary, will always be viewed as a temporary one. When he moves on, the Tottenham fans will need no bereavement counselling to get over the loss. Graham is professionally involved with Tottenham and personally involved with Arsenal, which is why he can quite easily justify retaining shares in Arsenal while manager of Tottenham.

A shrewd Tottenham fan like John Harris can see the situation with some detachment. 'There are very few players who are at a club they support,' he says. 'Most just pass by in the night. It is no different with managers. You've got to remember that George played for Aston Villa, Chelsea, Arsenal, Manchester United and Portsmouth. He was a coach at Crystal Palace, QPR and a manager at Millwall, Arsenal and Leeds. Arsenal may be the team he supports but look at his record.'

It is this ability to compartmentalize his professional and personal life that goes some way to understanding the man. At Arsenal he was always viewed as something of a contradiction. He was both chatty and laconic, charming and austere. He lived by the rule book yet stood by his wayward stars. He prided himself on engendering an unrivalled team spirit yet he cut a solitary figure who would rarely mix with the players out of hours.

He still cuts such a dash that, if you didn't know otherwise you would not realize that he and Jim Smith do the same job. While other managers favour the tracksuit look, Graham is a very much a bespoke suit man. He is Sean Connery dressed by Armani, and the fact that the Tottenham fans avoid chanting his name by singing 'Man in the Armani raincoat's blue and white army' is testimony both to terrace humour and to Graham's impeccable dress sense. After ninety harrowing minutes racing from dug-out to touchline and back, all the while hollering at his players (which is when his Scottish accent is at its most pronounced) most managers look as if they need a good soak with their players. Not Graham. He invariably looks groomed for a night out on the town. He can stand on the touchline and rant and rave for as long as he likes, yet that tailored jacket still hangs perfectly on his shoulders and there is seldom a hair out of place.

Away from White Hart Lane his standards never slip. Confront him in his office at Spurs Lodge training ground on non-training days and he will be as immaculately turned out as ever, sitting behind his desk, invariably dressed in black with the occasional nod to brown or grey. No bright colours here; his is an understated style. His designer label shirt will be beautifully pressed. His shoes will be so well polished that if Gerry Francis was wearing them and employing his usual interview technique – he studiously avoids looking at the camera – he would see his mirror image from the reflection. His trousers . . . well suffice to say that Graham is surely one of a rare breed of men able to make cords appear well-cut.

He looks good and he knows he does. Yet there is more than just ego at play here. He has high standards and his 'professionalism' extends to every last detail. If you feel good about yourself, he would argue, then you are better equipped to do your job well too. And you have to admire his fervour, even if on occasions he appears a little too desperate for his pound of flesh. At the end of the Premiership fixture between Tottenham and West Ham at White Hart Lane in December there was a perfect cameo that underlined the different approaches of Harry Redknapp, renowned for his geniality, and Graham. As the whistle blew on the scoreless draw, Redknapp turned to give Graham the customary managerial handshake, only to find his opposite number was more concerned with berating the fourth official for, according to Graham, blowing the whistle thirty seconds before time was up. Redknapp could clearly be seen shaking his head.

Yet strip away the front and underneath lurks a far more compassionate character than is ever apparent to those who judge George Graham merely on the snapshots they see of him in the media. When it comes to people or causes he feels strongly about he can be unstintingly generous. At the start of the season, for example, he asked Tottenham for some balls and shirts which he and the players subsequently autographed (rendering them worth several hundred pounds) and used to swell the testimonial funds of players in the lower divisions. When Cyril Knowles died tragically in 1991, Morris Keston turned to his friends in high places for help in organizing a testimonial. Terry Venables, then the managing director, allowed Morris the free use of the ground but refused to put his kit on (after retirement the only exception was as an occasional ringer for Morris's friendly park games). George Graham, on the other hand, not only brought the full Arsenal first-team squad – who had just been dumped out of the European Cup by Benfica – but endured the cat-calls by turning out with his Double-winning colleagues in the warm-up game. As a result of this generosity Morris was able to present Cyril's family with a cheque for £100,000.

Perhaps the most discernible differences between the Graham of old and the modern-day version are a little less hair and a far more rounded perspective. At Arsenal Graham was obsessive, totally consumed by the club. 'Everything was football,' he admits. 'Now I think I've got the balance right and I make sure I take a couple of afternoons off now and again. It makes me fresher for the next day's training.' In his personal life, too, he couldn't be happier. He is back in a sumptuous new house in one of London's most select roads in his favourite part of the world, Hampstead. 'It gives you the choice,' he says. 'If you want the countryside you've got the Heath; if you want the West End it's only twenty minutes away.' Not bad for a bloke from a working-class background who left school at fifteen with no academic qualifications.

Away from football Graham relaxes on the tennis court (he is a member of the David Lloyd club in Finchley) and like many football players and managers is no mean golfer (his handicap is twelve). He does, however, draw the line at squash. A man whose playing style earned him the sobriquet Stroller was never going to warm to a sport where you have to break that much sweat. But you sense, from the tone in which he talks about it, that he is at his most relaxed when he is pottering around his garden. A psychologist would doubtless have a field day here, but what is obvious is that Graham's garden affords him a miniature playing pitch: the bulbs and flowers are his players – the way in which he chooses to plant them and bed them in, his formations. He certainly pays the same assiduous attention to detail and organization designing his garden as he does training his team. 'My bulbs are not exactly planted in formation – I had to laugh when I read that one – but I do love creating things in the garden,' he admits. 'There's nothing lovelier than planting things and seeing them come up several months later. You think: I actually did that, and it's very satisfying. You can play with the garden for ever, constantly changing things, probing, watching it evolve all the time.'

There, the similarity to the work he does on a real-life pitch ends. Graham can tinker with his garden to his heart's content, but when it comes to watching events unfold and evolve on grass at White Hart Lane, he has neither as much time, nor as much autonomy to fashion his ideas. On the one hand there is Graham, pointedly referring to his fruitless search for players; and on the other there is Pleat, who believes that the very worst thing Tottenham could do is panic-buy in a transient quest for success. 'We might be looking for a short-term fix for a position and I'm saying we should wait until summer for a long-term player,' says Pleat. 'We urgently need a front player but we shouldn't panic. When they [Tottenham] were panicking about not having enough strikers two years ago they paid £6 million for a thirty-year-old player – and Les Ferdinand has had to carry that burden. At Luton I would have played one-up [as he did as Tottenham manager in 1987, playing Clive Allen as the lone striker], or thought of a different system. One of my big tasks here is to keep the mediocrity away. Tottenham in the last few years have signed mediocre players.' Quite what the board make of this is anyone's guess, although one wonders whether they share the views of many fans who consider there may be too many cooks in the process; recalling what Brighton manager Chris Cattlin once observed about his own situation twenty years ago: 'There's a rat in the camp trying to throw a spanner in the works.' At Tottenham all the Director of Football says with regard to his relationship with the manager is that 'we can have differences of opinions'.

Having predicted from day one that the Tottenham rebuilding process was 'going to be a continuing thing' you would hardly expect George Graham to walk away in the short term, especially considering that he appears more mellow at White Hart Lane than he ever was at Highbury. Some Arsenal fans have already voiced their indignation over the fact that he seems so much more animated on the touchline at Tottenham and celebrates each goal with so much more gusto than he ever did at Arsenal (those with a cynical disposition claim it is part of his act aimed at ingratiating himself with the Tottenham fans). 'It was *the* Arsenal, the way *the* Arsenal did things and the way *the* Arsenal expected you to behave. The dignified way,' he acknowledges. 'I believe sometimes the club is too stuffy and staid . . . me getting out of the dug-out and waving is not the Arsenal way of doing things.'

Yet one wonders how long a man with George Graham's pride will stand for the lack of ambition at Tottenham before he accepts that he has done all he can with what has been made available to him and considering his age – fifty-five – decides to make one last move to a club where he would be more appreciated. 'I still want to get the plaudits,' he says, 'the trophies that probably I deserve. I still want to win Championships. Hopefully it will be at this club. I want to put Tottenham back among the big boys, but only time will tell.'

But you do have to question where he would go should he leave. His options appear limited considering his admission that he no longer hankers after a European club, but his CV – despite the blot on it – would surely be welcome on the desk of any chairman in the world. Coaching a national side is probably out of the question for a man who thrives on the day-to-day involvement on the training pitch. On the managerial merry-go-round it is so often a case of right time, right place, and since staying in London is clearly vital in the equation Graham would surely be tempted by the offer of making the short hop across the capital to Stamford Bridge. Although some might view a move to Chelsea as hopping out of the frying pan and into the fire, it is likely that Graham would find Ken Bates's bluntness a mere inconvenience after Alan Sugar's comparative frugality.

As the Tottenham fanzine *Cock-a-Doodle-Doo* summed it up: 'Whatever his shortcomings, Graham can't be labelled a failure' (at Tottenham). Many supporters can appreciate the good he has done: nurturing youngsters like Carr and Young. Ian Walker has even been taught to kick a ball properly for heaven's sake . . . and of course, winning that trophy, and being more likely to gain a UEFA

Cup spot than a Nationwide League one. But what does concern the Tottenham fans is the quality of the football. They do not want to see the wings of their team clipped. They do not want to see the back four automatically raise their arms to claim offside whenever the opposition strikers break clear, as Tony Adams and co. did so robotically under Graham at Arsenal. Tellingly, Adams described himself as having been 'under orders . . . to perform in a restricted way for the good of the team'; but this is what Graham appears to want from Campbell. There are certainly some observers at Tottenham who feel that he has been made into a less effective footballer in much the same way since Graham arrived. He certainly makes fewer surging runs from the back these days, and like Ginola, he is often the source of the manager's intense frustration when he apparently fails to carry out the specific instructions to the letter.

Former Tottenham director Douglas Alexiou recalls Graham admitting to him that 'I love winning 1–0,' but of course back then in the early 1990s it didn't matter, for Graham was manager of Arsenal and if that was the Arsenal philosophy then that was fine by Tottenham, because they were still playing free(ish)-flowing football in patches under Terry Venables and Ossie Ardiles, before Gerry Francis arrived and the rot set in. But it matters now, because Tottenham fans do not want to see their team hustle and harry and hope to nick a 1–0 win. Passion alone is not enough. They want their team to put its collective foot on the ball and spray a few passes around the pitch, just like Tottenham have always done. And those who have claimed that the glory, glory tag is a fanciful notion would do well to remember that even in the 1984 UEFA Cup-winning season when the hard graft of players like Graham Roberts, Paul Miller and Steve Perryman was so crucial, Tottenham still had the virtuosity of Hoddle and Hazard and Ardiles too.

No one can ever deny George Graham his achievements. The record books will forever testify that his brand of football was successful at the top level for the best part of a decade. However, the game has changed now. It is not just about power and percentage football. All the successful modern teams possess flair allied to a strong backbone. Just look at Manchester United, Arsenal and even Chelsea. Yet all the evidence suggests that midfield creativity is just not a Graham priority. Even in the absence of Darren Anderton, the

Algerian Moussa Saib, who had been bought by Christian Gross because he had performed at the highest level in France and Spain, was quite simply frozen out, despite his skills he was regarded as a liability in the Tottenham midfield of 1999.

So does Graham have the credentials to manage Tottenham long-term, or have the club already seen the extent of his influence? And if he does remain, will Sugar give him enough financial backing to enable him to recruit the necessary quality? Because while good husbandry and canny motivational skills are commendable, it's a fact that in the Premiership of today you will be found wanting if your pockets are not deep enough. Graham must surely cast the occasional envious glance to his old domain where Arsenal have extravagantly backed Arsène Wenger. Wenger, he concedes, has assembled 'a wonderful bunch of players . . . but I can't believe they didn't do better in the Champions' League. People say they've been unlucky [in Europe] but you can't be unlucky three years on the trot. In the first year [in the UEFA Cup] they lost to a Greek team who were half-way down the league. I would have won something with them.' He is certainly dismissive about the friendship between Wenger and Dein which he suspects allows Dein to 'play with his toys' in a way that he would never have sanctioned. He preferred to keep the vice-chairman at arm's length when it came to playing matters, yet he does acknowledge Dein's allegiance to Arsenal, which may bring into doubt Alan Sugar's comparable sense of duty to Tottenham.

Of course, they see it very differently at Highbury. 'If George had not gone then we'd never have got Arsène Wenger,' says Arnie Dein, brother of the Arsenal vice-chairman. 'We'd never have seen the quality of play that we see now, when if we score two we expect four, and if we score four we expect six. That never happened under George. This is the best football I've ever watched [in fifty years] at Arsenal.' And it is totally in keeping with football's evolution that it is a thin, bespectacled Frenchman rather than a lean, dapper Scotsman who should be the catalyst.

Yet Arsène Wenger would be the first to admit that his job is made easier by his working rapport with David Dein. 'It is so easy,' he says, 'just to work with one person.' The two men are clearly of the same mind regarding any business concerning the club, so much so that they can act independently of each other, knowing that there is no chance of one stepping on the other's toes. So it is that, five-and-a-half years on from that summer trip to USA 94, David Dein is relaxing at home one Sunday afternoon, taking in the midday Nationwide League offering, the Serie A game on Channel Four followed by the Super Sunday game on Sky. Naturally, his telephone does not remain silent throughout this triple-header, and among the callers on this particular afternoon is Dein's friend, the theatre producer Bill Kenwright, who has just become the proud owner of Everton.

The two men exchange pleasantries before moving on to talk football, and it emerges that while Kenwright is hugely optimistic about Everton's future, the lack of a quality left-sided midfielder remains a problem. On hearing this, Dein immediately says: 'Well, what about Stephen Hughes?' (Hughes had just worked his way back into the first team after a period on-loan at Fulham). Kenwright appears to respond positively to this suggestion, and within a matter of minutes the two directors have as good as sanctioned the deal. By mid-March, following some protracted negotiations over his personal terms, Hughes is an Everton player. Fait accompli. Of course Dein wouldn't have acted unilaterally, but unlike his relationship with Arsenal's former manager, the present one is so comfortable that Dein describes it quite simply as 'a double act'. And unlike the triumvirate at Tottenham, it's a double act that is serving Arsenal well.

CHAPTER SIX
LE TECHNICIAN ALSACIEN

The West Stand of Tottenham Hotspur plc is sheltered from the Tottenham High Road by a pair of ornate entrance gates and a small forecourt that is made to look even more cramped by the gleaming motors parked bumper-to-bumper on its tarmac. There are no marble halls here, just a functional glass-fronted building that houses the various administrative departments and a variety of rooms and suites, among them the boardroom, the ante-room (where the directors and their guests mingle before and after matches) and the Oak Room (for less-exalted VIPs). In keeping with the rest of the building these are fairly modest rooms, the black and white photographs of the great Tottenham Double- and Cup-winning teams of the past dotted around giving the clearest indication of the tradition and history of the real business that goes on within these walls.

It was in the directors' ante-room at a Christmas fixture in the late 1980s that Arsène Wenger first trod on Tottenham turf. The slim, unassuming figure was unfamiliar to most of his fellow guests so few of them afforded him little more than a cursory nod. Certainly, had anyone present that day turned their attentions from a football to a crystal ball and predicted that this foreigner was destined to be a major player in shaping the future of English football they would have been ridiculed. In fact, a reply as dismissive as: 'Next you'll be telling us that George Graham will manage Tottenham one day,' would have probably been in order.

Yet there were two men in the room that day who were well aware

of Wenger's potential, although even they could never have envisaged that he would end up dictating the state of play quite so significantly. One was the agent Dennis Roach, who effected the intro-
ductions between the then Monaco manager and his hosts that day,
and who was instrumental in the sales of both Glenn Hoddle and
Mark Hateley to Monaco. The other was the Tottenham chairman
Irving Scholar, who was delighted that Wenger had taken the opportunity afforded by the winter break in the French season to travel to
White Hart Lane to see the workings of English football at first
hand.

For a few years Scholar had been domiciled in Monaco and being
a football enthusiast whose knowledge of the game extended far
beyond the boundaries of his own club, he was well aware of
Wenger's reputation as one of the most *avant-garde* coaches in
France. Scholar was the first of his ilk to envisage how English football might look freed of its parochialism, and he fancied that
Wenger would make an ideal Tottenham manager – if not now, then
certainly at some point during the next decade.

It was not that Tottenham were in the doldrums. Admittedly,
they had disappointed in 1985–86, finishing in tenth place in the
League (after coming third the previous campaign) and exiting the
FA Cup and League Cup early on during the second season of Peter
Shreeves's leadership. Shreeves was an affable man and a perfectly
capable coach who had graduated through the ranks at White Hart
Lane under his predecessor Keith Burkinshaw and had stayed true
to Burkinshaw's principles in attempting to play free-flowing,
attacking football. He had also bought well, most notably Chris
Waddle and the tenacious Paul Allen, the latter from right under the
noses of Arsenal and Liverpool. Yet in appointing Shreeves, Scholar
had clearly been anxious to cause the least disruption after the acrimonious split with Burkinshaw, who on walking away from
Tottenham was reputed to have uttered the memorable words:
'There used to be a football club over there.' Shreeves was probably
not Scholar's idea of a long-term manager and he had had no
compunction in using mediocre results as an excuse to replace him
with David Pleat.

Pleat had earned a reputation as a miracle worker by keeping
Luton Town in the First Division, despite being hampered by a

meagre budget and the continual sale of the club's best players. Given more scope at Tottenham he immediately made an impact. His brand of exciting, attacking football – he played five across the midfield and benefited from a fit and in-form lone striker in Clive Allen, who scored forty-nine goals that season (1986–87) – propelled Tottenham to third in the League, the semi-finals of the League Cup (which Arsenal won, after a marathon tie) and the final of the FA Cup (which they lost, after a bizarre deflection that was the inspiration for the Coventry fanzine – *Gary Mabbutt's Knee*).

Yet two months into the following season Pleat had gone after allegations about his private life. His successor was indeed a man with an expansive knowledge of the European game: a manager who was acknowledged as one of the most enterprising coaches of his generation; a manager who had twice been the subject of unsuccessful approaches from Arsenal. But this manager was not Arsène Wenger. It was of course Terry Venables, whose tenure coincided with the most traumatic period in Tottenham's history.

While Tottenham's start to the 1990s was characterized by frequently heated exchanges outside the High Court and even more frequent visits to the hospital bedside of a certain Paul Gascoigne, Arsène Wenger was quietly drawing up a pretty impressive coaching record. In his first full season in charge at Monaco the club won the French Championship, progressing as far as the semi-finals of the European Cup the following season. In 1991 they won the French Cup, then reached the final of the Cup-Winners' Cup in 1992, losing to Werder Bremen (which was hardly surprising as friends and family of the players had been involved in the tragedy at Bastia when a stand collapsed on the eve of their big day). Significantly, however, Wenger made his reputation as much for the effect he had on the club off the pitch as for the results he achieved on it.

His conspicuous influence was demonstrated by staying in the Monaco hot-seat for an unprecedented seven years – which is almost unheard of in France. Most coaches stay no more than three years at most at any one club; with freedom of contract pre-dating the Bosman ruling there is a history of a greater fluidity to the French system than in Britain, and both players and coaches move on at regular intervals. Only Wenger, and Jean Suaudeau and Guy Roux at

Nantes and Auxerre respectively, have remained in situ for far longer than is customary (Roux for an incredible thirty-five years), and it is surely no coincidence that all three clubs are blessed with flourishing youth systems that have produced many of the country's top players.

At Monaco, Wenger profited from the support of Prince Rainier and his son Prince Albert, who are true fans and viewed the football team as much of an asset to the Principality as the symphony orchestra. Despite averaging home gates of little more than 5,000, *L'Association Sportive de Monaco* was considered important enough to be granted the finance to fund both a thriving youth set-up (Emmanuel Petit, Lilian Thuram, Thierry Henry and David Trezeguet all emerged under Wenger) and the purchase of star players. As a result, Monaco were regularly among France's representatives in European competitions. It was clearly a mutually beneficial relationship. It was Wenger's knack of being able to balance short-term success and long-term goals that ensured that the royal largesse paid off, and marked him down as more than just a jobsworth coach. Moreover, his appointment might have been considered as something of a gamble considering that he had not exactly arrived at the Louis II stadium boasting a proven track record. Thanks to a comparatively undistinguished playing career he was still a relative unknown in France. He played most of his career in the lower divisions, initially at Second Division Mulhouse and Third Division Vauban, before reaching his apogee as a central defender with Racing Club de Strasbourg whom he joined in 1978 as a player-coach, the season they won the Championship. However, the successful manager or coach who never cut it as a player is no new phenomenon. There is an endless list of nondescript professional – or even amateur – players who became eminent managers, such as Bertie Mee (who was a physiotherapist before he moved into management), Lawrie McMenemy, Graham Taylor, Carlos Alberto Parreira (who managed Brazil to their 1994 World Cup triumph) and perhaps most significantly of all, Arrigo Sacchi, who never even kicked a ball in anger (except, perhaps, when he had cause to berate his players) but who, as coach of the Dutch-inspired AC Milan side of the late 1980s, freed *calcio* from the constraints of *catenaccio*.

So at twenty-eight Wenger got his first break, as head of the youth academy at his home-town club and like George Graham, he took to life on the other side of the touchline like a duck to water, later describing the experience as 'finding my niche'. From Strasbourg he went south to Cannes to spend a year there as assistant coach before going to Nancy to take up his first fully fledged managerial post. Nancy, the Charlton Athletic of the French League, who are seemingly forever yo-yoing between the First and Second Divisions and who are celebrated for being Michel Platini's first employers (and Tony Cascarino's last top-flight club), rely on sound house-keeping and a strong youth system for survival, and Wenger thrived on his hands-on remit until, after two years in the job, he was sounded out by the likes of Monaco and Paris St-Germain. It left him torn between a desire to remain at Nancy and see the young players he had nurtured progress to the first team – and ambition. 'In the end I decided to go to a big club and see if I could make it,' was how he unpretentiously explained his eventual choice.

His passion had developed early, as a kid growing up in what he describes as a 'modest family' in Strasbourg. 'I was in everyday contact with football,' he recalls. 'It was a very important thing in my life for as long as I can remember and my dream was just to stay in football. I became a manager because I loved doing it. It was a very natural progression.' That he was one to watch was evident from the character references that accompanied him to Monaco. They variously described him as a go-ahead, intelligent manager with an open and enquiring mind, a coach blessed with admirable man-management skills whose teams played efficient and entertaining football. And within months of his arrival in 1987, Monaco were reaping the benefits.

His association with Monaco and his president, Jean-Louis Campora – who as a doctor of medicine and a government minister possessed both status and power – was an unprecedented success. However, there are few relationships in life as frail as that between a manager and his chairman (or in this case, president), and in 1994 Campora decided, shortly after rejecting Bayern Munich's overtures for his coach, that Wenger was dispensable after all. It was football's equivalent of the seven-year itch and there was little sentimentality to cloud the issue. It is typical of Wenger's sanguine outlook that he feels no bitterness that he missed out on the chance to coach Bayern; Campora, he recalls, told him that he had to see out the remaining year of his contract at Monaco yet had no qualms about firing him after a terrible start to the 1994–95 season.

Those who suspected the dismissal would inexorably dent Wenger's confidence grossly underestimated him. According to Xavier Rivoire, the UK football correspondent for the French sports newspaper *l'Équipe*, Wenger was ready to jump even before he was pushed. 'Campora was clearly not giving Wenger the backing he once had,' Rivoire explains, 'and that was partly why Arsène felt that both he and the club needed a change. But he also left Monaco because he has a global vision of the game. There are so many people in France who think small, who view the world as a little village and want to stick to their roots where they have been successful. But Arsène is not like that. He knew Japanese football was not the greatest but he knew that he could do well there, simply because he was going to bring something new to them and learn something himself from being in Japan, not just from a footballing perspective but from a cultural one too.'

Stuart Baxter, head coach of AIK Solna, echoed those sentiments when he was questioned about his friendship with Wenger before Arsenal's Champions' League fixture at Wembley against the Swedish champions. The two men had encountered each other in 1989 when Wenger was at Monaco and Baxter boss of Halmstads in Sweden, and when Wenger arrived at Nagoya Grampus Eight in 1995 he turned to Baxter for advice (it must have been good advice, for Wenger was sufficiently impressed to offer Baxter the assistant manager's job at Highbury when he moved to London). He has no doubt that Japan shaped Wenger as a coach – 'it was a challenge for a coach to adapt to a different culture' – but maintains that Wenger was a revolutionary in football terms long before that. 'When we met in 1989,' he recalls, 'we found we were both into sports psychology, dietary analysis, flexibility training and other ideas which were new back then; things I used to mention to other English managers and be told, "Don't speak to me about all that bollocks." Thankfully the blinkers are off now in Britain and it's for the better, and a lot of that is down to Arsène.'

For such a footballing luminary as Wenger, Japan was the perfect pick-me-up after the put-down by Monaco. In footballing terms Japanese football is akin to a nursery school, its players childlike; at

Nagoya Grampus Eight Wenger found pupils as willing to learn as he was to teach. 'It was amazing to feel that people around you want so much to be successful and want so much to improve,' he recalls. 'If there's one thing I'm proud of it is having chosen Japan to be the next stage after Monaco. I learnt a lot there and accomplished some really good things for Nagoya ... on a personal and professional level I took a lot of satisfaction and above all a lot of pleasure.' Once again, his impact was immediate. Grampus Eight were floundering in the J-League when he arrived, yet they finished the season in second place and won the Japanese Cup. Wenger fondly recalls that 'we had such a great time'.

And then, midway through 1996, came the call from David Dein. Dein and Wenger had first met some years earlier when he had this time chosen Highbury as one of his destinations during the French winter break. Had he not got lost inside the bowels of the stadium and fate come to his rescue, history might have taken a very different course. In those days directors' wives were not allowed inside the boardroom but had their own room across the corridor. Stumbling into the hen party, Wenger was rescued by Mrs Dein, who took him to meet her husband. The two men struck up an immediate rapport and kept in touch throughout Wenger's stay in Monaco where Dein was a frequent visitor, having a yacht moored a few miles down the coast at Antibes. Wenger reflected some time later that: 'without David Dein I wouldn't be at Arsenal because he was the one who believed in me at a time when I was not well known, and who convinced the board so that they came to see me in Japan and persuaded me to come over here.'

Arsenal had ended season 1995–96 fifth in the Premiership but gone out of both cups early on, which nevertheless was a distinct movement in the right direction. However, it gradually emerged that there was a fundamental clash of styles within the club: a mismatch that was more about what had happened off the pitch than what hadn't happened on it.

Manager Bruce Rioch had a reputation for being a taskmaster, a martinet, which ought not to have been an obstacle; after all, Arsenal's players were used to having to toe the line under George Graham. However, whereas Graham could make allowances for wrongdoing from players who were doing the business for him when it mattered, Rioch simply couldn't accept that his sergeant-major style did not wash with certain players, most notably Ian Wright. Maybe Rioch was feuding with Wright in order to establish his authority. However criticisms of the player slacking in training, not pulling his weight in games and even of his colourful language came to a head with major dressing room confrontations. Wright eventually asked for a transfer which was rejected. Perhaps the shock of a favourite son wanting to leave convinced the directors that trying to fit Rioch into the infrastructure was like trying to force a square peg into a round hole.

However, high-profile managers were pretty thin on the ground at this juncture, and the Arsenal board, criticized for their conduct in the Graham affair and now abruptly terminating their liaison with Rioch, knew that they could not afford another unsuccessful appointment. The upshot of it all was that they faced something of a conundrum ... that is, until David Dein mentioned the name of Arsène Wenger.

Before dismissing Rioch, it is worth noting how his tenure paved the way for Wenger's reformation. Rioch was the rebound relation-ship, the man who picked up the pieces after the distressing split with Graham, who gave Arsenal the chance to come to terms with the break-up and open their minds to life after George. Rioch broke the pattern so to speak. There is every chance that had Wenger been Graham's immediate successor he would have faced even greater resistance than he actually did. (On another level, Rioch helped Arsenal to a UEFA Cup place and, working in conjunction with David Dein, bought Dennis Bergkamp.)

As it was, there was no welcoming party for the man from Japan. Far from it. Instead, Arsenal got it in the neck for the way in which they had dumped Rioch (whose sixty-one-week term was the briefest ever by an Arsenal manager) and chosen his successor (they had apparently sounded out Wenger long before Rioch was sacked). The whole saga was a sorry one, strung out by a ludicrous debate over the identity of the new manager that began as soon as Rioch was shown the door and didn't end until Wenger had actually set foot in England.

Almost all of the money had gone on Johann Cruyff to be the nineteenth Arsenal manager (Bobby Robson had been on the short list before Rioch was appointed but, though willing, couldn't leave

Portugal. Now he was ensconced at Barcelona and was off-limits, as Newcastle found out). One fan remembers visiting the club shop the day before Wenger's position was made public and being so convinced by the salesman's assurance that Cruyff was indeed going to be the new man that he almost had the Dutchman's name emblazoned on the back of his new shirt. Wenger's name only materialized when Cruyff insisted that he was not in the running, but even then no one was any the wiser. The *Evening Standard*'s back-page headline on the day of the announcement of his appointment didn't help the antipathy. 'Arsène Who?', it screamed, adding to the general sense that this was more cloak-and-dagger intrigue than a red-carpet welcome. Nor did the attitude of certain Arsenal players, most notably Tony Adams, who were highly sceptical of this unknown Frenchman.

Wenger did nothing to appease Adams's initial scepticism by appearing in the dressing room at half-time during the UEFA Cup away leg against Borussia Mönchengladbach (Arsenal had lost the home leg but were still in with a chance in Germany) and changing the system from 3–5–2 to a more conventional back four, whereupon Arsenal lost the game and the tie (with Adams being substituted in the second half). Not, it has to be said, a very auspicious start.

Arsenal had been anxious to keep the appointment confidential until it could be made public under the terms of Wenger's existing contract with Nagoya Grampus Eight; as it was, one of their own inadvertently let the cat out of the bag. A week before Wenger was officially confirmed as the new Arsenal boss, the club signed French Under-21 midfielder Patrick Vieira from AC Milan for £3.5 million and Rémi Garde, a thirty-year-old midfielder, on a free transfer from Strasbourg. As if the recruiting of two hitherto unknown French players was not a big enough hint in itself, Garde's declaration that he was 'delighted to have the chance to work with Wenger' as good as confirmed what had become football's worst-kept secret. Once made official, it was a huge anticlimax. What fans felt was needed was a different personality, a different attitude. According to one of them, 'Wenger looked like a 1970s throwback French professor . . . mmm, nice choice, Mr Dein, was what we all thought. He appeared on the screen before the Premiership game against Sheffield Wednesday and was unconvincing.'

It was not until 1 October that Wenger officially took charge, by which time you'd have been hard-pressed to find anyone outside the boardroom at Highbury who gave him a prayer. Much of the cynicism was linked to English football's xenophobic attitude towards the perceived standard of football played in the J-League. If Wenger was that good, his detractors questioned, then how come he wasn't managing a crack European club? The Manchester United manager Alex Ferguson stoked this particular fire when he reacted angrily to a reported press comment during his early days in the job, retorting: 'He [Wenger] comes over here from Japan [Ferguson practically spat the word out] and starts telling us how to run English football.'

Before his fellow countryman had actually set foot in England, Xavier Rivoire was bombarded with phone calls from English journalists desperate for information. Most were in the dark. 'No one seemed to know anything about him,' admits Rivoire. 'They kept calling to ask me: "Who is this man? Where has he come from? How come he's French, yet he has a German name?" It was all very odd.' In fact, the intrigue surrounding Wenger's arrival – and indeed his name – was peculiar. 'Arsène' is a singularly exotic first-name – it's a bit like being called Hercule, as in Poirot. In fact, the only other well-known 'Arsène' in France is Arsène Lupin, the fictional creation of Maurice Leblanc, who wrote detective thrillers set around the turn of the century. Imagine a Sherlock (as in Holmes) O'Neill, leaving Leicester to take charge of Olympic Marseille, and you get the picture.

But there was nothing fictional about the size of Wenger's task. He had the players to win over, the fans to convince, the press to persuade . . . as if that was not bad enough, his problems were exacerbated by some hugely damaging personal allegations which hit the back pages almost as soon as confirmation of his hiring had become yesterday's news. In truth the rumours had preceded his arrival, but the full impact was not felt until days into his Arsenal career, when a bizarre defamatory message that ended by predicting that Wenger would not see the week out as Arsenal manager appeared on the Internet. It disappeared almost as quickly as it had been posted, but enough people had seen it to ensure that the rumour spread like wildfire throughout the footballing fraternity. By mid-morning on the same day the media vultures were on their way to Highbury.

Amy Lawrence remembers it as a hugely upsetting incident for everyone connected with the club. 'As fans we obviously hoped that it was rubbish because fans always try to protect their own,' she admits. 'Arsenal's detractors were hamming it up but it was nothing but rumours, really. It wasn't going anywhere. It was just the kind of nasty stuff that does the rounds in football, and the person gets labelled for evermore, but that's all.' What started out as idle gossip quickly escalated into malicious slander; that it died an equally swift death was down to Wenger's foresight and courage. He realized that lying low would only fan these particular flames and incite the chasing pack; as things stood they just had scraps to feed on, half-formed allegations, and it was unlikely they would leave it at that were he to shirk the issue and say nothing.

Not for the first time, Wenger got his tactics spot on. At around lunchtime that same day he appeared on the steps of Highbury, visibly shaken by what had happened, but steadfast. He effectively dared the media to tell him exactly what this skeleton was that he was supposed to have lurking in his cupboard. He didn't rant, he didn't even shout. He just very calmly threw down the gauntlet and waited for the challenge. Of course, there was none, given that the allegations were without substance.

This stand-off between the pack and their perceived prey afforded a first glimpse of Wenger's strength of character, and most neutral observers liked what they saw. Here was a man who was clearly prepared to speak up for himself, who was not, as they say, going to let the bastards grind him down. His stock went up further when he later revealed that he had ignored the well-meaning words of wisdom of the club. 'They advised me not to react and to keep a low profile, but I couldn't help myself,' he admitted. 'At the time you tell yourself that it is so base that it will not have any effect but all it needs is for one paper to make allegations which don't have any substance to encourage the whole world to get involved. I was very sorry to disappoint those who had spent time researching my background, my sexual habits amongst other things. I remember a telephone call I received from a journalist who told me that he had photos of me with three other women and others with men and that his paper was going to publish them that Sunday. I replied: "Don't wait until Sunday because you risk someone stealing the information." After the event people told me I was done for now, that the press would never leave me alone, but I slept well that night. It was part of the teaching I acquired in Japan. When I returned home I could look at myself in the mirror. In the final analysis, instead of "killing" me, the papers apologized. I later learnt it was all part of the assumption that "Wenger would not last three months"; when Arsenal's results were good a campaign was launched to unnerve me. But I must say that I got over it quite easily.'

It is rare for a manager to stand so public a trial so early on in his occupancy, but two factors clearly contributed to the personal attack. Firstly, Wenger was 'a foreigner' and was therefore, in the insular conservative industry that is English football, subject to more scrutiny that most; secondly, he is an intensely private man in a very public arena and the cynics suspected that he valued his privacy because, frankly, he had something to hide. However, taking what some disparagingly described as being a sabbatical by going to Japan, he had obviously prepared for the cauldron in which he now found himself. In response to those who questioned his judgement in jumping off Europe's managerial merry-go-round, he claims: 'To leave Europe was a wise decision. One can learn by taking a step back and the time I spent in Japan was like a retreat from my life, from my family and friends. I was completely alone in Japan – Annie [his partner] used to come out during the school holidays but the rest of the time I had to be totally self-sufficient. I would spend whole afternoons on my own, thinking about what was important in my life. It was during that time that I realized how many things demand your time in Europe on a daily basis that you just don't need, and how in Europe the lifestyle is so competitive that no one is polite and no one speaks to anyone else, yet in Japan, one of the richest countries in the world, everyone is polite and has respect for each other. I was glad I was out of it and able to watch from a distance. It gave me strength and I returned with a completely different view of the subject. It was good for me to live in a different society with different values. On my return I was more clear-headed, more objective, calmer. I felt as if I had spent two years carrying out my job in a convent.'

He couldn't have chosen a bigger contrast than Highbury, where disillusionment was the order of the day. Yet it became crystal clear during the first few weeks of Wenger's managerial reign that he possessed self-belief by the bucketload. Without it he would never have been able to restore some of Arsenal's credibility and confidence so swiftly against a backdrop of such hostility, with no one save his employers backing him up. But it was the way he effected the transformation that was so startling. In stark contrast to George Graham, who arrived at White Hart Lane informing the players that they were going to do things his way, Wenger refused to lay down the law. He talked about 'the need to change without disturbing' (which was totally at odds with his precipitous and disastrous tactical change at Mönchengladbach). He had obvious respect for those who had been at the club longer than him and he clearly felt that he could learn from them as much as he hoped they could learn from him. It was 'a conscious decision', to win the confidence of the established players and lean on them to get his ideas across. 'I chose,' he explained later, 'to work straight away with them rather than against them. I opted for dialogue between us. It was the only viable option.' It was all about rebuilding bridges across which to transpose ideas, not about knocking them all down and starting again from scratch, as is so often the case at the start of a new managerial regime.

Initially, the key word was compromise. Wenger listened to the players' views and took them on board (with the aid of Pat Rice, who 'helped me when I wanted to do something uncultural. He knows the heart of the English players so well'). He agreed to extend the morning training session instead of training mornings and afternoons as was his wish; and he acceded to their preference to continue playing with a back five during that first season (it was only in the Double-winning season, by which time Wenger had bought in Overmars and Petit to balance the side, that Arsenal switched to the more conventional 4–4–2). It was a softly, softly approach which produced instant results. Arsenal's first official game under Wenger ended in a win up at Ewood Park. Two games later Arsenal topped the table as Leeds were comprehensively beaten at Highbury and the prejudices began to fade. When Tottenham were taught a footballing lesson in November, with Wright, Adams and Bergkamp netting in a superlative display, it would not have been surprising had the Arsenal fans launched into a hearty rendition of '*La Vie en Rose*'.

Modestly, Wenger claims that he was 'lucky at the beginning. If we had not won the first matches under my control everything would have been different. To be accepted, you have to win. If you tell players who were successful before that now you must do it this way they may enjoy it, but if they lose they will say: "We enjoy it but we don't win" so maybe they will have a reluctance to do it. If they win of course things are easier.' That he talked, too, about his serenity was significant; it was evidently this as much as anything else that had helped him through the first few turbulent weeks of his Arsenal career and enabled him to distance himself from peripheral events.

Yet he was realistic enough to realize that Arsenal were helping him as much as he was convinced he could help them. He was grateful for their offer. He knew that it had come at the right time for him, that personally and professionally he had fulfilled his remit in Japan and that, had he turned Arsenal down he would have risked being viewed as some kind of footballing oddity, as being unable to stand the heat in the kitchen (which is an accusation that could perhaps have been levelled at Bruce Rioch when he most peculiarly went to assist his former assistant Stewart Houston, who was now the manager at QPR). That said, there were certain criteria that had to be fulfilled for him to take the job. Money, it seems, was not a major factor, even though Arsenal had undoubtedly put an attractive financial package on the table. No, the overriding factor was Wenger's need to be sure that the framework he would be working within was right; that he would hold, as he put it, 'a full hand of cards' so that he would be able to make any changes he wished. That he was entirely happy with his terms of reference emerged when he later admitted, in talking about the future, that 'it would be difficult for me to return to a system where I would lose part of the control I have today. At this time I am at one of the biggest clubs in Europe and I am able to apply my ideas. In comparison the alternatives that are available are very limited. There has been talk of me going to Real Madrid but I will probably never have the same freedom that I have here. In order for a French, Italian or Spanish club to tempt me it would be essential to offer me the same type of responsibility that Arsenal do.'

He had obviously done his homework, for it was clear early on that he had a very precise point of view on what made Arsenal tick. Xavier Rivoire recalls the first press conference he held after his appointment, and remembers Wenger attaching great importance to what he described as 'l'ossature de l'équipe' (the spine of the team). 'Arsenal had this bone structure,' says Rivoire, 'and I can still picture him now pressing his pen on the table at each mention of the names: Seaman, Adams, Wright. He saw those three guys as the most important players at that time. He stressed that the legendary back four would remain, and also that there would be no *chasse aux sorcières* (witchhunt). It was his way of emphasizing that he wasn't going to get rid of Tony Adams just because he drank. He has always been very positive like that.' Yet at the same time Wenger admitted that he wanted to make a clean sweep of what Rivoire refers to as a 'British amateurism' within the club. His first-choice signing of Rémi Garde might have appeared strange initially, but according to Rivoire, Wenger was always going to go at the outset for a dependable player he could trust rather than a star he may not be able to handle. Having tried to sign Garde in the past he knew that his spirit was good and that he would fit in. An added bonus was that Garde would also be an able disciple in Wenger's attempts to instil fresh ideas into his new charges.

Anyone attending Wenger's early training sessions would have been left in no doubt that they were privy to the start of a new and very positive era. It was not just what Wenger said to the players gathered round him – his words were only audible to them, but the gist of it was that he wanted to make them as good professionals as possible, that he would respect anyone as long as they were committed – but the way in which he conducted the sessions once the talking was done. He ensured that the ball was always on the ground, which had not always been the Arsenal method. He would stop the exercise if he thought that kick-and-rush tactics were taking over, urging the players to take one touch – two at most – then move forward. He timed everything meticulously with a stopwatch. Training sessions were short but very sharp. They generally lasted no more than forty-five minutes, including a stretching and warm-up routine and a run around the pitch to finish off. The players poked fun at first on the onus he put on these stretching routines, but nothing convinces a cynic more than success and they very quickly realized that there was method in this foreign madness.

In contrast to Graham, who seemingly was only bothered about a player's life off the pitch if it encroached on his performances on it, Wenger is concerned with making his players better men as well as more accomplished footballers. He admits that he deemed it necessary to alter some of the habits of the team as a whole and that 'I had great luck that just before I arrived Adams came out and said he was an alcoholic. He wanted to change so I used him as an example. I thought that the other players should help him change and that the best way to ensure that happened was to ban alcohol completely so that they had to behave like he behaved.'

Thanks to a coaching apprenticeship which embraced physiology, Wenger understands how a professional footballer can function at his optimum level. It has been said that he can assess the extent of a player's fitness simply by watching him run, and he appreciates the prerequisite of being both mentally and physically in tune in order to be able to cope with the rigours of a full-blooded ninety minutes. When Adams was struggling for fitness at a crucial stage midway through the Double-winning season, Wenger sent him off for a week's rehabilitation in the South of France instead of pressing him into action for 'the good of the team', as many more myopic managers might have done. How many sob stories have been told about players who've been given injections to enable them to play through the pain barrier, with no thought given to their longer-term health? Wenger is aware that long-term gain is better than long-term pain. (Adams proved him right, too, returning to action at the end of January 1998 and scoring in a home win against Southampton, after which he was almost ever-present until the end of the season when he used his last reserves of energy to lift first the Premiership trophy, and then the FA Cup.)

Of course, it was not just Adams who benefited from Wenger's new regime. Lee Dixon, Nigel Winterburn, Steve Bould and Martin Keown, all of whom had had their footballing epitaphs written long before Wenger arrived at Highbury, claim that he has added years to their footballing lives. Two years to be exact according to Bould, now at Sunderland but still going strong at thirty-seven. By his own admission it took Wenger just a handful of training sessions to discover that many of the players surprised him. 'I had a poor view of their technique,' he says, 'but they were far better than I had imagined.' But it is nevertheless remarkable that he managed to instil new disciplines and promote a more wholesome approach in players who were extremely long in the tooth.

The exercise and diet regimes were seized upon by the press and served up for public consumption, all too obviously becoming the signature of 'Arsène's Arsenal'. However, don't be fooled into thinking that the brave new dawn coincided with the players suddenly being able to touch their toes and stomach platefuls of pasta and pulses. When your aim is to fine-tune an athlete then of course every little thing helps, but increased flexibility and a shift from junk food to wholefood was just part of the picture. On a wider scale Wenger paid attention to every nuance that concerned Arsenal Football Club's well-being, rendering it, in the eyes of many observers, almost unrecognizable from the club under George Graham's control. 'It's quite unbelievable the way the club has moved on,' says Lee Dixon. 'Every single aspect of the club has changed and I can't emphasize enough how much Arsène has had to do with that. Certainly the club would have moved forward but I don't think it would have been possible to go forward at this pace under anybody else. The team, the facilities, the stadium, just the professionalism in the way the club runs itself, everything is spot on.'

The embodiment of this attention to detail is manifest in Arsenal's new training ground at London Colney. It was designed to make the players feel as comfortable as possible and Wenger worked with the architects and was party to almost every aspect of the masterplan. Whereas the usual idea of attention to detail involved traditions such as the design of the club shirt, Wenger was far more concerned with practicalities. It was he, for example, who determined which chairs would best suit the players' needs, having worked out which made both ergonomic and economic sense; his thoroughness is illustrated by David Dein's comment that 'Arsène was involved right down to the last teacup'. He chose the colour scheme, opting for the calming influence of whites, greens and turquoises as opposed to red, which symbolizes fire and passion (there are some AFC red tiles in the shower room, but that's the extent of it). He also recommended that the entire complex had underfloor heating, and suggested that the vista from the gym should look out onto a tranquil waterfall.

To paraphrase the advertisement for the Sony Playstation (vital hand-baggage for so many footballers, but probably off-limits to the Arsenal staff since Sega became the club sponsor) – do not underestimate the effect that Arsène Wenger has had both on Arsenal and on English football, despite the odds being so heavily stacked against him from the start. On one level you have to admit it was hardly surprising that few people welcomed him with open arms, not when you reflect on the unsuccessful foreign managers who have presided over Premiership teams (the likes of Venglos, Ardiles and Gross). The fact is that Arsène Wenger is the first foreign coach who has been able to couple those traditional English characteristics of grit and determination with European technique – and emerge with a winning combination, whose leading lights shone on the biggest stage of all.

Remember France '98, how Seaman and Adams were among England's leading protagonists. Remember the roles played by Overmars and Bergkamp, who scored one of the goals of the tournament in the quarter-finals against Argentina. Remember – as if he would ever let you forget it – Petit streaking away in the last minute of the World Cup final to score France's third goal, and Vieira's coming of age on the world stage during the tournament. For Arsenal fans it was a defining occasion. 'Arsenal have always had an inferiority complex about their global standing thanks to an abysmal European record,' according to Amy Lawrence, 'but suddenly everyone was talking about these players with the same reverence reserved for real greats and I remember realizing that these were Arsenal players they were talking about. And it hit me – remember we'd just won the Double – that Arsenal were big now. You've got to put a lot of the credit for that down to Arsène.'

Wenger's Arsenal are a side whom the neutral observer would pay to see play. That boring, boring tag has been consigned to the dustbin of the past, and you would have to canvass opinion for a long while up and down Avenell Road before you came across a fan who does not believe that the football on show today is as good as it's been for years. Crucially, Wenger's way has attracted exciting, skilful artists like Overmars, Kanu and Henry, players who might not

Bergkamp, Dixon and Parlour overwhelm Ginola as Arsenal win at
White Hart Lane in May 1999 to keep their championship hopes alive.

Typical poses: victory celebrations for Arsène Wenger… *(below left)*
… and frustration for George Graham. *(below right)*

Nicolas Anelka in happier times with Emmanuel Petit, Tony Adams
and Patrick Vieira.

The Tottenham defensive wall of Sherwood, Freund, Ginola and Iversen,
together with Leonhardsen and Carr, fail to prevent Ian Harte scoring
for Leeds at White Hart Lane.

An all too rare occurance, Dennis Bergkamp scoring in 1999 – 2000 (against Middlesbrough). *(left)*

Sol Campbell – head, shoulders and body above the rest. *(right)*

Ian Walker fails to stop Ryan Giggs scoring in the home match against Manchester United. But Tottenham had the last laugh on this occasion. *(left)*

Dennis Bergkamp and Patrick Vieira are disconsolate as they leave the Wembley pitch after being eliminated by Fiorentina from the Champions' League. *(right)*

Steffen Iversen and Tottenham flatter to deceive as usual,
in the 1-1 FA Cup third round draw at home against Newcastle.

Kanu reacts to missing a close range header as Arsenal can only
draw against Wimbledon at Highbury in December 1999.

The showman prepares…

… to be substituted again, this time after a virtuoso display
against Watford on Boxing Day.

Lee Dixon, still going strong after all these years,
scores a late equalizer at Villa Park.

Sir Alan Sugar, businessman and football club chairman. *(below left)*
David Dein, the action man of Arsenal, the FA, UEFA, etc. *(below right)*

Back in the days when Darren Anderton played a full season for Tottenham – being challenged by you know who. (above)

Jay Bothroyd, hopefully a star in the making, against Leeds in the FA Youth Cup. (left)

A star of the season, up against Tottenham after scoring
at Highbury in March and …

… down and out after Arsenal lose against Galatasaray
in the UEFA Cup final in Copenhagen.

have thrived under a previous set-up, when visiting fans dubbed Highbury 'The Library', so boring and bookish was the spectacle. And no wonder the stars want to work with a manager whose philosophy is based on football as a vehicle for innermost expression. Wenger's pleasure comes from 'the way the game is played with fluency and passion. For me passion is like communication between people. That means something happens when the ball is passed quickly. It is beautiful when there is fluency in the game and that's what I like. Tactically I enjoy intelligent play but I love creative games when everything goes well and the players enjoy themselves.'

Tony Adams's rejuvenation as a player since Wenger's arrival is testimony to the manager's philosophy that his players share his enjoyment of the game. It was only when Wenger told his defenders that if they wanted to stay at the top they should respect what brought them into the game in the first place – a love of playing football – that Adams shook off the shackles that had bound him over the years and actually convinced himself that he was a pretty able technician. Wenger likens the renaissance to giving a voice back to someone who has been mute for years. 'Suddenly, he can now speak having been told to shut up for years, and he finds that he likes it. He can express his feelings now and his views of the game and he enjoys it . . . and now players have discovered that they are much better players than they thought they were. Especially the defenders, because in a pressing game there is always a reluctance by a manager to push their defenders to play. [There are two options]: either you don't take a gamble and you are direct or the second possible response is "let's play" and that develops the technique of the defenders. In England there is so much pressure to win the game that the most instinctive response is that you don't take a chance at the back. Make a mistake and the opposition will kill you. What has changed things is that the pitches are so much better so it is more difficult to pressurize a good defender than it was fifteen years ago. So if you are a good technician you can play.'

He makes it sounds simple, which of course it isn't. As in any new relationship Arsenal and Arsène took time to gel. 'Arsenal are a huge traditional body and it was not easy for them to accept that they were to be guided by a foreign manager,' he says. 'I could sense some reluctance when I arrived but I tried to do my best and that's all I could do.' The concept of change is not embraced by the English professional. Tried and trusted methods laid out by managers who put their international caps on the table rather than UEFA coaching certificates was what the players had come to expect. In the tradition of scintillating dressing-room wit they first nicknamed him Clouseau (just because of his nationality) and 'Windows' (because of his glasses), and then in belated recognition of his status, 'the Professor'. They found his subdued, almost minimalist team-talks somewhat unnerving after Graham's diatribes and Rioch's lectures. Graham's detailed pre-match analysis of the opposition would often run to pages; Wenger, by contrast, prefers to concentrate on the strengths and weaknesses of his own squad. Steve Bould admits that 'his methods came as a bit of a shock at first because match-days were very quiet whereas George used to have his team talks and rants and raves. When Arsène first came we were all sitting there wondering, you know, is he going to say anything? But he didn't have to. He did it a different way. With so many world-class players I suppose you can do that.'

The difference is that Wenger encourages his players to take responsibility for themselves, on and off the pitch. According to Bould, he even told the players that if they couldn't already play at this level then he couldn't teach them; in other words, he gives them credit for having a certain level of intelligence and ability which, frankly, is not always the case. The reason why managers have bawled and bellowed and thrown teacups over the years is because these methods have proved successful in administering the proverbial kick up the backside to lackadaisical and ignorant players. So having been indoctrinated by the George Graham school of management, it was no surprise that the English contingent underwent a culture shock. Used to dire threats, they were unnerved by such rationale, friendly advice as 'try and be careful today, Lee', even though the recipients probably felt that it would have been more effective if they had occasionally been told in no uncertain terms exactly what was expected of them.

Perhaps Wenger's soft-pedal approach contributed to a lack of understanding within the squad during the early days. There were certainly several clear-the-air team meetings in which Wenger questioned his players' collective desire and they, in turn, questioned individual appetites. There were also rumbles of dissatisfaction when Wenger showed scant regard for time-honoured customs. Some traditions have become unwritten rules where football clubs are concerned, hence the reason why Arsenal never trained the day before a semi-final. But that cut no ice whatsoever with Wenger, who scheduled a training session the day before the 1998 FA Cup semi-final clash with Wolves, only for Mother Nature to have the final say and intervene with a thunderstorm. But it was a clear indication that he was not prepared to pander to superstitions if he thought that there was a better alternative course of action.

Nor was he scared of making the unpopular decisions, as he demonstrated at the start of the 1997–98 season, by selling Paul Merson to Middlesbrough. At the time it was a gamble because the players he had bought had yet to make a telling contribution. Patrick Vieira had shown startling promise the previous season, but neither Marc Overmars nor the Monaco duo of Gilles Grimandi and Emmanuel Petit, having only arrived in the close season, had bedded down yet, while Nicolas Anelka and Christopher Wreh were unknown quantities. However, when you consider the facts it is hard not to arrive at the conclusion that Wenger did shrewd business in offloading Merson. Where, for instance, would he have fitted in? Not on the right or left wings, not in central midfield, and probably not upfront, either, since he lacked the pace and consistency to be an effective central striker. Wenger explained that he thought that Merson was 'too old to play on the flanks and although I would have tried to play him on the right-side instead of, maybe, Ray Parlour, I thought longer-term that the defensive balance would have been too weak'. Furthermore, there would have been limited opportunities for Merson to play his preferred position just behind the front two given the overriding claims of Dennis Bergkamp. On the basis of that analysis Wenger would have erred if he had turned down £5 million for a twenty-nine-year-old with a history of addictions.

Rather, Wenger proved to be over-conscientious when it came to retaining players. At thirty-plus, any one of the back five might have been considered surplus to requirements by a more ruthless manager; as it was, he claimed he was 'particularly surprised by how competitive they were . . . I could see huge quality and I knew they had top spirit, that they were not finished'. He should not have been surprised. Arguably more than any other unit, Arsenal's legendary defence has exemplified those quintessential English characteristics over the years – pride, passion and perseverance – and it was these same qualities that had lured Wenger to England in the first place. 'The impression is that English football is different from other football,' he says. 'This isn't a value judgement but simply that the English, when they play, or when they support a team, give everything. It's not the same elsewhere. I was always ready to give my life to win,' he continues, without a hint of self-mockery, 'but I sometimes had the feeling that in France I was the only one who felt that way. What I saw here, from the very first game I watched, was that my passion is shared by so many people. I didn't learn in England that you have to fight to win; what I did learn is that this is a football country. There is so much passion. When I leave England I will remember for a long time what I have lived through here, the feeling and the atmosphere which is integral in the grounds.'

Obviously, passion alone is not enough. It is more a sad indictment on the scarcity of innate ability available in this country, not to mention the inflated price-tag any potential talent carries, than xenophobia on Wenger's part. He has repeatedly been unable to buy British (youngsters Jermaine Pennant and Matthew Upson being notable exceptions) and has instead chosen to hop back across the Channel to tempt the likes of Petit, Anelka, Grondin (loaned back to Saint-Étienne), Diawara and Wreh to follow him to Highbury. He must have amassed enough Air Miles to last him a lifetime considering his shopping list has also taken him to Holland (for Overmars), to Italy (for Vieira, Kanu and Henry), to Spain (for Suker), to Germany (for Malz), to Austria (for Manninger), to Sweden (for Ljungberg), to the Ukraine (for Luzhny), to Portugal (for Boa Morte), to Switzerland (for Vivas) and as far afield as Brazil (for Silvinho), but those who criticize him for championing overseas personnel to the detriment of the home-grown should consider that English football has only itself to blame. Given £5 million to spend and a choice between Marc Overmars and Paul Merson, it's a pretty safe bet that most people would go Dutch (and not only because they'd have some spare change as well). Arsène Wenger has been unable to buy British for the same reason as everyone else; these days it is just not a viable market for prudent housekeepers.

Like most successful managers Wenger makes few mistakes in the transfer market, although not all of his buys have paid off. Stefan Malz, for example (who was not a regular in the Munich 1860 side when Wenger bought him), does not look an adequate replacement for Stephen Hughes, who on his day has a wonderful left foot and vision to match. (When Arsenal's reserves played Tottenham's reserves in 1996 Hughes stood out for one observer, who remarked to Arsenal director Danny Fiszman: 'Who's that? He's not an Arsenal player.' Fiszman retorted: 'You checky sod,' before adding, 'We sent him to the finishing school down the road . . .') In Luis Boa Morte, meanwhile, whom Wenger bought from Sporting Lisbon, he obviously saw a young player who had all the makings of a fine prospect – pace, skill, athleticism and attitude – but who failed to live up to expectations. Still, you can hardly blame Wenger for wanting to try, not when he can list the development of players like George Weah, Lilian Thuram, Petit and Thierry Henry on his CV. When Weah received the European Footballer of the Year award in 1995 he immediately dedicated it to Wenger, going so far as to invite the man he describes as his mentor and guru up to share the podium and his moment of glory.

Weah's cousin Wreh, meanwhile, is one of those players who divides opinion. Opposing fans will forever label him a dud, as will many Arsenal fans with short memories. But it is not too far-fetched to say that without Wreh, Arsenal would not have won the Double, simple as that. Not Bergkamp, not Anelka, not Adams . . . but Christopher Wreh, a little-known Liberian striker brought from Guingamp (where he was on loan from Monaco). As evidence they cite his winning goal on that wet Wednesday night at Selhurst Park in March 1998 – on the same night that Manchester United were held at Upton Park and three days before Arsenal went up and won at Old Trafford – which revitalized Arsenal's Championship challenge. Every supporter who witnessed that win will recall the Arsenal players going berserk after the match, which told its own story. Then, following that cathartic victory Arsenal went to Bolton, who at the time were scrapping for their Premiership lives, and Wreh did it again, scoring the only goal of the game with a memorable strike from outside the area. Another three points in the bag. He then scored the winner in the FA Cup semi-final against Wolves that took Arsenal to Wembley and, ultimately, the second leg of the Double. Three goals that were instrumental in securing the Double for the knockdown price of £300,000. *Merci, merci beaucoup.*

Look down the list of players Wenger has bought and a pattern of sorts emerges. It is his habit to target certain players then move quickly to sign them once his mind is made up. Back in 1987 it took him barely a day to sign Glenn Hoddle from right under the noses of Paris St-Germain, who had been negotiating the transfer for weeks. He recalls returning home from watching Hadjuk Split to learn from the daughter of the Monaco President that Dennis Roach had telephoned to say he wanted a decision. 'At 5.30 a.m. the following morning I called Roach and told him I wanted to sign Glenn,' Wenger remembers, 'so instead of flying to Paris to sign for PSG Glenn flew to Monaco. We met over breakfast at the Beach Plaza Hotel where Campora and Roach agreed a £750,000 fee while I told Glenn what I wanted from him.' The contract was signed at dinner the same day. (Incidentally, the PSG coach at the time was Gerard Houllier.) Clearly, Wenger has never regretted his choice. Of Hoddle he says simply: 'I discovered an amazing player. He was a leader by example. He had two such great feet that you didn't know which was the best.' Furthermore, Wenger maintains that Hoddle 'made George Weah'. The relationship between the two players on the pitch was such that when Hoddle was injured, Weah's goal tally dropped significantly. According to Wenger, Weah would 'come in every day and ask whether Glenn's knee was better'.

Similarly, the deal with Real Madrid for Davor Suker was done and dusted within twenty-four hours, in stark contrast to the inactivity at Tottenham, who had failed to take up an earlier option of signing Suker. It is possibly because 'the professor' has an encyclopaedic knowledge of players that he instinctively recognizes those who will fit in with both his system and his style. Football managers are renowned for this but Wenger is better informed than most. Steve Rowley, the Arsenal scout, once spotted a talented seventeen year old playing for the Ivory Coast in the World Youth Championships. Rowley subsequently mentioned him to Wenger, who proceeded to reel off a series of facts and figures about the youngster. Rowley admits he was flabbergasted, but the truth was that Wenger had attended the Championships, and what's more, had been one of the few foreign coaches to do so.

He also appears to favour those rare individuals who are blessed with virtuosity and a controllable ego; players who are not necessarily established stars but whose untapped aptitude he feels can be coaxed – and coached – out of them. His forte is that he can see what a player might offer his team, even before that player has realized his own worth. He had long been tracking Patrick Vieira before he actually got his man, from the time when Vieira, at eighteen, broke into the French First Division with Cannes. He knew that there was this accomplished defensive midfielder in Serie A whom AC Milan appeared to deem expendable – Vieira was not a regular at the San Siro – and took advantage of the fact that the Italian side was going through a transitional stage to make Vieira his second signing.

It was much the same story with Petit, who joined Arsenal from Monaco for £3.5 million at the start of the Double-winning season. (Again it was a case of capitalizing on Tottenham's hesitation. Petit had attended an inconclusive meeting at White Hart Lane and after another 'we'll think about it' response, asked for a taxi. Thinking he was returning home Tottenham obliged, but instead the driver was instructed to go to Highbury whereupon the player and his former manager were reunited in England. 'I wouldn't have minded so much,' Alan Sugar told David Dein after the transfer was announced, 'But I paid his bloody cab fare.' Dein could have replied, think of it this way, at least you didn't have to pay the fare to the airport.) At the time it would have cost Arsenal in the region of £5 million to bring in an established British midfielder: say, David Batty or Paul Ince (who was repeatedly linked with the club). But Wenger was well aware of Petit's prowess, having nurtured him at Monaco into a player who, at twenty, had already been capped by France, albeit as a defender. Under Wenger's guidance Petit has stepped forward into midfield and matured into one of the most astute and effective midfield players in Europe. What price now the Vieira and Petit double act?

Like a film director casting for his big-budget movie, Wenger obviously has clearly defined roles for each player he enlists. Petit was bought specifically to add that extra man in midfield so that Arsenal could revert to a 4–4–2 formation, while Overmars added width. But Wenger's instinctive ability to assess a player's potential is such that he can envisage a role for a certain player, regardless of whether or not they have filled that role before. Take Gilles Grimandi who, like Petit, arrived at Highbury as a defender but who now doubles up as a useful enough midfielder. Wenger's game-plan for Thierry Henry always involved moving the erstwhile out-and-out flanker into the central striker's berth. After investing £10 million, Wenger continually stressed that he saw the makings of a front man in Henry's raw pace and power, and if his progress at the start of 2000 is anything to go by, all the signs are that the manager's instincts will again be proved right.

It is in keeping with his belief that players at the top level have an innate intelligence that Wenger should subscribe to the maxim that 'the bigger the talent, the smaller the gamble'. By that token he obviously felt comfortable taking a chance on Nwankwo Kanu, whose career – not to mention his life – had been threatened by a heart irregularity; and on Davor Suker, who was out of favour at Real Madrid and desperate for more first-team outings. Suker is not a guaranteed starter at Arsenal, yet Wenger undoubtedly regards him as an asset to his squad, not just his first team. Suker's experience is without question, and as such he is an invaluable role model to the younger players like Jermaine Pennant and Jeremie Aliadière, the French Under-15 striker who Wenger snapped up via the French National School at Clairefontaine.

He courted controversy with that move back in France. The French Federation were livid that Wenger, as they perceived it, was robbing the country of its best assets. It began with Nicolas Anelka, when he exploited a loophole in the French system which has since been amended by a ruling which states that a young player must sign his first contract with the club that trains him. Wenger's perspective is rather more rounded, as befits his global vision of the game. 'If your seventeen-year-old son was asked to go and study at Oxford,' he retorted, 'then you would all clap, so why should football be any different? Europe is an open continent after all.'

However, it wasn't just the French who stigmatized Wenger. He has also come under fire from critics who disapprove of the increasing influx of foreign players and question the policies of managers such as Wenger, Houllier and Vialli who appear intent on creating foreign enclaves on fields that they think should be forever English. But Wenger plays a straight bat to that charge, laying the blame fairly and squarely at the door of English football and its obsession with the short-term. 'I was unfortunate to find on my arrival at Arsenal that, like a number of other English clubs, the youth policy had not been prioritized,' he says. 'Therefore, when you decide to rebuild you know it will take five years and that is a problem. If I compete to have the best French, Spanish, German and English players it is because I do not want to be obliged to spend £15 million (taking a chance on a big-name transfer) every year on the toss of a coin for the future of the club and its identity. I have preserved the future of the club with the older players but when they leave it will be a big problem. Pennant, Aliadiere, Volz [a German], Galli [an Italian] and Noble – all under seventeen – are in my opinion the best in the country. That means that when they are nineteen or twenty they will probably play for me. Not all, perhaps, but some. Then perhaps there will be a year of transition. You should remember that at twenty David Beckham wasn't the player he is today. Manchester United's luck is that their young players emerged at a time when the standard wasn't as high as today. To win the English Championship now you have to be *costaud* [mentally and physically strong].'

Anyone who has witnessed the manager's intense conversations with Arsenal's head of youth development Liam Brady would be convinced that he will give youth a chance when the time is right. Besides, Wenger does acknowledge that the foreign players who come into the English game have to, as he puts it, 'bring a plus. When a club is composed just of foreigners there is a loss of identity, not because they do not compete but, because the spirit of the team is foreign, there is less homogenous stability. I strongly believe in this stability. I could not believe in a team that changes every year. For example, there is a limit to the number of Frenchmen because not all Frenchmen will adapt to England.'

The likes of Aliadière, Galli and Pennant should consider how Anelka developed as a player under Wenger's tutelage and count their blessings that they have been singled out. 'He sees talent like he might see a rough diamond glinting in the river and he wants to grab it and make it shine,' was how Xavier Rivoire eloquently described Wenger's pursuit of youthful *savoir-faire*. It was certainly so where Anelka was concerned. There is absolutely no question that Wenger made Anelka into the player he has only occasionally been since leaving Highbury; it was not Wenger's fault that Anelka and his brothers had set their minds on leaving. The player himself, who infuriated everyone connected with Arsenal by his initial refusal to acknowledge his former manager's influential role in his development, only recently faced facts. 'Regret, no,' he said, on being asked whether he now considered leaving Arsenal to have been the wrong decision, 'but perhaps I made an error by leaving a great coach like Arsène Wenger.'

There is, however, no escaping the fact that Anelka's departure left Arsenal vulnerable at the beginning of the season. Neither Bergkamp nor Kanu are prolific front men; Suker has not been given a long enough run in the side; while Henry, it was felt, was always going to need time to adapt to a new role. Therefore Wenger has been forced to chop and change his forward line constantly, in contrast to the previous two seasons when Bergkamp and Anelka's partnership proved so complementary. Although this is not particularly unusual in modern football – Wenger certainly believes in the squad rotation system and has maintained that the most successful manager (in the Champions' League) would be the one who managed to rotate his squad most efficiently – it can undermine the team and in Arsenal's case it has certainly caused disquiet among the fans who feel Wenger is mistakenly reluctant to drop certain players who are clearly out of form, most notably Dennis Bergkamp. Why, for instance, did Wenger leave it so late in that crucial Champions' League fixture in the Nou Camp – seventeen minutes before the end of the game – to replace an ineffectual Bergkamp with Barcelona's nemesis, Davor Suker? Why, too, was Suker overlooked until the seventy-second minute against Tottenham at White Hart Lane when his eagerness to get on to the pitch contrasted with Bergkamp, who cut a disconsolate figure? Even when Suker did get the nod it was Kanu who came off, which astonished many Arsenal fans.

Notwithstanding the fact that Wenger feels Suker has 'lost a yard of pace', he obviously sees Bergkamp as the more influential player, which is why he will invariably be selected even when he's not at his best. He accepts the criticism as 'fair', but by way of justification explains that 'a manager is often in a situation where he knows that a player can come back to his best if you play him and I thought that Henry was not ready and that Dennis would come back to form. Maybe I did keep him in sometimes when I shouldn't have but there is always that problem when you have a super-talented player like Dennis.'

Yet the feeling persists among the Arsenal faithful that the manager should bite the bullet and select players who are in form rather than in favour, that he has been too slow in blooding the likes of Luzhny and Silvinho in place of the veterans, Winterburn and Dixon. The case for the defence might cite Silvinho's recently accomplished performances in the left-back position, in contrast with his somewhat shaky appearances earlier in the season, which suggests that Wenger has been justified in allowing him time to acclimatize. 'It has taken him six months to get used to the game here,' Wenger admits, 'but he is one of those young players who I am convinced will make it.'

Perhaps Wenger is simply being canny. It will be difficult enough for Arsenal to deal with the day when the back four reach the end of what has been a very long road. By phasing players in he appears to be going for smooth transition rather than the short, sharp shock. 'The day that they are in decline will be a big problem for Arsenal,' he acknowledges. 'That's the moment that we can say that we're at the crossroads. It will be very difficult. But the club must go forward and as long as the players achieve good results then I'm not worried for the club. The player's age does not concern me. I only take account of their performance on the field. Names, nationalities . . . it does not matter. I choose one or lots of players who, in my view, on the day of the match are the undisputed number ones in their position. This can change overnight but the day that Dixon, Adams, Winterburn and Keown can no longer play at the highest level . . . yes, that will be difficult.'

Manchester United did it, of course, successfully phasing out Gary Pallister and Steve Bruce in defence and adapting seamlessly to the sales of Andrei Kanchelskis, Paul Ince and Mark Hughes in 1995, as well as the loss of Cantona after the 1996–97 season. In 1999 they had to adapt to life without Peter Schmeichel, and while replacing the keeper has proved more problematic, they still managed to set the Premiership pace and reach the quarter-final of the Champions' League. It is debatable whether this is the sign of true champions or whether United are the beneficiaries of what Wenger has sarcastically referred to as their 'mid-winter break' in Brazil for the World Club Championships. He disguises his misgivings about the FA's ruling allowing Manchester United to pull out of the FA Cup by addressing its impact on his club. 'It gave them the opportunity to rest in December. But I am someone who always defends the football in the country where I find myself. Because I am proud of where I work, when Manchester United lose on the international stage it doesn't make me smile. I have to question myself and say, "They have the edge over us, they are stronger than us and they lose. That shows there is a problem domestically." That is to say, I also have a problem because they are in front of me.'

Certainly, on the domestic front, there has been little to choose between Arsenal and United since Wenger arrived at Highbury (in 1999 it was just a penalty miss and a point). The rivalry between the two sides and their managers over the last three years has intensified into football's own version of the north–south divide and the media have revelled in building it up and personalizing it, depicting it as the northern traditionalist versus the southern – and foreign – upstart. The impression is that in Wenger, Ferguson has perhaps met his equal. While Kevin Keegan was culpable in wearing his heart a little too prominently on his sleeve and allowing his emotions to get the better of him, Wenger is astute enough to know when to take a step back. He recognizes the verbal jousting for what it is – a sprinkling of spice into the melting-pot. 'It is a little bit of comedy but I enjoy it because I play to win and it is just that love of winning the games that we share,' he says. 'In the end that is what is important, and that the game is fair and that the best team wins.'

Yet the truth is that Wenger and Ferguson share more common ground than is superficially apparent, most notably an intense and almost obsessive will to win. Taken at face value they could not be more dissimilar. There is Ferguson, this growling and fiercely combative Scotsman, who will read the riot act at half-time if he deems it necessary, and who is spiky enough when provoked to think nothing of ordering a journalist from his press conference (as he did during the World Club Championships in Brazil). Then there is Wenger, the erudite Frenchman whose style is both calculating and methodical, as befits a graduate in Economic Science, and who prefers his dressing room to be low on decibels, high on deliberation. Never mind the teacups; Wenger believes in the benefit of restorative liquid before he makes any necessary observations.

His candid and expansive manner, meanwhile, has endeared him to the media who are used to feeding on the scraps tossed to them by cagey campaigners like Ferguson, who will not countenance interrogation and have become past-masters at stepping round questions designed to trip them up. With Manchester United being the flavour of the month, every month, a compliant press is the order of the day at Old Trafford. Yet in Wenger they are spoilt by someone who actively seeks to prolong a press conference, such is his desire to indulge his favourite subject matter. It is his habit to address the media at the training ground the day before a game, and it is not unusual for him to continue talking for five or more minutes after one of Arsenal's press officers has instructed that there should be 'one last question'. This candour has occasionally got him into hot water, however. When he claimed, as he did before the Premiership clash between United and Arsenal at Old Trafford in January 2000, that 'Mark Bosnich was no Schmeichel', it was taken out of context and contorted into a gratuitous criticism of Schmeichel's replacement, which enraged the United camp. Wenger, though, was not saying Bosnich was rubbish. He was merely stating the commonly-held view – that Bosnich was not as good as his predecessor.

Out on the training pitch Wenger runs a well-structured and precise regime in which his stop-watch is his most vital prop. He believes that players can over-train, and recalls having to hide the balls from his Grampus Eight players, so keen were they to stay on after the practice was over. Ferguson, meanwhile, is consumed by an inbred work ethic and sees no harm in players wanting to perfect their techniques by additional sessions. Wenger stresses the importance of diet and supplement, and employs an osteopath, a conditioning coach and a masseur to help keep injured players on the right track. Conversely, old habits die hard in Ferguson. He'll come down on his players like a ton of bricks on occasions. (He famously cut short a dinner engagement in Blackpool to tear back down the motorway to Manchester and break up a party hosted by Lee Sharpe and attended by Ryan Giggs and several other of United's young stars. He tore them off a strip, later justifying his actions by claiming that 'a manager, like a parent, has to put his foot down pretty firmly when things get out of hand'.) Wenger prefers to view his players as adults and expects them to know how to behave off the pitch as well as on it.

Scratch below the surface, however, and it is clear that there are similarities between Wenger and Ferguson which extend far beyond the fact that both are nicknamed after fictional detectives – Clouseau and Taggart respectively. In essence, they share a boundless enthusiasm for the job that both unites and divides them. Both are footballing workaholics, seldom able to switch off from the game that is their lifeblood. Both will return from European fixtures and re-run the video incessantly until the early hours, still managing to be back behind their desks early the next morning. When asked what he did with his leisure time Wenger famously replied: 'I watch football,' which was no exaggeration. In fact, it is unlikely that Wenger has many occasions to turn off Totteridge Lane down the A41 and into the West End other than on the odd evening when David Dein has persuaded him to go to the theatre (which is Dein's other abiding passion).

Certainly, anyone visiting *chez Wenger* in the leafy north London suburb of Totteridge (his nearest neighbour of note is David Ginola, whose house is infinitely more imposing than Wenger's comparatively understated abode) could not fail to notice the huge screen that dominates the front room, and would almost certainly see Wenger viewing whatever game he has been able to pick up (naturally, he has digital television so is able to watch Canal Plus regularly, as well as games from all over Europe). As television goes this is very much top-of-the-range, and the cinematic screen is totally at odds with the contemporary décor and subtle colour scheme in the rest of the room, in which there is no sign whatsoever of football memorabilia. Indeed, aside from a small sticker in the window of an upstairs room (presumably, his daughter Léa's bedroom) that encourages passers-by to 'Support the Arsenal', one wouldn't presume any football connection. Certainly, the family cars, a middle-range Merc and a Renault People Carrier, are not the usual predilection of somebody who is a captain of his industry or a resident of Totteridge.

It is possible that Wenger has not come across the proverb about all work and no play. He is more a work hard, play hardly at all kind-of-guy, yet it would be unfair to suggest that he might be more familiar with what happens to Jack when he works too hard. Wenger is not a dull man, although he has been accused of lacking warmth. He has a dry sense of humour that occasionally gets lost in translation, for which he cannot be blamed, just as one can hardly blame him for wanting to keep his private life exactly that.

Having said that, his life outside the game is a relatively simple one. On days off, when his long-standing partner Annie and three-year-old daughter Léa can prise him away from the screen, Wenger might go for a stroll *en famille* across Totteridge Green to feed the ducks at the bottom of the road. Occasionally, he takes a walk across the fields with David Dein, who lives a long ball away and who is fiercely protective of his manager on the grounds that he has little enough time at home, so what he has should be entirely private. These excursions, however, are about as adventurous as it gets. In fact Annie, a very friendly lady who also exemplifies French chic, claims that they go out so rarely that her knowledge of London is superficial compared to that of her friends. Léa attends a local Montessori school for a few hours every morning, but aside from that they seem content to wait for Wenger to return home, which clearly is not as often as they would like. During one interview at home 'Papa' was distracted, first by Léa – who Annie explained was 'excited because he isn't home much during the day' – as well as by a live game on Canal Plus between Nantes and Lyon (he kept interrupting the dialogue to eulogize about Nantes, who were 3–0 up within fifteen minutes). A possible third distraction, the phone, was ignored. 'If I take the phone I never stop,' he admitted.

The cynics would say that this obsession with winning has got out of hand to the extent that the philosophy which Wenger first stated in 1997 – 'I want positive aggression. If you are too soft you don't win many games' – has been pushed far beyond acceptable limits. George Graham's belief that Wenger lets his players get away with too much petulance would appear at first sight to be a case of the pot insulting the kettle until you consider that Arsenal had only half as many red cards during Graham's eight seasons in charge at Highbury compared to Wenger's three seasons to date. Certainly it's a worse record, but that is largely a result of the higher disciplinary standards FIFA has demanded, which many feel have given rise to high-handedness and inconsistency among referees.

However, it is strange that such an urbane and upstanding principal has not weeded out the problem by now. He has this open and honest bearing – critics might call it self-righteousness – that suggests a typically British attitude towards fair play, yet he has continually been unable to distance himself from his players and admit their culpability. It is probably because he feels that double standards are at work here, particularly with regard to Manchester United on the one hand – a recent analysis showed that they received a mind-boggling 75 per cent of decisions in their favour at Old Trafford – and against foreign players on the other. So while he has managed to instil new levels of professionalism in hardened English pros like Dixon and Winterburn who were previously prone to retaliate when provoked, it is now some of the leading lights of the foreign contingent whose behaviour consistently threatens to disable his side and undermine the progress he has made thus far. Even Ian Wright, whose rash aggression eventually caused him to seek the services of a rage counsellor, certainly seemed more in control of his anger towards the end of his Arsenal career. Instead, it is the likes of Petit, Vieira and Grimandi who have too often attracted the wrong kind of headlines.

Wenger ignores this perennial problem at his peril, for any failure on his part to root it out could tarnish his success. His stubborn stance does not sit easily with his upright image of a manager who believes that 'winning by respecting the rules is what makes football beautiful', and whose disillusionment with the corruption scandal in France involving Marseille while he was Monaco manager contributed to his decision to come to England, where he believes the game 'is straighter'. Anyone who knows him well will tell you that Wenger would never follow the example of some of his continental counterparts and devote time to teaching how to pull shirts and get away with sly and underhand methods. That is not Wenger's way. He sincerely believes that it is because his players are so wrapped up in the game that they lose their rags. However, as long as Wenger continues to resemble what David Lacey memorably described in the *Guardian*, as 'a head of the science faculty enthusing about the exam results, while down the corridor his students are attempting to blow up the laboratory for the umpteenth time,' Arsenal may never be the finished article while they cannot come to terms with refereeing mistakes.

Of course, when their legendary solidarity is channelled in the right directions then the results are unfailingly positive. All the talk before the needle match against Manchester United at Old Trafford on the night of Monday 24 January concerned the sparks that could fly, given that Vieira, Keane, Vivas and Butt had all seen red over the last sixteen months of these heavyweight, hot-headed contests. Yet Arsenal, severely weakened by the loss of several key players, more than matched their hosts for both skill and stamina – all the more surprising considering United had had a month's break from domestic football – and were unfortunate not to return home with all three points.

Wenger had acknowledged before the game that this match could turn out to be 'the turning point of the season'. United, he pointed out, had three games in hand over Arsenal but the same number of points. 'We have,' he stressed, 'got to get something out of it. We know we have the potential to beat them and that we are at our strongest with our backs to the wall. We just have to show we are strong enough to beat Manchester United.'

Perhaps as much for his sense of worth as anyone else's, he had to demonstrate that he could get something more from a team which, by his own admission, had been 'unbelievably disappointing over Christmas'. On Sky TV before the game he was asked if he could throw any light on the reasons why; if he could explain how it was that Arsenal had only managed fourteen points out of a possible thirty away from home, and conceded thirteen goals on their travels, one more than they had let in through the whole of the previous season? Wenger went so far as to admit that 'it is our away form that has cost us,' but stopped short at revealing what he referred to as a 'problem' with his team. 'I would prefer to keep that to myself,' was all he would say.

The suspicion was that Wenger was referring to his side's desire – its will to win. He has made no secret of the fact that he believes it was a collective hunger on the part of players who were fed up with playing second fiddle to Manchester United that was instrumental in driving Arsenal towards the Double in 1998. Some, like Vieira and Anelka, had never won anything at all. Two years on and Wenger clearly had cause to question the desire, the inner resolve that has always bound Arsenal sides so tightly. At Old Trafford his players answered him back as emphatically as they knew how.

Henry heads on, Stam should clear, the ball didn't bounce kindly for him. Ljungberg dispossesses him, beats the goalkeeper and Arsenal are ahead at Old Trafford. Eleven minutes gone . . . and is the dream alive in the Theatre of Dreams? Not given a chance, not given a prayer . . . could this be the first big League shock of the new millennium?

Jonathan Pearce, commentating that night for Capital Gold, is renowned for being able to talk up any game, yet his enthusiasm was spot on this time. Arsenal's target of pilfering a precious three points from under United's noses, just as they had done in the Double-winning season when Overmars scored the only goal of the game, was in reach, thanks to the combination of a wicked bounce which wrong-footed Stam and bravery beyond the call of duty by Ljungberg, who thrust his head in the way of Stam's half-hearted clearance before slipping the ball past Bosnich to silence Old Trafford and the majority of the record Premiership crowd of 58,293. From then on the small section of Arsenal fans in the corner of the ground never let up. 'You should have stayed in Brazil,' they chanted throughout a first-half in which Arsenal looked like the side that had enjoyed a twenty-six-day break from onerous Premiership duty.

This, then, was Arsenal at their defiant best, exemplifying the cohesive tenacity that has served them so well over the years. They arrived in Manchester with a wretched record of four League defeats in ten games on the road, and still smarting from an agonizing FA Cup penalty shoot-out defeat to Leicester. Hardly the ideal preparation for the most significant domestic game of the season. Yet backs against the wall and written off from the start is just the way Arsenal like it. Never mind that they were shorn of the services of Adams,

Bergkamp, Overmars, Suker and Kanu. Never mind that Wenger resisted the temptation to throw rookie striker Graham Barrett in at the deep end and instead started with only one recognized striker in Henry, with Ljungberg playing just behind him in a 4–4–1–1 formation. Somehow Arsenal managed to turn adversity on its head and it was the decision to employ the Swedish midfielder in that withdrawn role that proved to be the catalyst. Like a pick pocket in a crowded street Ljungberg made a real nuisance of himself. He hassled and harried, stealing countless loose balls and so frequently unsettling Stam that Keane was time and again forced to drop back and help out his beleaguered defence, which in turn left space for Arsenal's midfield to exploit.

Keown will chip it to the half-way line, Ljungberg glances it on, and this is Henry for a second Arsenal goal. Into the penalty area and Bosnich saves, and I wonder if that, after thirty-seven minutes, will prove to be the turning point of the game.

It was. 'We had 2–0 for the taking on a couple of occasions and I thought we were always in control in the first half but then we conceded a stupid goal,' Wenger acknowledged. 'I don't want to tarnish what was an outstanding performance in terms of character but we've got to have some regrets about not taking all three points.' Instead United, rallied by Keane, upped the tempo considerably in the second-half before replacing Cole with Sheringham in the sixty-fifth minute. Nine minutes later, United were level.

Ray Parlour has it, trying to find Dixon with a ball sneaked down the line but Giggs blocks, in towards Dwight Yorke who prods it back to Roy Keane. Keane chips it forward into the Giggs run. Parlour goes with him towards the dead ball line. In comes the cross at the far post, Seaman claws it away, it drops for Beckham who pokes it back in . . . it's 1–1 and it's that man who has levelled it up. On as a substitute, the Arsenal fans bated him because of his connections with Tottenham Hotspur but it's Ready Steady Teddy who makes it Manchester United 1 Arsenal 1 and I thought he was the danger and he has been. And Sheringham loves to score against Arsenal.

Oh the irony of it. Anyone, anyone else at all could have scored that goal and it would have been a blow, but nothing like as hard and true as the one which Sheringham administered to Arsenal when he side-footed nonchalantly past Seaman. There is absolutely no love lost between Sheringham and the Arsenal fans; their taunts during the warm-up had provoked him into holding up three fingers in their direction and gleefully hoisting three imaginary cups to remind them of his trophy haul the previous season. That he should have been the player to strut off the bench and rob them of their glory constituted a full-blooded knockout punch.

Yet even Sheringham's equalizer could not detract from the fact that Arsenal had not only taken the game to United, but had played well enough to have won. Wenger must have taken great heart from the accomplishment, despite the fact that the major beneficiaries from the result were Leeds, who were three points clear at the top with a game in hand over his team. Privately, he might have allowed himself to believe that he could still win the title, but his hopes were soon to be shattered by his side's capitulation against Bradford five days later and their 1–0 home defeat to Liverpool in the following fixture.

Unlike the Double-winning season, when the 1–0 win at Old Trafford had so galvanized Arsenal that they did not lose another game or concede another goal until the Championship was secure, Arsenal's mettle was now tested and found wanting. Against Bradford they simply did not possess the killer instinct. Against Liverpool, meanwhile, they looked stale and off the boil, out-thought and out-fought by a side who simply had a greater will to win. That Wenger chose the aftermath of defeat to bawl them out was illustrative of his disappointment with their apparent apathy. 'They deserved it,' he claims. 'If you do it too often it has no effect, so you must choose your moment.' And it would not have escaped his notice that Liverpool were steadily gaining a solidarity and an ability to function efficiently as a whole without its most potent parts – Owen, Redknapp and Fowler – which was always one of Arsenal's quintessential qualities. What's more, Liverpool had done it under the guidance of a fellow countryman who had acknow-ledged Wenger's part in facilitating his task at Anfield by paving the way for a foreign manager to be accepted at a high-profile English club. Arsène Wenger had been the pioneer and now Gerard Houllier was reaping the rewards. As Paul Hayward wrote in his *Daily Telegraph* match report: 'Wenger and his spiritual ally passed on football's *escalier* yesterday. Houllier was travelling sweetly up, Wenger bumpily down.'

Wenger is far too much of a winner to bail out and wave *au revoir* at the merest whiff of trouble, but by Arsenal's own high standards the talk of a mini-crisis was no exaggeration. Arsenal's stop-start League campaign had been characterized by a lack of consistency and conviction, and as Wenger pointed out after the Worthington Cup defeat against Middlesbrough, 'potential counts for nothing . . . it is consistency that gives us the chance to win something and we have never been able to string together defensive consistency and offensive efficiency.' In both cup competitions they failed to progress beyond the fourth round, while most significantly, they made a humbling exit from the Champions' League.

There is no doubt that Arsenal's failure to perform adequately on the biggest stage yet again when they appeared to be far better equipped both mentally and physically than ever before was a tremendous blow to the manager's professional pride, one which has caused him endless soul-searching. At the time he admitted he and his side were at their lowest-ever ebb. The disappointment must have been so much greater than the previous year because of the calibre of the reinforcements to the squad. Once again, the theory about that European inferiority complex resurfaced. Football is a game of habit, played out in the head as much as on the pitch. It's the snowball effect, about the striker on a roll, the team on a winning run. And frankly, Arsenal under Wenger have got into the habit of losing key European games.

There are no hiding places, no excuses. Not even Wembley, even though in retrospect it was definitely a hindrance. While Wenger is undoubtedly right when he berates English football for its short-sightedness in not aiding its European representatives with the help of a less-congested fixture schedule – he complained that 'the English Premiership is the only one that doesn't protect its clubs which are involved in European competition' – the proliferation of European games has for once put the English clubs on the same footing as their continental counterparts. Consequently, their experience in the number and intensity of domestic encounters should have given them a competitive edge. However, there are times when one just has to hold one hand up (as the Arsenal back four of old did so well) and confess. The brutal truth is that 'the professor' has not yet come up with a solution to liberate Arsenal from this mental block that prevents their European emancipation at the highest level, and that must go down as a big blot on a copy-book that is, save for the indiscipline problem, otherwise unblemished.

He doesn't need anyone to tell him so either. For a man whose work and play are so intrinsically linked he will be perturbed by his inability, hitherto, to solve the problem that prevents Arsenal taking their place among Europe's élite, which ultimately hinges on them reaching the knockout (quarter-final) stage of the Champions' League, at least. He will be well aware, too, that next season is a crucial one, both for the club and for himself. Handicapped as they are by what, by continental standards, is a small stadium (even if they wanted to reconsider the ill-fated Wembley experience, the redevelopment of the national stadium means they have Hobson's choice), Arsenal can ill afford one fallow season. Failure to qualify for the Champions' League could well result in the dissatisfaction and ultimate departure of those star players who could earn more money playing fewer games at a higher level of competition in a more convivial atmosphere. There is still the UEFA Cup, of course, but unless you win it or at least reach the final that's like buying *vin de table* when your taste is for Veuve Cliquot.

Wenger's halo is in no danger of slipping yet. From the boardroom to the family enclosure he has unequivocal support. No one has ever indicated a readiness to jump on his back, never mind a desire to see the back of him. As far as Wenger himself is concerned, there is perhaps just one job that might tempt him away from Highbury in the short term and that is managing a national team. But he is still probably *persona non grata* as far as the French FA are concerned – primarily for persuading Jeremie Aladière to leave the French National School at Clairefontaine to go to Highbury – so the likelihood of him being offered the position in the near future is as remote as him accepting it, considering how much he relishes the day-to-day involvement of club football. Besides he doesn't consider the national team to be more fulfilling than a club 'because you have more influence over a club'. What Wenger could have added is that there has to be more than the specific assignment itself for optimum job satisfaction. So just as Japan gave him equanimity, the Bundesliga, a home from home on his doorstep, would provide a fitting climax to his coaching career.

Talking long-term, he has admitted that 'the desire to coach hands-on will diminish. [Everyone] has physical and psychological limits. But whatever happens I cannot see myself living without football.' He speculates that 'one day I could see myself returning to France, but in the role of administrator', which suggests that he could be welcomed home as the national technical director or the president or general manager of a leading club, if not as the national coach.

However, *Monsieur* Wenger has already signed an extension to his original contract at Arsenal which, barring a major catastrophe, will tie him to Highbury until 2002. Say it softly, but according to the high standards Arsenal have set themselves, failure to qualify for the Champions' League for one season is a major catastrophe. Whether that occurred or not, given the painful end to his stay at Monaco it would not be surprising if Wenger regarded the last year of his contract as unduly favouring his employers, who could dismiss him at a whim without heavy financial penalty. So if he is not offered, or indeed does not sign, a new contract in 2001 then Arsenal's loss could be the Japanese national team's gain, just in time for a little local event they are co-hosting with their neighbours – the 2002 World Cup.

CHAPTER SEVEN
THE GREAT DIVIDE

It is 2 p.m. on a Friday afternoon and Pat Rice is pottering around in his dressing gown, a regulation white towelling robe with the Arsenal club crest embroidered on the chest. This is no sudden, out-of-character show of indolence on the part of Arsenal's assistant manager. He and Arsène Wenger have just finished putting the players through a penultimate training session at London Colney before the forthcoming derby against Tottenham, and while the players have showered and are gradually dispersing to wherever it is players go when their few hours' work is over for the day, Rice obviously has club business to attend to and is in no great hurry to get going.

Instead, he pads cheerily around the training centre, happening to spot Thierry Henry, nattily dressed as always in designer jeans, expensively cut crew-neck sweater and top-of-the-range trainers, exiting with a bulky wad of newspapers tucked under his arm. 'I need them to improve my English,' Henry explained to press officer Amanda Docherty, who was not altogether pleased to catch the player leaving the reception armed with the club's full quota of daily reading matter. But Henry is not about to be stopped in his tracks by the friendly admonishments of any club official. He does, however, turn on his heels at the sound of Rice's bellow from across the hallway.

'Oi, Thierry, we'll find out just how much of a Gooner you really are on Sunday,' shouts Rice (who knows a bit about these things, having been at Arsenal boy and man; Arsène Wenger says he is 'the link between the past and the future' and describes him as 'deeply, deeply Arsenal'). Henry, in an engaging manner wholly appropriate in one who knows he can currently do no wrong, laughs out loud before disappearing, unabashed, out of the door (although it is debatable whether he is actually intent on spending the rest of the afternoon absorbing the 'literary' fare on offer in the pages of *The Times*, the *Daily Mail* and, inevitably, the *Sun*).

Just over forty-eight hours later, Henry has answered Rice back in the best possible manner *and* guaranteed the back-page headlines in the following day's papers. Succeeding from the penalty spot – where eight of his colleagues had previously failed during the season – Henry was instrumental in securing a 2–1 victory over Tottenham in the 126th north London league derby (not to mention shepherding Chris Armstrong into a position inside his own box from where he could not help but head an Arsenal corner into his own net).

On a very basic level, there is nothing that endears a player more to his supporters than a blatant act in a derby match, be it scoring the winner or flooring an opponent. It is not even so much what you do as how much you mean it, and so it was that Henry (or 'TH14' as he is referred to by those Arsenal fans who converse on the Web), whose stock was pretty high even before the game thanks to his recent hot goalscoring streak, assumed cult-hero status after his wholehearted contribution in what was his first derby in Arsenal colours. As Arsenal fan Alex Chung, who was among those rejoicing in an adoring Clock End, observed: 'It's plain to see Henry is a wonderful player with enormous potential whose heart is in exactly the right place – below the cannon on his left breast.'

The 'smiling boy wonder' Chung called him, and no wonder. Henry had mentioned beforehand that he had the impression that this derby was 'some kind of a war', and his celebrations could not have been more triumphant, nor a more appropriate rallying cry. After the penalty he raced to the fans in the Clock End behind Ian Walker's goal – eyes bulging, shirt pulled down to expose the cannon – before wheeling away to milk the congratulations of his team-mates and the rest of the stadium (save, of course, for the small pocket of Tottenham fans at the South End, whose jubilation at getting back on level terms had been painfully short-lived).

Par for the course now, these gung-ho celebrations of Henry's.

Every striker has his way of commemorating a goal and the Arsenal fans had been spoilt by Ian Wright's wacky repertoire over the years. However, Henry has taken up Wright's mantle on this front and toasts every single goal with gusto. It is his custom, which began when he and his Monaco team-mate David Trezeguet played together for the national Under-21 side, to wiggle his hips en route to the corner flag, where he then puts a forefinger to his lips as if asking for a quiet moment to contemplate the done deed. He also occasionally indulges in a mysterious elbow-rubbing routine, the origin of which made for an engaging debate on the club web site (after numerous suggestions the conclusion was that it was some reference to solidarity and teamwork, given that the French expression for that is *serrer les coudes* (literally, 'close the elbows'). In response the fans have taken to serenading Henry with a chant set to the tune of an obscure instrumental number entitled 'Tom Hark' by the 1980s group The Piranhas, that was originally a hit in 1958 for Elias and his Zig-Zag Jive Flutes. Strange, but true.

However, as goals go Henry's penalty was especially significant. Firstly, it meant a vital three points in the bag in Arsenal's quest for a Champions' League place next season. What's more, it ensured revenge for the 2–1 defeat at White Hart Lane in November. Yet the truth is that Henry's exuberant performance was really all that illuminated what was a particularly drab affair. Arsenal looked jaded after their exploits three days earlier in the UEFA Cup against Werder Bremen, while Tottenham – whose reputed playmakers David Ginola and Darren Anderton made precious little of the play – lacked the necessary guile to exploit their opponents' tiredness. It was a game that left the Arsenal fans once again praising Arsène Wenger's foresight in making Henry the club's record signing in the summer, and sent the Tottenham fans home mortified that there was no player wearing white and blue on the day of comparable effectiveness.

Henry, at twenty-two, appears to have the lot. Pace, power, a great first touch, fine close control and two cultured feet. He can cross and head the ball with aplomb. He even takes free-kicks, even though there are a few dead-ball specialists among the Arsenal ranks. However, they don't make the best use of them, perhaps because Bergkamp and Petit may not be as good at set pieces as some other people who take them; they are not in the class of Beckham and Zola, and Silvinho and Henry should be moved up the pecking order. But most crucially for a front man, his finishing has improved beyond recognition from the somewhat reluctant striker whose profligacy in front of goal in his first few appearances in an Arsenal shirt caused many to question Wenger's judgement in asking a player who had spent four years out on the wing (at both Monaco and Juventus, as well as for the French national side) to take centre stage. The winner against Tottenham took Henry's tally to sixteen and left him two goals short of Anelka's total for the whole of last season, with nine league games still left to play. Not bad for a player whom Wenger claims 'was convinced when he came that he couldn't score goals'. Wenger was obviously convinced he could, and he has been proved right. Asked if he was surprised by how well he had performed as a striker Wenger responded: 'Not how well, but how quickly, because when you consider the type of player he was in terms of finishing at the beginning of the season and the way he finishes now, the change is amazing.'

But then Wenger would probably win *Mastermind* if he chose Thierry Henry as his specialist subject. He had, after all, been instrumental in developing the teenager through the ranks at Monaco, so it was not quite as much of a gamble as some imagined, this chucking Henry in at the deep end. 'He played as a striker when he was young, otherwise I would never have bought him to play the striker's role,' admitted the man who gave a seventeen-year-old Henry his debut, and whose departure from Monaco led to the player being shunted out wide permanently by Wenger's successor (and the man who alongside Platini, Giresse and Fernandez in the French national side formed one of the greatest midfield quartets of all time), Jean Tigana.

The astounding thing about this success story is that Henry the winger was good enough to win a French Championship with Monaco (in 1996–97) and become a World Champion in 1998 with France, for whom he top-scored with three goals. Too much too young perhaps, as Henry was later to as good as admit. 'When you are a champion of the world at twenty the hard thing is to remain at the top for eight or nine years,' he acknowledged. At Monaco he went, if not off the rails then certainly off the boil. His form slumped, yet he was simmering nicely again by the time French coach Aimé Jacquet selected his World Cup squad. Yet even then Henry's detractors were still on his case, and had he not completed what was a lengthy rehabilitation process under Tigana's watchful eye he might have buckled under the weight of expectation. He describes what he experienced in the build-up to the World Cup as 'real pressure. I was only nineteen, yet all the talk was about whether I was the right person for the job. It was very hard to handle. I was slaughtered if I had a bad game or missed a goal. I felt my career was going to be finished before it had started. But I came through that and learnt how to handle that kind of situation. It made me a lot stronger in my mind.'

It was his performance on the biggest stage of all that inevitably attracted the roving eyes of Italian giants Juventus. His sojourn in Turin was short (he lasted just eight months in Serie A) and not very sweet – hardly *la dolce vita* – but character building none the less. Now Henry maintains that 'Juve was not a regret. Under Lippi [his first coach] I did not play but under Ancelotti [Lippi's successor], I did. In Italy the games were tight, there was restricted space unlike in England where it is more open, and the defenders were more calculating. I learnt a lot which has helped me.'

All of which goes some way towards explaining how Henry was not only able to withstand the inevitable comparisons with Nicolas Anelka when he arrived at Highbury, but how his arrival almost immediately had the effect of ridding the club of the sour taste left by the Anelka affair. By mid-September the fans had begun to realize – after Arsenal beat AIK Solna in the Champions' League clash at Wembley thanks to late goals by substitutes Henry and Suker – that here was a player whose enthusiasm was the perfect antidote to Anelka's protracted and acrimonious departure.

Yet at the time of his transfer there was a concern that Arsenal were simply paying a lot of money to replace like for like. Here, once again, was a young Parisian (eighteen months older than Anelka) who had come through the National School at Clairefontaine but who, more significantly, had similar first-hand experience of the pitfalls awaiting those whose talent enables them to abandon their roots but whose immaturity can hinder their ability to deal with the subsequent fame and fortune. 'Why have we bought another Anelka when he pissed us off so much?' the fans questioned. 'He had no respect, so what is another French teenager going to do for us?'

Vive la différence. And the difference in this case is that while Anelka, for all his undoubted talent, was a loner who seemed to prefer his own company to that of his team-mates, Henry appears imbued with a rampant *joie de vivre.* He is eager, animated and gregarious, and possesses what Wenger likes to describe as a 'generosity of spirit' (hence the reason he has been able to pass off the constant comparisons with Anelka as 'OK, because Nicolas is my friend'). Wenger has identified the similarities between the two players as 'speed, explosive power, finishing, desire, physique and age', but the truth is that Anelka came across as a thoughtful, if sometimes indolent player as compared with Henry, who is a verit-able bundle of energy – all darting runs and gazelle-like leaps, a blur of both physical and mental speed (reminiscent of another former Arsenal striker whose natural enthusiasm and unpredictable nature, both on and off the pitch, endeared him to an entire generation of fans).

There is a Canal Plus film entitled *Dans les Yeux des Bleus,* a docu-mentary of France's World Cup-winning exploits, in which the clips of Thierry Henry perfectly encapsulate his character. Seasoned observers maintain that the inclusion of effervescent young players like Henry and Trezeguet in the squad was a calculated ploy on Jacquet's part to lift the mood among the more seasoned *habitués.* If so, it worked a treat, because Henry in particular views football as 'a group thing first and foremost. You can assert your individuality afterwards. We win together and we lose together.' The philosophy was no better illustrated than when he was injured after sixty-four minutes of France's second-round match against Paraguay and was carted off, his ankle iced up, to a medical room somewhere in the bowels of Lens' Felix Bollaert stadium.

For one so absorbed in the game as Henry, it was sheer purgatory. The camera shows him agonizing over the fact that he cannot witness the events unfolding out on the pitch, and the viewer winces as his inability to bear the frustration any longer forces him to hobble to an adjacent room where he can at least follow the proceed-ings on a television monitor. As the games wears on he increasingly resembles a jack-in-a-box, a bundle of nerves and pent-up energy, reaching such a state of high agitation that he is unable to contain himself when Laurent Blanc eventually scores France's 'golden goal' after 114 minutes. After giving the team doctor an enormous bear hug he limps in obvious discomfort back out onto the pitch to embrace his team-mates, to be a part of the celebrations. This in-group fervour perhaps goes some way towards explaining why he has fitted in so well at Arsenal, a club where team spirit has traditionally been the highest common denominator. 'I owe a great deal to Arsène Wenger,' he says, 'but not forgetting the quality players at Arsenal. Football is a collective sport. You don't succeed on your own.'

It seemed inevitable that Henry would eventual follow Wenger to Arsenal. He had, after all, publicly angled for a move to Highbury before Juventus snatched him away from the Principality, Arsenal's bid having been rejected. Yet the lure of Arsenal offered him more than just the chance to team up again with Wenger, whom he describes as 'very, very intelligent and very calm and wise'. When you consider that at Monaco he played to an audience which seldom amounted to more than 6,000, and that at the other end of the spectrum, at Juventus, he was just another fish in what was a very big pond then it becomes easier to understand why the middle ground of Arsenal held such appeal.

Players at both ends of the fame scale can tailor Premiership football to suit their particular lifestyle. How they deal with the publicity it can bring depends upon the disposition of both the individual and his club – they can choose to lap it up (David Beckham-style) or leave it (à la Dennis Berkamp). Couple this with the fact that the Highbury crowd has long enjoyed a reputation for being more respectful and tolerant than most and you have the perfect balance for a player like Henry, who quite clearly enjoys the public adulation his on-the-pitch exploits afford him, but who also values his privacy and anonymity. He lives in Hampstead and obviously appreciates being able 'to walk about where I want and people leave me alone. In fact, they are sometimes frightened of bothering you. In Italy that is not possible. Taking a quiet walk around the shops is not possible. Every time you go there are photographers. I feel very at ease here.'

By the same token he appreciates that the fans did not get on his back in the early days when his finishing left an awful lot to be desired (his first goal was the cracking winner against Southampton on 18 September). The English are 'more patient. In my first match against Leicester . . . they saw that I tried, that I was willing,' he says of the Arsenal fans. 'In Italy they were critical straightaway, questioning why they [Juve] spent that money.' At this juncture it is worth pointing out that Henry might not have fared so well had he gone to White Hart Lane. Arsenal fan Danny Peters summed up the difference by maintaining that 'everyone supported Henry, even when he was missing sitters, but look at the way Tottenham fans have treated [Chris] Armstrong. Crap or not you shouldn't boo him. If he's in a Tottenham shirt he should have your support. From what I've seen of him he always gives 100 per cent.' Indeed, the contrast between the ecstatic manner in which Henry celebrates a goal and the downcast reaction of Armstrong only serves to make the point, although in defence of Tottenham fans it is perhaps easier to tolerate one particular player's profligacy when he plays in a successful side and there are a number of other gifted individuals who are capable of hitting the target. At Tottenham there are no such luxuries. There is also the point that both sets of fans are less critical of their imports. Steffen Iversen is at times just as ponderous as Armstrong but doesn't have to suffer anything like the same level of abuse. Similarly at Highbury, Ray Parlour's mistakes are seized upon as evidence of a lack of technique, in comparison to his more illustrious colleagues, which is unfair, and also ignores his enthusiasm, workrate and positive intentions.

So the Arsenal fans can give themselves a collective pat on the back for the part they have played in allowing Henry enough time to acclimatize, although judging by Wenger's early-season prediction that it might take him a season to adapt fully to his new role he is obviously ahead of schedule. The fact that Bergkamp, Overmars and Kanu have been rendered peripheral figures by injury and international duty, while Suker has not been a regular-enough starter to stake a permanent claim to one of the striking berths, is further power to Henry's elbow. So well has he shouldered the striking responsibility, in fact, that whereas at the start of the season he was probably fourth in the pecking order, now Wenger's first-choice attack reads Henry plus one, and the Arsenal fans expect a goal every time he plays.

However, the footballers who do not have to work at perfecting their art can be counted on the toes of one foot and Henry has certainly toiled unstintingly to reawaken the predatory goalscoring instincts that had lain dormant during the four years that he spent hugging the touchlines. Shortly after arriving in England he admitted that he needed to 'rediscover the scoring instinct, that automatic reaction in front of goal', and to do that he worked with Wenger after training, studying videos to learn how strikers moved and what positions they took up. He also picked the brains of defenders like Martin Keown, who told his new colleague that the striker he most feared playing against was the one who made continual runs behind his back. 'If you come too deep defenders are happy because they can see you,' Henry learnt. 'When you play on the wing you have to come back and you touch the ball more. The most difficult thing is remembering not to do that, but to stay nearer the defender to make the run.' At Juventus, Henry's attacking instincts were dampened by regularly having to retreat to counter attack-minded full-backs like the Roma pair of his countryman Vincent Candela and Cafu. 'That,' he says, 'was not my natural game. I like to score goals and make them and I can do that now.'

However, it was evident from Henry's performance against Tottenham that he had added a physical element to his game. Frankly, he and Kanu took the supposedly immovable rock that is Sol Campbell 'on a tour of the pitch', as one Arsenal fan was later to recall it, 'and made him [Campbell] look quite pedestrian at times'. But then Henry probably looked at Alan Shearer, at Emile Heskey, even at Michael Owen – who despite his size can stand up for himself – and realized that to be a successful striker in English football you have to put yourself about a bit. No wonder, he admits, when 'in every team you are confronted by huge defenders like Campbell. You must learn how to tussle.' English football, he says, is like 'a game of street football – three tackles in a row and they're in seventh heaven', and it was that which forced him to adapt his style. In practice, it was brought home to him in no uncertain manner by Martin Keown's practical demonstration of what he would be up against. 'As a result,' he says, 'I have learnt to succeed by winning heading duels and knocking the ball down for my teammates.' Not only that, but by using his elbows and shoulders to good effect, too, as he demonstrated with one hugely effective shoulder charge against Campbell which knocked Tottenham's captain off the ball – no mean feat that – and elicited a huge roar of approval from the Arsenal fans.

'TH14' and most of Arsenal's fans are members of a mutual appreciation society. He has very quickly become their talisman, and rather sweetly described the crowd in the derby game as being *chauffé à blanc* ('really into it'). There is no doubt that the Arsenal fans are seeing the best of Thierry Henry when you listen to him admitting that 'I try things I wouldn't have attempted in France because the fans push me into it and you want to give everything for them. There is a wavelength between the players and the public at Arsenal, probably throughout England, which doesn't exist elsewhere.' No wonder, then, that he was so amazed to be confronted whilst out meandering around London by a smartly dressed businessman, who stared at the player for ages before unbuttoning his shirt to reveal an Arsenal shirt concealed underneath. 'He didn't even talk to me,' recalled Henry. 'He just showed me the shirt and walked off. It was incredible because the guy was in a suit with a briefcase. In France some fans don't even like to put on the team shirt to see the game.'

He was just as surprised by the pre-match atmosphere at Arsenal. 'I can't remember the song but in the dressing room before the first leg against Werder Bremen, Martin Keown danced in front of everyone and we sang and danced and applauded. It's strange to recount this because in France there is a different approach, an effort is made to concentrate. It doesn't perturb me though because I don't like to focus until I hear the whistle.'

Arsenal supporters won't thank anyone for mentioning Henry and Steffen Freund in the same sentence, let alone the same breath, not when you consider that Freund isn't every Tottenham fan's favourite beverage. Yet leaving aside his apparent shortcomings – which included, in his early days in England, a propensity for gamesmanship which annoyed fans of all persuasions as well as officials (one referee claimed that the Tottenham midfielder was 'always stirring things up') – Henry and Freund do share some common ground in that both have been overwhelmed and consequently galvanized by the reception afforded them by English fans (although it is tempting to say that Freund must have had low expectations, because he certainly does not have a comparable fan base at White Hart Lane to Henry's at Highbury).

When Freund flew in from Germany in December 1998, a £750,000 purchase from Borussia Dortmund, he arrived alone at Stansted airport without his family (who didn't join him for another three months). Now Stansted is not the most welcoming of airports. It's stark and miles from anywhere, and has none of Heathrow's characteristic hustle and bustle. Yet any trepidation Freund might have been feeling was dispelled by a Tottenham fan at the airport who, on recognizing his club's latest signing, went up to him, shook him by the hand and said: 'Thank you, Steffen, for coming to my club.'

Freund was flabbergasted. In Germany no such rapport exists between the players and the fans, whose tendency, he feels, is to be hypercritical. 'That would never have happened back home,' he says, maintaining that 'the fans are only happy when you win 5–0.' Given the lack of empathy, it is no surprise to hear Freund claim that Bundesliga players 'only move around for money'. It clearly bothers him how the fans react towards him, and he recalls almost wistfully the reception given to him by the Tottenham supporters when he took his seat in the stand for the derby at White Hart Lane (when suspension ruled him out of contention). 'They were singing at me and shaking my hand and waving and I was so happy,' he explains. 'It was heaven. I had goosebumps and my heart was beating very fast. As long as the Tottenham fans are happy, so am I.'

It's an admirable sentiment, but a small section of fans does not adequately represent the majority view. Tottenham fans used to feasting their eyes of the likes of Hoddle, Ardiles and Gascoigne had found it hard to warm to the midfielder whose bark, they believed, had been far more prevailing than his bite since his arrival at White Hart Lane. He had not exactly won many 'freunds' among the Tottenham support; they considered him to be over-excitable, prone to rash challenges and unable to dominate in midfield as they had hoped. It had baffled them that Graham, on signing Freund, had described him as 'the German Roy Keane'. Wishful thinking on Graham's part, surely? So far Freund's suspect temperament was the only thing he appeared to share with the Manchester United captain, who was his team's undeniable driving force. Freund, for all his enthusiasm, fell way short of Keane's standards on that front. In fact, Tottenham fan Mark Jacob, writing in *What's the Story, Boring Glory*, admitted amazement on meeting some fans 'who actually thought Freund was a good player'.

But it wasn't just Freund's ability that the fans questioned. It was his manner. They hated the way he would go down under the slightest challenge, as if the only thought in his mind was to get the perpetrator of the 'crime' punished. He had a nasty habit of getting involved in any feud that concerned his team-mates, and of brandishing imaginary cards, which in the vernacular of English football was 'just not on'. It had disgusted many Tottenham fans to see both Freund and Allan Nielsen doing just that during the Worthington Cup final in an attempt to incriminate Leicester players. Frankly, Freund paled in comparison with his compatriot and erstwhile Tottenham idol Jürgen Klinsmann (although it would take some player to match up to Klinsmann, whose popularity at White Hart Lane knew no bounds).

It certainly wasn't behaviour that Tottenham fans were used to, and some feared that the 'all for one, one for all' mentality that had been characteristic of Graham's Arsenal sides was beginning to prevail at Tottenham. Tony Adams recalls that under Graham Arsenal players would on occasion surround the referee in an attempt to harass him into giving a decision their way, while former Arsenal midfielder David Rocastle has admitted that 'if someone got tackled in a game then we all used to stand up for him and get rough'. Rocastle recalled being horrified at the sight of Patrick Vieira getting heavily tackled in his first derby game and no one on the Arsenal side going to help him. Rocastle admits to thinking: 'Hold on, what's going on here?'

Tim Sherwood has stood up for his midfield partner, claiming that 'if the opposition like Steffen then he is not doing his job properly'. Fine, but then there are plenty of players around who do their jobs properly without resorting to gamesmanship, and Freund's conduct during the Premiership match against Manchester United at White Hart Lane in October left much to be desired. First, he collapsed under the 'weight' of Roy Keane's challenge. He then ran thirty yards across the pitch to confront Keane, whose tackle on Taricco he took exception to, before wheeling away at the last minute with three United players in hot pursuit (which earned him a booking for 'threatening behaviour'). Taken at face value it was behaviour that would not have looked out of place in the playground but which had no place on a Premiership football pitch, although Freund later attempted to explain his actions – which would have been comical had they not been so hostile – by claiming that 'Keane fouled in a way that could have caused injuries.' And it must be said, this was another case of double standards as far as Manchester United were concerned. Alex Ferguson fumed about Freund's behaviour while his own players, Keane and Beckham, were guilty of reckless fouls.

It is so often said in defence of players who let their anger get the better of them that if you curb the aggression you lose the very essence of that player. So as witness for the defence, step forward former Germany coach Berti Vogts. Freund was a regular choice under Vogts in the German national side, so Vogts is better equipped than most to comment on what English fans perceive to be an undesirable trait that is being imported to the Premiership. Vogts says he watched the match (against Manchester United) on television and admits that 'Steffen did some things that I don't like to see. He is a typical German. He plays the German way and English people don't like that. He is temperamental and demonstrative but that is his way. He will be angry at times, running around the pitch and getting involved in everything but he has to play that way otherwise you will never see the best of him. Diving and trying to get opponents booked is not something I like to see but it is part of the German game and something a lot of players do.' Vogts added that he did notice Freund go up to Keane afterwards and offer his apologies. 'As far as he is concerned the game is over and there is no need to be enemies.'

Freund certainly has a problem channeling his exuberance in such as way that doesn't annoy both sets of supporters and the opposition, not to mention his own team-mates (he once had a well-publicized row with German international colleague Andreas Möller, who accused Freund of having an over-inflated ego). Yet in his own defence, Freund refutes the accusation that he is a dirty player, although he does accept that he is prone to over-reaction. 'I always go for the ball,' he claims. 'Passion, emotion, you can call it what you want. It's football. If I hurt a player when I am playing that makes it a bad game for me. I have respect for the other players on the pitch and I never go out of my way to hurt anyone.' In fact, it might surprise his critics to learn that he is often so troubled by his image that he seeks a second opinion on his behaviour (he admits that his wife, no less, rebuked him for his antics in the Keane incident). Besides, those who witnessed his reaction to being booked for a rash challenge on a Southampton player in the league match at White Hart Lane in March, when he accepted his punishment without any show of dissent before going across to shake the hand of his victim, suggests that, perhaps, the deutschmark is beginning to drop.

A player can temper his hot-headedness without compromising his ability, as Patrick Vieira has shown since his return from his seven-match ban. But unlike Vieira, who is as demure off the pitch as he is combative on it – there is an emotional edge to Freund which when viewed in the context of his personal life is positively endearing. Take him away from the charged atmosphere of a football match to a more relaxing environment and he is earnest, almost effusive in his emotions. Listen to him talk at length about his experiences in English football over a Dover Sole, at one of his and David Ginola's favourite haunts, Al Fresco in Whetstone High Road, and a picture begins to emerge of a man who is almost childlike in the intensity of his passion.

Those who know Freund well have attributed his desire to succeed to his background as a foundry worker in a sheet metal factory in his native East Germany. To get to the advantaged position in which he currently finds himself has been no easy journey. There are only a few East German footballers who have made their mark (not to mention their deutschmarks) in the west, Freund's mentor Mathias Sammer being arguably the most celebrated of them, and Freund is understandably so eager to justify his manager's faith in him that he will at times overstep the line.

However, kudos should be given when it's due. There are far too many foreign imports who come to England with no intention of doing what the Romans do in Rome. Like Klinsmann, who might just as well have been granted the freedom of London so unreservedly did he embrace the culture, Freund clearly loves his home from home, and got to know the city well during the first three months when he was staying in the Swallow Hotel in Waltham Abbey and travelling everywhere by Underground (he now drives a Mercedes, which is somewhat inevitable given his line of work but more excusable given his nationality). He is currently renting Ramon Vega's old house in Totteridge, in the road adjacent to David Ginola's, and his children are settled at the same school as Ginola's kids in Mill Hill. He is also extremely happy with his choice of Tottenham as his third major club (he started his Bundesliga career at Schalke 04 before moving to their fierce rivals Borussia Dortmund). 'I had been over five years at Borussia Dortmund and I was too cosy there,' he explains. 'I could have gone to Bayern Munich, say, but I had the feeling that I must change my country. That is a very important experience. If you stay your whole life in your own country then you can't understand the mentality or philosophy of another footballing nation. Spurs were the first club to come to me and I liked what I saw – the stadium, the training ground, the infrastructure [he struggles a bit with the language and this choice of word obviously pleases him]. It was better than Dortmund's. It was hard at first but I never had the feeling that I needed to cry [which is Freund's rather quaint way of explaining that he has never regretted the move to Tottenham]. I had said yes, so I give it 100 per cent.'

And, unquestionably, he is delighted to have ended up under the tutelage of George Graham, who he describes (after much searching around for the suitable English word) as a man who displayed an 'aura' that convinced Freund he was 'a winner'. He maintains that 'you can see it in his [Graham's] eyes. He wants to win titles and he wants success. Straight away I had the feeling that we could work together, that our philosophy was the same.'

Given this assessment it hardly needs stating that Freund's footballing credo is based on the group coming before the individual – 'Once you have the team working as a unit then the wonderful player like David Ginola becomes important,' he says, 'and that is when you win things.' Because, not to put too fine a point on it, Steffen Freund is as much George Graham's ideal player as Graham is Freund's ideal manager. In footballing terms they were made for one another. Just as at Arsenal, where Graham put great faith in his midfield workhorses, so he was inevitably going to be looking, as he told Freund, for 'two players in central midfield to influence the game from that position' for Tottenham. The appreciation is obviously mutual – given Roy Keane's reputation as Manchester United's talisman no manager will liken a player, as Graham has with Freund, to the United captain lightly – while for his part, Freund has complete faith in his manager, on and off the pitch. 'Rune Hauge [back in business after his FIFA ban, brokered Freund's deal with Tottenham] told me that George Graham came over to watch me playing against Kaiserslautern and immediately said yes for me. He is the most important person at the club, the main man.' Freund makes this statement with absolutely no hint of disingenuity. 'If I have a problem I would go to him and if he has a problem he comes to me. It is a compliment to me to hear him say that he didn't need to be able to talk to me because the most important thing is how you communicate on the pitch. He has the experience and it is important to have players who understand. If my head is not free then I play bad football. But I have had no problem with the football from day one. I give everything.' Definitely what the manager wants to hear.

Yet unfortunately for Freund, he suffers in much the same way as Tottenham's Argentinian full-back Mauricio Taricco, who has so far been found lacking when compared to the couple of pretty useful fellow countrymen who graced White Hart Lane in the late 1970s. Freund has a huge task to match, let alone eclipse, what Jürgen Klinsmann achieved. For a start, Klinsmann's travels via Monaco and (Inter) Milan rendered him more sophisticated and worldly-wise than most footballers, whereas there is about Freund a certain earnestness. He is almost too intense, too eager to please, although in mitigation he is hampered by the language barrier, which for Klinsmann was 'for sure' never a problem; when asked who he roomed with on Tottenham away trips he let slip that he had 'slept with' Korsten, Nielsen, Vega and Taricco. In essence, his sentiments off the field are as easily misinterpreted as his actions on it, and his reluctance to express his opinions for fear of being misrepresented is wholly understandable.

That said, his exuberance and his dedication to Tottenham's cause should never be called into question. Like most of the foreign imports he is hugely conscientious; he will not, for example, conduct interviews the day before a match because he says he needs to rest and focus on the game ahead. He is a good trainer, too, and runs daily of his own accord (if David Ginola were to look out of one of his numerous windows he might well spot the baseball-hatted figure of his team-mate jogging along the undulations of the South Herts Golf Club). Moreover, contrary to the somewhat xenophobic image of Germans that exists in this country, Freund has proved to be anything but set in his ways, as manifest in his acceptance of the English belief that the body needs time to recuperate after a game. 'For the body it is better to do nothing,' he acknowledges, 'even though for the head it is better to run.' He also goes to the gym at the same David Lloyd club that George Graham frequents, although Freund has not yet encountered his manager out of hours.

Those who judge a footballer purely by the image he presents on the pitch might have cause to take issue with this point of view, but Steffen Freund is essentially a thoroughly sound bloke. How many players would have responded in the way he did towards a family who confronted him at his local restaurant. Two kids, a brother and sister, brought over a paper napkin for his autograph. 'I can't sign this,' he exclaimed. 'Wait here,' he told them, and got up and dashed out of the restaurant, returning with colour photographs that he had ordered specially from the club and proceeded to inscribe two personal dedications. Unfortunately, however, the photos weren't the only thing he brought back from his car. He found that he had just got a £30 parking ticket, yet he actually seemed as pleased to be asked for his autograph as the whole family were with his kindness and consideration. (One Arsenal fan, on hearing the anecdote, remarked: 'I wish I'd never been told that. I don't want to like the bloke.')

Of course the cynics will say that he knows the value of good PR, in which case he obviously took that particular leaf straight out of Klinsmann's book. (Incidentally, Freund did not consult Klinsmann before he made the decision to sign for Tottenham because he wanted to 'have the right feeling on my own first'. However, he did call his compatriot on the day he signed the contract, to learn from Klinsmann that there were good people on the staff who understood football – although Klinsmann was obviously not referring to Graham, of whom he had no experience, but to long-serving employees like club secretary Peter Barnes and press officer John Fennelly, who was particularly helpful. (Klinsmann was particularly appreciative of Fennelly's efforts on his behalf, as unsolicited, he had taken the trouble of finding out Fennelly's address and sending him, as a memento, his 1998 World Cup shirt.)

But unfortunately for Freund, his attempts to curb his naturally combative tendencies have failed to diminish his proclivity to attract bad PR on the pitch, which is certainly what he did at Highbury. Mind you, if a footballer intends to pull in his horns he is hardly likely to come over all meek and mild on the occasion of a derby, and this was probably the one occasion in which the Tottenham fans would have excused Freund displaying the more irascible side of his nature.

What he actually did was snap at Vieira's heels in what appeared to be a calculated attempt to irritate the Arsenal man. It's easy to picture what his manager might say in the dressing room before a game, perhaps something about winding his opponents up in the hope that they would not be able to handle it. But if that was the case in this instance, neither Graham nor Freund had reckoned for Vieira's newfound composure. In fact, his admirable restraint, and the manner in which he exacted revenge on his undesirable shadow by exerting his customary influence on the match only served to highlight the difference in quality between these two defensive midfielders. Vieira was classy, constantly breaking up Tottenham's play and looking for the probing pass. As for Freund . . . well, A-plus for effort but somehow, like his team-mates, not up to scratch on the day. A frustrating set-back after their last result.

Tottenham had come into the derby following a 7–2 mauling of Southampton, their highest league victory since 1977 (when they scored nine without reply against Bristol Rovers). The game was a significant step on the path to rehabilitation for the much maligned Chris Armstrong, whose double strike suggested that he had at last rediscovered not only where the goal was, but his missing confidence too (one cheeky back-heel on the edge of the area almost set up Anderton for what would have been a beautifully crafted goal). Arsenal, moreover, would definitely be tired after their 2–0 victory over Werder Bremen three days beforehand in the first leg of their UEFA Cup quarter-final tie and besides, they had, according to one regular, 'a strange team out': no Seaman, Winterburn or Keown at the back; Ljungberg dropped in place of Parlour; with Bergkamp continuing his comeback by starting on the bench.

Stuart Preston in the *Gooner* also drew attention to the 'anxiety around Highbury until and unless we score'. 'If we concede,' he wrote, 'which we have been doing at an alarming rate recently, you know there is a mountain to climb.' Recalling Herbert Chapman's quote about a goal being merely the conclusion of a successful move, Preston lamented the fact that unless Arsenal score then 'all of our possession and passing and movement counts for nothing'. But he was not the only Gooner using the pages of the fanzine to sound off about the team's perceived inadequacies. Elsewhere, the 'Highbury Spy' claimed that 'Parlour will have to fight for his place next season with a top notch, right-sided creative player whose priority is to score goals'; that 'Ljungberg is the only midfielder who looks remotely like scoring and that's not good enough'; and declaring that 'if Suker can't hit a barn door from two yards with his wrong foot then sell him. This is AFC not Totteringham Resthome and it's about time Arsène felt a few collars and stopped pussyfooting around when it comes to getting the best out of the "untouchables".'

The Tottenham fans would give several limbs each to have such worries. Yet this apparent disquiet regarding team selection at Highbury served to give Tottenham heart where none might otherwise have existed. In fact, all except the profoundly pessimistic might have understood their optimism. They could certainly point to some good omens: Armstrong's return to form; Anderton's return to the side; Sol Campbell's pledge – according to a headline in *Sport First* – that despite alleged interest in him from Arsenal, he would 'never join [the] Gunners'. However, as is so often the case the headline told a different story to the one underneath, which reported that what Campbell had really said was that 'it would upset all the Spurs fans if I went to Arsenal – not that I am going to. I'll start thinking about my future at the end of the season. It's silly to let it affect me now.'

Ironically, the same Tottenham fans who had spent months complaining that the club had failed to sign a new striker were mightily relieved that Wimbledon's John Hartson had failed a medical in the week and was not now lining up for his debut against his old club in a Tottenham shirt. That scenario would have given the Arsenal fans another reason to poke fun at their rivals, since Hartson was never universally popular at Highbury.

Now there are times when one has to bow to a manager's better judgement when he signs a player who, in the fans' estimation, is not exactly what the doctor ordered, because on many occasions the manager does get it right. It's what he's paid to do, for heaven's sake. Conversely, there are times when fans can be forgiven for questioning their manager's sanity. On the evidence of Harry Redknapp's previously ill-advised foreign purchases, for example, who could have blamed any West Ham fan who had chosen to berate Redknapp when he signed the temperamental Paolo Di Canio from Sheffield Wednesday? (On this occasion the manager's gamble paid off for Di Canio has become the hero of the hour at Upton Park and was even a contender for Footballer of the Year.)

But the Tottenham fans were not prepared to give George Graham the benefit of the doubt on this one. They knew they didn't want Hartson playing for their club and they knew why. It wasn't just that he used to play for the Arsenal (of course that didn't help his cause, but then look at who they had been forced to accept as their manager). No, it was the fact that Hartson, who had inexplicably cost nearly £15 million in transfer fees since leaving Luton Town in January 1995, was simply not thought of as a Tottenham type of player. According to season-ticket holder Paul Stern he was 'a big bruiser'. As his father David asked: 'Where's the guile? We need to allay the fears that Spurs are no longer a big club by signing a world-class player like Sergei Rebrov to send out the right message.' As Ian Ridley questioned in the *Observer*, was it not now 'a waste of time' touting the Tottenham name abroad, about as fruitless as trying to export Rover cars?

It's a charge that one would expect the club to deny, and indeed David Pleat insists that 'it's still a great name.' But the fact that

Tottenham had been prepared to pay £6 million for Hartson smacked of desperate times calling for desperate measures and desperate money. Arsenal had picked up Kanu for a good deal less than that, while Leeds had paid £1 million less for Michael Bridges, a self-confessed Tottenham fan who had snubbed White Hart Lane for Elland Road where he had made an immediate impact. But the rumour was that the fans were not the only ones who weren't keen on Hartson. It was unsubstantiated, of course, but allegedly there were people at the top of the Tottenham hierarchy who had considered the transfer fee for Hartson exorbitant and had found a way of scuppering the deal; if that was so then at least they and the fans were singing the same song on this occasion, even if their agendas were totally different.

The rumour was fuelled by Jonathan Barnett, Hartson's agent, who claimed that Mother Teresa would have had difficulty passing the Tottenham medical. Presumably he was using her reputation for saintliness as a metaphor because physically even John Hartson was in better shape. But according to David Pleat, he was not sound enough to carry out the role 'to shake people up, knock people about' that George Graham had in mind for him. David Pleat recalls that 'we x-rayed his ankles and his knees, we never even got as far as his groin [he was actually sidelined with a hernia ailment] and we saw something very serious and it was a problem that hadn't been treated'.

In the event, Hartson's non-arrival at White Hart Lane delighted the fans but depressed the manager who had originally paid Luton £2.5 million to make him the country's costliest teenager. Ironically, the rout of Southampton came at the end of the week in which the deal fell through, but Tottenham's feat of scoring a goal more in one game than they had managed in the previous nine was fooling no one, least of all Graham, who pledged to keep up his search for added firepower. 'This won't make any difference,' he avowed in the post-match conference. 'We need more players and I'm looking to build now for next season. It's a slow process.' This was something of an understatement, considering the number who had been rumoured as coming to Tottenham during the course of the season but who had never actually got anywhere near the place.

Besides, it was only Southampton, once again resisting the spectre of relegation, who had been on the receiving end of a rout that Graham claimed 'had been coming for a while; we were due to give someone a hiding' and the reality was that in the early stages of the game there was precious little to choose between the two teams in terms of which abject defence was the worse. Had Glenn Hoddle had the rejuvenated Kevin Davies at his disposal, or more faith in the ability of Matthew Le Tissier to consider it worth bringing him on earlier then the story might have unfolded differently. As it was, there were more than just a few Tottenham supporters echoing the view of one of their number who described it as 'the worst 7–2 victory I have ever seen'.

So it was really only on paper then that Tottenham's chances against Arsenal appeared auspicious. But to add to the belief that this might finally be the season in which they landed their own scaled-down version of the 'Double' there was Graham's reputation as a past-master at organizing his teams for vital one-off games to throw into the equation. Perhaps Arsène Wenger recognized that, because he certainly tried to play down the game beforehand and take the wind out of Tottenham's sails by claiming that 'Chelsea are our huge rivals now because of their position in the table'. In theory he was right, but in practice these realities tend to be forgotten on derby day, when League placings and current form are consigned to the back burner for ninety minutes.

The Highbury clock read 3.01 p.m. when the first chant of 'Stand up if you hate Tottenham' rang out. Yet according to Arsenal fan Chris Parry, writing on the Arsenal web site, 'there was something very anti-climatic to a Spurs derby game that showed all the fervent atmosphere of a Wimbledon game . . . the players were crying out to be carried over the finishing line by a passionate crowd, but sadly apathy prevailed.' Parry went on to recall what he described as 'the hearty reaction of the Spurs fans to their win in November as compared to our feeble effort. Could it be that the Highbury crowd have become too blasé, or are such highly charged occasions a thing of the past?' Certainly Arsenal fan Mark Whitford thought so. 'It's just not the big game any more,' he said. 'Bring on United any day, a guarantee every time of a hard-fought, skilled encounter with a highly charged atmosphere.' A case, perhaps, of too many games, too much success.

Arsenal definitely had other things on their mind. Following the first-leg victory over Werder Bremen, perhaps they already had one eye on the semi-finals of the UEFA Cup, and there was still the prize of a Champions' League place to be claimed. Whatever the reason, the message appeared to be that Arsenal had bigger fish to fry. Gone were the days when the two sides were fighting for such consequential rewards as a Cup final place; against Tottenham there were once again just points and pride on offer.

 Of course, one of the traditionally spicy elements of a derby encounter is the feeling of antipathy that certain players instill in the rival sets of fans. Tottenham supporters have an aversion in particular towards the likes of Dixon and Winterburn, viewing them as competent rather than world-class performers yet for so long their defensive nemesis, as well as Bergkamp, conversely, because of his undoubted class (there is nothing like ability to encourage hostility). But the sobering reality for Tottenham was that their current squad contained only one comparable target. Whilst acknowledging Ginola's skill, what really gets the Arsenal fans going is what they see as a propensity to dive. Campbell on the other hand has earned their respect. 'Brought up as we are,' as Alex Phillips points out, 'to appreciate the art of defending ... where Spurs have recently got away with 0–0 against us it is as if he single-handedly kept us at bay.' However, there is no such grudging praise for Sherwood and Freund who are disliked by the fans for performing in much the same way as Graham Roberts and Paul Miller used to do.

Any sense of animosity felt by the Arsenal fans towards Ginola probably stemmed from the legacy of his ongoing spat with Lee Dixon. However, the two players were denied the opportunity to continue their hostilities on this occasion by Graham's canny ploy to play Ginola on the right wing in order to, as he put it, 'see just how good a defender Silvinho was'. The tactic certainly took Wenger by surprise. 'I expected Ginola on the left,' he said afterwards, 'but maybe George Graham knew that Lee Dixon knows Ginola very well, and in fairness Ginola made their goal.' But Graham's confession that 'I still don't know [how good Silvinho is]' was a thinly-veiled admission that Ginola's impact on the game had been as muted as that of his team-mates, none of whom was able to take advantage of Arsenal's lacklustre second-half display.

Naturally there were a few rare cameos from Ginola – the odd flash of dexterity, the odd sublime back-heel which found its target – but at this level that is not enough. Notwithstanding the fact that Ginola in top form and full flight is still a joy to behold, there may well be a case to be brought against him, particularly away from White Hart Lane, where he is inconsistent – breathtaking one minute, anonymous the next. What's more – and this criticism has even been whispered this season at White Hart Lane, where any slur against Ginola is akin to heresy – he looked to be carrying more weight than is beneficial for a player who relies on turn of pace and an ability to run rings around the opposition. Silvinho stood off him too much at times, notably in allowing him time and space to whip in the cross from which Armstrong scored, but generally it was a frustrating afternoon for Ginola, whose every touch was booed, and every misplaced pass or unsuccessful trick cheered.

'The boys showed good character today,' was about the extent of Graham's summing-up. 'We just need a bit more quality, because the commitment and attitude is definitely there.' Anyone listening must have felt like telling him to change the record, because he'd trotted out the same explanation so many times before this season. The fact that Tottenham could only muster two shots on target told its own story. For quality read guile and style, attributes that are conspicuous by their absence from the locker of N17's finest these days. Granted, Carr was characteristically energetic (even showing the more fiery side of his character in the scrap with Grimandi which resulted in the Arsenal player becoming the third man wearing red to see red in a north London derby in the season), but his team-mate on the opposite flank, Mauricio Taricco, was less effective. Taricco was Graham's first signing, which suggests that his manager is a big fan, but he has had a spasmodic impact on the side – good in patches – and does not appear to have the full quota of attributes that Tottenham fans have been looking for in a full-back for years. Yes, he loves to attack, but in defence he is less convincing, which is dismaying given that defending is precisely what he is paid to do. He naïvely chopped down Ray Parlour to concede the penalty which won Arsenal the game, and on one occasion he attempted a blatant handball – jumping for the ball as Alex

Manninger came out – that brought to mind the actions, fourteen years ago, of a certain, more celebrated Argentinian.

Frankly, no Tottenham player managed to stamp his authority on the game. Armstrong showed willing – his fourth goal in as many matches was a cleverly executed header – while Les Ferdinand, as one Arsenal fan put it, 'made a nuisance of himself' when he replaced the ineffectual Iversen after sixty-one minutes. However, in general the front men lacked any decent support from the midfield areas, where Freund and Leonhardsen spent most of the afternoon snapping at heels and chasing shadows as the sun gradually sank over the West Stand.

As for Darren Anderton ... wasn't this game set up for him? Wasn't this the perfect stage for him to signal his intent to the supporters that Tottenham was the club that he wanted to play for and win things with, and that they had better not think it was all just about money because that was not what motivated him at all. But Anderton did not take the chance. Far from being the leading light, he was almost inconspicuous, the game passing him by almost as if he wasn't on the pitch at all – which he hasn't been for 50 per cent of the time he has been on Tottenham's payroll.

Anderton's protracted contract talks, coupled with the revelation that he was allegedly holding out for a pay deal that would make him one of Tottenham's highest earners, had caused the fans to label him greedy and alter his nickname from the perennial 'Sicknote' to 'Banknote'. There were even fans who suspected him of shirking his duty, or deserting the colours: utter nonsense according to Anderton. 'I understand the fans are frustrated because they haven't seen me play as much as I would like. But how do they think I feel? It amazes me that there are people who think I don't want to play. That's too ludicrous for words. All I've ever wanted to do is to be fit to play for Tottenham.' Before the Spurs Lodge training ground opened, injuries were treated at White Hart Lane and Anderton can remember that after his session he would walk up the players' tunnel and stand on the fringe of the pitch in the empty stadium, imagining what it would be like to once again run out to the acclamation of the crowd on match-day. As his team-mate in distress Les Ferdinand has said: 'The best thing of course is to play. Failing that you want a place on the bench but if you are injured the nearest you can get to feeling a part of the action is to stand in the tunnel.' Smartly attired in a sober suit, Anderton could be seen supporting his team-mates from this vantage point. However, so bleak did the future sometimes appear that he would often drive the three hours to Southampton to the bosom of his family, making the return journey to White Hart Lane for physiotherapy the following day, to avoid sitting and brooding at home. Hardly the actions of a player who enjoyed his lengthy convalescence.

Indeed, five years ago when he was in a rich vein of form for both club and country, he admitted that dangerous tackles were what he hated most in the game. 'I've worked hard to get where I am,' he said, 'and it would be scandalous if some idiot went and ruined it.' But while it is undeniable that injury has cast a blight on Anderton's career since the start of the 1995–96 campaign (though he did manage 31 League games in the 1998–99 season before breaking down again just a month into the 1999–2000 season), one can understand the supporters being irate at someone who had been absent so often asking the club to pay him so much.

Many fans may have come round to the conclusion that he was just a 'fancy dan' and that the club would be better off cashing in on a player who, they joked, risked pulling a hamstring just by tapping the console on his beloved computer games rather than risk losing him for nothing at the end of the season. 'I'd boo him even if he signed a ten-year contract,' complained one fan moaning on the Tottenham web site. 'He's no playmaker. The only place he should play, if at all, is on the right wing as he is good at the early ball, but even that has become a rarity nowadays.' (Perhaps even this fan would have smiled had he came across the dramatic news flash which announced: 'Anderton signs contract' but continued underneath with the details: '. . . but fails the medical'.)

However, there had been glimpses of the versatility that had been missing presumed lost both during the few games Anderton had managed earlier in the season and since he had returned to the side in mid-January, which was no doubt what finally cemented the deal that gave him a one-year extension to his contract. He had actually hit back at the accusation that he was greedy when talking to Garth Crooks on BBC TV's *Football Focus* the day before the derby. Crooks didn't beat around the bush. 'Are you greedy?' he asked Anderton, who retorted: 'Obviously not. It's not just about money. There are other issues. I want to know if the manager's going to get the backing to strengthen the squad. I know he wants the top players here but that does cost a lot of money.' When Crooks asked him where he thought he would be playing his football next season he said: 'Tottenham. I think Tottenham. I'm very sure it will be Tottenham.'

Anderton did end up signing his contract – and a one-year deal was about the best he could have hoped for given the stop-start nature of his career – which suggested that he had been given the assurances he had been seeking over Tottenham's future. But it might not have escaped the notice of avid Tottenham watchers that Anderton had asked the same questions five years ago, when Manchester United had made overtures towards him. 'I spoke to Gerry [Francis] at length about it,' Anderton had revealed, 'and he said he wanted to build the team around me. I think that with a couple more players and a decent squad, we'd have a chance.' The same old song or what? It was this perennial shortfall in ambition that eventually forced Teddy Sheringham to pack his bags and take the route north to Old Trafford and the Treble that Anderton declined.

Still, Graham must have been pleased to retain Anderton's services for a further year at least – he had once likened having Anderton back in contention for a place to 'signing a new player' – although the same probably cannot be said for his chairman, who one can safely assume did not crack open his best bottle of bubbly while watching the ink dry on Anderton's new contract. He might have kept his mouth shut on this occasion but he has not done so in the past, once describing the player as a 'waste of space' who had cost Tottenham greatly in terms of lost potential. He probably wouldn't have been sorry to see the back of him, at a price. He was aware that in the words of David Pleat, 'a dangerous precedent might have been set. One year extra: where's the loyalty?' But in Pleat's view it was 'the best deal for us at the moment – if he plays he gets extra money. [Moreover] we have given George a breather; he has another quality player – a canny player, a continuity player – for a further year.'

To be fair, if the judgement of the last three England managers is not wrong (Kevin Keegan is also a self-confessed Anderton admirer) then a fit and in-form Anderton is a desirable commodity, although it does remain to be seen whether injuries have taken the edge off his ability. On the field he is blessed with an intelligence that enables him to spot the early ball and make the early run. That is undoubtedly why he dovetailed to such devastating effect with Teddy Sheringham, who won the domestic Golden Boot in 1992–93 thanks in no small measure to the fact that Anderton landed so many pinpoint crosses on his head. It is always said of Sheringham that he runs the first two yards in his head, and Anderton is similarly quick thinking (although as a former schools cross-country champion he is obviously no slouch either). According to a friend who watched Anderton develop during park kickabouts in Southampton, where he grew up, there is 'something special about the way Darren thinks about the game. His brain talks to his feet so quickly, just like when he plays on the computer and his brain talks to his fingers. That's why he's so good.' The assessment of Dave Hurst, the Portsmouth scout who spotted this scrawny kid with knobbly knees doing the business for Southampton Schoolboys, was that 'he couldn't run, couldn't tackle and was all arms and legs. He got knocked off the ball easily and didn't dominate games. But he could pass the ball perfectly and we had a feeling he was going to be a late developer.'

Anderton eventually played himself into the nation's consciousness during Portsmouth's 1992 FA Cup run, inspiring the Second Division club to a semi-final replay against Liverpool at Highbury where he scampered in from the wing to score a memorable opening goal (before Liverpool equalized and went on to win the tie on penalties). Several members of that Portsmouth team (such as John Beresford and Kit Symons) were snapped up by bigger clubs after that Cup run, but Anderton was the undoubted star of the show and it was no surprise when Terry Venables was first to get his foot in Pompey's door, paying £1.75 million for a player whose skills appeared ideally suited to the White Hart Lane stage, and whose loping gait and coltish, willowy frame led to immediate comparisons with a former favourite son, Chris Waddle.

Like Waddle, Anderton is at his most effective when cutting inside from the wing, but it is because he is a master of two trades that he suffers in the same way as David Beckham. Despite the fact that Sheringham (who might now have changed his mind having benefited first-hand from Beckham's accuracy) once described him as 'the finest crosser of a ball in the country', Anderton himself reckons he is more of a playmaker, so he was thrilled when Gerry Francis persuaded him to play a more central role during the 1994–95 season (as a member of Ossie Ardiles's 'Famous Five' he was more often given a role wide on the right). He is no shrinking violet when it comes to demanding the ball and clearly prefers the involvement of the midfield to being stuck out on the wing, where he claims 'you might not get a kick for fifteen minutes and have to rely on someone else to get you the ball'. However, George Graham will only say that 'Darren wants to play in the centre so I've given him a run there', which suggests that Tottenham's manager remains unconvinced that Anderton possesses the necessary attributes to be a key playmaker.

Anderton now had a major point to prove to both Graham (to whom he was grateful for his backing, not to mention his generosity in allowing Anderton sick leave in November which he spent in the Caribbean, returning reinvigorated and praising Graham's man-management) and to Keegan – with Euro 2000 just a few months away he was a player in a hurry. So no wonder he eagerly assumed responsibility for the majority of Tottenham's set pieces (they used to be Ginola's assignment, of course, and it may be more than pure coincidence that Ginola, who thrived on his star billing, had gone off the boil since Anderton's return to the side). Anderton had a decent claim, of course, for he can strike a ball sublimely, as Tottenham fan Bill Moth noted in an article in the Tottenham fanzine *My Eyes Have Seen the Glory*. 'It seems to me,' Moth wrote, 'that it is not just the Tottenham team that is going through a transformation into Arsenal circa 1987, but our fans as well. All this vilification of Anderton is unbelievable. What has the bloke done wrong? Got injured too much ... and wants the club to be more ambitious. He's reportedly settled for less than half what Manchester United pay Roy Keane. Not bad for an England international. Have people forgotten how good he was and will be again if he keeps on playing? Who else can strike a ball like the goal he scored against Leeds in the FA Cup last year? What disturbs me most is the way he was booed at White Hart

Lane while he was warming up recently. Here we have the grotesque spectacle of Tottenham fans presumably schooled in the tradition of quality touch players of the Anderton genre watching a Spurs team which includes the likes of journeyman worker-ants like Freund, Leonhardsen and Armstrong actually booing one of our last remaining class players. I doubt if the philistines would know that a bloke called Blanchflower once played for Tottenham. Anderton and Ginola represent the type of player that Danny meant when he talked about "doing things with a flourish".'

Anderton would no doubt react to the criticism by trotting out that most ubiquitous and infuriating of footballing clichés, the one about letting his feet do his talking. But in the modern game that is no longer enough. It used to be said in defence of footballers that they were paid to express themselves on the field, not off it, but the game has evolved into a far bigger beast now and the insatiable appetite of the press and its public, coupled with the hefty financial rewards on offer to those fortunate enough to play at the top level, means that players now have to fulfil their fair share of public ob-ligations whether they like it or not. In other words, Anderton has a duty to communicate with the fans, yet the feeling persists that he has constantly chosen to hide rather than come out and nail his colours to Tottenham's mast, except when a new contract is in the offing. Perhaps that is hardly surprising considering that Anderton is essentially a shy man who epitomizes the boy-done-good image of a footballer who has achieved a schoolboy ambition that once seemed unattainable.

To be frank he is not one of the game's most engaging personali-ties. He is not as personable and articulate as, say, Les Ferdinand, and he lacks the presence and confidence of John Scales. Moreover, his somewhat awkward manner, not to mention his appearance – the square, angular chin, the gauche frame – means that his shyness could never be passed off as being cool, unlike Sol Campbell who is unusually quiet but who exudes a quietly confident air none the less. At times he has resembled a kid let loose in a toy shop who can hardly believe his luck; he once admitted that he finds it 'weird to have all this money at such a young age', although that hasn't stopped him enjoying the financial trappings of his stardom. Far from it. Before he moved to his current home in London's

Docklands he lived in a large suburban house in Hemel Hempstead – it was recognizable from the outside by the lawn, which (his friends joked) Anderton had mown in circles to look like Wembley – with several of his mates, one of whose job it was to cook for the boys (having done the weekly shop with the 'housekeeping' provided by Anderton, playing the role of some benevolent, wealthy overlord).

It was a great life, if you like that sort of thing. The boys spent their leisure time playing endless computer games in a room Anderton referred to as 'The Museum' (it was a veritable shrine to his career, festooned with pictures of Anderton playing for Portsmouth, Tottenham and England, and with pennants and framed shirts), or driving around in the same model of brand new dark blue convertible Mercedes (a 500 SL without personalized number plate for fear that 'some Arsenal fan would have a go', but in Tottenham colours; his mum refused to let him have a green one) as Anderton had bought as a surprise for his dad. At the time he claimed that the only downside to his footballing lifestyle was the possibility of getting drawn into a scrap with Arsenal fans on a night out – 'you know, it's Arsenal this and Arsenal that and then it's all over the papers that you started a fight' – although he may now have changed that opinion given the catalogue of injuries that have left him out in the cold for so long. But now he had his new deal, and claimed that his plan was 'to put in a real solid conclusion to the current campaign, keep myself ticking over in the summer then have a good pre-season'.

However, such an agenda was likely to do team-mate Allan Nielsen's Tottenham career no good. Anderton had definitely profited from Nielsen's misfortune considering that the Worthington Cup match-winner was perhaps the one midfield player at the club to come anywhere near Anderton in terms of stamina and all-round support play. Yet Graham was clearly no fan of Nielsen's. Despite Tottenham's lack of strength in depth, the Danish international had started only eight games during the season, even though the likes of Leonhardsen, Freund, Anderton and Sherwood had all been out for lengthy spells. Most people expected that come the end of the season he would be expendable.

Not that he would complain, not if a move gave him the chance to resurrect his career (like Espen Baardsen, and Alex Manninger at Arsenal, he knows his chances of being selected for his country are limited by not playing regularly for his club). Talking after the game at Highbury, for which he was even overlooked for a place on the bench in favour of Stephen Clemence and Willem Korsten, Nielsen was remarkably sanguine about being given the cold shoulder by Graham. 'It's the manager's decision,' he said. 'He just doesn't fancy me. It would be all right if he played the squad system so you get thirty minutes here and there but this is totally unsatisfactory.' Unlike Baardsen, who was refused the opportunity of some first-team action with Chelsea earlier in the season, Nielsen was belatedly loaned to Wolverhampton Wanderers a few days after the Highbury defeat, giving him an outside chance of a bizarre 'double': selection for his country's Euro 2000 squad and helping the Midlands club into the First Division play-offs.

Korsten, meanwhile, had been given the moniker of the 'disappearing Dutchman' since arriving from Vitesse Arnhem (via Leeds). Injury had ruled him out of contention for a first-team start throughout the entire season, and he had little chance to make an impact in the derby, coming on with just four minutes left in place of Ginola after Luke Young had earlier replaced Campbell. Ominously the Tottenham captain left the field clutching his hamstring, although he had initially been forced to play on after Graham appeared to signal to him that he had to stay on the pitch. At one point Campbell even went over to the bench as if preparing to be substituted, only to turn back again, to the great amusement of the Arsenal fans. 'They must be desperate if Campbell has to play on when he's crocked,' jeered one fan, who had long since decided that Campbell was not as good as everyone else was sure he was anyway. 'Sol Campbell? No thanks,' he sneered. 'Henry and Kanu have torn him to shreds.'

Mind you, the Arsenal fans were less than happy that Wenger failed to take advantage of Campbell's injury by throwing on, say, Bergkamp or Suker to create a bit of havoc in Tottenham's penalty box, but instead replaced the tiring Henry with Nigel Winterburn. That left Arsenal with no outlet upfront and meant they were under considerable pressure in the last fifteen minutes, although

Tottenham were still unable to make their possession count. It bore all the hallmarks of a what-we-have-we-hold game-plan, which wasn't surprising considering that Arsenal had to travel to Germany for the second leg of their UEFA Cup tie against Werder Bremen four days later. Besides, they had done enough. The victory moved them up to third in the Premiership, two points behind Liverpool, and the irony was that Arsenal under Wenger had done what Arsenal under Graham became so adept at doing – ground out a victory without playing well.

They knew they had under-performed (with the exception of Henry, whom Wenger said 'had a tremendous game') and Wenger knew it too. 'I was pleased to just get through this and get three points,' he later admitted. Graham, though, also knew it, and in the away dressing room after the match his disappointment was almost tangible. 'He felt we had a good chance to win,' disclosed Steffen Freund. 'He told us: "Today was the day we could have won." ' Later, Graham replied to a journalist who put it to him that they – meaning Tottenham – had no midfield (which was why they failed to capitalize on Arsenal's tiredness): 'That's right, they were there for the taking,' not realizing he was talking at cross-purposes. The penalty he described as 'a killer blow'.

Later on, up in the VIP lounge at Highbury, Graham – who is not one for letting things lie easily – clearly had a point to make during 'a Tottenham meeting' (as he referred to it) to debrief his henchmen – Theo Foley, Chris Hughton and David Pleat – who were huddled together, deep in conversation. At least, Graham was deep in conversation; the others simply listened. He kept his voice low but it did not take a rocket scientist to work out that Graham was vexed that Tottenham had not taken advantage of Arsenal's below-par performance, and one suspects that the main source of his displeasure was once again David Ginola. You could hardly blame him for feeling let down by his player, after the decision to switch Ginola to the right wing had so obviously caught Arsenal on the hop, and after Ginola's cross for Arsmstrong's goal had got Tottenham back into the game at 1–1. That both Ginola and his team-mates had failed to seize the day was obviously going to ruin Graham's weekend.

Watching from the stands that afternoon was one former

Tottenham manager who had a very clear view on exactly what the problem was. For Peter Shreeves, it was ninety minutes spent watching a side who bore little resemblance to one he led to third place in the League in 1984–85. 'It's not the team I know,' Shreeves mused. 'I know George has made them tenacious and committed but where's the flair? There was no creativity from the midfield. George has made them a mid-table team. At least we had flair.' Like Alan Nielsen, Shreeves was also the recipient of a short-term assignment that came out of the blue. One minute he and his wife were chatting with Graham, Pleat and co., the next he was on his way to Sheffield to replace the sacked Wednesday manager Danny Wilson and attempt the extreme long-shot – preventing another of his former clubs from being relegated.

It was faintly ironic that Steffen Freund, so obviously hampered by the language barrier, should manage to sum up so succinctly just what was wrong with Tottenham's performance from a player's perspective. 'We had as good a team spirit as Arsenal,' Freund claimed, 'but we need one or two more strikers because you work so hard to close players down and win the ball and then you create the chance – and you need a world-class striker to put it away. I am not saying we don't have good strikers but if you want to be the best . . .' His voice trailed away momentarily before he offered this suggestion: 'Look at the Arsenal squad and you understand what I mean. It is important that we get the last step.'

One wonders what impressions of the Tottenham performance Alan Sugar took away with him from his vantage point in the directors' box in the East Stand. It was certainly a glum-looking Sugar who attempted to make small talk in the directors' lounge after the match, although Arnie Dein had some superficial success in lifting his mood. 'I went to the cemetery this morning,' Dein told Sugar, 'and as I was looking down at the people in the ground I had the thought that as long as you can look upwards, then you will be OK.' Sugar was forced to agree, although it is questionable as to whether he and the supporters agree as to what 'upwards' means for Tottenham. They will crane their necks and see the likes of Manchester United, Liverpool, Leeds, Chelsea and Arsenal forming an exclusive club at the top of the Premiership, with Tottenham desperately trying to cling to their boot laces. For

Sugar's critics, 'upwards' relates more to the price of Tottenham's shares.

Still, not everyone in the Tottenham camp was full of doom and gloom. Chris Hughton, who as a Tottenham regular during the FA and League Cup-winning seasons of 1981 and 1982 has known considerably better days, was put on the spot after the game when asked if he could still enjoy the job. Without hesitation he replied: 'Of course. I'm just happy to go to work and enjoy the fresh air, working with the first team, the reserves, the young players – they are all important if we are going to have a solid base.' Then he continued: 'It's been a better year than most, anyway, as we can see some players coming through and that's the yardstick for us.'

So could David Dein, as he watched his youth team put one foot in the final of the FA Youth Cup two days later by beating Middlesbrough 1–0 in the first leg of the semi-final, at Highbury. The club's young stars lived up to their burgeoning reputation, but there was another Arsenal player who caught the eye on the night, although not for his performance on the pitch. The increasing importance of Thierry Henry to the Arsenal cause was perfectly encapsulated in a vignette that involved Arsenal's man of the moment, and the club's vice-chairman, who bumped into the player on his way back up to the directors' box for the second half of the game.

It was as if Dein had been waiting for the appropriate moment to act out this little scenario, for looking around him for witnesses to what he was about to announce, he threw down the gauntlet, a twinkle clearly evident in his eye: 'I've never said this before, but here goes: it's 167 to go and five seasons to do it in [Henry has a five-year contract with Arsenal], starting from now,' he said. The momentary look of embarrassment that crossed Henry's face soon passed, to be replaced by a smile. 'OK, I understand,' he simply said, which he obviously did. Notwithstanding the fact that Henry has admitted to 'never setting myself targets', there can be few people connected with Arsenal who would fail to understand such an obvious reference to Ian Wright and his all-time club goalscoring record, least of all the player whom everyone – and not just the fans – is as one fan so categorically put it, 'desperate to become the new Wrighty'.

His point made, Dein turned away uttering the aside: 'I'd adopt him as my son, but then he'd want a rise.' After the events of the last few days Henry probably deserved one already.

CHAPTER EIGHT
BELIEVE IN ME

As an affluent, good-looking twenty-two year old residing in one of the most cosmopolitan cities in the world, Thierry Henry could have been forgiven for seeking amusement somewhere a good deal more convivial on a cold Tuesday night in the middle of March than Highbury, where the spectacle on show was Arsenal's Youth Cup semi-final first leg against Middlesbrough. Arsenal are, after all, his employers, and most employees would never dream of returning to the workplace out of hours unless the invitation was strictly compulsory (although it has to be said that for most, working days do not finish at lunchtime).

Yet after the Arsenal directors and club officials, journalists, scouts and mums and dads had finished refreshing themselves at half-time with the tea and sandwiches on offer in the East Stand (2,663 fans were congregated in the West Stand), many of them were amazed to be confronted by a tall, lanky figure loitering in the landing that separates the directors' and VIP lounges from the press area at Highbury. And, judging by the number of people who thanked Henry for his support, this was a particularly singular occurrence. 'I've rarely seen that before, a first-team player at a youth game,' said Amy Lawrence. 'Not even Tony Adams. It's a measure of how Henry feels about the club, of how much of a cult figure he's becoming, that he can be bothered to turn up.'

At what, if only in football terms, could be described as the ripe old age of twenty-two Henry had a good four years on the callow bunch of Arsenal youths who beat Middlesbrough that night, which in the context of life as a whole is a mere blip. There is really no discernible difference between an eighteen year old and a twenty-two year old other than a little more stubble and slightly more disposable income. Yet in this respect football has created its own ageism. You only have to look at Henry's impressive case history to realize that four years represents a long enough timespan for a footballer – if he's good enough – to assemble a decent collection of medals, a whole heap of experience and a very healthy bank balance.

So Thierry Henry was very much the elder statesman at Highbury that night. Clearly an interested observer he was, none the less, not just present to set a good example and make up the numbers. Of course, Henry might simply have been displaying unusual empathy, given that he was once a teenage star himself. However, the most significant factor about his presence on the night was that he represented the link between Arsenal's present and its future. However much the here and now mattered, the future was pretty damn important too, and those preoccupied with short-termism had better not forget the old adage – and the currency we're talking here is in footballers – about the pounds taking care of themselves if you look after the pennies first.

In other words, it is all too easy to claim that a football club is in rude health simply because its first team have enjoyed a productive season. The longer-term prognosis is significantly affected by the quality of the players coming up through the ranks. How many can realistically be expected to climb to the top of the pile instead of being tossed onto the scrapheap? If Arsène Wenger is to be taken at his word, there is at least a chance at Highbury. On learning that Manchester United were prepared to break the British transfer record for PSV Eindhoven forward Ruud van Nistelrooy, he was moved to say: 'We will not be spending £18 million on a striker. We are more likely to spend £1.8 million or even look for him in our youth team.'

A club can bring in costly reinforcements all it likes but in these days of spiralling transfer fees and wage bills it is the young players who also represent the lifeblood of a club. Consider what happened to Newcastle when they infamously disbanded their reserves under Kevin Keegan's management, so fixated were they on the more immediate success of the first team. It was a move that left non-playing first-team squad members feeling disenchanted and distanced, and young players coming through without a means of assessing their readiness for first-team action. It took two seasons of heartache – not to mention a pile of dirty laundry regularly being washed in public – before Bobby Robson's arrival immediately restored some equilibrium and the importance of a playing structure beneath the first team at St James's Park.

Actually, Henry's commitment to the cause was not really surprising. On the contrary, it was typical of the dedication that flows through Arsenal, as exemplified by the fact that the club directors were once again out in force on the night. Looking like plutocratic soul brothers in their matching navy blue overcoats and bright red scarves, Messrs Dein and Fiszman sat alongside managing director Ken Friar in the directors' box. There was a constant stream of chatter concerning the merits of the play and the performers which occasionally involved Liam Brady, the head of youth development, turning round from the row in front to add his invaluable two-pennies' worth.

At Highbury they have always placed great store by the youth, long before a side containing five home-grown players won the League so memorably up on Merseyside a few years ago. So those supporters who watched Don Howe's shaven-headed boys outmanoeuvre and out-muscle Middlesbrough on the night – Arsenal's 1–0 scoreline flattered the visitors – would have realized the importance of being able, as one fan succinctly put it, to 'look to the future and feel good about it'.

However, even having got this far (with the creation of academies in 1998 boys can be attached to clubs from as young as nine) these footballing apprentices can only ever possess potential. Not even the most astute coach can predict just how a schoolboy superstar will react in front of 40,000 hostile fans; and the fact that around three-quarters of players taken on by clubs at sixteen are not rewarded with a full professional contract by the ages of eighteen or nineteen (by contrast Ajax, who set the standards by which other youth policies are both judged and then fall short, estimate that over half of their young players will make the grade) points up the harsh reality behind the glamorous façade. The route to stardom is littered with the names of those whose dreams were never realized: England internationals like Terry Venables, Steve Perryman, Clive Allen and

Martin Peters – all Tottenham players, ironically – who also represented their country at schoolboy level, are few and far between.

Yet notwithstanding the long odds of a top-flight future, there was obvious class running right through Arsenal's side, class which had underpinned their success throughout the tournament. Youth coaches are always loath to highlight their prodigies for fear of overburdening them, but it would be an atypical fan who was not roused by the sight of a promising youngster, particularly nowadays when so many clubs opt for the quick-fix afforded by an experienced (yet sometimes distinctly average) foreign player instead of risking an inexperienced yet talented kid.

So Arsenal appetites were understandably whetted by the versatile German full-back Moritz Volz; by Italian centre-half Niccolo Galli, who appeared to possess the full quota of characteristics one readily associates with Arsenal centre-halves – including dominance in the air and steely commitment – and looked a more than competent footballer; by David Noble, brimming with imagination and improvisation in central midfield; by the outstanding Jermaine Pennant, whose wing-play was a joy to behold – the modern game is poorer for the dearth of that breed nowadays – and left no one who witnessed it still questioning Arsenal's sanity in spending more than £1 million on a sixteen year old; by the honest endeavour allied to mental and physical speed of Irish Under-21 International and Youth Cup captain Graham Barrett (who had already made his first-team debut). And by the craft of England Under-18 forward Jay Bothroyd.

There are those in the game who erroneously write off the FA Youth Cup as a meaningless competition. However, while the Youth Cup is something of a misnomer in that the players – drawn from both the Under-17 and Under-19 sides because there is no official Under-18 league – are unlikely to be regular team-mates, it is actually so competitive that if Arsenal get past Middlesbrough (and Middlesbrough can boast in their line-up their own million-pound player for that is how much Argentinian Carlos Marinelli cost) and win the cup, then they are entitled to feel pretty good about the future judging by the fate of the immediate past winners. Just look at West Ham, who swept Coventry aside in 1998, inspired by the gifted Michael Carrick and a kid called Joe Cole who looked pretty useful too (both players have now starred in the Hammers' first team). Or at Leeds, whose 1997 nucleus – Jonathan Woodgate, Harry Kewell, Stephen McPhail and Matthew Jones – is now an integral part of David O'Leary's first-team squad. Or at the Liverpool class of 1996, which included youngsters like Jamie Carragher and Michael Owen, now crucial cogs in the Anfield resurgence.

Liam Brady sums it up when he admits that 'at this age, results don't mean a thing, but they can demonstrate that you have good players and good coaches'. Brady is the man charged with nurturing the Arsenal stars of the future; as such, he has what David Dein describes as 'the most important job at the club'. Yet Brady, in that typically under-stated way of his, plays his role down, which isn't to say he underestimates its importance to the club's long-term success. 'I do have a very important job,' he affirms, 'and I think we are making really good progress. In the next two years I hope to have the satisfaction of seeing the boys get into the first team. That's always the criterion, but at Arsenal there's a double criteria – they have to be good enough to win trophies. They are not there to get into the first team and get sold on.'

Stephen Hughes might disagree with that. Hughes spent four seasons with his foot stuck in the first-team door at Highbury, but after being loaned to Fulham was eventually sold to Everton (where he is likely to be a guaranteed starter) for a sum which might eventually amount to £3 million, despite the existence of a gap on the left of Arsenal's midfield which prompted Arsène Wenger to buy Stefan Malz (who on the evidence of his Arsenal career to date is some distance from commanding a first-team place). In the club's defence Brady claims that 'we did not have a player ready for Stefan Malz's squad place, but next year we will'. Furthermore, that he believes that Arsenal have 'not produced the right kind of player in the last seven years', and that 'at the end of the day Hughes was not good enough. We have to produce better than him as often as we can' says something about the comparative standards required to make the grade at Highbury and at Goodison Park.

Brady, of course, knows what it takes to make the grade, although he was fortunate to be born with a talent that earned him the right to be talked about in the same breath as other virtuosos like Hoddle and Platini. A waif-like figure with unexpected physical strength, sublime natural balance and an even more sumptuous left foot, Brady waltzed into Arsenal's first team in 1973 at a time when the successful side of the early 1970s was in transition. And if *Carpe Diem* ('Seize the Day') is the motto for any aspiring young footballer on the brink of a breakthrough, then Brady did just that. 'When I came in, Arsenal's team was maybe suffering a hangover from the great years that had gone before,' he recalls, 'but I just wanted to get out there and show people what I could do. If you're going to have a career in football you've got to be able to handle so-called pressures, things like playing in front of a big crowd for the first time . . . all I could think was what an opportunity – let's make the most of it.'

Don Howe, the former Arsenal manager and England coach brought back to Highbury as head of youth coaching by Brady (who describes Howe as 'one of the best coaches I've ever worked with') claims that it was Brady's will to win as much as his sublime skills that made him such a complete player. Courage is never one of the first attributes that springs immediately to mind in recollections of Brady the player, but Brady had bags full of the stuff. In Italian they call it *coraggio*, and the Juve fans will forever remember how in 1982, with Juventus needing to beat Catanzaro to win the Scudetto in the final game of the season, they were awarded a penalty. All Juve's all-star side except Brady cowered in the face of such pressure and he stepped up, took the kick and scored to secure the 1–0 win. And this from a player who had just found out from the agent Dennis Roach (not even from the club itself) that he had been rendered surplus to requirements by the purchase of Michel Platini, and would not be playing for *la Vecchia Signora* the following season.

No wonder then that for Brady, character is as crucial in the armoury of any young player as touch, pace, control or any of those attributes that might stand out among a bunch of raw fourteen year olds but which count for nothing if he then cannot handle the demands that are an occupational hazard for professional footballers in the twenty-first century. 'Most people can spot talent,' Brady acknowledges, 'but it is how it develops and the personality and character . . . different positions have different requirements and it's about having the expertise to spot real potential and work on weaknesses to make them complete. It's no good having first touch and control if you don't have the brain to use the ball the way it should be used.' Unsurprising this, from a player who gave the impression he could deliver the ball onto a daisy-head with his eyes closed, but vision is paramount, and he maintains it 'is evident in a player from a very early age. I could take you to an Under-13 game and tell you which player had it and who didn't. It's something that can be improved on. It's all about thinking about the game.'

There was and will always only ever be one Liam Brady, so more than just a few young players will fail to live up to the high standards demanded by him. When you were that good you are bound to be disappointed by young pretenders, and perhaps Hughes came into that category – for he is undoubtedly a gifted player. There is a suspicion, too, that Jay Bothroyd may be about to emulate Hughes if he is not careful; that in Brady's book there might just be a question mark against his attitude. Technically-speaking he is a thrilling prospect. What's more, he has, according to Brady's right-hand man and former Gunner David Court, 'as good a left foot as you'll see'. But he is also languid, and Brady – who has taken more knocks on the managerial merry-go-round than he ever did on the pitch and is therefore more hardened and cynical than he ever was in his playing days – probably doesn't like languid very much.

However, just as Brady will not single out any individual for especial praise, so he will not criticize any either, preferring to take the more tactful line that 'Jay has good vision but needs a bit of time yet.' What he will say is that 'it is our job to iron out the weaknesses so that they don't have problems when Arsène Wenger gets them. This is a performance-related industry – it's the same at Aldershot as at Arsenal – and if you get into the squad you have to take your chance. I'm confident we have the players to do that. Looking down the age scale I'd say every position is covered. The benchmark is what Alex Ferguson did at United. In striving to get his first team right he made sure his youth policy was following on behind and we want to get ourselves into that position. I think we can.'

On a personal level the transition to the other side of the touchline was not smooth sailing. Brady returned to his spiritual home in August 1996 after two unhappy managerial sojourns, the first north of the border in charge of Celtic – which was a thankless task given

Rangers' total domination, and exacerbated by internecine bickering in the Parkhead boardroom – and following that, down on the south coast at Brighton. For a man whose playing career had reached such heights – a seven-year odyssey in Serie A incorporating Juventus and Inter – these were lows of the kind that he had never before experienced. It is telling that he now admits to missing the dressing-room banter, but never 'the sleepless nights, the problems with newspapers bending stories or players asking for transfers, or the highs and lows of winning and losing'. His appointment suited Arsenal as much as it did him, and although it went largely unnoticed the significance of the 'signing' could not be overstated. As one fan put it at the time he was 'Arsenal by name and European by nature', and thus the perfect ambassador to impress upon prospective starlets the special status of the club.

Once in place, he discovered a bunch of young players who were 'good quality, but nothing exceptional'. The years since Arsenal won the Youth Cup in 1988 (with a side that included Alan Miller, David Hillier, Steve Morrow and Kevin Campbell), and the Championship the following season with the likes of Paul Merson, Micky Thomas, Tony Adams, David O'Leary and David Rocastle, had seen the production line grind to a near halt; of the victorious Youth Cup-winning side of 1994, only Stephen Hughes had progressed to the fringes of the first team, so Brady makes no bones about the size of the task that faced him. 'I knew we had to invest substantially in our youth policy,' he says, 'to get better quality boys and improved standards of coaching. I looked at the situation for several months and decided to bring in new coaching staff – notably David Court, who is an excellent administrator, and Don Howe.' The choice of Howe was crucial given that Brady's remit does not include day-to-day coaching. 'I wanted someone of real calibre and it's a bonus to have him [Howe],' is Brady's view on his former boss, who presides over a network of coaches responsible for players aged from nine to nineteen.

The investment, in terms of time, effort and no little cash has brought about, in Brady's words, 'a tremendous improvement in facilities [which will be further augmented by the completion of a new training complex at Finchley in north London equipped with five- and seven-a-side facilities, and two artificial pitches] so that we are now really attractive to boys in terms of their development.' However, the key for Brady is that a boy should want to come to the club, not because of the facilities or the financial rewards that might one day be his, but because of what Arsenal stands for. 'When you grow up with a club and you end up winning things, you are from that club,' he has said. 'I was produced here, formulated here. I'd been coming here since I was thirteen and I only ever wanted to sign for Arsenal. When we brings boys over from Ireland or other parts of the country it's important they get to like the club immediately and they say, "When I leave school I would like to come here." That's what I call the "treatment" I had at Arsenal.'

The success Arsenal have achieved under Arsène Wenger has enhanced the club's profile within the game to such an extent that Brady's idealistic goal is no longer the pipedream it might have been viewed as in the dark days, when every mention of Arsenal was automatically prefixed by that 'boring, boring' tag. However, before the establishment of academies – which came into being following FA Technical Director Howard Wilkinson's Charter for Quality – there were so many grey areas surrounding youth football that a club could no longer rely solely on kudos and clout when it came to procuring the best young talent. In fact, it had started to mirror the senior game to such an extent that the idea that a player might choose a club for love rather than money became totally passé. Laughable even. Notwithstanding the fact that there were regulations governing transfers, the brown envelopes and bungs that characterized the era pre-Premier League became as prevalent in youth football as they were in the senior game. Once the academies were up and jogging, the grey areas were gone and in their place – reality. Brady himself spells it out in black and white. 'Football has changed,' he admits. 'Once the name of Arsenal was good enough for a boy to want to join, but things changed when you could offer a boy a professional contract [which becomes operative on his seventeenth birthday]. These days, if you want to secure the top talent then they would have to have a contract clearly in place by seventeen or eighteen, whereas before I arrived they wouldn't be offered a contract until after they had proved themselves. So the ones who were sought after – like Nick Barmby – would go elsewhere'; the implication being that there were substantial rewards 'elsewhere' that were too good to ignore. The fact that Barmby was wooed and lost by Arsenal as a schoolboy was 'a huge disappointment' according to David Dein; that he went to White Hart Lane just added insult to injury.

In theory no club can line a boy's pocket until he reaches sixteen, when if he is retained he gets offered a standard three-year scholarship (which replaced the old YTS scheme) which gives his club time to assess whether or not he is likely to succeed. The best of the bunch will be offered professional contracts early during their apprenticeship, and while there are three levels of pay according to age – modest three-figure sums here – there is the promise of more to come as and when potential is fulfilled and it's fair to say that a Joe Cole will overnight earn the equivalent of a senior manager in industry as a result of his first professional contract.

At the other end of the scale, the majority will be released, and many of those end up drifting away to clubs in the Football League where the grounding they've had invariably stands them in good stead. Brady cites the example of former Arsenal youngsters David Livermore, now at Millwall, and Richard Hughes and Jamie Day, who both went to Bournemouth, predicting that 'they'll find it easy, because it's hard here.' The point is that just as it always used to be said of boys schooled in the best tradition of Tottenham Hotspur, they were technically gifted enough to flourish at a lower level should they fail to become first-team regulars at White Hart Lane (the likes of Jamie Clapham at Ipswich and Darren Caskey at Reading prove the point), so now the same is true of boys whose formative footballing years have been spent at London Colney. Indeed Livermore, a useful enough defender, was apparently destined to turn professional with Tottenham until he defected to Arsenal, whereupon it transpired that almost the only contact he had had in two years with Tottenham's head of youth football John Moncur was when Moncur discovered that the player was turning his back on Tottenham in favour of their rivals. Given that Tottenham's attitude was allegedly so slipshod, it was no surprise that Livermore's father raved about the set-up he encountered at Highbury, although it should be remembered there are usually two sides to every anecdote. On behalf of a brother of an Italian friend who was a semi-professional footballer back home, Arsenal fan Alex

Phillips wrote to about twenty clubs in the south to ask if he could come over for a trial. The only reply he got was from Theo Foley of Tottenham, who personally rang him up.

Bill Hollingdale, who spent years spotting players for Brady's predecessor Terry Murphy, talks almost wistfully about Arsenal's youth set-up under Murphy, who instilled in his posse of coaches and scouts an attitude that Arsenal were different. Arsenal were the establishment club who exemplified the old school. Arsenal didn't have the flash-Harry attitude that characterized some of their rivals. Antiquated though it may now sound, Arsenal's image was one of benevolent aristocrats who were extraordinarily solicitous of those in their employ, and they firmly believed that the club's name and reputation should be enough to lure any aspiring young footballer to Highbury.

Which was all well and good until money – and bags of it – began to flow into the game following the creation of the Premier League and the subsequent commercial revolution that gave football a draconian face-lift. As other clubs began to realize that money was going to be the key to success at all levels of the game – which did not preclude paying veritable fortunes for boys who were hardly able to tie their own laces – Arsenal kept their feet firmly routed in the past. Murphy, who Hollingdale describes as 'an excellent man who really cared about the kids and was a superb judge of character' apparently failed to keep up with the times in being reluctant to offer the kind of 'incentives' that would keep the most talented boys at Highbury. Murphy wasn't being precious – there was a practical point to his principles as well. Referring to today's cradle snatching, he reflects that of the many youngsters he cast his eye over 'only four fourteen-year olds – Tony Adams, Stewart Robson, Nicky Barmby and Michael Owen – showed the maturity and strength of character to convince me they could go the distance . . . Paying money is a gamble,' he hesitated to take, 'because the best at sixteen are not necessarily the best at eighteen.' As a result, many flew the nest. 'I remember Michael Owen well as a thirteen year old,' Hollingdale recalls, 'because he was considering Arsenal at that time. He starred in a game between the north and south when the south lost 6–5 and he was so downcast at losing that you'd never have guessed he'd scored all five goals. So we knew he was going to be special even then.'

Not special enough, evidently, for Arsenal to try to secure his services in the now accepted manner of modern football, for which Murphy eventually paid the price. He was sidelined during Bruce Rioch's managerial regime, and although David Dein kept him on to help set up Arsenal's academy, he eventually severed his ties with the club and took his expertise south of the river to Wimbledon. 'In the end,' Hollingdale recalls, 'the people Arsenal wanted had to be pragmatic – more in touch with the idea of buying young talent. But do they really understand youth football? You have to be brought up in it to understand how it works.' Hollingdale worries that the buying in of players at both senior and youth levels blocks the progress of home-grown talent, and also risks creating dissension in the ranks when the players Arsenal have invested heavily in are seen to be getting favourable treatment. 'I watched an Arsenal reserve game recently in which a number of Arsenal's Under-19s were playing, along with Martin Keown, who was rehabilitating after injury,' says Hollingdale. 'Because they have more time and space at that level, the likes of David Noble made Keown – who was their midfield partner that day – look a donkey. These young players should be encouraged and given their chance, yet what do the club do? They buy Stefan Malz and then play Nigel Winterburn in midfield, so what chance is there for young players seeing that, and watching their peers being favoured because they cost a lot of money?'

Brady, though, has a definitive answer to that criticism. 'If we bought a player with a big reputation and guaranteed him a contract, yet he didn't look any better than any of the others, then we would have a problem,' he agrees. 'But anyone can see that Pennant has the potential to go all the way. He has a high level of skill and speed. You might not see him for long periods in the game but when he has a spell it can be a match-winning spell.' That Arsène Wenger clearly views Pennant as another from the stable that has already produced Nicolas Anelka and Thierry Henry – players who possess a devastating combination of speed and skill – is evidence enough to suggest that Arsenal deemed it worthwhile investing an inordinately high sum of money for what at this stage is still only exceptional promise, as well as time and effort into helping Pennant overcome what Brady describes as 'a difficult upbringing, and teaching him the professional side of football'.

Hollingdale's is an honourable sentiment, but an outmoded one none the less. The knowledge that he must wake up and wince at the news that Arsenal have spent over £1 million on a slip of a lad is not going to prick the conscience of the Arsenal hierarchy, who have long since adopted the stance that if you can't beat them, then not only must you join them but you must show them the way forward too. Arsenal are now recognized as being in the vanguard of both fostering and forking out for the best young talent at home and abroad, and if there are those out there who cry foul at this practice then they only have to consider the progress Arsenal have made at every level over the course of the last five years to realize that their protests will fall on deaf ears.

Seventeen-year-old full-back Volz was originally spotted by Arsenal scout Steve Rowley playing in a tournament for Germany's Under-16s and persuaded to choose Arsenal, thus becoming the first German youth player not to sign for a Bundesliga club. He's just one of a plethora of young footballers to have come into this country from the continent, now a regular recruiting ground for British clubs, but the trend has caused controversy. Last year the French Sports minister Marie-George Buffet pleaded for 'the trade in children to stop', claiming that 'young talented players are treated like commodities. The trade raises serious questions about sporting ethics.'

At face value, one has to question the morality of uprooting young foreign players when the ink on their passports is barely dry and their command of the language so limited (although in some cases their vocabulary is considerably better than their English counterparts). Is it really fair to expect them to settle far away from their families and friends, particularly given that the likes of Pennant – who at least is English and can live with his family (he actually lives with his aunt) – can find the going tough in what is a high-pressure industry, even at this level?

David Court, however, refutes the suggestion that this is improper practice. For a start, Arsenal's 'bread and butter' is still predominantly London. Moreover – and he does wonder if the club have been lucky in this respect – the foreign boys on Arsenal's books are 'incredibly mature and a delight to work with'. Niccolo Galli, whose presence at Highbury is down to the friendship between Brady and Galli's father – a goalkeeper who played for Internazionale and Torino, as well as for the national side in the 1986 World Cup finals – speaks perfect English and lives with Paolo Vernazza's family (Vernazza himself is a London boy through-and-through but his antecedents are Italian so at least there is, as Court puts it, 'a cultural link'). Volz too (who lodges with team-mate Graham Barrett) speaks fluent English and along with Galli and two of the other imports attends Westminster Boys tutorial college in South Kensington, where they arc 'keen students'. Besides, as Court points out (without a hint of superciliousness), 'Most of our boys are internationals so get to go home regularly to play for their countries anyway.' Clearly, while Arsenal is not exactly home from home for some, every effort is made to ensure that the boys feel at ease within the fold of the same 'Arsenal family' ethos that left an indelible impression on a certain young Dubliner all those years ago.

Arsenal's attention to detail is such that they have even established a relationship with a comprehensive school, Highams Park, whereby a dozen boys attend that one establishment as opposed to any number of disparate schools. That arrangement affords the club, in Brady's words, 'more quality coaching time with the players'. Not even Leeds, whose academy – established by Howard Wilkinson – has regularly been cited as the standard-bearer for this new generation of footballing breeding schools, enjoys the benefits of a similar set-up to Arsenal in that respect.

Alan Hill, the Leeds United Academy director, undoubtedly speaks for all his colleagues when he states that the aim of the academy is 'to produce top quality Premiership players, but failing that we hope we can produce people who are able to obtain a quality job away from football having had a good broad educational base. It is all about developing good professional footballers and good members of our society.' Hill goes further, maintaining that the academies are 'the best thing that's happened to English football'. He cites one of the key reasons that the Europeans have been so far ahead of us technically is that 'they've had access to kids for the last twenty years, whereas we've only just started. But I looked at our Under-8s last year and again last week, and the difference in a year makes the hair stand up on the back of my neck. I'm sure we will be a world force in eight to ten years as the academies will produce the type of players we're looking for.'

It was clearly a series of exemplary academies such as those run by Arsenal and Leeds that Les Reed envisaged when he first began assimilating information gleaned from the set-ups at Ajax, PSV, Barcelona and the two Milan clubs in order to come up with what he describes as 'an academy model for England'. Both Arsenal and Leeds, according to Reed, along with Liverpool and of course Manchester United, have 'gone right the way down the academy concept. They have taken the bull by the horns and invested heavily in terms of both staff and players, and as a result their infrastructure and their facilities are spot-on.' They have in fact become what Reed describes as the 'super academies'.

A softly spoken and thoughtful individual, Reed was originally in the FA's employ in the mid-1990s, as regional director for the southeast, but his frustration at the inflexibility of football's powers-that-be at the time – and the fear that his avant-garde ideas on the game's reformation might never see the light of day – prompted him to leave the FA and take on the role of first-team coach of Charlton. Whilst at the Valley, he was able to nurture a thriving youth policy – even though he also suffered from a serious illness which did nothing to dent his unbridled enthusiasm for the game, and from which he has now thankfully fully recovered – and when the call came from Howard Wilkinson offering him the opportunity to use his expertise on a much bigger stage, Reed felt that 'although it was a big gamble, I would never have forgiven myself if I'd passed up the chance'.

As the FA's director of technical development, his role alongside Wilkinson was crucial to the academy cause, both in terms of 'selling' the idea of academies to the clubs and, subsequently, establishing and maintaining the standards at those clubs who have embraced the concept. Reed estimates that there will be more than 50 in operation by the start of 2000–01, since 'many more clubs have taken up the challenge than we expected. It's a good thing, but it has created a monster which needs servicing all the time. In five years we might have the best facilities in Europe, if not the world, and we have to make sure we keep up in terms of our training, standard of coaching, programme development, educational welfare and so on.' He predicts that over the next ten years those clubs who find they cannot sustain the financial support for an academy will drop back in the Centre of Excellence scheme – which is to all intents and purposes the academy second division – leaving around thirty 'super academies' to attract the very best players and ensure, as Reed puts it, that 'the cream will always float to the top'. The next challenge, he declares, 'will be to maintain that as a healthy youth development programme'.

On the basis that few would argue with the assertion that a Dutchman or a Frenchman is born with the same inherent skills as an Englishman, then it had to be the English system – rather than the kids that was the obstacle. As Reed maintained at the time: 'I've worked with boys all over Europe, and nobody's telling me that their eight and nine year olds are any better than ours. It's just when they get moved up our pyramid that they get crippled.' Trevor Brooking, one of the most naturally gifted English footballers of the last three decades – who cares that he 'stung like a butterfly' (according to Brian Clough) when he had all that vision and poise – supported Reed's declaration by claiming that 'by the time the boys turn professional they've got into such bad habits that coaches have to work on basic techniques like controlling the ball. So the clubs are taking the boys younger and younger because at sixteen they're not up to scratch. They'll be at the maternity wards next.'

The predicament was exacerbated by the quality of coaching in this country at that time (and which is only now starting to be adequately addressed thanks to the latest blueprint to come out of the FA under new chief executive Adam Crozier) and also because clubs had such limited access to schoolboys, who came under the jurisdiction of the English Schools Football Association (ESFA). Under the old scheme, the professional clubs continually had to grovel to the ESFA, whose insistence that football was of secondary importance to a decent education meant that any time that was granted was strictly limited to a couple of hours a week. As a result, even the gifted boys relied for their early footballing tuition on well-meaning but ill-qualified teachers, or the dad of their mate who ran the local Sunday League side in his spare time, where 'Get stuck in' was about as constructive as the advice got.

Consequently, it was not uncommon for the most promising young players to have to endure a gruelling schedule. Southampton's Sheffield-born striker Kevin Davies, who was given his chance by former Tottenham striker John Duncan at Chesterfield, recalls training three times a week after school at Sheffield United's Centre of Excellence, and playing two matches a weekend for his Sunday League side Brunsmere Athletic and Sheffield Boys side. With a schedule like that was it any wonder that Davies was eventually rejected by the Blades for 'lacking pace and aggression' – not qualities that a thirteen year old should be assessed on in the first place? How was it that most English clubs placed so little store by their youth policies and those who staffed them – it's doubtful that Davies would have been rejected for lacking the afore-mentioned qualities by a coach with a better-trained eye for what constitutes potential in a thirteen year old – while in France, for example, a modest club like Nantes managed to be so far ahead of the times?

Nantes had been reaping the benefits of its *Centre de Formation* – an academy set up to discover and develop young talent – for over a decade before the penny dropped with English clubs. Its recent roll-call of honour include Marcel Desailly, Didier Deschamps, Christian Karembeu, Patrice Loko and Reynald Pedros – interna-tionals all. (Incidentally, the success of the Nantes prototype prompted the French Football Federation to rule that every club should have a *Centre de Formation.*) Auxerre, under the astute management of Guy Roux, are renowned for a similarly productive set-up which has elevated the club from the equivalent of Ryman League standard to the Champions' League in under twenty years.

Even the Scandinavians have recognized for some time that a flourishing breeding ground makes sound economic sense. According to Lars Andersson, a director of Swedish Division One side Landskrona Bols, selling to survive is the principle that governs the existence of most clubs in Sweden's lower leagues. As such, Andersson admits that 'we have established for some years now football schools run by the club for players as young as six and upwards'. As ex-Tottenham defender Gary O'Reilly, who works in Nike's youth development programme, noted in his piece on the subject for *Match of the Day* magazine, it was 'bad enough that the Swedes have given us Ikea, Volvos and Ulrika Jonsson. The realiza-tion that they're now giving us better footballers – and will continue to do so for years to come – should be substantive food for thought.'

It was clear that there had to be change to the structure of English football. Years out in the wilderness after Heysel, and the collective – and eventually cathartic – soul-searching that was a consequence of the Hillsborough disaster meant that English football re-entered the European fray at the start of the 1990s to find that its former sparring partners had moved up a weight. This was the footballing equivalent of Rip Van Winkle. Europe had stolen such a march on England in terms of coaching that factors such as diet, alcohol intake, training regimes and more holistic methods of rehabilitation had all been embraced by Europe's top clubs in an attempt to step up a gear and steal ahead of the chasing pack. The English game, for all the clichéd 'fire in its belly', had been left floundering in the wake of this cultural revolution.

As a result, Italy, Holland, Spain, Germany and France dominated the final stages of European club competitions during the 1990s. Sweden and Bulgaria, traditionally regarded as footballing makeweights, got as far as the World Cup semi-finals in 1994. Germany and the Czech Republic contested the final of Euro 96 (although England reached the semi-final, those with non-selective memories will note that they actually got lucky against Switzerland, Spain and Scotland – who knows what might have happened had Gary McAllister not missed that penalty – and failed once more to beat Germany, and that their only victory of note, although it was a high note, had come against the Dutch). France, meanwhile, won the World Cup on home soil in 1998 with a blend of seasoned campaigners like Desailly and Deschamps, products of the afore-mentioned youth scheme at Nantes, and young, talented players like Henry, Pires and Trezeguet. Frankly, it was no good English football boasting to the rest of the footballing world that its Premier League was the biggest and the best when both its clubs and its national side were conspicuous by their absence from winners' rostrums.

The obvious solution, of course, was for English clubs to foster enough – and more crucially – good enough English talent to enable them to promote from within rather than having to purchase from abroad. And that, in short, is the rationale behind the academies. As yet they are still in their infancy, but there's plenty of evidence to suggest that the tide is slowly turning, that English football's approach to youth development is no longer an easy target for those worthy critics who still lambast the English way. On the contrary, Les Reed discloses that there has been 'a lot of interest from abroad about our academies, many foreign visitors wanting to come over and learn from our set-ups'. Not surprisingly, a good deal of those interested parties have come from Germany, where the national game is currently experiencing a steep decline in home production. Long term, that might actually mean that England's manager – whoever he might be in 2006 and beyond – will not have to 'watch the First Division for a lot of his players' as the current incumbent Kevin Keegan recently predicted, but will have a large pool of talented, academy-groomed Premiership players at his disposal. Reed sums up the progress thus: 'We obviously couldn't send the boys down to the beach to play, or start recreating shanty towns, but we could do something to start catching up in terms of the technical development – the number of games, the structure of the syllabi, the quality of the coaching – of boys between the ages of eight and twenty-one. And with the academies, we have done that. At last we have a good platform and it's looking good for 2004, 2006 and the future. We are moving into being European and world leaders.'

The fundamental idea of the academies, of course, was that for the first time clubs should have total control over their hand-picked boys from the ages of nine to nineteen so that they could control their tuition – on the football field and in the classroom – and hopefully instil in them the necessary skill and spirit to make it all the way to the top, to the ultimate benefit of both club and national side. In other words, as Peter Suddaby, Tottenham's Academy Director puts it, the 'academy ethos is to look after the whole boy, not just the footballer in the boy.'

Suddaby, a remarkably young-looking fifty-one, is as far removed in footballing terms from Liam Brady as it is possible to get. While Brady knew, almost from the moment he could feel movement in his left leg, that it was to be a footballer's life for him, Suddaby was ambivalent. Brought up in North Wales, he admits to 'playing football every spare minute', but only because 'that's what kids did; we never thought we could earn a living from the game, especially since football didn't play a major part in the environment' (the nearest 'major' footballing city was Chester). In fact, having been turned down by Arsenal at 17 he claims he was 'not too disappointed because I was always going to university. All my mates were going and it was a natural progression.'

It wasn't until he was twenty-two, having obtained an honours degree in mathematics at Swansea University and a Certificate of Education at Oxford, and represented both the British Universities side and England at amateur level, that Suddaby signed professional terms for Blackpool (he was originally spotted playing centre-half for Skelmersdale in a side that included future Liverpool stars Steve Heighway – now the club's Academy Director – and Brian Hall). 'Blackpool offered me three years but I only wanted a one-year contract,' he reveals, 'which amazed them. But I wanted to be sure that if I didn't like it, I could leave. I only signed for £5 a week more than I could earn as a teacher so it wasn't the golden goose. The rewards were nowhere near as great as they are today. But it worked for the first year so I played for twelve.' Those twelve years took in over 300 appearances for Blackpool and spells at both Brighton and Wimbledon; after retiring Suddaby graduated to coaching, and was for a while Alan Mullery's first-team coach at Brighton (this was at a time when Blackpool and Brighton were not the small fry they are today) before coaching Tottenham's Under-15s on a part-time basis for six years and fulfilling roles within the youth set-ups at both QPR and then Chelsea.

Given Suddaby's perception of football as just part of life – albeit a very important part – rather than life itself, he is an ideal choice to oversee an establishment from which there is bound to be a high fall-out rate. Like Brady, he would never underestimate the importance of his task, which he defines as 'producing good team players for Tottenham'; it's just that he is anxious to play down the hype that would have the academies churning out Michael Owens by the cartload. 'There is no guarantee that an academy will produce a Ginola or a Joe Cole,' stresses Suddaby. 'They are extreme talents who don't come along every year. Of course we're always looking for the gems – and who's to say we don't have some in the younger age groups – but what we can produce are good solid Tottenham Hotspur players with a feel for the club, players who might never be man of the match but who will always be the first name on the team sheet.'

There is a distinct echo here of the George Graham philosophy as evinced by his purchases since becoming Tottenham manager.

Moreover, the cynics would suggest that Suddaby faces Hobson's choice because of the dearth of quality young players in Tottenham's ranks, in stark contrast with the abundance of talent at Arsenal. Where, in other words, are the Hoddles and Campbells of the future when you need them, as Tottenham so clearly do? Is the problem that the name of Tottenham is no longer a big enough draw for wannabe footballers, who look at the way Tottenham teams perform these days and do not like what they see?

That, precisely, is what Chris Waddle fears. Personifying the style which used to be Tottenham's, Waddle admits that he joined the club from Newcastle in 1985 simply because 'I loved the way they played'. In those days, Waddle maintains, the club 'had a reputation for producing excellent footballers. Good technical players, but players who were also entertainers, like Glenn [Hoddle] and Micky Hazard. Clubs knew that if they took on an ex-Spurs kid that he'd have had a good football education, but there's been a steady decline at Tottenham over the years and because so many other clubs are playing good football now Spurs have found it hard to trap decent players. Sure, they seem to be investing heavily, but other clubs are investing more. Besides, it annoys me that they have to buy in young players, particularly foreign ones. When I was at White Hart Lane it was always us and Arsenal, neck and neck, but I can't see Spurs either producing a player as talented as Glenn or investing millions in a player as gifted as Thierry Henry. And that's sad.'

You wonder if Suddaby might be about to dodge the issue in claiming that football is cyclical, and that the barren spells that clubs suffer at first-team level can also afflict them lower down the ranks. After all, he asks, 'when was the last time a kid broke through at Manchester United? You can't repeat success like they had year after year and we've not done too badly when you consider that Ian Walker, Sol Campbell, Luke Young, Stephen Clemence and Stephen Carr have all come through.' But he is pragmatic enough to admit that Tottenham do not currently have a crop of players, particularly at Under-18 level, that is comparable to Arsenal, or even West Ham. 'I am not going to sit here and say that we are on equal terms,' he admits. 'We have a bit of a lull at that age group, perhaps because we weren't as aggressive in scouring the place for the best kids in the past. But that's changed now. We've also become more aggressive financially in competing for young players and working rewards into their scholarships.'

And about time too, observes Gary O'Reilly, who points out that 'if Crewe Alexandra can reach the semi-final of the Under-19 and the final of the Under-17 academy league [Tottenham fell at the first hurdle in both play-offs which follow the 22-match league season] then there is no reason why Tottenham should not do just as well. The next eighteen months will show whether Tottenham can match the immense leap forward shown by Arsenal.' (Crewe, of course, have long since realized that their livelihood depends on them regularly producing and then selling on quality young players like Danny Murphy and Seth Johnson to Premier League clubs. Yet if Crewe were a French club then they would doubtless have benefited from the democracy of the French League and emulated the success of a like-minded club such as Nantes.)

It sounds incongruous, this idea of Tottenham employing financial clout to secure the services of young players, given that they have been so conspicuously niggardly in beefing up the first team. But Suddaby's revelation does explain why David Pleat, who has the final say on young players, has recently taken his personal pot of spending to almost £5 million with the signings of Anthony Gardner (from Port Vale), Matthew Etherington and Simon Davies (from Peterborough), Dave McEwen (from Dulwich Hamlet), Swedish Under-17 captain Jon Partin and, most recently, Gary Doherty (from Luton Town). Quite simply, it would appear that there are not enough young players of sufficient quality on the Tottenham conveyor belt. It is not just that the club are unwilling to highlight individuals – which is an admirable enough sentiment – just that there are no individuals worthy of highlighting, save perhaps for 18-year-old Johnnie Johnson, the only professional to be taken on from the academy this year, whose performances on the left side of midfield have impressed George Graham, and who has featured in the reserves as a left-back.

The Under-19 side, comprised in the main of Under-18s because it is the club's philosophy to encourage the Under-19s to fight for a place in the reserve team which Suddaby maintains is 'better for their development', had 'a mediocre season'. Then there's this 'bit of a lull' at Under-18 level – Tottenham made little impact in the

Youth Cup, put out by eventual finalists Coventry in the fourth round – and it wasn't much better at Under-17 level, where only seven boys were taken on this year and the side did 'quite poorly' over the course of the season. No wonder George Graham has acknowledged that there was 'more work to do at Tottenham than when I took over at Arsenal'.

But in defence of this poor record Suddaby points out that the Under-17 side was essentially an Under-16 team, while the same applies to the Under-18 and Under-19 sides – both apparently handicapped in terms of results by virtue of them being packed out with younger players. In other words, results can distort the real picture and damage a club's image, so much so that Suddaby has even campaigned against the publication of league tables at this level. 'Fans,' he points out, 'will look at the tables in the programme and think that the youth teams are not up to much, but they do not appreciate the full story. Firstly, no team plays the same fixture list as the other teams within their academy league – you play twenty-two matches, of which about twelve are within your own division, but the rest are against teams from outside that division. Secondly, the teams are packed with under-age players, so no wonder they do not compete as well. You have to ask: what are we trying to do? What is the point of the academies? Not to win their respective leagues, but to produce some really good players for the first team.'

If Suddaby is at pains to hammer home this point it is because 'I got my fingers burned in the past over this issue'. It's all very well having a star team that sweeps all before it at youth level, he reasons, when the reality is that players from one particular team very seldom progress together through to the senior ranks. 'I had one of the best Under-15s that has been at this club for a while,' he recalls (this is his second spell at Tottenham), 'with Quinton Fortune, who we brought over from South Africa as a fourteen year old [and who is now at Manchester United]. But out of that team very few really good players emerged. They complemented one another as a team, but the bottom line is that they were never going to progress as an entire eleven. They move on as individuals and then have to stand out on their own. You can say, "Well, he can do this, but not that" and that's not good enough. In the end the smallest number of trainees ever was picked from that outstanding team. The objective is to develop players as individuals, and if as a by-product they win their league then so be it. At youth level it's all about development, whereas in the first team it's all about results. Yes, it's about entertainment too, but if you entertain but keep losing, then people will very soon get fed up.' What is left unsaid is that at Tottenham people will get fed up even sooner if you hardly ever entertain at all.

The problem, of course, is that development takes time, and time is a precious commodity at any level of football nowadays. 'Give us time' should be the mantra for all football clubs and their managers because people – be they supporters, directors or shareholders – all want success and they want it now, not one, two or five years down the line. And yet the academies are still very much in their infancy; as Suddaby concedes, there is 'a lot of tinkering and fine-tuning to be done before we can all sit back and say, "Yes, this is working really well." That won't be until ten years down the line. We are still making mistakes. After all, we were so far behind and all of a sudden the idea of the academy has come in and the clubs have been given this huge responsibility and it's quite daunting. Frankly it's a massive change and we aren't going to get it right now. It would be conceited of us to think otherwise.'

An indication of the size of the task facing those entrusted with establishing the academies came when the FA announced, in 1995, that they were raising the age of children playing small-sided football from nine to ten. Hardly revolutionary this, considering it had been common practice on the continent since the year dot, yet well over 300 parents protested vociferously outside Lancaster Gate and had to be placated by then England manager Terry Venables, who asked them: 'If you didn't have a ball would you use a tin can?' and 'If there were no goalposts would you use jumpers?' When they answered yes he said: 'So why are you worried about the size of the pitch if you'll do anything to play football?'

Further evidence of how long old habits take to die has been provided by the academy directors, who will tell tales of being approached by parents, anxious that the shift away from the treadmill of Sunday League and schools football on full-sized pitches to the academy method – where the emphasis is on carefully controlled training and five-a-side games to maximize technique – was actually going to harm the development of their precious (and maybe even potentially priceless) boy. It is clearly a long road ahead, even more so if one accepts Suddaby's description of the thrust of the academies as 'a culture of learning'.

Of course the predicament particular to Tottenham is that the 1990s was a decade of such steep decline – from high stock to laughing stock in ten years – that it would never have been possible for a manager to blood a crop of youngsters even if there had been a decent enough crop to blood. In essence, it's fine to introduce young players if the first team is doing well, but frankly, that has not been the case at White Hart Lane since Gerry Francis's side tottered around the top of the Premiership towards the end of 1995, and even then one got the impression that Tottenham were never going to last the pace, because they never do. The fans do not tag it 'White Hart Pain' for nothing, and in these days of high-intensity, high-scrutiny football there is too much at stake, too much riding on every game for clubs in precarious positions (like Tottenham) – the manager's job, the chairman's reputation, the star player's contract – so the easier option is to buy tried and tested players who will do the business immediately and never mind that their stays are usually transitory, their commitment transient. (Although when the established players have manifestly failed, the fans would probably be more tolerant of the team's performance if the manager was brave enough to ring some youthful changes.)

Suddaby actually believes that the ultimate aim is to drip-feed young boys into the first-team squad and if you can achieve a rate of one per year then 'you are doing quite well'. But it does, he stresses, 'depend on the manager and the climate at the club. If the club isn't in a comfortable position then it's very difficult to introduce young players because the pressure is so great. Look at Arsenal. Having won all those trophies they've every right to introduce some youngsters, whereas if you're fighting relegation and you bring in youth and it doesn't pay off, then you're hung. Besides, Arsenal have been very successful under Arsène Wenger but I'm not so sure that many of their players have come through the youth system ... everyone says it's very good but if the manager is not conducive to using talented youngsters then what's the point?'

The point is, of course, that the appointment of Wenger was crucial to Arsenal, both in the short and the longer term. Almost immediately, Wenger managed to amalgamate his foreign signings with the incumbent home-grown stalwarts to devastating effect – the Double – while longer term he has fashioned the club according a philosophy which translates itself at every level. Thus, in the image of their first-team elders and betters, the successful Youth Cup side is an eclectic cocktail made up of local brew – youths like Bothroyd, Jerome Thomas and Noble – laced with an exotic twist, as represented by the likes of the Italian Galli, the Brazilian Da Silva Filho and the French youngster Aliadière.

Graham's apparent reluctance to give regular first-team football to Leeds' youngsters Jonathan Woodgate, Alan Smith and Stephen McPhail, all of whom made an immediate impact at senior level after David O'Leary gave them their chance, led to Graham receiving widespread criticism. However, Suddaby dispels the notion that Graham does not favour throwing young players in at the deep end by inferring that it is just a popular misconception. 'You have to question,' he muses, 'whether those kids were really ready while George was at Leeds? It is always a gamble to blood them – even Alex Ferguson got lucky in that his hand was forced by injuries when he risked that group of youngsters in the Coca-Cola Cup in 1994 and they played brilliantly, making it impossible for him to ignore them. There's certainly never been any suggestion here that George is anything other than very enthusiastic about incorporating the young players, and he is in contact with us every day, keeping an eye on the boys' progress and asking questions.'

However, it is no coincidence that Woodgate, in particular, made his Leeds debut almost as soon as Graham's bag was packed, and very soon played his way into the full England squad too. Yet in Graham's defence he can hardly be blamed for the lack of any Tottenham fledglings of note – striker John Piercy got the occasional run-out earlier in the season but has subsequently taken a back seat once more – and the insufficient quality of the players knocking on the first-team door explains the recent influx of young players like Etherington, Davies and McEwen, none of whom took long to make their first-team debuts.

This is a crucial point, though, particularly if one subscribes to David Pleat's view. For all his reputed failings – and the Tottenham faithful would have one believe, somewhat unfairly, that he has many of them – Pleat does have a justifiable reputation for having a marvellous eye for a young player and an inherent appreciation of what will make or break that player. He claims it's 'all about opportunity, about getting sympathy from a good coach; that's what will make Gardner, or Etherington or Davies. Talent stands out, but it is the manager's reaction to that talent and how he encourages it that's key. If a young player doesn't get his chance between the ages of eighteen and twenty then you might as well say goodbye. There is a period when a boy has to have that opportunity otherwise you lose him. He gets dispirited and despondent and goes down a scale.' As an example Pleat cites the case of Danny Hill, who made just a handful of first-team appearances in a decade for Tottenham before being loaned out to various clubs. It is Pleat's opinion that Tottenham 'kept him too long in the reserves'. Could the same be said about Stephen Hughes at Arsenal?

To be fair to both club and manager, the one player widely tipped to make the breakthrough in 1999–2000 was defender Ledley King – heir apparent to Campbell if you believe the hype – but he has been sidelined through injury and as Suddaby explains, 'That kind of setback can mean the difference between people saying the youth system is good or bad.' It only took one tip-off from Tottenham Under-19 coach Pat Holland, who told Graham he thought King 'should be thrown in', for Graham to throw King in at the deep end – and they don't come much deeper than Anfield, in front of 44,000 (at the end of the 1998–1999 season). King, 6ft 2in, and blessed with as much composure as you will find in a twenty year old, is in Holland's words 'a real footballer' in that he can play the ball out from the back, so there is the merest glint of a silver lining in the cloud that hang's over Sol Campbell's possible departure.

King is not the only one, maybe just the only truly promising one. There's also nineteen-year-old defender Alton Thelwell, who has been loaned to a Swedish club to gain experience, and striker Peter Crouch, twenty, although there seems to be some doubt over whether he will have the physical attributes to mix it at the highest level. Yet one gets the feeling that had either of these been good enough they would have been considered old enough; that new boys like Etherington and Davies have jumped ahead of them in the pecking order tells its own story.

In fact, following the defeat at Highbury, abysmal performances against Watford (1–1) and Middlesbrough (2–3) encouraged the promotion of the former Peterborough pair to the first-team team sheet and they made their Premiership debuts as substitutes during the 2–0 loss at Anfield. They were emulated by Dave McEwen a couple of weeks later in the 1–1 home draw against Derby at the end of April. It could therefore be argued that Tottenham were even ahead of Arsenal in espousing the cause of the young as their counterparts were unlikely to feature as prominently in *Monsieur* Wenger's end-of-season plans. But then, seemingly as always, Arsenal had something to play for: a Champions' League place and a UEFA Cup final. Moreover, as Gary O'Reilly comments, 'Arsenal will look to buy in above (the Under-19 Level) but they will expect maybe four or five to graduate to the first team and even if they don't they will get their money back', since the Arsenal youth squad, Jermaine Pennant aside, cost a fraction of what Tottenham have had to pay to fill the gap at and above Under-19 level.

This latest emphasis on buying in youth is pertinent, however, if Tottenham are to continue firing blanks in their attempts to make the high-profile signings. Alan Sugar's recent outlay to add quality to the youth ranks – which is totally in keeping with his philosophy of building a team without any 'irrational cheque-book madness' – has even led to some sniggering in various sections of the media that he is attempting to create a veritable boy band of footballers. But Suddaby maintains this could not be further from the truth. 'I have never been told, 'he claims, 'that I have to produce a whole team of Tottenham youth players. No doubt Alan Sugar is thinking that the future of the club lies in its youth system, which is true because of the current prices. But I don't feel pressure to put young kids through.'

Sugar has apparently been 'very positive in terms of financial backing, and he obviously has a vision of how he'd like it to be here, which involves spending a few million pounds'. But Suddaby is sure that 'the questions will come if we don't produce sooner rather than later; it just depends on what people think sooner is. The academy has only been going one year and it's rather like asking how long you'd give a manager to change a mediocre team into a good one?'

Judging by Sugar's reaction to what he witnessed one unseasonably sunny Saturday morning in April, when Tottenham's Under-19 and Under-17 sides entertained their Birmingham counterparts in a friendly fixture, Sugar might come questioning sooner than Suddaby envisages. An infrequent spectator on such occasions, Sugar spent most of the match chatting on the touchline to former Tottenham striker Ronnie Rosenthal (who is now an agent), occasionally glancing up to see what was occurring on the pitch. He clearly didn't think much of what he saw, for as he left he remarked to Tim Sherwood and Ramon Vega, who were watching the game during a break from fitness training (both players were rehabilitating after injury): 'You don't have to worry about your first-team places next season, not judging by this lot.' Hardly a vote of confidence from the man at the top.

However, credit where credit's due. There is no doubt that Tottenham are working very hard at this level to get their house in order. That view is endorsed by Les Reed, who claims that the club's youth programme suffered because of the dent to the club's image over recent years, coupled with the resultant huge turnover in staff and the knock-on effect at youth level. Furthermore, that Tottenham dragged their feet in finding a suitable site for their new training facilities meant that they were, according to Reed, 'slower to get off the ground because planning problems hindered their progress'.

However, Reed concurs whole-heartedly with the image of Suddaby as an academy director who is totally committed to the cause; so committed, in fact, that it was only the idea of working within an academy that enticed him away from his part-time coaching post at Chelsea back to Tottenham (he had left six years previously, not least because 'the travelling was getting me down'; this was before the North Circular was fully built, although whether its completion has actually made much difference is a moot point among those who regularly get stuck on it on match-days). 'The youth system had never been able to function on its own before,' he explains. 'We'd never been able to design programmes for youth alone; they'd always been tied in with the first team. That meant that if the first team didn't do well on the Saturday then all the young players had to come in on the Sunday too, which didn't seem quite right. We don't want to be totally separate but we do want to be able to make decisions for the good of the youth.'

This autonomy is a vitally important aspect of the academy philosophy. For years British clubs had their feet kicked from under them whenever a manager got the boot, and his entire backroom staff – which inevitably included the youth coaches – went with him. It meant starting from scratch every time a new manager was appointed. Now, the academies are run along the same lines as in Holland, where youth coaches are given long contracts and are unaffected by any changes at the top of the club's managerial hierarchy. Hence, none of the Tottenham academy staff – who include head of academy recruitment John Moncur, Under-19 coach Pat Holland, Under-17 coach Ricky Hill, technical coach Bob Arber, academy physiotherapist Tim Williamson and Robbie Stepney, facility manager for the 9–16s age group – are Graham's appointees. Suddaby also believes in keeping it in the family where possible to engender a true Tottenham spirit, so ex-Tottenham players Micky Hazard, Paul Allen and Mark Falco are also on the coaching staff.

That said, Suddaby clearly feels that the stability Graham has brought to the club has rubbed off from top to bottom. 'The academy idea is very exciting and we are slowly fulfilling the remit here,' he insists. 'We're planning a new academy building here [at the Spurs Lodge training ground] to house all the facilities for the 9–19-year-olds, the idea being to take the academy boys a few hundred yards away from the first team so they have something to aspire and progress to. We are trying to build something permanent here and you can only do that when the club is stable. The next step is the hardest one. After underachieving under Gerry Francis and Christian Gross, we're ready to have a go now.'

Having a go means having to compete for players within an area that is fiercely competitive. Tottenham's hunting ground overlaps not only with Arsenal's, Chelsea's and West Ham's, but also with Charlton's, QPR's and Watford's, as well as with Ipswich's and Norwich's for older boys (if the boy is under fourteen he has to live within an hour's travelling time to the academy; those over fourteen must reside with a ninety-minute radius. The only way round the regulation is to create a home-from-home, but at such a tender age the risk is only worth taking with exceptional prospects). Therefore the attraction has to be strong between boy and club, both in terms of status and, because this is football in the twenty-first century, financial reward. You do wonder why a boy would choose N17 over N5, E13, SW6 or even SE7, since Charlton have an estimable youth set-up. But Suddaby refutes suggestions that Tottenham are nowadays the poor relations who must rely on pickings from the scraps discarded by the likes of Arsenal and West Ham. 'Spurs are still a big club,' he contends, 'and they have a reputation of playing the right way, but it is very competitive and the lure of money can turn anyone's head. Hunting players is so intense, even at this level. We're playing the same game as with the first-team players here, because a player could be tapped up by any other club during that time or he could let his scholarship just run out and walk away. It's similar to the situation that existed with Darren Anderton. Not as much money involved, but the same ethics.'

Welcome to a world in which a fourteen-year-old schoolkid can cost £500,000 – for that is what Tottenham have just paid Wycombe Wanderers and Charlton in compensation for strikers Michael Malcolm and Owen Price respectively – and where an agent will think nothing of touting a boy of fifteen, who has been assiduously brought up under the watchful eye of a lower league club, from one Premiership fat cat to another in the hope of realizing the astronomical price-tag that has been slung around his neck. It's a scenario that is indicative of the competition for players at this level, but it nevertheless begs certain questions about what is right and wrong for the long-term welfare of a minor or teenager. At least the selling club receives a tidy sum in compensation for the gem they have apparently unearthed, dusted down and polished up – there really would be something amiss with a system that allowed the big clubs to pick the best of the bunch for mere peanuts, although if some of these boys turn out to be half as good as predicted then their eventual worth could be substantially higher than any compensatory fee paid. Yet cynicism still lingers around these deals, which go through with alarming regularity, such is the desire of the big clubs to corner the market in footballing prodigies and the desperate financial predicament of most clubs outside the Premier League.

Is it right, for instance, that football should be sanctioning what is fundamentally a 'trade in teenagers', and touting boys who are still at school? What incentive does this leave for the smaller clubs, who have traditionally relied for their survival on the provision of potential top-class players to the big clubs? Is it right, furthermore, that boys of this age should have an agent at all? And is it naïve to wonder why a boy cannot stay with the club that has invested so heavily in his footballing education until at least the age of sixteen, when a little added maturity might make all the difference when it comes to deciding his future? After all, there is a lot to be said for remaining at a smaller club as opposed to bailing out in search of fame and fortune to a Premiership club, where first-team opportunities are inevitably restricted.

David Manasseh of Stellar Promotions, who acts for many of the country's top young players (including Stuart Taylor and Paolo Vernazza at Arsenal and Crouch, Thelwell, Gardner, Etherington and Davies at Tottenham) insists that while it is not his custom to move young players around from club to club, there is now so much at stake that it is imperative for a teenage footballer to enlist the help of an agent. 'When you go to watch an England Under-18 match these days, you won't see a player on the pitch who doesn't have an agent,' says Mannasseh. 'If you're eighteen and are offered a five-year deal with a Premier League club, that takes you through until you are twenty-three, and that's a long time in a footballer's life. It has to be right and that's where we come in.'

Manasseh, who has been in the business for six years, is unquestionably a scrupulous operator, but there is absolutely no excuse for an agent who makes it his business to go turning the head of a young player who is relatively settled at a modest club with talk of untold riches, when it is hard enough these days to keep feet on the ground and egos in check and prospects in perspective. There is nothing wrong with allowing a boy his dreams, for that is called ambition and those who lack it may not make the grade, but it is unethical that an agent should be allowed to use his inexperienced client as a vehicle to land himself a bumper pay-day, and short-sighted that the big clubs should be allowed to siphon off the cream from the smaller academies and centres of excellence, thereby removing their incentive. That the odds are heavily stacked in favour of the Premiership clubs already is obvious considering that Stevenage were refused permission to set up an academy because it would have been within Arsenal's orbit.

Of course geographical restrictions have prompted British clubs to go shopping even further afield for raw recruits (and Leeds to consider an alliance with Oldham in order to muscle in on the Manchester clubs' territory). So it is that the line-ups of certain clubs in the academy leagues and youth cup matches have begun to resemble their respective first-team squads in terms of the number of nationalities represented. Arsenal, Tottenham and Chelsea have all recruited several foreign boys, while even Fulham can boast a Florentine youth, a *ragazzo*, among their number. The result is that the progress of young English talent has been hindered, not just by the increasing number of foreign first-teamers coming into the country, but by the growing number of youngsters being plucked from foreign fields to continue their development in England, despite the fact that the *raison d'être* of the Charter for Quality was to produce good young players for the national team.

Les Reed believes that part of the problem is that 'we are not experienced enough in this country in identifying potential'. He does not subscribe to the current fallacy that if a player is 'an international, foreign and cheap then he must be better than anything on offer here', and cites as an example the case of Mark Kinsella, an Irish Under-18 and Under-21 international whom Charlton bought from Colchester for £200,000. 'Following Kinsella's success at Charlton at least half-a-dozen Premiership clubs informed us that they'd been looking at him,' Reed reveals, 'but had all rejected him for a variety of reasons. It makes me think that we are not good enough at spotting the potential in players like Kinsella. Instead, the game is littered with young foreign players who have proven to be failures.'

Peter Suddaby admits that Tottenham have recruited some foreign boys – they have a promising striker in eighteen-year-old French striker Yannick Kamanan – but echoes Liam Brady when he stresses that the priority is to recruit an English boy every time. 'We would love to have an academy full of English players but the rules make it quite hard,' he maintains. 'If we want to strengthen the Under-16 squad, for example, then our chances will be slim as the likelihood is that any player who is any good will already be attached to a club. But my job is to do whatever I can to strengthen the playing ability of Tottenham Hotspur so we do look at foreign players. However, that player would have to give us something that we haven't already got. We are trying to say to English kids that it's you we want, but if a hole appears and we can't find an English player then we look overseas. But the foreign player has to have pedigree. We won't watch *Monsieur* Joe Bloggs unless we are tipped off that he will definitely be an international, but we will watch Mr Joe Bloggs even if he's not. Ideally we want the best British kids because if you have them for a little bit longer they do "become Tottenham". The foreign kids are the icing.' (Interestingly, Suddaby reveals that because boys leave school at eighteen in mainland Europe in contrast to Britain, where the school-leaving age is sixteen, the parents of a foreign boy are always far more concerned about the educational prospects for their boy than their English equivalents, whose first question, Suddaby says, is invariably: "How much will he earn?" ') As David Pleat points out: 'Unless they are outstanding like Galli at Arsenal, the risks are obviously greater. You have to allow the boy time to acclimatize – we've been disappointed in some instances but you have to allow them a second year' (when strictly, on performances, they haven't earned it).

Of course, parents can prove potential spanners in the academy works, as highlighted by the case of Owen Price who was championed in an article in *Sport First*, instigated by his parents against the advice of the club. Under the headline 'The New Owen', the article claimed it was 'revealing the youngster who is being compared to Best, Beckham and his namesake Owen' and described Price as 'the hottest property in schoolboy football'. Price, who was originally attached to Charlton but disliked the set-up, eventually ended up at Tottenham after attracting Leeds, West Ham, Aston Villa and even Manchester United. He was apparently drawn by Tottenham's proximity to his home and by their 'impressive set-up; oh, and there was the not insignificant fact that 'the club has David Ginola, one of my heroes'.

But Tottenham are not prepared, as Suddaby puts it, 'to isolate one boy. That article caused us lots of problems because we have a lot of fourteen-year-old boys with potential – but that's all it is. The fans are waiting to hear about the next young star but we daren't talk about him because the minute we hold him up as the great hope then the pressure becomes too much. There is a lot to go wrong between fourteen and nineteen and we don't want the best players at fourteen; we want the best at nineteen and twenty. It might not be exactly what people want to hear, but we have an interesting group coming through and that's all I am prepared to say.'

He's right of course. Trawl back through the England against Germany schoolboy fixtures over the years – for that has traditionally been the showpiece event at this level – and it is rarer to spot a player who has made it big than one who hasn't. The casualties are many because as Suddaby says: 'It is easy to pick out the best player at that level but we are not looking for the best player. He might be the biggest and the strongest but when everyone grows to be as big and strong as him then he may not stand out any more. We are looking, in racehorse parlance, for the boy who will train on, who's coachable, who will get better and better.'

They were also looking for a boy with both character and confidence, because frankly, a shrinking violet is not an advantageous trait for a footballer. Even Sol Campbell, a reserved soul off the pitch, exudes an air of supreme confidence on it, and in such a pressure-cooker industry that is a crucial attribute. 'You can have training matches and academy matches, any match you like,' argues Suddaby, 'but you just don't know how a player will react when they step out there in front of thousands of baying fans. They have to be confident, an arrogant beast. In a perfect world, the minute a player crosses that white line he becomes arrogant, and when he returns he is nice. That's the perfect template for a footballer.'

Whisper it, for he is only sixteen, but there is an English boy who fulfils the above criteria. An English boy, moreover, whose ability to combine defensive and creative attributes suggests that he could become the composite modern-day midfielder. 'We are always wondering whether we should pick two David Battys and one Paul Scholes, or one Batty and two Scholes,' says Les Reed, whose wide-ranging remit within the FA means he works with England players across the age spectrum, 'so part of the strategy is to develop players in positions that we lack, such as a midfielder who possesses both sets of qualities.' During the recent UEFA Under-16 tournament in Israel Reed claims this particular player stood out a mile, and while one must not forget the caveat – that at this age we are only talking about potential – the fact that the boy apparently has an outstanding professional attitude, a supportive family background, a level head and a refreshingly low profile means that he has as good a chance as anyone of going all the way. Remember the name: Ben Bowditch. And remember his club: Tottenham Hotspur.

One boy, however, does not an academy make, and if one was to take Alan Sugar's glib comment at his word one might question his faith in a youthful future. So what will Peter Suddaby say in defence of Tottenham's fledging academy? 'Nothing is ever certain,' he admits, 'but all I can say is that I look at the evidence and feel quite pleased with the way things are going. All we can do is try to lead the boys in the right direction. It's a hard job in that it's never finished – there's a lot of input and a minefield of problems to nego-tiate before you can say: "Go and fly now" – but there is enough in the age groups to suggest that there might be something for Tottenham in the future.'

Nevertheless, Tottenham fans will doubtless have noted that Arsenal had won the Youth Cup almost at a canter, beating Coventry 5–1 on aggregate over the two legs. Not only that, but the Under-19s and Under-17s had reached their respective academy finals, due to be resolved at the end of May. And they will doubtless fear that, just as their first team are rarely a match for Arsenal's any more, so their youth policy is failing to keep pace with the pace-setters. It can be no fun to be a Tottenham fan and see Arsenal's future looking comparatively rosy.

Don Howe was being ironic when he declared, after Arsenal's 2–0 victory at Highbury had finally killed off Coventry's resist-ance in the Youth Cup final, that 'all they have to do now is be good players'; but at this level there was no doubting his players' ability. This Coventry side was a year older and wiser than the one which was humiliated 9–0 (on aggregate) by West Ham, yet Arsenal were always in command of the tie, right from the moment at Highfield Road when Jerome Thomas cut in from the left edge of the penalty box to open the scoring. That first leg had finished 3–1, and although Coventry, like Arsenal, had a reputa-tion for performing better on their travels than at home, it would have been a brave punter who dared put his money on the Sky Blue youngsters making up for last year's misery at that stage of the game.

After all, Arsenal had Jermaine Pennant back for the second leg at Highbury, and Volz too. It had been to Arsenal's chagrin that Pennant had missed the first leg of the final because of England Under-16 commitments. David Dein admitted they were livid that the FA had refused to overrule and allow Arsenal to retain Pennant's services for the sake of what was, after all, their own competition. In the event, Coventry kept Pennant relatively quiet for much of the second leg at Highbury, so the crowd of 14,706 had to make do with a few late runs down the right touchline and one mazy dribble which culminated in Pennant hitting the side-netting with a near-post drive.

The player who really caught the eye was David Noble, the England Under-18 international. The sublime piece of skill on the edge of the box that took him to the byline to set up Steven Sidwell for Arsenal's second goal alone justified any praise that had been heaped upon his slender shoulders prior to the match. Jay Bothroyd had scored the first, capitalizing on a defensive mix-up to nick the ball over the Coventry keeper with a typically audacious flick before knocking the ball into the empty net. He made it look easy, which is what they say about Dennis Bergkamp around these parts.

The victory put Arsenal's young stars into seventh heaven – with academy league finals to come there was the distinct possibility of a memorable treble to sustain the euphoric mood – yet it brought Don Howe, as he put it, 'down to earth. I've won a great deal in the game, but never anything at this level, and the experience has been good for me.' Doubtless it was good for Liam Brady too. At least his crop of Arsenal youngsters had superseded their mentor in one respect, for Brady never reached the Youth Cup final as a player; he was in the Arsenal side that reached a semi-final, but the arch-enemy Tottenham had ended that particular dream and gone on to win the competition that year.

So Arsenal's kids had ended the course in triumph, but what was the true significance in terms of the greater good of Arsenal Football Club? The basic truth is that there's still a question mark hanging over the success of the youth policy, and will be until the first-team ranks are infiltrated by some of the home-grown stars. Wenger is unquestionably keen on youth, but will the risks involved in integrating a raw youngster or two and allowing them time to gel be too great until Arsenal undergo a fallow period (which is unlikely) or the games start coming thicker and faster than they already are and the current squad system is unable to cope?

The case of Ashley Cole might go some way towards bucking the trend that has seen Arsenal buying big as opposed to promoting small. A nineteen-year-old left-back who has spent the latter part of the 1999–2000 season on loan to Crystal Palace – where he has undoubtedly gained in maturity during the club's battle to stay in the First Division – Cole would return to Highbury when the season was over, where according to Brady 'he has a tremendous future and will probably get his chance [in the first team] next year'. Ironically, it is only thanks to the perspicacity and consideration of the old-school stalwarts Hollingdale and Murphy that Cole is still on Arsenal's books at all. Hollingdale recalls Cole starting out as a thirteen-year-old striker who 'fell behind in terms of his height. It was touch and go whether he would be kept on and I remember Terry asking all the other coaches for their opinion. One by one they advised against retaining him. When Terry turned to me I told him I thought Ashley had a lovely touch. So Terry gave him another year and he hasn't looked back. Now he's probably going to be number two in that position behind Silvinho, which could signal Winterburn's departure.'

Hollingdale would doubtless feel some small sense of satisfaction at such a scenario, as would Don Howe and Liam Brady if one or more of their Youth Cup-winning charges were to grace the Premiership stage. Asked after the game whether he thought that was a reality next season, Howe replied: 'I don't know. I really don't know. This club has to win things and we are in the Champions' League again and Mr Wenger has that on his plate and I can see his point of view. But I do hope he introduces one or two of these young players. They need the opportunity to go out and show what they can do at the highest level.'

For Les Reed, the ideal would be to remove the risk factor for a manager by producing players skilled enough to ensure that the transition from what is essentially a footballing playground, to the Premiership, is a smooth one. 'We need the fellow in charge of the first team to follow the club's philosophy, but we have to take the gamble aspect out of it too,' Reed states, because in essence, it is a manager's willingness to give young players a chance, not just the system that produces those young players in the first place, that is crucial. Under the old regime, which unquestionably had its virtues, whether or not a boy progressed was largely dependent on an empathic head of youth development. Nowadays that is less paramount thanks to a far more sophisticated and professional system – more money, a far larger pool of players and a higher level of competition have all become influencing factors. Yet never before have managers been under such pressure to deliver, short-term, which paradoxically affords them less room to manoeuvre than ever before. And therein lies the dichotomy.

CHAPTER NINE
THE BITTER SWEET YEARS

To his friends, Morris Keston is 'Mr Tottenham'. There was a time when Morris would literally go to the ends of the earth to follow his club. On one occasion he actually changed his religion for Tottenham.

In the early 1960s, Tottenham were the glamour team, and as such were invited to be the opposition in a special celebration match against the Egyptian national side in Cairo. Back then, obtaining an Egyptian visa when you had an Israeli stamp on your passport was usually an insurmountable obstacle, but if you intended to accompany the players every time they played then it was just another challenge to be overcome. Only one thing for it – write 'C of E' on the application and be prepared to be teased by greetings of 'shalom' from Jimmy Greaves and company when you came down to breakfast at the Nile Hilton. In fact, Bill Nicholson had to restrain the Tottenham players from taunting Morris in case they blew his cover.

Still a West Stand season-ticket holder – he hasn't missed a home game in fifty years, although it's difficult to maintain the same level of attendance for away fixtures once you've reached your sixties – Morris complained recently to his long-time mate Terry Venables that 'the buzz has gone out of football'. Venables told him he was mistaken. 'The buzz hasn't gone out of football,' he said. 'The buzz has gone out of your team. When your team is playing well you'll get the old feeling back.'

How many times would Morris's pals and the club's former heroes, men like Jimmy Greaves and Steve Perryman, have to question what had happened to the Tottenham they used to play for before someone – and that someone knew only too well who he was – would sit up and take just a little bit of notice?

It might be tempting fate to ask, but could the penny gradually be dropping? For after yet another season spent craning their necks to catch a glimpse of the high-fliers at the top of the Premiership, the Tottenham hierarchy have finally realized you have to be in the Champions' League. That means you have to speculate to accumulate, something Alan Sugar has been reticent to do. He has constantly reiterated his belief that spending money won't guarantee you success in football but has refused to acknowledge that not spending enough money will guarantee a lack of success.

This is the chairman who replaced the hapless Christian Gross with the parsimonious George Graham attracted by, amongst other qualities, Graham's reputation as a past-master at working on a shoestring budget. On three counts – a former Arsenal manager, tainted by the bung scandal, with a reputation for boring football – it was an appointment that appalled the fans, but Sugar didn't care. As lifelong Tottenham fan John Harris says: 'You are in this situation and you don't want to fork out a fortune. Who's the best man to have? George Graham. Who's the most hated man you could bring to Tottenham? Bugger that. Let's bring George here. He'll get the whip out. But I don't want that. I'm looking for another Irving Scholar with £200 million, not £10 million, to blow. Sure Alan Sugar hasn't lost his money (on the contrary he's quadrupled it) but what profits a man who has a terrible football team? There's no thrill, no excitement in that.'

At the Tottenham AGM in December 1999 Sugar publicly inferred that the club's policy was to rely on Graham's adroit use of the players already at his disposal – plus any funds he might generate from disposing of those he wasn't keen on – to scramble into the top six (Graham and Pleat also trotted out the same line repeatedly, even though finishing sixth is really no different than finishing tenth – it doesn't get you into Europe). 'I genuinely don't believe that rushing out with a pile of money trying to get the best players is the best solution,' Sugar said. 'I am very confident with Mr Graham's road map for the way forward.' By the New Year, however, that policy had clearly gone down the pan. First, financial director John Sedgwick clearly stated the club's objective when he admitted that 'as a business we have got to be in the Champions' League. That is probably the only way to make this club a lot bigger. There is a genuine recognition that we are not going to get into the Champions' League on managerial acumen alone. Everybody knows we have got to buy some quality players. If you look at how much we've paid out and then you look at the performances, the two things don't correlate.'

That statement was then backed up by David Pleat, who outlined what the change of heart would entail by admitting that 'it's going to cost up to £25 million to get three players, plus another free transfer who we have in mind on a Bosman ... then it's down to whether Alan is prepared to stump up the money'. Having rejected the idea of securitizing gate receipts (money upfront to be paid back over time from match-day revenues) and the overtures from media companies ('a tempting carrot' but not to be taken according to Alan Sugar, because 'in return for the investment you have to give away the shop' with 'lucrative' developments such as the Internet and ppv about to come on stream – though with Tottenham already closely associated with Sky through Amstrad, UEFA Cup television rights and the Internet there was every reason for Rupert Murdoch to believe that he would have Sugar's support; and of course Tottenham was out of bounds for the competition like NTL), it was finally time for Sugar to put his money where his mouth was.

One can imagine Sugar, phone tucked under his chin (as it constantly is – he makes at least fifty calls a day), turning his attention to David Pleat who has once again shuffled into the office to broach the subject of the big money deal, and barking something along the lines of: 'Yeah, yeah, just get on with it then. He'd better be top drawer, mind, for that money.' This was a new dawn for transfers that hitherto disappeared in the Bermuda Triangle that existed between Sugar, Graham and Pleat, whose lines of communication seemed interesting to say the least. According to someone who has worked closely with the club, the reason why there has been 'sound and fury signifying nothing' on the transfer front is because the three men indulge in their own version of Chinese Whispers and the message invariably gets lost somewhere along the line.

Essentially, Graham will tell Pleat which player he wants whereupon Pleat informs Sugar, who says he will think about it. Then it goes quiet. Eventually, a frustrated Graham asks Pleat what's happening so Pleat goes back to Sugar, who could be excused for thinking that they'd forgotten all about it – by which time, of course, it's too late and they've missed the boat. That seemed to have been the pattern, but the club was adamant: things were going to be different from now on.

It was another astonishing volte-face on the part of the man who had infamously slagged off foreign footballers as 'Carlos Kickaballs' – and then re-signed Klinsmann; who had poo-pooed the idea of spending £4 million on a twenty-eight-year-old Les Ferdinand – then promptly paid £6 million for the same player when he was thirty; who had time and again looked to sell the club – only to change his mind when circumstances changed; and who after rubbishing the financial rewards in Europe, described as 'awesome' at the 1999 AGM the money on offer to participants in the Champions' League (mistakenly telling the shareholders it was £30 million – this only comes your way if you reach the final – which 'explains how Chelsea have defied the laws of gravity').

This latest change of heart was just one more example of Sugar's quixotic nature, which not only alienates the fans but also unsettles his employees, which is how he views his players. How can a team expect to show consistency when the man in the driving seat is constantly changing direction? Yet paradoxically Sugar's problem with Tottenham, unlike his other businesses, is that he does not seem to move in time with the times. He appears reluctant to embrace change, rather it is forced upon him by events so that when he does finally come round to the universally accepted way of thinking he finds that others are way ahead of him.

Former director Douglas Alexiou, who actually has no reason to speak up for Sugar, does so by explaining that 'if I was taken out of my job here [he is a senior partner for an old, established firm of solicitors] where I do things in a certain way and told that I had to go and run another business then I'm bound to go and use methods I've used before because I don't know any other way. We are all products of our past environment and it's natural to do what we do best in a different environment. It may not work but it's not unreasonable that one tries to apply the same principles, and for Alan Sugar that's focusing on the balance sheet, the profit and loss account and the turnover. And who can blame him for that?' Thus, Sugar's vision of the football industry is conditioned by his business successes and his opinion of himself that 'I have never failed at anything – well perhaps my charisma O level'.

Despite a market value of more than £1 billion at its height in the late 1980s, based on value-for-money word processors, personal computers and hi-fis, Sugar broke up Amstrad in 1997, leaving him with a personal fortune estimated at £140 million. That elicited a rare show of emotion from its founder, who admitted at the time that 'it would be a terrible knock emotionally if I thought Amstrad was gone, and from a corporate point of view that is obviously the case [Amstrad was replaced in part by a company trading as Viglen Technology]. But in my mind it will not be gone at all. This is not the end of Amstrad, it is the rebirth' (and indeed, the Amstrad name has been revived through diversification). Failure is not an option for Sugar, which explains why he has become so adept at pulling rabbits out of his hat in search of the next quick hit. Now the signs are that he has done it again. When, early in the year, it was announced that Viglen would be investing in the Internet, Sugar's majority stake in the company soared in value by over £100 million in just a few hours.

The fundamental problem, of course, is that Alan Sugar is not a football man. (Irving Scholar recalls asking Sugar what he thought he might pay for a player whose transfer fee was being adjudged by tribunal, only to be told: 'I've no idea. I know more about schmaltz herring than I do about football.') As befits a man whose single-mindedness catapulted him from the back of a lorry on to Millionaires' Row, he is focussed on the bottom line. 'Show me the money,' he growls in a manner resonant of Cuba Gooding Junior's character in the film *Jerry Maguire*, 'that's my plan. At the end of the rainbow, show me the money. It's not about getting the bloody share price up, flogging some shares and pissing off to the South of France. It's about creating a sound company.' Sugar is involved in the business of football, not in the football game. He appears to be more concerned about profit and loss than winning and losing. Progress is defined by an increase in Tottenham's stock market valuation, not according to whether or not David Ginola has turned in a match-winning display. (However, even by that criterion the financial returns could be better. Tottenham Hotspur plc will claim that the share price had outperformed a stagnant market, but considering they went public as long ago as 1983, the share value in recent times has been disappointing, and moreover, for the last couple of years no dividend has been forthcoming.)

Which is not to say that he has not become a fan. His enthusiastic reaction to Allan Nielsen's late League Cup-winning goal at Wembley in 1999, for example, was proof that he can be moved by the occasion. Yet one could never say that Sugar has been bitten by the bug, as were so many agnostics after Gazza's tears in Italia 90. Yes, he was born just a few miles from Tottenham, and it is true that his older brother Derek has always been a passionate supporter of the club. But when Nathan Sugar took his youngest son Alan to his first match at White Hart Lane the boy was distinctly unimpressed. He would, he decided, far rather be pursuing his photographic interests, or thinking up a money-making scam, so that when Tottenham were doing the Double the youngest Sugar was completely oblivious to what it was that had sent his brother into raptures.

To be fair, Sugar has never professed undying love for the club. He does not dine out on tales of freezing away trips to Bolton and Preston. He does not claim to 'jump out of my seat, leaping up and down with joy when we score . . . or stand up clapping, singing or waving scarves'. (In his defence, it has long been the etiquette of the Tottenham directors' box – pre-dating Alan Sugar – that you don't stand up and cheer when Tottenham score, and guests' cards are marked to that effect. Polite applause, however, is permitted.) You would be hard pushed to find anyone who could claim to have heard Sugar eulogizing about a Klinsmann bicycle kick or a Ginola dribble or a last-ditch Campbell tackle, and it's safe to assume that he has never returned from an away fixture in Europe (notwithstanding the fact that there have been precious few of them during the last decade) and immediately re-run his video machine, as David Dein is wont to do. 'That is me,' he admits, 'never one to show any emotion.' He sticks to a piece of PR advice he was once given, namely never to laugh or be seen to be enjoying yourself in public because there is a danger that you will be photographed doing so and it will come back to haunt you when a malevolent media juxtaposes your happy countenance with a critical story.

Perhaps that is why, although he may have mellowed a little so that he can at least enjoy a satisfactory working relationship with David Pleat, he could never enjoy the unique intimacy that Dein shares with Arsène Wenger; nor could one imagine him wearing his heart on his sleeve in the manner of Peter Ridsdale, who celebrated Leeds's defeat of Roma in the UEFA Cup by racing onto the pitch and leaping into David O'Leary's arms. Sugar is far more withdrawn. Perfunctory congratulations are more his style.

He will say though, that Tottenham 'has become a passion', although he immediately tempers the admission by adding that 'it is a business whether people like it or not'. Sugar views Tottenham as 'a commercial enterprise that has to be run properly and have tight financial controls, so you can't say to hell with everything, let's just enjoy the football'. His revelation that his reason for becoming involved in the club was 'to be the custodian of this great institution that reminds me of my early days' indicates that his overriding motive was to get the club out of debt and back on its feet again. According to die-hard fans Sugar was not concerned with putting the flair back into Tottenham, with bringing back the glory nights to White Hart Lane. They felt there was no emotional pull involved. 'He's got no feel for the history,' contends John Harris. 'He's not speculating, he's earning money, and don't confuse the two issues. He's very successful at earning money and he's doing it at Tottenham.' As Sugar himself said at the time of his takeover: 'I will take care of the £11 million at the bank [a reference to the Tottenham debt] and he'll [Terry Venables] take care of the eleven men on the field.'

One has to give him credit for spotting the commercial revolution coming, but that's hardly surprising given his eagle eye for a business opportunity. At Amstrad it had become his *modus operandi* to try and succeed on the hop by discerning trends and then producing value-for-money products for the masses, and his range of low-cost, user-friendly word processors was responsible for introducing a predominantly computer-illiterate British public to the age of information technology. In 1989 he climbed on board Sky's bandwagon when he agreed to make satellite receivers for

Rupert Murdoch, and two years later teamed up with Venables to buy Tottenham for less than £10 million – pocket money for Sugar but a small fortune for El Tel. The upshot was that when Sky and ITV came to bid for the rights to the Premier League contract in 1992, Sugar's pressure on Sky to up the ante and 'blow them [ITV] out of the water' was instrumental in ensuring Sky won the day. A side-effect was the increase in value of Amstrad because of the increased demand for satellite equipment.

He must also be given credit for maintaining his stance against the climate of extravagant spending that football clubs have indulged in ever since, despite the break it has put on his own team's momentum. 'We have got to be careful,' he warned at the time of the bidding war for the second Premier League contract in 1996, 'that the television money doesn't go through us like a dose of salts. It's like a laxative and we, the clubs, don't see the benefit. It just gets passed on in higher wages and transfer fees.' In fact, David Pleat maintains that 'Alan Sugar talks more sense around the Premiership table than all the others. He has a vision of the future and he knows that if you get £1 you should spend 80p and save 20p so that you have a reserve fund.'

Yet for all his wise counsel on this front, seemingly Sugar has not taken full advantage of the Tottenham brand. There is an anecdote regularly cited in marketing manuals about the managing director who, when asked what he would take with him if he had to leave the company, admitted that he would ignore the infrastructure and just take the brand names. It is one of the cardinal rules of a business that depends on customer loyalty, that the brand is key; it bestows a value far beyond the performance of that product or service. However, the club's marketing policy appears to ignore the fact that in Tottenham Hotspur they possess one of the strongest brands in the football business, and that the Tottenham brand is unique. It has a rare history and heritage. Push and run, the Double side, Nicholson, Greaves and Gilzean, Hoddle, Waddle, Ardiles, Gascoigne and Klinsmann. Entertaining football played with style by a team liberally sprinkled with stardust. The Tottenham way. Simply by not investing in top-class players Alan Sugar is not keeping the faith, to the ultimate detriment not just of Tottenham Hotspur FC but also of Tottenham Hotspur plc. Conversely, the more the fans believe in the brand, the more value the brand returns to its owner.

Sugar's policy has a limited horizon based as it is, according to his son Daniel who controls the commercial side as well as being the family's full-time eyes and ears at White Hart Lane, on 'a strong manager, a strong business team and a strong chairman' – and he never even mentioned the players. This is undoubtedly a proficient operation. In the last five years turnover has doubled and cumulative profits at £38 million are second only to Manchester United. Yet is the customer satisfied? In response to a journalist who took him to task in 1996 about the fare on offer at White Hart Lane he growled: 'I think the fans have demonstrated that they're quite happy with us in as much as we're packed out for every home game. When I took over we had an empty ground and now we're being forced into rebuilding the North Stand to accommodate more and more people who want to watch the "dross" you're talking about.' (Yet the reality is, of course, that the club has been swept along on the tidal wave of general euphoria that accompanied the inception of the Premier League and the commercial revolution.)

The club currently reaps the rewards from a record number of season-ticket holders and members. White Hart Lane's boxes in the West, East and North Stands number 120 (in comparison to the 54 boxes in Highbury's Clock End) – and the holders include blue chip companies like British Telecom, Tesco and Mitsubishi. Additionally, there are the corporate enclaves of the Centenary Club, the Cross Bar club, Legends, the Corner Flag, the Touchlines and the Hotspur, as well as hospitality areas such as the Bill Nicholson suite, so that when the ground is full, as it is for most home fixtures, the corporate guests and VIPs number more than ten per cent of the capacity. So while it rankles with the traditional fan that the corporate customer has encroached on traditional home areas in all four stands, he suffers the double whammy of having to pay substantially more for his season ticket (although prices have been frozen for 2000–01). And there is nothing to be done about it. How do you resist price increases from a monopoly? On a good match-day then, White Hart Lane's 36,200 capacity, comparatively small by actual and planned Premiership standards, might take a cool £1 million – and that's almost £250,000 more than Highbury, which accommodates over 38,000.

However, John Harris fears that 'there will be a point when the fans suddenly start getting sensible and stop coming. Just as worrying is that the sponsors will stop coming too.' As yet there is no sign of either scenario happening. On the contrary, it speaks volumes that in industry circles Tottenham's cachet remains high enough to attract companies of substance. The deal with adidas, for example, is better than the previous contract with Pony and, according to Daniel Sugar, the club stores sold almost as many new adidas kits in the launch month as they did Pony kits during the whole of last season. Furthermore, the sponsorship with Holsten, reassociated with the club after an absence of five years, is worth significantly more than the tie-up with Hewlett Packard. Throw in the fact that Tottenham sold their UEFA Cup rights for a sum that was considerably higher than either Arsenal or Leeds managed to negotiate, and all the evidence suggests that the Tottenham 'brand', despite the knocks, is in rude enough health. As finance director John Sedgwick explains: 'Despite the lack of success on the field people do want to come and be associated with Tottenham Hotspur. It is a kind of blue chip name and we try and play on that in everything we do.'

The accounts back up Sedgwick's assertion that Tottenham possess 'an affluent supporter base because of their great heritage' and that is manifest in an operating profit of around £9 million. Sedgwick, incidentally, is unique among the Tottenham hierarchy in that he is a committed fan who describes his job as 'a privilege', and who will readily reveal his true colours. 'I'm not as anti-Arsenal as some,' he admits, 'but you will never see red anywhere on me.' By contrast, some of his colleagues have little or no concept of the club's heritage, and while one cannot expect every club employee to become a die-hard fan, there is no excuse for the Tottenham executive who, after being at the club for a number of years, is still unable to identify any of the players (apart from Dave Mackay) – not even Blanchflower, Smith, Jones or Norman – in a picture that was taken during the Double-winning season.

Yet from a business point of view it is clearly a veritable boon to have Sugar and co. around. 'We play on the club's reputation and the chairman's reputation, which is solid,' Sedgwick explains. 'When you go to a bank for money or someone for a deal, if you get Alan to come to the meeting that alone pushes the price up.' Sedgwick admits that 'at one time we lost sight of Tottenham as a big club. We try and give our customers service and behave as though we are looking after them, whereas perhaps three or four years ago we didn't do that. It may have been, "just put the ticket prices up as much as possible and see how far we can go". Now we try to be as commercial as possible in everything we do. As far as I know we are the only club that is paid by Sky for them to have the privilege of producing our web site which will be the best site in the Premier League, I guarantee it, so we are giving the fans a good service and we are being paid a lot of money.'

Given his loyalties, Sedgwick understands better than most the need to rebuild bridges with the fans. 'In the past,' he admits, 'people have been critical that if we haven't been able to make a profit out of it then we don't do it.' But he immediately recognizes the harsh realities. 'I think we've got to get more kids wearing Tottenham shirts. It's not fashionable because Arsenal and Manchester United have been so successful. But we are trying. Against Middlesbrough we opened a block in the South Stand for 800 and sold tickets at £5 to schools, with each adult accompanied by one child. If I know we are not going to be full up then I will do everything I can to fill the stadium. In the past we've given tickets away through our community scheme and we are getting round the schools a lot more. We give free coaching. We've invested £10,000 in a local police-backed boxing school, and our membership is 37,000, which is second only to Manchester United's.'

This is creditable stuff which deserves wider recognition. The club should take a more proactive PR line on positive developments like this. However, taken on a step it begs the question: in terms the club purports to understand, are they making maximum use of the brand's heritage? And how much untapped potential is still out there? The club may well have exploited commercial opportunities, but surely, if they want the kids to wear the Tottenham shirt, then would not the simplest option be to improve the performance on the pitch, to bring back some of the pizzazz and panache, so that those kids have something to aspire to?

Given that Amstrad never established the same empathetic relationship with its clients as Apple, it's hardly surprising that Tottenham's fans have been marginalized in the pursuit of a better business. Buying into Tottenham afforded Alan Sugar a level of prestige and recognition that he had never got from his other business interests – except when it came to the fans, whom he found loyal but impossible to fathom. It mystifies him how he is still being viewed as the spanner in the works despite the fact that he is acknowledged to have saved the club when it was believed to be on the brink of receivership (although that is a myth: the Midland Bank had actually extended credit on the basis of the sale of Paul Gascoigne to Lazio and the club's involvement in Europe in 1991–92), straightened the books, seen off both Venables and the FA (who in 1994 initially deducted Tottenham twelve points, banned them from the FA Cup and fined them for irregular payments to players), significantly improved the stadium, hired a manager with a proven track record – albeit with Arsenal connections – and spent £72 million over nine years, recouping £28 million. 'What is it?' he asked, in a recent interview given to the *Sun*, 'that people have in their minds that makes a certain minority scream at me as if to say I am ruining something or not providing something? Is there a vision that all the gate money is going into my pocket, all the TV money and sponsorship money is being hoarded in some kind of war chest? Because if so it is totally wrong!' Yet as Alan Sugar is no doubt aware, even his harshest critics have never questioned his propriety. Inventing a spurious argument and then rubbishing it won't, though, absolve his transfer record from closer scrutiny.

Take the figure at face value and £44 million (the net outlay on transfers) sounds a quite considerable sum – until you read between the lines and realize that £44 million over nine years amounts to a net annual expenditure on players of around £5 million. And £5 million will not buy you stars. Players like Jason McAteer, Nathan Blake and Ashley Ward all cost around £5 million and they play their football in the First Division, having failed to save Blackburn from relegation. Moreover, Tottenham's transfer spending is entirely covered by profit. And over the last five seasons, unlike Newcastle, Liverpool and of course Blackburn – who all have a cumulative (profit/transfers) deficit of over £30 million because of unrealistic expenditure – Tottenham actually have a profit surplus of nearly £6 million. However, Sugar would doubtless defend himself by citing the £9 million he made available to Ossie Ardiles in 1994 and ask where that got the club. A case for the chairman of once bitten.

In hindsight, this was not a match made anywhere near heaven, for Ardiles's romantic notion of how football should be played was never going to dovetail with Sugar's more pragmatic, results-related approach. John Harris maintains that it was Sugar's inability to appreciate the aesthetics of football that sounded the death-knell for Ardiles, whose hiring Harris says 'thrilled everyone at the time. It was a Tottenham appointment.' Of that there was no doubt, but in the euphoria of the moment, his patchy coaching record was largely overlooked. Sugar, says Harris, 'is the finest chairman you'd ever get for the plc but for the football club? No. Look at the ten years before he came, and since? One League Cup. He had Ardiles and had he been a football man he could have said: look, Ossie, we love you going forward, so take Don Howe. I'm sorry, Steve Perryman has been a wonderful servant for this club and we'll find something for him but you've got to have Don Howe and then the world's your oyster.

Instead, Sugar fired Ardiles and replaced him with Gerry Francis, who suited Sugar right down to the ground. In Francis, and later in George Graham, he enlisted the services of managers who, had they been Amstrad employees, would have found themselves taking the fast-track route to foreman status. They were sidekicks who could be considered as footballing versions of 'Sugarlumps', which was the collective term given to his erstwhile managers at Amstrad. Both were forthright, self-assured and largely impervious to outside criticism. In other words, they were as thick-skinned as their boss, who knew that he could rely on their caps-on-the-table authority and trenchant game-plans to elicit the best from the workforce. But football is a very particular beast, and while Sugar may be able to control the costs of his business operations – when you are producing PCs for a clearly defined market you can churn out units ad infinitum – but it's when you try to apply the same operating profit principles to football that you very quickly become unstuck. Sugar's players are not his PCs, and whoever he puts in charge of them he himself ultimately has no control over Ginola's temperament or

Campbell's commitment. He cannot foresee there being a divot in the pitch or a hostile referee. In short, he cannot totally control this business of football.

As far as Gerry Francis was concerned, there was a fundamental problem: he was not a Tottenham appointment. As a London boy and a former England international he was well aware of Tottenham's heritage, but his own teams, while they were always efficient and workmanlike, were not picked to thrill. He had worked wonders on a shoestring budget at QPR and before that at Bristol Rovers, but Tottenham fans had higher expectations. His inability to get on their wavelength was underlined in a conversation he once had with John Harris, a man who has an entire room in his house filled with Tottenham memorabilia called The John White Memorial Library, and who on the occasion of every home game leaves his car, goes to the ground to buy a programme then returns to his car to store the programme away in a specially appointed briefcase before re-entering the ground. (While this pre-match routine may not be the expected behaviour from a middle-aged accountant, and even calls his sanity into question, it should not detract from his acumen on matters Tottenham.) Harris was talking to Francis about the honour of being captain of Tottenham, whereupon Francis replied: 'What do you mean? I was captain of England, now that's an honour.' Harris, almost apoplectic, spluttered: 'Captain of England! That doesn't matter. Being captain of Tottenham, like Ron Burgess, Danny Blanchflower and Gary Mabbutt (a man who turned down the chance to go to Liverpool when he was out of contract, ultimately spent sixteen years at White Hart Lane and was described by Peter Shreeves, one of his managers, as "the sort of boy every parent wants their daughter to bring home") . . . now that's the greatest honour in the game.'

One man who would share Harris's sentiment is Sugar's predecessor Irving Scholar. It may be difficult today to give credit to someone who was prepared to bring Robert Maxwell to Tottenham Hotspur but Scholar was quite simply a football visionary. He was the first chairman to recognize that the clubs needed a showcase top division, and that in order to attain that it would be necessary to forge an alliance with television. He had high aspirations for his club – aspirations that would ultimately lead to his demise as the plc diversified disastrously into non-football industries. The irony was that Scholar only took Tottenham to the Stock Exchange to wipe out inherited debt and provide the wherewithal to ensure that those glory, glory nights could once again become a regular feature of their fixture list.

It is an understatement to say that his heart was in the right place. He considered himself to be a hugely privileged fan, and he never let his status obscure his love for the club. 'Irving Scholar,' said Nick Shaw, 'was a financial nightmare but he loved the club as much, if not more, than me, and that is saying something. I remember flying to the first game of a season, Sunderland away, and Scholar loved to sit with us, the ordinary fans, and conduct a quiz about football. What a guy. He knew everything about football and was an expert about my beloved Spurs. I immediately respected the man.' Contrast this with Sugar, who back in 1996 said: 'I look at some of our fans as children. They are always asking their dad for new toys and I have to explain that we can't afford them. I'm hoping that they will grow up with me and understand that my medicine is good medicine.' Nearly four years on, and the chairman's reply to a supporter who told a tale of woe about his trip to Kaiserslautern in the UEFA Cup was 'sounds like you had a bad night then'. End of story. So no change there then, and one department where a bit of inconsistency would have been welcome.

Gary Briggs, a thirty-seven-year-old shareholder and season-ticket holder, speaks for many Tottenham fans when he maintains that the club appears to have shown 'a constant lack of feeling for the supporters. They can sell season tickets or convert them to corporate seats quickly so they don't seem to give a damn.' Sugar's one-liners, Briggs maintains, 'don't do him any justice because he is perceived to be a strong leader with a definite plan in mind, and oh to give a little bit back in the way of understanding how the fans feel'. Yet it is a vain hope, surely, when one hears stories such as the one concerning the longstanding supporters – some of them invalids – who in the interests of keeping the Oak Room for guests of the management had their passes to the one lift in the West Stand taken away. (They would have had to cross the VIP area to get to their seats.) Consequently most have had to reorganize their match-day schedule in order to climb the sixty-four stairs at their own pace to avoid the jostling of the latecomers. What's a little inconvenience, after all, when you are compelled to follow your lifelong obsession?

This apparent belittling of the fans has not reflected well on the management, in particular the installation of the new ticketing system, which was so poorly thought out that hundreds of season-ticket holders still hadn't received their new books in time for the opening day of the season. But it's not just the supporters who have been sidelined, cast in bit-part roles in a show which is more *Rocky Horror* than *Starlight Express*. Tottenham players past and present have been treated in a way that Scholar, who in the presence of his players was always starry-eyed, would never have sanctioned. He told the Double team at a reception he organized for them: 'You think you are forgotten but every time this ground is opened some-one thinks of you.' He had already demonstrated that he had lived up to his word by making it his priority on assuming control to arrange a testimonial match for Bill Nicholson. He revelled in being in a position to help his heroes. When he received a call before the 1987 FA Cup final from Terry Dyson, whose tenacious wing-play had been such a contributory factor to the success of Bill Nicholson's side, saying that he'd never asked for a favour like this before but could someone possibly sort him out two tickets for himself and his son, they were immediately forthcoming.

A decade on and although one cannot blame the top man, Tottenham do seem to be out of touch with the needs of former play-ers. The club was asked if they could possibly help finance a hip operation for Bobby Smith, who had fallen on hard times. Considering that Smith's ailments almost certainly stemmed from his playing days – he was the archetypal old-fashioned centre-forward: big and burly and brave – it seemed the least the club could do. When someone took the club to task over their lack of action club secretary Peter Barnes's defence was that 'if we did it for Bobby Smith then we'd have to do it for Alfie Stokes too' (Stokes was a versatile striker who spent seven seasons at White Hart Lane in the 1950s). 'Well, so they bloody well should,' came the reply. Barnes was clearly embarrassed and his silence spoke volumes when his acquain-tance fumed: 'It's because they bloody well don't know who Bobby Smith is. It's shameful.' (He had only top-scored in the Double-winning season and netted over 200 goals in a lilywhite shirt.)

The irony, however, is that while Scholar's heart was in the right place the fact is that Tottenham had become a plc with a duty to its shareholders and the dual role took him away from his primary interests. He was a man who fought shy of publicity and he tended to hide behind the plc when it came to making the decisions that affected the football club. Deep down Scholar must have realized that Tottenham Hotspur football club should never have diversified as it did into ladies knitwear. Replica shirts, books and videos were fine, of course. Indeed, along with Edward Freedman, later to revolutionize Manchester United's merchandising, Irving Scholar can justly claim to be one of the fathers of the commercial revolution. The football club on and off the field was thriving; it was just that the plc blew the dosh, as Alan Sugar would say. And in a role reversal that was never envisaged, the plc came to the football club to bale itself out.

This is not to say that mistakes were not made under Scholar's regime, and the Arsenal fanzine that harshly nicknamed the Tottenham chairman 'Urban Squalor' had a point. The rebuilding of the East Stand was cocked up (its legacy still apparent today in those two hideous pillars obscuring countless sight lines), undermining in the process what Scholar called 'the best standing view in London': the Shelf – in the interests of yet more corporate boxes. And the selling of the Cheshunt training ground, in the light of today's requirements, looks with hindsight like an act of lunacy.

Yet just as the Scholar set-up was ultimately incapable of handling affairs off the pitch so the Sugar regime has been unable to emulate their record on it, so that it may be now 'a well-run business but a poorly run football club'. The ideal, of course, would be to create a balance and that is why fans like Nick Shaw and John Harris crave a composite chairman. Shaw pleads: 'Give me Alan Sugar's money and business sense and Irving Scholar's love of the club and then we would have the chairman of our dreams', while Harris puts it thus: 'The trouble was Irving didn't have the money. Sugar has the money but not the heart. I don't think you'll get someone with both of them any more.'

Terry Venables once said that 'in any other business you show a £10 million profit and you're a success, but show it in football – and get relegated – and you're a complete and utter failure'. Sugar does appreciate how disastrous relegation would be for the club, but what is crystal clear is that at some point he took a long hard look at Tottenham's one-time partners in the Big Five and decided that he would not aspire to the likes of Arsenal, Manchester United and Liverpool, but to Wimbledon. The Dons, he reckoned, were financially sound, possessed an enviable youth set-up, invariably occupied the middle ground in the Premiership and might even scramble into Europe. However, what Sugar doesn't understand, claims Gary Briggs, 'is that Wimbledon have a spirit but Tottenham have a style. Wimbledon have insufficient ability and can win on spirit alone, but Tottenham have never relied on spirit alone and sometimes ability is enough to win a game.' And besides, the Norwegian take-over has ripped the heart out of Wimbledon and just look where they are now.

That is what the fans fear, that Tottenham will go the way of Wimbledon and become a mere shadow of its former self. The process is already well under way if one subscribes to the view of the TAG (Tottenham Action Group), which actually began life as a one-man band, namely financial journalist Joff Wild and his fax machine, which was employed in the interests of providing the media with a considered anti-Sugar view and now numbers several hundred agitators.

TAG's commitment is commendable, yet the reality is that a few aggrieved fans – which was about the extent of a demonstration outside White Hart Lane earlier in the year – is hardly going to frighten off Alan Sugar. His disdain was evident in his mock applause from the boardroom window, and he later dismissed TAG by claiming in an interview given to the *Sun* that '99 per cent of fans are ordinary decent people ... who have the best interests of the club at heart. There is a minority we hear singing occasionally – 100 or 200 can make a very loud noise in any scenario – but I simply have to ignore this and get on with the job.' Besides, Daniel Sugar's revelation – for he 'sorts out all the old man's mail' – that 'many fans write to express their dissatisfaction with fans like TAG who seemingly exist to find fault with the club and with Alan Sugar in particular' suggests that TAG are out on a lonely limb. Besides, Sugar is well used to being the bad guy. He bewailed the fact that having been the backroom boy for two years while Venables was running the show, by the time he came to the forefront his image was so tarnished by media portrayals of him that 'people in the industry had a preconceived idea of me even before I met them'. However, it was just water off a duck's back to him.

He stated five years ago that he was 'quite happy to put up with aggro,' and has described the typically robust manner he would like to deal with it. 'In my mind I have this big baseball bat in my hand to knock it out of the way and as new things come long I just smack 'em out of the way, although regretfully it's not legal to take a baseball hat and smack it around the head of three beer-swilling yobs who are spitting at you and abusing you.' But he does admit that there is a limit to what he will put up with, and that is continued and increasingly hostile abuse directed at his family.

Back then, he did threaten to sell up under such circumstances. Then again, when the going got tough in early 1998 he was initially receptive to a call from journalist and broadcaster Richard Littlejohn on behalf of a group of wealthy Tottenham fans prepared to buy out the chairman's stake. David Fordham was at the Banque Internationale à Luxembourg, who acted on behalf of this consortium. Personally he feels proud to be able to say that 'we made a bid for Tottenham; as a fourth generation fan it meant a lot' but from a professional point of view he explains that the bank got involved because they had been casting the slide-rule over Tottenham and considered it to be one of the clubs that it would make sense for a financier to acquire.

Fordham remembers there was 'a group of investors, all people of substance, who wanted to make a bid for Tottenham as the club was having a rough passage under Gross. Alan Sugar was getting personal grief and the share price wasn't doing much.' Richard Littlejohn acted as a conduit to try and ascertain if Sugar thought it was time to step aside, and whether he was prepared to accept the bid (at the same time a similar approach had been made through ENIC, a company with a number of diverse investments in a portfolio of clubs, including Glasgow Rangers, Sparta Prague and AEK Athens). 'We never got to the position of making a full Stock Exchange bid but we made an approach for around 30 per cent of Sugar's shares,' discloses Fordham, 'with the proviso that he and his son would stay on the board. It was all very friendly. The plan was that the consortium would put in more money and raise finances and change the nature of the club.'

The bank duly sent a letter to Sugar outlining their proposals, and the plan was for Littlejohn to talk to Sugar over the following weekend to discuss the prospective deal. The weekend in question, however, was the very weekend that the BSkyB bid for Manchester United was revealed, which drastically altered the picture. 'Sugar may be many things,' says Fordham, 'but he is no fool and he realized that the Sky bid put a premium on all the Premier League clubs, and that whatever premium was added on top of the market-value of his shares in the invitation was completely out of the window. However, instead of saying to Richard or the bank that he was sorry and that the market had changed so the offer was insufficient, he came back incredibly aggressively, very hostile, treating it as a Mickey Mouse bid and claiming he had no interest in selling. It was a complete volte-face. We were stunned by the reaction.'

Anyone present at the Tottenham AGM, on 10 December 1999, would have come away with the impression that bowing to the pressure and baling out was, quite frankly, the very last thing on Alan Sugar's mind. There was a discernible air of disquiet at the start of the meeting stemming from the shortcomings of the side as shown up in the last two League games – a moribund scoreless draw at home to West Ham and an away defeat at Newcastle – but predominantly from the League Cup defeat at the hands of First Division Fulham nine days earlier. Yet within the first five minutes it became abundantly clear that Sugar was totally in control. 'He appeared to be as strong as ever,' confessed Gary Briggs. 'He beat back every negative comment and portrayed the future as being really rosy. The meeting had hardly begun but you could say he was very quickly 3–0 up and it was game over.' After that Sugar could afford to rest on his laurels – and throw out a few barbed one-liners for good measure. In reply to criticism that the TV cameras at White Hart lane were 'too high up', he quipped: 'No, it's your television that's the problem.' Later on, his quick-as-a-flash reply to one elderly lady who reminded him that she had 'paid a lot for my seat' was 'but not as much as I paid for mine', which was both funny and facetious (he does have 'a good sense of humour', which is the first thing David Dein will say in his defence).

Sugar held court for almost the entire meeting, save for a brief speech by Graham and the odd interjection by Pleat. 'He sold us the whole concept,' says Briggs. 'We had our doubts but he made us believe in the whole story. As Spurs fans we have been guilty of living in the past – for me it's always "Bring back 1981". But ten minutes with Alan Sugar and you almost start believing in his vision.'

Almost, but not quite. 'I'm half-way through my life,' acknowledges Briggs, 'and I've not yet had a glimpse of the Championship. There was one season, 1984–85, when I spent three-quarters of the season thinking we had a chance, but it wasn't to be [Tottenham finished third that season having never dropped below fifth place in the table]. As someone whose ancestors always say: "Look at what it was", I want to be able to say, "But look what it is now". I want to be part of a big club, a winning club. As Tottenham fans we keep getting appetizers but seldom a main course and never a dessert, and I don't see the set-up as it is now delivering.'

Of course it does deliver, but not where it really matters. As John Harris points out: 'Sugar's view [that today's players cost and are paid more than is healthy to sustain a business] is absolutely correct. They are millionaires now and how do you motivate millionaires? Historically millionaires were self-made men who motivated themselves; Sugar doesn't need motivation to make money and he wants to pay them by the appearance and by results. The only trouble is that I'm not interested in that view. I want to watch the best football. Now I'm paying £40 a ticket to watch Tottenham Hotspur when I can go to Arsenal and pay a bit less to see better football. It doesn't add up. All I would like is for someone to come along with £100 million and buy him out. I think he would sell for £100 million and then he could say that he bought for £10 million and sold for £100 million. That's fabulous. [Fine in theory, but a prospective purchaser would probably need double the amount in practice because not only would he have to make the same offer to other shareholders but he would also need investment capital and besides, many people have travelled down that road before, only to find the goalposts have been moved by the time they arrived at their destination.] Because what does he get out of it? He's not an enthusiast. I imagine he gets enjoyment from the way the game is going. It's not the excitement of the beautiful game. He would take enjoyment from the fact that a goal was a winning goal, not from the way in which it was scored.' But though it might offend the purists, what Alan Sugar gets out of it is entirely up to him.

So what is it exactly that makes Alan Sugar stick with Tottenham when so much mud is sticking to him? Why does he hang around when he could walk away at any given time having made a nice tidy profit from his original investment? He cannot enjoy sitting in the directors' box at White Hart Lane and having to listen to the fans calling for his head. He cannot enjoy reading in the press that he is the rotten apple in Tottenham's barrel, that he is the one who has been responsible for the last decade being, as TAG put it, 'the bleakest ten years in Spurs's history since World War Two'. He cannot surely go home after yet another dismal performance and tell his wife he's had a good day at the office. He can't get a buzz out of it all, can he?

Ironically, it is probably because he does not appreciate how good it was before that he is unable to realize how bad it is now. He may be cast as the villain, but what does that matter when you are the chairman of Tottenham Hotspur. The reality is that Alan Sugar is fiercely protective of the status he feels he merits. He positively wallows in the recognition that being Tottenham chairman affords him, for as Amstrad's supremo his profile was never this high. 'We could have been up there with the giants,' he said mournfully when Amstrad hit the rocks. Tottenham, on the other hand, buys him respect, for it provides him with a ready-made means of entertaining his friends and business acquaintances. Like the host at the head of a table he can wine them and dine them and then provide them with the ultimate in post-prandial amusement: a game of Premiership football. He is like a rich aristocrat who has purchased this great institution for himself and for his family and one gets the impression that he would, if he could, reflect his involvement in a personal legacy of some sort. 'This company is mine, those are my initials up there and it's going to be around for ever,' he said on launching Amstrad, and his pride stood out a mile. However, the day when football club owners start bastardizing the names of their clubs will be a sorry one on the road to sell-out. The Madejski Stadium and the Doug Ellis Stand are bad enough.

Sugar's is the ultimate rags-to-riches story – from son of an East End tailor to back-of-a-lorry trader to corporate tycoon to knighthood – so perhaps he can be excused for expecting the occasional pat on the back. But what becomes a mogul when money can't buy happiness? After receiving his knighthood for services to the computer industry and education he circulated a memo to the White Hart Lane staff advising them that henceforth he wanted to be addressed as 'Sir Alan' and his wife as 'Lady Sugar'. Sugar was 'tickled pink' to be awarded his honour. He reckons he's worked hard to get this kind of kudos and he's not going to let people forget that in a hurry.

He found it hard to stomach when Venables was getting all the plaudits. 'What about me?' he once reportedly asked, piqued at hearing yet another rendition of 'Terry Venables' blue-and-white army'. This was his club and he called the shots, not the players, not the manager, and not even the directors. 'Why would I want to listen to them,' he scorned, when advised that there might be something to be gained from taking counsel from the likes of Alexiou and Berry, men who had Tottenham in their blood.

Given Sugar's attitude, it was only a matter of time before both Berry and Alexiou were removed from the board in August 1998 (although they remain as club vice-presidents). Claude Littner was also moved sideways from his role of managing director although he remains on the board as a non-executive director (the chairman raised a titter from the audience at the AGM when he inadvertently called for 'Mr Littner's erection'). Although his methods of cutting costs and improving margins sometimes made him a hostage to tabloid headlines there is no doubt that Littner fulfilled his job function of turning Tottenham Hotspur plc into a well-run and extremely profitable business. Moreover, his devotion to duty couldn't be questioned, nor could his fortitude. He shocked his colleagues by the matter-of-fact manner in which he announced at a management meeting that they would not be seeing so much of him in the near future because he was suffering from cancer. They did continue to hear from him, though, as he bombarded them with telephone calls even while he was undergoing chemotherapy.

However, it appeared that as was the case with Alexiou and Berry, the law of diminishing returns had come into play. As Alexiou recalls, 'He [Sugar] relied on Tony and me when he first took over but it got less and less as time went on. For instance, we were very much part of the process of Ossie Ardiles's appointment – I even drove to fetch Ossie and we picked Tony up before driving to Alan Sugar's house – and then were consulted about Gerry Francis, but played no part in Christian Gross's appointment, and we had resigned before George Graham arrived.' Essentially they were Sugarlumps who had served their time. They were dissolved.

Considering that both men incurred the wrath of the anti-Sugar brigade by supporting their chairman against Venables in the High Court, they could be forgiven for bearing a grudge. But Alexiou, for one, is far too diplomatic and dignified for that. Once described as 'class in the boardroom', Alexiou is that rare breed in football – a true patrician. He may have Greek ancestry but he is very much the archetypal English gentleman, the perfect ambassador for a club which in his early days could still justify its place among football's élite. What's more, as a son-in-law of the former Tottenham chairman Sidney Wale – Alexiou's wife Shirley was first taken to White Hart Lane in 1956 – he understood what it meant to be a Tottenham man.

Therefore he considered it a 'privilege' to be invited to join the Tottenham board in June 1980, where he remained for eighteen years. It was an auspicious time. There were seven visits to the Royal Box in fifteen months as Wembley became almost like a second home to Tottenham during the succession of FA Cup and League Cup and Charity Shield appearances. There was the UEFA Cup victory in 1984, and no doubt a tear or two as Coventry upset the odds at Wembley in 1987. In 1991 Alexiou was back at Wembley again, but by then the club was about to change hands. Alexiou felt that it was imperative that Tottenham remained true to itself, and both he and Tony Berry briefed Claude Littner on the philosophy after Littner took over in 1993. 'I have always said,' Alexiou maintains, 'that the most important thing about Tottenham is that we have a soul and I fear that it is easy to lose that soul.' Tottenham, he recalls, 'were always there. You always heard about them, read about them. But now they are not "there" any more. They have under-achieved for a club of that stature.'

There could not be a more marked contrast between the way the club used to conduct itself, and today. Morris Keston recalls his friend Philip Isaacs, a director of Grand Metropolitan Hotels, needing to get back from a European match in the 1970s in Romania in time for a board meeting the following day. Mr Isaacs asked the chairman Sidney Wale if on this one occasion he could return with the directors rather than have to wait for his charter flight a couple of hours later, which would mean missing his meeting. Sidney Wale, who had actually been invited to a number of Grand Met functions by Mr Isaacs, politely refused, saying that he'd just turned down a similar request from Lord Ted Willis (a well-known Tottenham fan and a respected playwright of the time). Rules were rules. Only players and staff were allowed on the official transport. Morris and Philip were disappointed but not surprised. 'You knew where you stood,' said Morris. 'They [the board] kept rigidly to their own code of behaviour.'

It's the same today – except that standards have slipped. You can now pay for the privilege of sitting in the directors' box. And if you are Bill Nicholson you don't even get to sit in the Royal Box or 'the box seats' when the club that you built play at Wembley because you're below the sponsors in the pecking order.

By contrast Douglas Alexiou says: 'I considered that being a director was something to be cherished and used with responsibility. One of the great things was being able to give a bit of magic to people – taking a kid in the dressing room to meet a player or showing them the FA Cup. Not abusing that, for you have to retain a little mystery, but just taking time to make people feel they matter, whether it be the guy on the gate or the laundry lady or whoever. We are all part of the same team and without them that team doesn't function. I saw it as a duty to give and not just to take.' This is not just open-ended rhetoric; Alexiou would regularly drive from his Surrey home to attend functions on behalf of the club – he was even governor of a local primary school for two years – simply because he felt strongly that Tottenham 'should be represented and show that we cared'. During his time as chairman (after Scholar first took over and remained in Monaco for a year) he went to every pre-season friendly and on tour, as well as to all the first- – and many of the youth- and reserve-team – fixtures. 'I like to think,' he says modestly, 'that I made my contribution.'

Back in those days Tottenham were the glamour club of north

London. Arsenal, Alexiou recalls, 'were more dignified, they had this aura about them, but we had the style'. Tottenham were also, according to Alexiou, 'the most hospitable club around', and he recounts endless colourful tales of how the club entertained officials from the opposing team before European fixtures, often taking the trouble of learning whole speeches in their native language just to foster good relations. For Alexiou it was all part of a certain style, the sense that 'a big club should do the little things well'. Therefore it now saddens him that standards have slipped and that others have taken up where Tottenham have left off. He talks from personal experience, too. 'I have a friend, an Arsenal fan [an eminent QC],' he discloses, 'who was celebrating his wedding anniversary recently, so I called David Dein to ask if I could buy a signed ball to give him. Well the ball duly arrived without any prompting from me, along with a shirt which was signed by all the players, with my friend's name on the back, which I hadn't even requested. I thought that was a really considerate gesture.'

It is no wonder then, that Alexiou feels Tottenham 'have a long way to go' before they can recapture former glories, on and off the pitch. 'Do you know,' he remarks, 'I can remember David Dein coming up to me after we won the UEFA Cup, shaking my hand and saying: "Well done." I'm sure he meant it, but he must have felt envious. We were still good in 1987, too, but after that Arsenal went into overdrive and left us behind when they got Graham on board.' The irony is not lost on him, but while he refuses to condemn Graham for his past misdemeanours – he believes that 'if you pay the penalty then you are entitled to another chance' – you can bet your last pound that had either he or Berry been consulted as to whether or not Graham was the right man for the Tottenham job they would have muttered something about square pegs and round holes.

However, this is early 2000 and Graham has moved on up the road (or down, depending on your persuasion). Only trouble is, he's brought his baggage with him. The fact is that Graham can build you a good foundation. He can makes bricks out of straw, but perhaps he cannot build you today's luxury villa with all the latest mod cons because his approach is not flexible enough. Where is the ingenuity? The inventiveness? Ginola, the one player to possess any of these characteristics, has too often been marginalized, while as Pleat says, 'nowadays you can't just have a few players who can compete physically and attritionally. You have to have those who can turn the game, and we have not.'

It is hard to read Graham, for he hides his emotions well. But a man who had free rein at Highbury cannot be happy that the chasing of potential signings at White Hart Lane is done by others, and there have been definite signs that he is disillusioned with the confines of his role, not least that during the second half of the season Tottenham appeared to lack stomach for the fight, which is not a criticism that has previously been levelled at any of Graham's teams. The suspicion is that one of his greatest strengths, his motivational powers, has been weakened by the fact that that he is no longer dealing with errant players but with playboy millionaires who enjoy a profile as high as their managers. And does he not like that? John Harris worries that Graham seems to have 'come up against a brick wall with this particular bunch of players. Whether they have worked something out – they know how to play this guy so he doesn't work – or whether he has lost his drive, I don't know. But something has happened in the last few months and it is just not happening on the field. He says we have lost a lot of games by the odd goal but we shouldn't be losing games by the odd goal. That's what Graham is all about. The one thing he should be doing when he builds from the back and builds a solid team is to inspire those solid teams, as he did at Arsenal and Leeds, to go to places like Wimbledon and wipe the floor with them. Instead it's been one of the worst seasons I can remember.'

While Graham was around, even though he was struggling with arthritis, he at least had the respect – if not the whole-hearted appreciation – of the players. But when Graham went into hospital and Stewart Houston took over, perhaps the temptation to swing a bit of lead was irresistible. As March gave way to April the season petered out in an anti-climax, including two shocking defeats at home against Middlesbrough and Aston Villa. John Harris summed it up as 'a nothing season. They've been busy buying youth players but I'm interested in today.'

Buying youth players, as everyone knows, is David Pleat's bag, but that is not the whole story. The Tottenham fans who disparage

Pleat – and there are plenty of them – would do well to listen to his views on Tottenham and how the game should be played; and reconsider. For Pleat's love affair with Tottenham began back in 1960 when he was an impressionable England Schoolboy footballer who witnessed Nottingham Forest being taught a lesson in the art of football by Bill Nicholson's side, who were to win the Double that season. 'It was their thirteenth game after a winning streak of eleven games [Tottenham hadn't lost a game since the start of the season and had drawn only once, in the League against Manchester City],' Pleat recalls, 'and they were fantastic. The *People* gave every player ten out of ten. I still have the cutting in my scrapbook and I can even remember the goal John White scored, with Baker and Blanchflower playing passes in the six-yard box to get out of trouble. They were footballers, and nothing will ever change my thoughts, which are that football at Tottenham Hotspur is meant to be about entertainment. They may not win everything, or anything, but they have to entertain. Tottenham fans want to see a winning team, or a team that is about style and glory. Tottenham is special, and if you don't believe that then you might as well go and get the most defensive manager in the world. And I hope the chairman also understands that.'

Before Gerry Francis was appointed it looked as if Pleat would get the chance to turn the clock back, but given the opportunity to hire a foreman in his own image, Sugar probably decided Pleat wasn't hard enough to browbeat the workers to his satisfaction. Nevertheless, Sugar had occasion to appreciate Pleat's negotiating skills when he attempted to buy Andy Sinton from Sheffield Wednesday while Pleat was the manager. Pleat told him that '£1 million is not enough, Mr Sugar'. Sugar replied: 'Are you joking? He's on your bench.' But Pleat was adamant. 'Well, I'm telling you,' he retorted, 'you won't get another chance.' Dave Richards, Pleat's chairman, was keen to sell but Pleat told him: 'If it's in Gerry Francis's head that he wants the player, if results don't pick up dramatically they'll come back.' Sure enough they did, and paid £1.5 million. (Pleat must have been particularly pleased because it irked him the way Tottenham were playing under Francis. After the away fixture at White Hart Lane a couple of months earlier, he complained that 'if you wanted to follow the game from the bench you'd have to stand up', being that the ball was in the air for the most part.)

Voicing the opinion of many – just what does David Pleat do for his £300,000-plus salary – Sugar answered a shareholder's question at the AGM that it was precisely because of previous criticism of the lack of football expertise that both David Pleat and Martin Peters were appointed to the board. 'In an environment,' said Sugar, 'where millions are spent on transfers and salaries and on the development of our youth academy, we need people who know what they are doing.' He added the cliché about peanuts and monkeys and claimed that 'the fruition of his work [especially via the academy] will be evident in the ensuing years'.

Today it is Tottenham's good fortune that Pleat is Sugar's conduit between the manager and the players. He makes a point of regularly talking to Sugar, and the importance of the relationship was highlighted by the breakdown in talks with Michael Bridges, a collapse which wasn't helped by Sugar's manner. According to Pleat Bridges was 'a big Spurs fan, he even had pictures of my team from '87 on his wall'. But what were already delicate negotiations to begin with – for family reasons it was always unlikely that Bridges would be coming this far south – were not helped by a few typically blunt remarks along the lines of 'So you're the bloke who's going to cost me all this dosh then?' Perhaps Bridges decided that this was not a man he wanted to play for and he took himself off to Leeds for whom he scored twenty-one goals, a veritable bargain at £5 million. 'Alan didn't realize how highly I rated him,' Pleat says regretfully, his judgement being confirmed by a local contact who remarked: 'Sunderland don't appreciate what they've got.'

There is no doubt that Pleat is conscious of his role, that he respects the fact that there are lines over which he must not tread. 'I keep away from the first team,' he stresses. 'I don't want to be seen to be spying.' Moreover, he is grateful to have been given the chance to return to what he calls his spiritual home after his successful stint as manager was cut short when he pushed the self-destruct button after just one season. With Hoddle and Richard Gough gone, Ray Clemence and Ardiles on the way out and Clive Allen injured, it would have been a difficult act to repeat, and Terry Venables complained about the pieces he had to pick up. Ironically, Pleat points the finger at Scholar's obsession with Terry Venables as the defining factor in his demise. 'I remember we took the team to Spain to play a friendly against Real Madrid,' he recollects, 'and we all went for a meal: Irving, Terry and I. Irving was sitting there eating his Eggs Florentine and he suddenly said: "I never thought I'd see the day when I would be sitting here with Terry, my hero, and David, who I hope and pray does well for Tottenham." It was like hero worship. Terry was always in there. Even four years later when I saw Irving at Wembley for the FA Cup final, he was still talking to me about how clever Venables was. I said to him: "He might even be too clever for you." '

But Pleat is not a bitter man (even though he believes he was treated badly by Sheffield Wednesday, for whom he bought players of the calibre of Benito Carbone and Paolo Di Canio), and he acknowledges that he 'enjoys the job [at Tottenham]'. That does not mean, however, that he is entirely happy with his remit. He has the thankless task of trying to sell the squad players who clearly do not figure in Graham's first-team plans; as he puts it, 'I'm left trying to get rid of the mediocrity that was here before, players who weren't good enough for Tottenham', one or two of whom he was involved in bringing in. Furthermore, for a man whose ultimate job satisfaction lies in his ability to coach, he longs to see Tottenham play in the more expansive style with which they have traditionally been associated and it frustrates him that he cannot do anything about the fact that they do not. 'Some days I am stimulated,' he admits, 'like when we are doing a deal and I can let myself go and impose myself, but other days are just ordinary and without much satisfaction, like on a Saturday when I sit and watch the game and see things, yet I have no control in any shape or form.' You can imagine Pleat sitting in the directors' box and wincing when he sees Tottenham using a throw-in to gain ground, as opposed to switching the play and giving Ginola the opportunity to run at a denuded defence, and being creative. For that is his philosophy. But is it that of his club?

Post Venables, the question was posed: is Alan Sugar the problem or the solution? Years on, and Tottenham fans are none the wiser. Sure, the transfer and wages budget has been increased for 2000–2001 but is it too little too late? And who's ever heard of a successful *menage à trois*, although the continentals seem to manage it easily enough? Over at Highbury there are no such doubts. Everyone there pulls in the same direction to find the answer to the central question: just what will it take to stop Manchester United?

CHAPTER TEN

SHOW ME THE MONEY

There is no better time than the immediate aftermath of victory in which to indulge in a spot of overt back-slapping, and in the minutes following Arsenal's Youth Cup conquest of Coventry at Highbury, one of the club's former stalwarts clearly relished the opportunity to single out for praise those whose respective skills and dedication had realized this particular dream. Brian Marwood, co-commentating on the night for Sky, focused first on the triumphant players, looking every inch the consummate pros as they rejoiced with a lap of honour and extravagant gestures of affection towards the fans (young players copy what their elders and betters do off the pitch, too, and Arsenal's youngsters have had plenty of occasion to observe the seniors in celebratory pose over the years). He then turned his attention to Don Howe and Liam Brady, congratulating them on their past season's endeavours.

Then last but by no means least, Marwood homed in on a dapper-looking figure sitting in the East Stand next to Arsenal's soon-to-retire managing director Ken Friar, conspicuous by the ubiquitous red scarf tucked into the collar of his coat and the look of pure contentment spread across his countenance. There is not much that gives David Dein more pleasure than seeing Arsenal win, at whatever level, and this was his kind of nirvana. 'He deserves a special mention,' stressed Marwood. 'As vice-chairman he's spent many a Saturday morning down at London Colney watching the youth players, and I remember when I was on the playing staff, David was always very supportive; always encouraging the system and putting resources into it. He can take great satisfaction from this victory.'

These are good times generally for David Barry Dein. The club he loves – his wife Barbara has described Arsenal as his 'mistress' – is currently the second best in the country (if they could shake off the Champions' League chip that sits perennially on their shoulder they would be among Europe's élite, too). They can boast – and this is all down to Dein's foresight – one of the most coveted managers in world football, who in turn has assembled a talented squad of players capable of treating their supporters to some of the most attractive and free-flowing football ever witnessed at Highbury (Dein himself says he feels 'blessed' to be able to watch them perform). Furthermore, as a member of both the FA's executive and international committees, and a representative of an exceedingly rare species – an Englishman holding a senior post within UEFA (he sits on the UEFA Competitions Committee, so ironically was among those responsible for sanctioning the ridiculous decision to allow the fallout from the Champions' League, which of course included Arsenal, to enter the UEFA Cup) – his opinions hold great sway; the former Wimbledon owner Sam Hamman has gone so far as to describe him as 'the most influential figure in the modern game'. And of course, with Arsenal's stock currently riding high, he is sitting on a personal fortune of around £20 million which could take a quantum leap if Arsenal were to take on a media partner.

Yet for all his considerable wealth, David Dein could never stand accused of getting into football to make money. While he might possess worldly goods that are beyond the reach of most of Arsenal's supporters, he does share with them a love of the club – a cradle-to-grave affair which began in the late 1940s when, as an impressionable six-year-old he was taken by his uncle to Highbury and had his head turned by a characteristic Tommy Lawton header – which will undoubtedly continue until his dying day. Unlike Alan Sugar, whose marriage with Tottenham was essentially one of convenience, Dein married into Arsenal for love, and that is why the club will always be cherished while he remains one of the family.

For those of a Tottenham persuasion, this contrast with Sugar is a painful one. Both men belong to the new breed of chairmen. They are hard-nosed entrepreneurs who have superseded the old-style custodians and become omnipresent in the modern game. For their predecessors it was all about prestige, a case of keeping it in the family and upholding tradition, a seemingly quaint anachronistic notion – although with maximum wages of £25 per week for the players and decrepit stadia, where did the money go from the thousands who poured through the turnstiles? – but one that Dein is at pains to uphold. He is unquestionably ambitious, but he is also patriotic – a fan of England as well as of Arsenal. Indeed, so appalled was he by England's abysmal performance against Norway in that fateful World Cup qualifying clash in Oslo in 1993 that he urged the FA's international committee to take action to stop the rot, and his eventual realization that the most effective way to get a job done is to do it yourself has pushed him to extend his remit beyond Highbury.

Nevertheless, while at Tottenham under Sugar, two steps forward have been followed by one step back, Dein has moved Arsenal on a pace. Conscious of the past while being alive to contemporary ideas, instead of selling out and cashing in, Arsenal Football Club has retained its heart and its soul.

However, it is the infrastructure as much as the individuals that has kept Arsenal on the straight and narrow. Each of the directors has a specific remit. Richard Carr looks after the youth set-up, Danny Fiszman's responsibility is the new stadium, while Dein oversees team affairs and commercial matters, which means he is the one who liaises on a daily basis with Arsène Wenger. These two share such a healthy working rapport that Dein, as the link between the manager and the board, is more often than not able to present matters such as transfers to the board purely as a rubber-stamping process. That the mechanics of the set-up are invariably well oiled was revealed by Ken Friar's comment that 'we only have five board meetings a year,' to which he added the somewhat cryptic aside '. . . unless there is a crisis, in which case we have four'.

The truth is that Dein had far more in common with Irving Scholar than he has with his successor, which is not to say he has a problem with Alan Sugar. On the contrary he claims they 'get on fine', even though their friendship – which was enhanced by dint of the (now defunct) relationship between Darren Dein and Sugar's daughter Louise – was soured somewhat when Tottenham hired

George Graham. Dein was upset by the appointment, but he is not one for bearing grudges, so he will readily stand up for the Tottenham chairman by claiming that 'whenever someone is successful they are always maligned'. He also admits that Sugar 'makes me laugh', which is a trait Dein values highly, probably because he himself has a nice line in self-deprecating humour manifest in a steady stream of sardonic one-liners and amusing soundbites. Someone who knows him well describes him as a inveterate giggler; or on his better days, as 'the Jerry Seinfeld of football'.

Sugar and Dein are both forceful men but while the former is renowned for his bluntness, the latter shares with Irving Scholar a fan's enthusiasm which is far more becoming in a man of power. The comparisons, however, do not end there. In fact, Dein and Scholar's paths could have crossed in the 1950s when they were both grammar school boys in north-west London and played in the same Sunday youth league. Later, both men were to build up successful businesses, Scholar in the property industry and Dein in commodity trading. However, it was only when they took the same route into football in the early 1980s that they became acquainted, Scholar paying £600,000 for a 25 per cent stake in Tottenham in 1982 and Dein paying around £300,000 for a 14 per cent stake in Arsenal the following year.

Dein was an entrepreneurial teenager with an quick and enquiring mind. He understands the importance of quitting when you are ahead. It was a lesson he learnt as a youth. An acquaintance of his in those days recalls how Dein and his pals would meet occasionally on a weekday evening at the dog track which used to stand on the site which now houses the Brent Cross Shopping Centre. One evening Dein turned up half-way through the proceedings and bet £20 on one race, which yielded him £120. Immediately, he departed, leaving his friends to agree, 'that's the way to gamble'. When Dein's acquaintance learnt, some years later, that he had bought his way on to the Arsenal board he thought Dein had lost his touch.

In 1983 English football was in a mess. Hooliganism was rife, stadia were antiquated, attendances were falling – and the horrors of Heysel were just around the corner. It was hardly a propitious time to choose a football club as a bedfellow, as Peter Hill-Wood noted. 'Some rich men like to buy fast cars, yachts or racehorses, but David is more interested in Arsenal,' Hill-Wood commented when Dein took out his initial stake in the club. 'I'm delighted he is – but I still think he's crazy. To all intents and purposes it's dead money.' However, Dein's unmitigated joy at attaining a position beyond his wildest dreams was highlighted by his wife's description of him at the time. In answer to Irving Scholar's enquiry as to how he was enjoying his new role she said that David was 'like a drunk let loose in a brewery'.

Indeed, the only misgivings he might have had about shacking up with Arsenal concerned not his bank balance, but his background. Arsenal was the preserve of the old school tie, yet here was Dein, the upstart with the working-class roots, muscling his way in to rub noses with the Eton-educated Hill-Wood, whose family connections with Arsenal spanned three generations. Yet unlike Alan Sugar, who makes no bones about his humble origins and has lost none of his rough edges, Dein is guarded about his past and does not take kindly to any reference to his days as an enthusiastic seller of exotic fruit and vegetables in west London's Shepherd's Bush market. However, he has no reason to be bashful, for his entrepreneurial nature was most definitely honed beneath the arches off the Goldhawk Road, enabling him to climb the business ladder into commodity trading and make the fortune that was eventually to help him achieve the ultimate goal of claiming a seat on the board of his favourite football club.

Besides, he needn't have worried. Peter Hill-Wood was happy enough to let him have his head, and after initially finding the transition from fan to director difficult to make – Terry Neill called him 'starry-eyed' and blamed Dein's friendship with some of the players for contributing to his dismissal – it wasn't long before Dein realized, like Irving Scholar, that the big clubs were being held back by the archaic Football League structure. Reform, he reasoned, would not only help Arsenal but the national team as well. A long-time supporter of an eighteen-club top division which he felt would showcase domestic football and at the same time improve the national team, he was initially thwarted in his plans: removed from the executive committee of the Football League for favouring the big clubs in the 1988 ITV television contract and then, after doing a lot of the spade work for the establishment of the Premier League, outmanoeuvred by smaller clubs in both the structure of the new league and the division of powers within it, as well as in the award of the television contract in 1992 to BSkyB rather than ITV, whose cause he had championed. 'David Dein was so over the moon at getting his little Premier League ... he is only now beginning to realize what hit him,' remarked the Chelsea chairman Ken Bates. 'One club, one vote, no committees ... so you had no permanent chance to be in the corridors of power or have committee influence.'

As a result of his company, London and Overseas (Sugar) Ltd, suffering a bad debt in 1993, Dein arranged a management buyout, the company was wound down and he devoted his energies full-time to Arsenal, initially in a non-salaried role. Responsible for the commercial side and the redevelopment of the stadium, including the North Bank Stand (and the much loathed bond scheme whereby bond holders now pay as little as £250 or £300 for their season tickets, which represents exceptional value but obviously only favoured those wealthy enough to afford the upfront payments of more than £1,000), he has watched Arsenal's turnover grow from £15 million in 1993 to £49 million in six years. Arsenal fan Danny Peters says: 'When Dein first arrived it is probably fair to say that a lot of people thought he would be a disaster. I remember someone describing it as the barbarians arriving at the gates. Now you'll hardly find a Gooner with so much as a vaguely bad word to say about him. So he's made some money out of us ... who cares? I'm sure he's as passionate about Arsenal as I am, if not more so. He continues to lead the club with distinction, and anyone who can negotiate a £23 million deal for Anelka can't be bad. Anyway, his foresight got us Wenger. That's surely enough.'

In fact, you can imagine how Dein must inwardly have puffed up with pride on being told by a fan waiting outside Arsenal's training ground at London Colney that he was 'as important as the players'. A father with his young son was among a crowd of supporters waiting patiently to accost whichever player looked like he might be up to signing the odd autograph after his strenuous training session; on seeing Dein draw up, the pair nervously approached him, pen and book outstretched, whereupon an unusually bashful Dein commented: 'You don't really want my autograph.' The son looked nonplussed – one can imagine that the autograph of David Dein would have considerably less cachet in the playground the following morning than that of, say, Dennis Bergkamp – but his father had no hesitation in making Dein's day.

Thanks to the Premier League becoming the greatest show on earth (even if its cast was too large for his liking) Dein could adhere to his beliefs: namely, that Arsenal was first and foremost a football club, and that the creation of a successful football team would open a multitude of beneficial doors. 'Every morning when I look in the mirror to shave,' Dein reveals, 'I see the words written on my forehead: Get a winning team. When you've got that then everything else is comparatively easy. First and foremost fans want a successful team and they will even accept a team that is not playing well but winning. Now we have gone to a different level where not only have we got a successful team but we are probably playing the most attractive football with the most talented group of players I've ever seen.'

However, for a man harbouring Dein's level of ambition, this was never going to be the end of the story. He might have been forced to accept that his influence around the Premier League table was limited but he was not going to let it stop him in his stride. He would simply look for an alternative route and shift the focus of his attentions to some other corridors of power in an attempt to exert some influence on behalf of both Arsenal and England.

It did not take him long to get elected onto the FA's executive committee, or to get a foot in the door at UEFA. In fact, if one discounts Sir Bert Millichip, whose presence within UEFA was to all intents and purposes recognition of an elder statesman, no other Englishman has successfully gone that way recently. Perhaps Dein is now playing a canny game, for how else does one account for Arsenal's non-inclusion in the G14 pressure group formed by the big clubs – among them Real Madrid, Inter, Ajax and Manchester United – to lobby UEFA? Surely, if Dein really wanted Arsenal to have an authoritative voice, then round the G14 summit table was the place to have it? But in order to curry favour among UEFA's powers-that-be he has, of course, to toe the party line, and from there the pieces fall nicely into place. However, Dein has certainly flirted with Super League schemes in the past – indeed, Arsenal were wooed by Media Partners, the Italian sports marketing company, as one of their prime candidates for their breakaway franchise league – so an audacious attempt to run with the hare and the hounds should not be discounted.

Besides, if he has a craving for power then it is for all the right reasons. This is clearly not some ego trip, and to suggest that he might use and abuse Arsenal to further his own ambitions would be way off the mark. Arsenal's vice-chairman kept a deliberately low profile when the club received widespread praise for their 'sporting gesture' of offering to replay the controversial FA Cup tie against Sheffield United in February 1999 (after Overmars's winner had been deemed to contravene the principle of fair play). Dein was quite content to let Arsène Wenger take the credit, despite the fact that it was Dein, vacating his seat the minute the final whistle blew to seek out Wenger, who had actually recommended the course of action to follow. In short, it is the image of Arsenal and not the image of David Dein that comes first.

In the mid-1990s there was intense media speculation regarding Dein's future role at Arsenal after he significantly reduced his share-holding in order to make up a shortfall of millions of pounds created by the London and Overseas bad debt. However, his outstanding criterion was that if he had to effect the intervention of a third party it would be someone who would not threaten the relationship he has with the love of his life.

Enter Danny Fiszman. Ironically, he too was first converted to the cause by an 'uncle' who took him to Highbury as a boy, although in Fiszman's case this uncle was not a blood relation but a 'very dear family friend'. He'd become an acquaintance of the Fiszman family when they were living in Antwerp before emigrating to England ('the Germans entered one way and my family left by another' is how Fiszman describes the process), and this 'uncle' was forever impressing on young Danny when he was growing up in Belgium that there is 'only ever one foreign club: Arsenal'. Fiszman, himself born in Willesden Green in north-west London, was soon a devotee and a regular in the Upper East Stand (he is reluctant to reveal that most of his spectating as a boy was done from a sitting rather than a standing viewpoint, aware that there is a fallacious minority who claim that you cannot be an Arsenal fan unless you've stood on the North Bank for years), a vantage point which afforded him the opportunity to drool over the skills of heroes like Doug Lishman, Jimmy Logie, Danny Clapton and Cliff Holton. 'The noise of him hitting the ball stuck in my memory,' Fiszman admits. He is clearly imbued with a love of the game in its purest form and one gets the impression that he is grateful to have this common denominator that transcends a person's personal circumstances. 'There is something about football that brings all societies together,' he says. 'To be involved in a sport that does that is very special. It's a great equalizer.'

Yet because he is an intensely private person he did not immediately jump at the board's offer to take up an active role in the club. In fact, he says: 'I have been so lucky because I have been on the board during eight years of success and it's been a wonderful time, but it took some months of thought. I wanted to do it because it is every fan's dream but the question was whether I could stand the exposure. I have tried to limit it as much as possible.' He has done a good enough job of that, which is not surprising considering he has experience outside of football of how to keep a low profile. A diamond dealer by trade, Fiszman spends his days in a high-security office in Holborn in central London, which for the unsuspecting visitor smacks of a scene straight out of *1984*. As you enter, with the door closing stealthily behind you, you are confronted by a reception without a receptionist – just a bank of phones and a voice which appears to come out of the ether to request the nature of your visit. Once this has been established and then verified, a revolving lift which will only accommodate one person at a time, which is faintly reassuring after such a protracted ordeal, transports you to your destination. Fiszman claims that 'it's to protect people more than the diamonds', which serves as a reminder of just how much is at stake.

Aside from the diamonds, Fiszman also has considerable investments in property and technology which have rendered him a multimillionaire. Yet despite the wealth, he is not in the slightest ostentatious. In fact, like Douglas Alexiou, his contemporary at Tottenham (they went to the same preparatory and secondary school) he is a gentleman whose refined and civilized demeanour mirrors the image of his club, just as Irving Scholar's engaging and enthusiastic manner once summed up everything that Tottenham should stand for. Fiszman flaunts no rings or medallions, and although he, like Dein, is always nattily dressed, a sports jacket will often suffice on match-days whereas Dein is never without his suit. There is no flash motor, just a comfortable top-of-the-range BMW. He lives in Hampstead and has four grown-up children of his own as well as two step-children. That much we know. But that is as much as he wants us to know.

Fiszman would have to go underground if his profile was any lower, but it would be inaccurate to presume that he has taken one of the back seats on the Arsenal board. On the contrary, he had the unenviable task of calming the muddied waters of the bung affair, and the whole business left a bitter taste in the mouth of a man who has an unwavering sense of right and wrong. 'It was dishonourable,' he states unequivocally. 'I've been saddened by the things George has said and continues to say. With hindsight the board wrongly attempted to protect him as much as possible. I am disappointed he doesn't recognize this.' There's no doubting his bitterness, for he is a relatively placid individual who is not given to excessive shows of emotion. At the time of the scandal Fiszman made a point of keeping his head down and his mouth shut, letting others do the talking – for there were plenty who wanted their two-pennies' worth at the time.

However, one can safely assume that over the course of the next couple of seasons he will have to take several steps out of the shadows, for it is his task to oversee matters relating to the development of Arsenal's new home, which in all probability will be on the site of an old Islington Council rubbish dump at Ashburton Grove, just half-a-mile away from Avenell Road. There is no doubt that a move away from Arsenal's home is the only sensible choice. The only way the club could significantly alter Highbury's infrastructure would be to overhaul the West (and buy the homes that back onto it) and South Stands. Even then the capacity would be increased by just 7,000, at an uneconomical cost of around £40 million, and as Fiszman admits, 'It would only be a compromise.' Given that Old Trafford can now house 60,000 and is soon to be increased to 67,000, and that Arsenal felt compelled to play two seasons' worth of Champions' League fixtures at Wembley in order to accommodate more fans than can fit into Highbury's confined spaces, relocation is the only option.

If Ashburton Grove comes to fruition – Arsenal can submit a planning application in 2000 and if it is accepted they would hope to move into the new premises in time for the start of the 2004–05 season – it will be, promises David Dein, 'an all-singing, all-dancing stadium; the best in Europe'. The planned capacity is 60,000, with facilities for 150 executive boxes, conference and community centres, but mindful of the ordinary supporters, not to mention future generations, it is the club's intention to prioritize family enclosures and offer heavily subsidized tickets in certain areas of the ground. Slipping into each other's duties, Dein says: 'If I have my way there will be 20,000 seats at very reasonable price, no more with inflation than the fans are paying at the moment, but with far superior facilities,' while Fiszman is at pains to stress that 'we will be continuing to build the team whatever happens, that's the number one priority. Nothing can detract from the success of the team.'

It is an understatement to predict that a parting from their historic home is bound to be collectively agonizing for the fans after so long and so eventful an association. If one takes on board what Amy Lawrence maintains, that 'Arsenal is Highbury. Highbury is Arsenal. There is no other,' (although Bernie Kingsley of TISA (Tottenham Independent Supporters Association) puts the other side of the story; 'Arsenal, is Woolwich,' he says. 'They will always be south London immigrants to us'), then it is no wonder that many fans cannot entertain the idea of closing the door on a stadium that has been joined at the hip with the club for the last eighty-seven years. 'To me there is an aura and a beauty about the stadium that cannot be just left behind and re-created by building a plastic spaceship behind King's Cross or anywhere else,' says Greg Lowrie, while Paul Ward is adamant that 'to even think of leaving Highbury behind and all it represents is dicing with death'. For Martin Kearsey, however, the attachment to Highbury has as much to do with what occurs on the pitch as what lies beneath it. 'I know we have to compete, I know we have to move forward and wherever we move to, I'll be there,' he declares, 'but it would break my heart to move from Highbury. I'm not basing this response on my thirty-one years of football memories but the fact that the club gave me permission for my family to bury my dad's ashes by the North Bank goal in between Cup finals in 1993. Somehow it wouldn't be the same with a house on top of it.'

Amidst all the emotion, however, a more pragmatic view emerges, as exemplified by David Jacob, who reveals: 'I was born and brought up within five minutes of the ground. I attended my first game in 1961–62. I still remember my first glimpse of the pitch, how colourful the red and white shirts looked against the green. I still get a thrill entering the ground, or even looking at it from a passing train. Despite all this I favour a move to a new purpose-built stadium. If the board can come up with a magnificent stadium that I can be as proud of as Highbury I would be happy. Even if Highbury was sold for redevelopment that wonderful East Stand and façade would surely be kept in some way. This and the memories would appease me.' Indeed, according to Amy Lawrence the separation process has already begun. 'For a long time,' she admits, 'people had mixed opinions. Of course, the season-ticket holders at Highbury were quite happy; they had an "I'm alright Jack" mentality, whereas those without season tickets couldn't wait. They were demanding, "give us Ashburton Grove tomorrow". But in general now there seems to be an acceptance that Arsenal are in countdown mode. It's like there is a ticking clock to Ashburton Grove.'

Personally, she feels that nothing will ever replace Highbury, and she certainly does not subscribe to the opinion that a new stadium ought to commemorate an Arsenal legend. 'It's all right to name stands after people, but not an entire stadium,' she says. 'Besides, what would the criteria be? You could make a case for Herbert Chapman or Bertie Mee or Arsène Wenger, but how do you know that the best is not yet to come?'

But Amy Lawrence, and thousands like her, would doubtless be aghast to learn that there is more than just a half-chance that Arsenal could be tempted to sell title sponsorship to their new home which could be named, not after a former hero, but after one of the club's commercial partners, for instance one of the world's most famous sportswear manufacturers, Nike. It's a horrifying thought, exacerbated by the fact that Nike's core business is still athletic footwear and American sports like basketball, baseball and the grid-iron version of football. In mitigation, Arsenal would not be the first to take such a heretical step – Middlesbrough (the BT Cellnet

Riverside Stadium), Wigan (the JJB Stadium) and Bolton (the Reebok Stadium) are examples of clubs who have gone down that road already, but for purists these kinds of commercial collaborations are just one more example of a game more concerned with money than tradition, even if the income generated is used to reinforce the team.

Having said that, Arsenal are definitely facing a dilemma. The bottom line is that they will have to find more money than they've ever had to find before – the cost of their new top-notch home is estimated at £150 million – while simultaneously endeavouring to keep up with the Joneses. And because David Dein and co. are not, by training, marketing people (although Ken Friar's replacement, Keith Edelman, worked at Carlton TV and the Storehouse retail group) they might consider that selling the naming rights to the stadium is a new and much-needed revenue stream they cannot possibly ignore, when in fact it would be as misguided as the Oval cricket ground deciding to re-christen itself after an Australian lager. For just as Highbury has been an integral part of what has made Arsenal great over the years, so the new stadium should be an integral part of what will hopefully make the club great in the future, and it cannot fully fulfil that brief if it is called the Nike (or whatever) Stadium. Frankly, having a commercial prefix cheapens a stadium. It's contract football. The club would be mortgaging their future by sacrificing the value of the Arsenal brand.

To Arsenal fans Highbury will 'always be a special hallowed place,' says Danny Peters. 'A palace built from the success and dominance of the teams in the 1930s that showed the power and superiority that is Arsenal. It is where Arsenal won the League in 1953 and 1991, the Fairs Cup in 1970 and the Premiership in 1998. But it is also a physically magnificent ground. It is a fitting tribute that the East Stand is now a listed building. Anyone who goes on the stadium tour and sees this fantastic art deco building knows that it helps define what is Arsenal. The loss of the North Bank terrace was an enormous wrench but the new stand is impressive and a worthy neighbour to the East and West.' Evidently, if a new stadium is to stand any chance of being enthusiastically received, the board should ensure it captures the essence of the club as far as possible. Well, what better way to ensure that happens than to call Arsenal's new home simply: the Highbury Stadium? (The irony is that Arsenal's ground is officially called the Arsenal Stadium, but has come to be referred to as Highbury, just as West Ham's is universally known as Upton Park, which is actually the name of the nearest Underground Station, when its real name is the Boleyn Ground.) Not only would that embrace one of the key virtues of the club's history, but it would also assure a discipline for the future, because the board could surely never be tempted to over-commercialize the stadium if it was so-named?

Danny Fiszman maintains that 'we are conscious that we have to look after the brand', but do he and his colleagues really understand what that entails? If Tottenham can improve their brand simply by going out and purchasing better attacking players, thereby performing in a more entertaining and successful manner, the stakes for Arsenal are higher. The Arsenal brand could be said to deliver a standard of excellence because of the club's tradition and playing record, but is that standard being met? On the field, certainly, but that brings its own problems as expectations are higher year-on-year. Ironically, it is by getting its priorities right and managing well the core business of football that Arsenal has undermined its own brand values. Many more loyal users of the brand are currently being turned away than are accommodated (and those who are have to pay an increasingly high price for their loyalty). Hence the importance of the new stadium, which cannot, however, be built in a day. In the meantime, the brand users who show a level of loyalty any product or service would envy, are feeling let down. On a practical level parts of the stadium such as the Clock End and the video screens, the merchandise and the shops all fail to live up to the highest standards. So Arsenal are poised at the marketing crossroads. The new stadium will give them the opportunity to control their future by managing the brand off the field as competently as Arsène Wenger has done on it. But they will succeed best if they avoid the atmosphere of suspicion that was allowed to develop over the building of the North Stand; a genuine dialogue should be initiated, the fans' needs and wants researched. It would be a shame if a 'them and us' situation prevailed.

Highbury is Arsenal and Arsenal is Highbury. Ashburton Grove should come to be viewed in the same light. Sponsors are partners.

You don't allow them to dictate your brand policy. That means no extraneous naming of the stadium and, perhaps, no sponsor's name on the shirt either. Do BP allow Michelin to put their name on BP's fascia? Do Schweppes let Cadbury's Dairy Milk advertise on their bottles? Like the fascia and the bottle, the shirt is the most salient manifestation of the brand. How much more value, both intrinsically and in monetary terms, would it be worth if it was 100 per cent Arsenal? The board have a clear indication of what the home strip should be and have impressed this upon Nike, perhaps more than some other clubs have done with their supplier. (Nevertheless, if an alien came to Highbury for the first time he would be perplexed as to why the crowd wasn't chanting '1–0 to Dreamcast'.)

The same principles should also apply to a second strip, so why not establish them in line with what the brand stands for? (Arsenal have perpetrated some horrendous away strips over the years.) Similarly, look around the offices, stadium and training ground and there is a clutter of confusing identity. Different colours and even different names and symbols: AFC, Arsenal, the Gunners, the cannon, the shield. The best way to communicate is through a clear identity. How much greater would be the perception of what the club is and what it stands for if there was a consistency of impression? Sadly, like football clubs everywhere the sound of money talking through the vicious circle of wages and transfers equals success equals even higher wages and transfers, has drowned out any thought of a long-term brand strategy.

Arsenal might pull in around £25 million if they sold their soul to someone like Nike, but that is by no means their sole money-making option. They could float Arsenal plc (which, being Ofex listed, is already semi-public) on the Stock Exchange, but this is unlikely, for while it would make the directors seriously rich, none of them need the money. Besides, it would mean them relinquishing control, and that is exactly what they are trying to avoid. Dein and Fiszman enjoy an autonomy that directors at clubs like Tottenham and Manchester United renounced long ago, and that suits them fine, because they believe that they can run Arsenal better than anybody else. And one has to acknowledge that on the evidence of the last five years they are probably right. As journalist Myles Palmer noted after the last AGM in September 1999: 'If the Arsenal board hires a French manager who wants the club to buy some land near St Albans and build a state-of-the-art training ground, they can do it. If it cost £6 million David Dein does not have to consult with a plc board or City investors. He can say: "It is a capital asset, we need a top-quality training ground for our millionaire players and we trust Arsène to produce good young footballers, so let's get on with it." '

However, while the club could afford, in 1998, to spurn the advances of Carlton Communications who made an offer of £200 million plus for the club, they can no longer be so selective. As David Dein admits: 'Perhaps the time is right now to do a deal to make sure the money is there for the future. You've got to do this while you are successful.' In essence Arsenal need to compete with the financial firepower of Manchester United and taking on a media partner would be a way of doing this.

David Dein will no doubt look at Chelsea – who received £40 million from Sky – and adjudge them to have taken the money and run without heeding the long-term implications of a tie-up with a television company. Arsenal reckon that's too close for comfort and they want to keep their distance; that they cannot afford to shack up with any old Tom, Dick or Rupert. As Peter Hill-Wood admitted at the AGM: 'I can confirm that we have had talks with virtually every media company there is but we aren't convinced yet that it is advantageous to the club or its shareholders to pursue any of the proposals that have been made to us. We have an open mind and if an attractive proposition is made to us then we would certainly look at it. But we are not there yet.'

The truth is that Arsenal are not attracted by a broadcaster who might regard the club as just another part of its schedule, simply as viable alternative programming to *The Simpsons* or *The Bill*, ruling on where and when – especially pre- and post-season – they should play, and which channel they should sell their rights to. In fact, what Arsenal really want is to have their cake and eat it, too, for their ideal would be to link up with a company who could offer them invaluable advice and substantial amounts of money (they would hope for around £30–£40 million) but who would refrain from meddling in the club's day-to-day affairs and leave that to its directors. To that end they made an approach earlier this year to Octagon, a subsidiary of the Interpublic advertising group who specialize in negotiating television rights and sponsorship deals and who already have marketing agreements with Brazilian clubs Santos and Atletico Mineiro. They realized that they would not have to worry about any conflict of interests in terms of television rights, which would be the case if they were they to tie up with BSkyB or NTL, or any of the ITV companies.

However, they weren't to know that Octagon had just purchased a 19 per cent stake in Eintracht Frankfurt for £16 million, with an option to take a major interest. It looks like an astute acquisition (even though they inherited a £5 million debt too), given the club's heritage and large fan base (Frankfurt is Germany's sixth-largest city) and its location in what is a major European business centre. There was a touch of bitter irony as far as Arsenal were concerned because Eintracht Frankfurt, who won the German Cup a couple of times in the 1970s and again in the 1980s but not the Bundesliga in recent times, clearly had a great tradition and a great potential – but a recent history of gross under-achievement. Sounds familiar? Well, in essence Octagon had purchased a key role in the German equivalent of Tottenham Hotspur.

So David Dein and Danny Fiszman and the other Arsenal directors will have to think again. But the answer to their problems could be staring at them in the face. Literally. For if the bigwigs at the Premier League in their infinite wisdom had understood the machinations of pay-per-view television then surely they would have made available far more than just the forty live games in the latest rights package? And that would have meant a bumper pay-day for Premiership clubs big and small. 'If the technology allows you, then let the market decide,' says Adam Smith of the media buying company Zenith. 'I can't see what logic would lead you to the argument of restricting ppv to forty games. Every game should be up for grabs.'

As David Dein, who can see the merit in widespread pay-per-view, says: 'We've probably got one million fans around the country who can't see the team and we can only accommodate 38,000 at Highbury, so we've got an unsatiated demand for our product and we want to give our public the opportunity to subscribe for it [ppv] if they want to.' Currently, those fans who cannot get or cannot afford a season ticket at Highbury are at the discretion of Sky and its programming schedule in terms of how many times they get to see Arsenal play live each season. However, if widespread ppv was in operation then all of those excluded fans could watch their team home and away simply by purchasing an electronic ticket. And if half a million punters all paid, say, £10 a time (which would seem a fair enough price for an armchair seat considering it is much less than half the average price of a Highbury ticket) to watch their club home and away then you don't have to be a genius to work out that Arsenal would stand to make a serious amount of money (remembering, of course, that they only own the rights to their home games if there is no longer central negotiation by the Premier League). Moreover, apart from preserving their existing fan base and developing the future one, Arsenal would be spared having to forge commercial collaborations just for the money.

Pay-per-view on such a scale makes sense, but Vic Wakeling has his doubts. Wakeling is a genial Geordie who operates out of a modest office in an industrial estate just off the A4 on the old Heathrow Road, but don't be fooled by the setting. The head of Sky Sports, and arguably the most powerful man in English football, he fears that extending the pay-per-view options would erode football's grassroots support. 'The Premier League are slowly opening it up but if that's as far as they want to go then that's OK,' he declares. 'It's a fine balance because if every club could sell its rights then what would happen is that ourselves and every broadcaster would make a beeline for the big clubs and throw all sorts of money at them and never mind about the rest. Besides, if you suddenly start saying that all these games can be televised then what would that do to the gate? If it starts keeping young fans away then that's attacking football at grass roots level because it's too easy for them to sit at home. If someone's offered the chance of getting a few mates round to watch Manchester United at 3 p.m. on a Saturday for the price of a tenner then he's not going to go and watch Rochdale or Colchester or Torquay, is he? It's a very fine line between television exposure and the health of the game.'

However, Wakeling misses two crucial points. The first is that Rochdale fans, by definition, are primarily interested in watching Rochdale so it matters not one jot to them that Manchester United

or Arsenal or Tottenham are available on some pay-per-view channel for the price of a few pints because they don't want to watch any
old Premiership match in preference to their own team thank-you-
very-much. Football just doesn't work that way. They will be off
down to Spotland at 3 p.m. every other Saturday – except on the
very rare occasions in mid-winter when it might be preferable to
stay in and pay to watch Arsenal play Leeds as opposed to braving
the elements. The European experience shows that ppv doesn't
adversely affect attendances. In France, despite most of the national
team playing abroad, numbers have actually increased since ppv was
introduced, while in Spain and Italy, attendances have followed the
same static trend that has been apparent over the last few years. As
Deloitte & Touche have argued in their report on England's Premier
clubs: 'If anything, all the additional TV exposure has led to higher
attendances. This goes against conventional wisdom – and intuition
– that increased TV coverage must lead to fewer fans going to
games, given that they will now have the option of staying at home
instead . . . Perhaps the conclusion to be drawn from this is that, for
many fans, the television game is a completely different "product"
to the live one, and so, far from cannibalizing each other, broadcast
and gate revenues are symbiotic – they grow together.'

The second point is that a club can only own the rights to its
home games. Wakeling may be right when he says that the broadcasters will target the big clubs, but these clubs also have to play
away, and when they do so they attract potentially as large a television audience as when they are at home. Southampton, for example,
may have limited appeal when Bradford City or Derby County come
to town but Southampton also have to host Manchester United and
Arsenal and Leeds and Liverpool and Chelsea. And because the
supporters of all those clubs who don't have a season ticket and
cannot therefore follow the team in the flesh, would like to be able
to see their team play period, that means a bumper pay-day for
Southampton each time because the real point of pay-per-view is to
access fans who are currently missing out.

Of course the biggest clubs are obviously going to attract the
biggest audiences and therefore the largest slices of revenue, but the
smaller clubs will benefit as well. Instead of getting just a few
moderate appearance fees (£311,000 each time they are transmitted

live) from Sky as they did under the set-up in 1999–2000, Southampton would in addition profit from more and bigger pay-days each time they entertained the Premiership's star turns because ppv is a new revenue source that would supplement not replace the existing 60 live pay fixtures. They might then stand a better chance of living with the big boys without getting bullied, enabling them to pay decent enough wages to hang on to their existing players and also, occasionally, to fork out for the odd star.

Whether the deals are negotiated collectively as they are in France and in Germany, or whether the rights belong to the clubs as they do in Italy and Spain, the home club gets the lion's share of the receipts. (There is even an argument that the intrinsic revenue-sharing principle of ppv is an advance – more democratic – on the current practice of 'live' football which penalizes the small visiting club; all match-day income having been kept by the home club since the mid-1980s, thus depriving the likes of Southampton from getting any financial return from playing to full houses at venues like Old Trafford and Anfield.) The bigger clubs on the continent have regarded ppv as a means of reflecting their market value because the amount of money they generate, which is a lot more than they hitherto received from pay TV, is directly related to the number of people who pay to view them. So though there may be internecine arguments regarding the formula for distributing revenue, the abiding principle of club football is enshrined because the big clubs can't play in a vacuum; they need more opposition to play against than can be supplied by their equals. And anyway, they have to play and beat the lesser mortals in order to remain big and strong. So where there are non-exclusive contracts, as is the case in Italy, Spain and France, broadcasters have had to select both big and small alike to comprise an attractive programme schedule.

However, the Premier League missed the boat in terms of pay-per-view by excluding over 250 fixtures from being broadcast live, in essence treating pay-per-view as an event, which of course it may be for a Mike Tyson fight but is not for the weekly timetable of league football. Pay-per-view should be an integral part of the on-going schedule, just another available option, one more game from the electronic fixture list. And while there is obviously a limit to the number of fans who can fit into a stadium, despite the limited application of cable and satellite, millions can access the game through the small screen. So, not to accommodate the fans is a wasted financial opportunity and a dereliction of duty. The evidence from the continent shows that ppv has tapped a new market of armchair or bar loyalists. The largest revenue generators in Serie A, Juventus, derive 80 per cent of their ppv sales from season tickets for all their games, enabling thousands of their fans to follow their team for the first time live, albeit on television, every week. Far fewer viewers are likely to buy a Premier League season ticket of 40 games when their team is likely to be shown just a handful of times. And as Napoli has proved, Serie B status has not decimated their ppv appeal: the Neapolitan club attained higher revenues than all but a few Serie A clubs. Applied to England, it would be one way of minimizing the disproportionate wealth gap between the Premier League and the Football League, since Manchester City and Wolves, for example, would be able to capitalize on their large supporter base.

And Vic Wakeling knows this. When Sam Chisholm was his boss, ppv was certainly on the agenda and it is arguable that if the entrepreneurial Aussie had remained in his post as a consultant to the Premier League (he was fired with a pay-off of millions because he stood to earn an eight-figure sum from commissions), then through pay TV and ppv every live game might have been available. This scenario would of course have meant two broadcasters sharing an enlarged pay market as the competition authorities would not have permitted a pay monopoly. As it is, by winning a new Premier League contract (which has been extended to sixty-six live matches) Sky maintains its dominant position, with NTL picking up the consolation prize of the forty ppv games after Sky have picked their games.

Those who stand to lose most from this short-sightedness are, as usual, the fans. It is bad enough that admission to Premiership grounds has gone up by leaps and bounds (much more than the rate of inflation since the Premier League was introduced). Now, dedication will be tested to the limit by the fact that Sky have had to fork out £1.1 billion for the three-year contract and will have to pass on the cost to someone, that someone being the football fan. So a price rise in subscriptions looks inevitable, particularly as audiences for Sky Sports live coverage fell by more than 10 per cent over the course of the 1999–2000 season.

Since the summer of 1999 Sky has been giving away set-top boxes with the aim of increasing the number of digital homes and, taken in conjunction with the fact that it is also a programme provider via cable, Sky desperately needed to retain the pay TV contract, for European experience has shown that football (along with movies and video on demand) is the driver for the new pay services. For most of the 1990s Sky had a free run at the UK pay TV market. Now cable has consolidated into two main operators (NTL and Telewest) and ONdigital has entered the scene, all aiming for increased distribution. The answer for all of them is Premier League football. To the victor the spoils. But the intense competition may have pushed up the asking price to an unsustainable level. Like the award of the ITV franchises and the mobile communications licences, Sky may have won the auction but landed itself with the winner's curse.

The amount of money a household is going to pay for television isn't going to change dramatically in real terms as the years go by. Yet Sky have more than doubled the amount they have paid for the live rights to £366 million a season – more than £5.5 million for a live game. NTL have also paid a high amount, £328 million in guaranteed revenues, for the ppv matches. The easiest way for both companies to grow is by attracting new subscribers, but how are they going to do that unless the costs are underwritten? So far as Sky are concerned, with more than 50 per cent of their four million-plus satellite homes converted to digital, putting some or all of the Premier League exclusively on the digital channels with the added interactive facility could be their main edge in a market that is becoming ever more competitive.

With so much money at play in the pay television market, the switch of highlights from the BBC to ITV is almost a side issue, despite being the main news story after the award of the new contracts, which become fully operative in 2001. The fact that ITV paid £61 million a season for a Saturday and Sunday highlights programme, three times the amount of the existing BBC deal, emphasizes, along with the rest of the decisions, that once again money was talking loudest. The sealed bids procedure meant that the Premier League chairman didn't even have a vote and the presentation, history and tradition of *Match of the Day* counted for nothing. Just like Sky and NTL, the top bid won. The television earnings for a Premier League club can now be expected to triple from £8 million to over £25 million, with more to come as the clubs gear themselves to be the beneficiaries of technological changes. And that means yet another round of salary increases for the already obscenely wealthy Premiership players (who according to a recent survey each earn an average of £400,000 a year).

A decade ago Sam Chisholm served notice of Sky's policy – and showed a total lack of appreciation of football's finer points – when he reputedly asked FIFA agent Jon Smith to lobby the world governing body to, as he saw it, up the entertainment value. 'Whatever it takes,' he apparently said to Smith. 'Bigger goals, smaller goalkeepers, shoot-outs. We've got to get rid of these 0–0 draws.' (Sky may have changed the face of football as we know it but the idea that they might have the power to genetically modify a future generation of goalkeepers was beyond even them.) Perhaps Chisholm had been lulled into a false sense of security by the then FIFA president João Havelange's support for similar measures before the 1994 World Cup, in order to encourage the major US networks to broadcast the event. But considering that 'golden goal' is now an accepted part of the game, coupled with the fact that television ratings invariably soar during penalty shoot-outs, one has to wonder just how much life is left in the 0–0 draw?

Thankfully, common sense prevailed and both Sky and the game's governing bodies appear to have realized that they stand to gain more by keeping the faith and eschewing extraneous stunts. But that hasn't prevented Sky frequently having to answer the charge that they don't tell it like it really is, that they hype up matches that are all too obviously dull. Vic Wakeling, though, won't have any of that. 'Anyone who watches Sky closely will appreciate that we are like any set of fans who approach a game with an unashamedly positive attitude,' he says. 'But if it doesn't work out that way then we will admit that at some stage during a game. It's easy to write off a game as rubbish but the viewer expects more, needs someone to explain why it isn't working out on the pitch and our broadcasters will do that.'

'We are a partner of the game,' Wakeling claims, 'not its servant or its master. We are in this together. We want football to be successful. We want big stadiums with big crowds, and unless we work with football to encourage that then we will all miss out.' Yet it is hard to agree with him when television dictates the schedules to such an extent that kick-off times are littered so randomly across the week that pre-planned fixture lists are not worth the paper they are written on. They have also been tempted by technical gadgetry to the detriment of the game's spontaneity. Wakeling accepts this, but only up to a point. 'If you're watching a cracking game then sometimes you just want to sit back and let it happen,' he admits. 'But we have a young audience, many of them kids brought up on gadgets and toys that we can now give them. However, it does worry me that the attention span of this younger viewer isn't what it was and that we are contributing to that. We have to be careful because the most important thing is the match. But what we are doing with the interactive service is marvellous and it will be developed further so that the quality is better. I believe that being able to watch a game from a different angle and view patterns of play without losing the game itself can only help a viewer's soccer education. Since we started we've tried to be at the sharp edge and set the pace every season and we will continue to do that.'

However, despite the Premier League enabling Sky to retain their television pre-eminence, for the first time clubs will be able to flex their individual muscles because of the Internet. From 2001 they will be able to show their own games (home and away) on their own television channels and web sites after a short time period for ppv and pay TV, live and highlights has expired. Although the Premier League will be offering its own web site, this will be the first time their members will be able to control their own league fixtures. For the mega-clubs like Manchester United with a global following, the turnover – not just from recorded action but through the platform thus provided for e-commerce – could increase by 50 per cent.

Yet all such thoughts must have been lodging somewhere in the furthest recesses of David Dein's mind as he meandered down one of Copenhagen's more tranquil streets prior to Arsenal's UEFA Cup final clash with Galatasaray. This was a pretty satisfactory way to be wrapping up what was, in reality, an ultimately frustrating season for Arsenal, and a victory would partially make up for going out of the Champions' League so early, which he has admitted 'hurt a lot'. His anticipatory mood was further lifted when he was confronted by a group of Arsenal fans who, on spotting him, asked whether he would do them the favour of posing for a group picture. Dein may be wary of the media, and avoids personal publicity like the plague, but this was different. This was recognition and respect from his peers, because that's what he is: an Arsenal fan. Luckier than most, certainly, but as Rick Parry, the former chief executive of the Premier League emphasizes: 'He is utterly dedicated to the Arsenal cause.'

CHAPTER ELEVEN
THE WAY WE ARE

As the Spanish referee, Señor López Nieto, blew the whistle on extra time in the first UEFA Cup final of the 21st century, the Arsenal chairman Peter Hill-Wood rose to his feet and, turning to the Galatasaray president, extended his hand. 'Well done,' he said, warmly congratulating his opposite number, who, looking understandably bemused, stuttered: 'What do you mean, "Well done?" We haven't won yet.' At that, Hill-Wood gave a rueful smile. 'Oh yes,' he said, 'but you will win. You'll see. We never win in penalty shoot-outs.'

One could hardly blame Hill-Wood for his fatalism. Ever since that unholy trinity – Italia '90, Euro '96 and France '98 – the penalty shoot-out has become a mental stumbling block for every English football fan, yet Hill-Wood's pessimism was no doubt provoked by a more personal experience, for tortuous failures in penalty shoot-outs clog up the Arsenal fan's memories. In the Cup-Winners' Cup final of 1980 both Liam Brady and Graham Rix missed from the spot to give Valencia the trophy. Then, in 1999, Peter Schmeichel saved Dennis Bergkamp's injury time penalty in the FA Cup semi-final against Manchester United who went on to win the Treble. More recently, during this season Arsenal exited both domestic cup competitions because their players were less successful from twelve yards than the opposition's. Simple as that. First up, Middlesbrough in the League Cup, and never mind that Arsenal had put five without reply past the same opponents just days earlier. This time neither Nelson Vivas, Silvinho nor Matthew Upson found their range – so that was the least desirable piece of silverware out of reach for another season. Then, early in the New Year two dreary stalemates against Leicester City meant that penalties would decide this FA Cup fourth-round tie, and when both Lee Dixon and Gilles Grimandi failed from the spot, bang went Arsenal's chances of another day out at Wembley.

You could hardly say it was a curse, but when substitute Davor Suker and Patrick Vieira both missed their kicks against Galatasaray, Peter Hill-Wood had already prepared himself for the worst. Arsenal had been pre-match favourites, although that probably had as much to do with the fact that they were revisiting the scene of one of their greatest triumphs – it was in the Parken Stadium that they beat Parma in the 1994 Cup-Winners' Cup final – as with their form. Fact: no Turkish club had ever won a European trophy, while Arsenal had the European pedigree. Fact: Arsenal's prospective matchwinner was twenty-two years old and on fire, while Galatasaray's playmaker was thirty-five and supposedly on his last legs. Fact: Galatasaray's entire side cost less than the £7.5 million Arsenal had paid for Dennis Bergkamp. Fiction: Galatasaray had just come along for the ride.

The Arsenal fans' sense of superiority was clear from the chant that rang out during the early exchanges. 'We'll win, cos we're Arsenal', they reasoned, but you can seldom reason where football is concerned and in the event it was more shades of Paris '95 than Copenhagen '94. Then, in the Cup-Winners' Cup final against Real Zaragoza it had been Nayim who had done the damage in the last minute from the half-way line. Well, this time it was another former Tottenham player, Gica Popescu, who did the damage, with the last act of the game (he scored the decisive penalty) but this time from twelve yards. How to kick a dog when it's down.

Galatasaray had obviously done their homework. Coach Fatih Terim's clever tactics of stifling the Arsenal midfield by forcing the play wide, thereby denying Overmars and Henry the throughballs they so eagerly feed on, blunted Arsenal's attacks. Even after a six-of-one, half-a-dozen-of-another tussle between Adams and Hagi had resulted in the Galatasaray player being harshly dismissed in extra time, Arsenal couldn't exploit their numerical advantage. Before the game Adams had said: 'I quite like Hagi. He's a nice enough guy. He was captain of Romania when I captained England for the first time and I've got a framed picture at home of the two captains shaking hands.' After the defeat he must have reflected ruefully on his out-of-character, out-of-place scuffling, a reaction to a frustrating and unfulfilling day.

Yet the UEFA Cup had been rendered a worthless trophy long before the first ball of the final, for the rioting that had cast so many black shadows over the city in the forty-eight hours preceding the match undermined anything that the football might offer. And although the claims of commercialism doubtless took precedent over calls for UEFA to abandon one of their showcase events under such distressing circumstances, this match really was a non-starter.

It was as though the Arsenal fans had decided, early on, that if there was going to be no repeat of the glory night of six years ago then they just wanted to get the game over and done with and get out of Copenhagen as quickly as they had got in (instead of staying in the city a lot of fans, fearing the worst, had spent the previous night in disparate parts of Scandinavia before travelling to Copenhagen, while many more only flew in from England on the morning of the game). The ambience was certainly not a patch on what it had been before the encounter with Parma, when Arsenal's underdogs had just set out to enjoy the party, whatever the result. 'The build-up to the 1994 final,' wrote Stuart Preston in the *Gooner*, 'was probably the Arsenal fans' greatest hour. The reception they gave the team and the sheer noise and colour created by the travelling Gooners dwarfed the Italian contingent and gave everyone such a lift (which was all the more amazing given the usual atmosphere at Highbury).'

The contrast six years on could not have been more marked. The events preceding the Galatasaray–Leeds semi-final first leg in Turkey, when two Leeds fans were stabbed to death, had cast a cloud over the event and many fans stayed at home. In fact, Arsenal fan Alex Phillips believes that the 'poor atmosphere we fans generated during the game was why we lost really. It sounds melodramatic and almost superstitious but I genuinely believe that the crowd effect cannot be understated. We were very quiet. The violence had an effect'. (It did not help that the Arsenal fans struggled to make themselves heard above the Galatasaray supporters, whose numbers had been swelled by dint of Copenhagen's sizeable Turkish immigrant population.)

Ditto the players. 'We had Sky in our rooms,' revealed Martin Keown in his *Daily Telegraph* column, 'and were able to see the pictures of mayhem in the streets. It was sickening. What we witnessed was brutality on a grand scale, poorly managed by the police, ruining it for those paying considerable sums to be there. You can plead with the fans (real fans) not to get involved, urge them to stay away, but they want to be part of the game. But I came into contact with English supporters in Copenhagen wearing England shirts, not Arsenal shirts, who did not greet us in the normal way. We do not want these people. They have no part to play – in our success or failure.'

From Dublin to Marseille to Copenhagen, you can join up the dots and trace a trail of destruction by so-called English fans across the map of Europe. In imagining that the dark ages had been consigned to the past we have clearly been deluding ourselves. Frightful, frightful Copenhagen showed up the flimsiness of that belief.

The Arsenal players were undoubtedly affected by the pre-match hostilities; certainly, they collectively failed to perform on the night. Instead, the occasion was illuminated by Gheorghe Hagi. He and his partner Okan effectively ran the show, never allowing Arsenal's midfield axis of Petit and Vieira to settle. Indeed, Alex Phillips claims that one of the key moments in the game was when Vieira got booked, because 'after that he was treading on eggshells and we lost momentum'. Perhaps, for Arsenal, it was a sense of wrong time, wrong place. After all, the really prestigious event in UEFA's calendar was not due to take place until the following week, in Paris. Through their own inadequacies Arsenal were really just playing for one of the consolation prizes, as Arsène Wenger inadvertently admitted prior to the game. 'Today at a club like Arsenal the UEFA Cup is not enough to give you a complete season,' he maintained. 'The players have a feeling that they must be in the Champions' League. If they are not they feel that they are wasting their time and are not playing at the right level.' Of course, Arsenal's late nine-match unbeaten run in the Premiership – which began with the derby victory at Highbury in March, included a 4–0 trouncing of

Leeds and was prompted by the prolific form of Thierry Henry, who scored nine goals in the run-in – meant that they had pipped Leeds to second place in the Premiership (eighteen points behind Manchester United but, crucially, four points ahead of the Elland Road outfit), so their invite to next season's group stage of the Champions' League was already assured.

That being the case, perhaps they could have been excused for taking their foot off the pedal in the final League game of the season, a 4–2 reverse against Newcastle, especially after the Premier League had refused to allow their match to be brought forward in order to give them an extra day's preparation; the neat symmetry of everyone kicking off at the same time on Sky's last Super Sunday clearly took precedence over giving an English club a better chance to win the second-most-important trophy in Europe. So, when all was said and done, Arsenal's defeat ensured that Tottenham remained the last English side to win the UEFA Cup when they beat Anderlecht in 1984 – on penalties.

Arsenal's players and officials beat a hasty retreat from Copenhagen, and the flight home was understandably subdued. There were definitely no champagne corks popping – and that had nothing to do with Arsenal's more sober approach under Arsène Wenger. Some things, though, never change, and you can be sure that Tony Adams (despite his misgivings over his part in Hagi's red card) did his rounds, encouraging his team-mates to use the defeat for future motivation. But however much the UEFA Cup had been devalued, both by the violence and by the omnipotent Champions' League, no one likes to lose, least of all in a major final. Touchdown at Luton airport could not come quickly enough.

One Arsenal player, however, took a very different route home. It has been well documented that Dennis Bergkamp does not fly. His phobia stems from his days as an Ajax player, when several of the Dutch youth team he played with perished in an air crash, and was compounded by two incidents that occurred while he was with Holland during the World Cup in 1994. First, a security alert caused the plane in which the squad was travelling to be grounded for five hours; then, a Dutch journalist had a mid-air fit en route to Orlando and ran screaming down the aisle. It had a profound effect on Bergkamp, who admits: 'I have a problem and there is nothing I can do about it. It is psychological. I have tried but I just cannot fly. I just freeze up. It's like a mental injury. It's chronic and one I just cannot cure. It's not as it I haven't thought about therapy myself. I've tried everything. But people think there's nothing wrong with me and want to give me a little push to get me on an aeroplane. They get me really angry. Nobody at Arsenal will force me on to a plane or force me to go far away if it means flying. I'll never fly again, not for the rest of my life.'

However, there is no doubt that long, arduous journeys by train or car do take their toll (his fear of flying will obviously rule him out of the 2002 World Cup in Japan and South Korea) and Arsène Wenger faces a conundrum every time Arsenal play away in Europe as he has to decide whether or not to risk packing Bergkamp off with his passport down Europe's motorways and monorails. Ample recovery time at the other end is clearly a prerequisite. After a training session at London Colney on the Friday before Arsenal's Champions' League clash in the Nou Camp, a journalist asked when Bergkamp would be leaving, to which Wenger replied, 'He's left already.' But it is not always enough; against Barcelona and Galatasaray he might just as well have stayed at home.

He has presumably grown accustomed to winding his solitary way back home from overseas fixtures that are not regarded as being out of his orbit, so in that sense the trip back from Copenhagen wouldn't have worried him unduly. He is no social animal, and besides, this was a not too tiring land-and-sea route back from Copenhagen through Germany and from there into Holland and his home city of Amsterdam, where he almost certainly stopped off before continuing the trip back home to England.

But return journeys after a defeat seem interminable, and Bergkamp has probably had better trips. The depressing events of the past twenty-four hours and his own, lacklustre performance doubtless replayed themselves over and over in his mind, so that as late night turned into early morning and 18 May dawned, anyone wishing Dennis Bergkamp a happy thirty-first birthday might have got very short shrift.

The early thirties are a defining time in anyone's life. Somehow, the odd bout of irresponsibility and wild excess are fine when you're still in your twenties, but hit thirty and there's a subtle shift in emphasis that dictates a more sensible and rounded outlook. Those carefree teenage days seem a lifetime ago, while the big 'four-o' is no longer way over the horizon but lurking round the corner.

In the career of a professional footballer, moreover, this is a momentous time, not least because they have such short shelf-lives. A player in his late twenties is usually regarded as being at his peak – Luis Figo, Zinedine Zidane and Edgar Davids are cases in point – but a player in his early thirties? Well, unless he occupies the space between the posts then he'll invariably be talked about in terms that suggest he's seen better days. Paolo Maldini, Marcel Desailly and Fernando Hierro are all still wonderfully accomplished, but Anno Domini is beginning to take hold.

No player is immortal. Not even Dennis Bergkamp, although any football agnostic might have cause to think otherwise given some of the hallowed terms – divine, heavenly, blessed – that are used to describe him (not to mention the proliferation of Arsenal shirts with 'GOD 10' on the back). In *Perfect Pitch*, Hugo Borst writes: 'He is from another world, don't ask me which one, but he is not an inhabitant of the football world. Being different in football is only allowed if you are special. Fortunately he is.'

This was a theme taken up by Nick Hornby in an article he penned for the Dutch magazine *Hard Gras* in which he described the hat-trick Bergkamp scored against Leicester in August 1997 (which earned Bergkamp the unprecedented award of first, second and third in *Match of the Day*'s Goal of the Month competition). 'The first goal,' Hornby recalled, 'was a curving ball from twenty-five yards; the second a direct shot after an impeccable Arsenal move ... but the third. With his back to goal Bergkamp took the ball on one foot, played it round the defender with the other foot and shot it past the defender with ... does Dennis Bergkamp have three feet? Probably not. It only looked that way.'

Bergkamp himself has even fuelled this transcendental image by revealing that he sometimes senses he's being 'guided from above, that everything has been determined'. When he was in such irresistible form in the first half of Arsenal's Double-winning season he admitted to an intuitive, pre-ordained instinct about the way he was playing, almost as if he had no control over his actions. He brings himself back down to earth by insisting that 'I'm fairly human.

When I miss chances, for instance', although he does nothing to dispel the notion of some form of divine intervention by adding that 'at moments like that I think I'm being punished, and the other way around: when I'm lucky, it's a kind of reward or something'.

Nick Hornby may just have imagined that Bergkamp had three legs, but it is no illusory comment to claim that he does have three sides to his make-up. He can be mean, moody and magnificent, the conundrum being which trait will be on display: the spitefulness, the anonymity or the sublime skill. It might be fun to speculate that Bergkamp would probably provide an engrossing challenge for a therapist, and so unpredictable are the behaviour patterns of his three-sided personality, he should insist on a discounted group rate. Moreover, Arsène Wenger, who tends to have a bit of blind spot when acknowledging his players' foibles, has even managed to suggest a fourth side to Bergkamp's personality. 'He is one of the toughest players in the Premiership, a bit like the Björn Borg of football,' claims Wenger. 'They called him the Ice Borg because he never let it show. But to play as he does you must be competitive, you must love the game. And Dennis loves the game. That's what shows his strong feelings to me. Maybe we should call him the Ice Berg' (which begs the question 'why?' as Bergkamp vents his frustration by being spiteful).

Like Glenn Hoddle (whom he idolized as a kid), Marco Van Basten (his mentor, and the player whose mantle he inherited at Ajax) and Liam Brady (the last comparable Arsenal star), Dennis Bergkamp has enough God-given talent to ensure that when he plays and is fully fit and on form, he is a cut above the rest, and that is why so many journeymen defenders resort to foul means to try and stop him, because no other way will work.

He is sleek, muscular, finely tuned, quick off the blocks and blessed with an economy of movement that is apparent in the way he treats the ball. He will caress it, cushion it, juggle it, flick it, drive it and curl it. He will take free-kicks and corners (as he does for the Dutch national team), but he will also probe and provide in open play, as well as being one of the few players who can truly turn a game in an instant with a cushioned trap of the ball, a change of direction and a bending, curling drive that leaves an unsuspecting goalkeeper bemused.

He is no smug clever clogs, but technique is obviously something he ponders deeply. The way in which he will take an interested observer through the motions of a goal, such as the first of that trio against Leicester, is in marked contrast to the ubiquitous 'I've just looked up, seen the keeper off his line and I've hit it' line that is too often forthcoming from less cerebral players. 'I turned inside,' recalled Bergkamp, 'and tried to bend it around the goalie so he couldn't dive for it. There was no backlift. You just face the middle of the movement of the ball with the foot and it gets a curve round the goal. Of course you need a bit of luck but you know exactly that you don't want to curl it so he can touch it, so you curl it really wide. It's just technique. You should be able to do it with your bare feet.' So that's it then. Simple, really.

Technique was not the only thing that was ingrained in him during his years at Ajax. Bergkamp has none of the arrogance of some of his national team-mates (although he has more right than most to be cocky). Instead, he has an in-built self-confidence that was instilled in him by the Ajax system, which nurtures in its young players not only the physical attributes needed at the highest level but the mental strengths too. 'At Ajax,' Bergkamp remarked, 'we are young, we hold our heads up high and we go on to the pitch believing that we are the best … I began here aged eleven thinking only one thing: attack. I also learned of the perpetual competitive environment. Right from the youngest, when a player doesn't make the grade he is asked to leave. So when you stay at Ajax year after year you get the feeling you are the best. And the day you play for the first team you have all this history supporting you. You know that you are the only one to have succeeded when a hundred others have failed. The Ajax players will always have this pride, the drive to always be the best.'

Bergkamp knows, as do those watching, that even if most of the game has passed him by there is always a chance that he will suddenly produce a defence-splitting pass, or pull a twenty-yard chip over the keeper out of his hat. And that is why, when other players would be castigated for their ineffectiveness, Bergkamp will invariably be excused. It is the mark of a truly great player, to be able to dip in and out of a match to such devastating effect. Yet – and there was a time when one would have had to whisper this within earshot of Highbury – Dennis Bergkamp can really be very ordinary indeed. Hugo Borst writes that 'occasionally, Dennis lands on earth', but the reality is that these days he all too often treads the same turf as his less gifted contemporaries. Arsenal's number ten circa 2000 shows only glimpses of his talent. It does not even emerge in dribs and drabs, but rather in short sharp bursts, so that he will be amazingly and memorably effective during the course of one game, then anonymous for the next few. In mitigation, a profusion of calf and groin complaints have taken their toll on him, but the jury stays out progressively longer to deliberate each time he returns after a spell on the sidelines.

Arsène Wenger, however, steadfastly refuses to take off his blinkers so far as Bergkamp is concerned. He waited as long as he could in the Nou Camp before removing him from the fray, obviously holding out for a moment of magic to turn the game. Similarly, in the derby at White Hart Lane in November Wenger kept Davor Suker on the bench in favour of starting with an out-of-sorts Bergkamp. He admits that maybe sometimes he erred in persevering with Bergkamp. Yet knowing 'when you have a super-talented player like Dennis' there is a temptation to go against your better judgement. Besides, appearances, he maintains, can often be deceptive. 'There have been some games when I thought Dennis didn't do a lot, yet when I watched the tapes of the games I noticed that in the two or three moves from which we could have scored, it was always him who was involved. So I thought I couldn't leave him out because we would then lack the final ball. We have a working midfield but for that final ball we rely on only one or two players.' Yet as Arsenal fan Kevin Whitcher says: 'When he does something special that changes the game, sometimes it's the only thing he does. If you don't get that special moment he can be anonymous.'

Actually, there is a case for maintaining that Dennis Bergkamp has always been a sporadic performer. 'The British press,' the writer Simon Kuper notes, 'are always applying the cliché "Dutch Master" to Bergkamp. Well, the most obvious Dutch master is Rembrandt, but he's no Dennis Bergkamp; the *Nightwatch* is a picture you can't miss – giant and imposing. Without doubt Bergkamp is Vermeer, the miniaturist, the man of the tiny brush strokes, the technical perfectionist – and the paintings of Vermeer are as rare as the works of Bergkamp.' (Laterly.)

We do not know how knowledgeable the former Barcelona coach Louis Van Gaal is on the works of Vermeer, but he is certainly better qualified than most to comment on Dennis Bergkamp's career. For it was Van Gaal, whilst coach of Ajax, who supervised Bergkamp's transition to star status (he also brought on Overmars and Kanu). Van Gaal is renowned for pontificating so it was no surprise to hear him say, on the eve of Arsenal's Champions' League clash with Barcelona in the Nou Camp, that 'Dennis is still a fantastic player, but I believe he was better in my team at Ajax. In those days he could make and score goals. In the Ajax system of the time he was top scorer with twenty-five goals a season. Now he doesn't seem to score as many. Why? These days both he and Arsenal seem happy enough that he is more of a creator, a playmaker operating behind the main striker. Now his profit for the club is not as great. And the bottom line of how much you produce is always the most important thing.' (Precisely, which is why Arsenal fans might beg to differ by pointing out that Bergkamp showed his versatility when Wright and Anelka were around to take on the primary striking roles.) Van Gaal rubbed salt in Bergkamp's wound by citing Overmars as the opposition player he would most like to have in his side given the choice (although that may have simply been an indication that he was concerned about the lack of pace down Barcelona's left flank).

But Van Gaal is not the only one who is not blind to Bergkamp's faults. Simon Kuper admits he 'can't head the ball like Alan Shearer ... He's weaker and slower than Ronaldo, less intelligent [a footballer] than Zidane and he misses as many chances as Kluivert. When he's off form the defender just has to push him and he'll fall over, and sometimes, when he's scored a goal from twenty-five yards that the keeper didn't even see coming he'll spend the rest of the game hanging around in the centre circle like an clerk waiting until 6 p.m. when he can leave the office.' Not only that, but his left foot is not half as well educated as his right, as Liam Brady alluded to when he remarked: 'I wish I had his right leg, but I think he'd like to have my left.'

In other words Bergkamp has weaknesses. Even Arsène Wenger thinks so. 'He could improve his heading. He is strong and could use this against defenders in the box. I would like to see him get five or six goals a season with his head but he doesn't like it. He was brought up at Ajax where they did everything on the ground. When you look at the goals he scores they are mainly from outside the area. He scores goals like a midfield player not like a forward.' Bergkamp reluctantly concurs. 'Ian [Wright] is one of the best for having a killer instinct,' he once said of his former striking partner. 'If only I had something like that ...' (His modesty absolves him from the abuse that fans will gleefully dish out to opposition players acknowledged as having a superior talent but a supercilious attitude to match. Admitting one's faults is a very human trait after all, and while Bergkamp's good and he knows he is, he also knows he's not perfect.)

Unfortunately, what he does have in common with Ian Wright is a tendency to transgress. For while he generally keeps his head down and his mind on his football, there is another side to him – he can appear irascible and tetchy – that occasionally surfaces when someone pushes him too far. Then something snaps and the self-control goes.

You would think that being a marked man ought to qualify him for extra protection from referees, but instead he has found himself on the receiving end of more yellow cards than is customary for a front man. Of course he gets his shirt pulled, his ankles clipped and his legs taken from under him. It's an occupational hazard if you are Nureyev on a football pitch (as one Arsenal fan described him) and the rest of them are just jobbing dancers not fit to share the same stage. Besides, you have to sit up and listen when that self-styled hard man of football himself, Vinnie Jones, comes to Bergkamp's defence. 'It's crystal clear that Bergkamp is just not getting the protection he is entitled to from referees,' said Jones, after the striker had received his fifth caution of the season (in his eleventh game) against Crystal Palace in October 1997 for kicking out at his marker. 'If he's had someone kicking his ankles for ninety minutes it's impossible not to retaliate.' However, Bergkamp's propensity for over-reaction is at odds with his skilful image, which only serves to increase its shock value.

The Premiership has probably added a nasty edge to Bergkamp's make-up, but he had mastered the art of giving as good as he gets long before he arrived in England. He says he learnt from Marco van Basten 'how to give out and how to "play" with a defender.

Small things. Hook his foot if the ball's not around. Dirty little things like that which make the guy lose concentration.' Of course, you can get away with sly, underhand tactics when the referee's back is turned but some of Bergkamp's retaliatory measures have been far more in-your-face. Literally. He could say nothing to excuse his flailing elbow after he gave Steve Lomas a bloody mouth at Upton Park in March 1998, even if he did later apologize, maintaining that 'it was just a reaction on my part. He pulled my shirt and I did not realize the consequences until after it happened.'

There was no alibi, either, for the elbow he planted in the face of David Hughes during the game against Southampton in August 1997, although Wenger rather too conveniently overlooked it, claiming instead that 'when he got frustrated and was fouled [Francis Benali indulged in a spot of shirt-pulling to put Bergkamp off his stride] he had the right reaction and finished well. He becomes so determined that nobody can stop him. It is difficult for strikers when they continually get pulled by the shirt and the referee doesn't whistle. Rather than get nasty he shows that he doesn't accept it and he is ready to revolt against it.' However, Bergkamp was lucky to remain on the pitch, subsequently scoring Arsenal's third goal, and his performance in that game perfectly illuminated the Jekyll and Hyde lurking within him.

It was during France '98, however, that Dennis Bergkamp laid himself bare. In the space of a week – from Holland's second round match against Yugoslavia to the quarter-final against Argentina, then on to the crunch semi-final encounter with Brazil – Bergkamp displayed the good, the bad and the ugly (a film, incidentally, that he professes to like) sides of his split personality, cracked open for all to see. First, he carelessly trod on the prone Sinisa Mihajlovic of Yugoslavia, which would have resulted in a red card had the referee spotted it. Then came that goal – the goal of the World Cup. Frankly, football fans have to sit through a good deal of dross but it is moments like the one Bergkamp produced that make it all worthwhile.

Having disposed of Yugoslavia, Holland were pitted against Argentina in the quarter-finals. Twelve minutes in, and Kluivert scores for Holland. Several minutes later, López equalizes. The game ebbs and flows without further score and extra time looks a certainty until, on ninety minutes, Frank De Boer spots a team-mate making a run down the right-hand side and lofts a last-ditch ball sixty yards. It's inch-perfect for Bergkamp, who kills it dead with his first touch, wrongfoots his marker with his second and with his third, bends the ball with the outside of his right foot from the corner of the penalty area round the goalkeeper. At that moment Bergkamp's ice cracks and he wheels away, hands covering his face, sheer unadulterated joy etched across his features. Not only had he won the game for his country but he had also become Holland's leading all-time goalscorer. Talk about doing it in style.

The story did not end there of course. Bergkamp had been mean and magnificent; now cue moody. Three days later Holland faced Brazil in the World Cup semi-final and he was a peripheral figure, unable to exert any influence on the outcome of the game, which Brazil eventually won on penalties. His dispirited display high-lighted his self-imposed handicap: the need to feel 'in the mood' before he can perform like a classical pianist before a recital. But football is a team game where such self-indulgent luxury cannot be tolerated. So while Bergkamp will sometimes go for the easy option when he is not in the mood taking the set pieces rather than taking the game by the scruff of its neck, other players play even better when carrying an injury as it forces them to concentrate on the basic tasks in hand. Fortunately for Bergkamp anonymous displays are quickly forgotten. It is only the gems that remain, vivid in the memory.

Arsène Wenger is a lucky man, for not all incoming managers find their predecessor's players so much to their liking. But in marked contrast to the way in which George Graham has made it clear to Tottenham's talisman David Ginola (who was signed by Gerry Francis) that he will only be accepted if he adapts to Graham's terms, Wenger has made it clear that he will accept Bergkamp even if he plays on his own terms. In fact, the way in which Wenger has compromised in order to accommodate Bergkamp has even annoyed some of the fans, who believe that Wenger's persistence with Bergkamp has been on occasion detri-mental to the team as a whole. 'It's frustrating for me as an Arsenal fan,' admits Kevin Whitcher, 'to see the ritual standing ovation when he is substituted because sometimes he doesn't deserve it.'

Yet he knows why Bergkamp elicits such a response. 'They have a special love for the player because of what he can do.'

Kevin Whitcher's viewpoint in no way suggests that Bergkamp has fallen from grace at Highbury. Bergkamp, it is said, made Arsenal into a beautiful team. He arrived in June 1995, aged twenty-six, thus becoming one of the first players to come to England with his best years still ahead of him, and he was the first truly international-class star to sign for the club in years. 'I can think of no other top European club that has kept this prize from its fans for so long,' reflected Nick Hornby shortly afterwards, 'which is why it had become ever more difficult to describe Arsenal as a top European club.'

They had to wait seven games before he scored, during which time he had to withstand the customary pressure that is heaped on star signings. The *Daily Mirror* was especially vociferous in its criticism, running the headline 'Hartlefool' when he failed to score in the League Cup against the Third Division side and even starting a Bergkamp clock watch. But the Arsenal fans will tell you they knew 'Dennis' (the special place he holds in their affections appears to encourage the familiarity) would come good, even though he had flopped during his time with Internazionale. They had to be patient. He was merely competent in his first season, and during the second flickered only intermittently, scoring a wonder-goal in the FA Cup against Sunderland and a gloriously executed last-minute third in the 3–1 defeat of Tottenham at Highbury when the manner of his celebration – he peeled away and slid to his knees with a rapturous expression on his face – cemented his place in Arsenal's folklore. The real turning point, however, came on a gloriously sunny day in August 1997 when he scored two goals against Southampton: the first, a sweet strike across the keeper; the second a twenty-five-yard drive after he had left two defenders trailing in his wake. Arsenal's assault on the Double had begun, and Bergkamp embarked on a string of performances which earned him both the players' and the football writers' Player of the Year award. Perhaps he had been stung into action by Tony Adams's suggestion that for a man of his ability it was about time he delivered in spades.

When Arsenal fans fantasize about dream teams and players, their ideal performer is surely a composite of Adams and Bergkamp. And maybe, in addition to some of Ian Wright's old rapaciousness in front of goal, perhaps he could be blessed with a smattering of Wright's natural ebullience, too. Because although one has to respect that Bergkamp is naturally introverted, his cool, clinical demeanour means that when he takes his final curtain call he will never (outside Highbury and Holland, at least) receive the encores that have been afforded to Eric Cantona, with his swaggering poise and posturing two-fingers-up-to-the-establishment attitude; or even to David Ginola, who wants everyone to know how much he loves playing football. Bergkamp, on the other hand, invariably wears the expression of a man who is carrying the weight of the world on his shoulders, and often seems pallid and wan. He seldom appears enthused by the game and rarely smiles, so it is not easy to warm to such a self-contained customer. Unless that is you are a fan like Liam Doyle who points out that 'the joy of watching Bergkamp is that of watching a player attempt things others wouldn't. He is so consumed by the seriousness of this task that he has no time for extravagant, extroverted gestures.'

His lifestyle is as about as far removed from the tabloid portrayal of a footballer as it is possible to get. After training, all he has to do is to drive ten minutes from London Colney and he is back in Hadley Wood, where he lives with his wife Henrita and their two young children. Situated between Barnet and Cockfosters in Hertfordshire's green belt, Hadley Wood is certainly not for the impoverished, and although the Bergkamp residence is no mansion, it is definitely large enough to ensure that the likelihood of he and his neighbour exchanging pleasantries while they mow the lawn or dead-head the roses are slim (even slimmer when you consider that one of his neighbours is journalist and self-professed Tottenham fan Richard Littlejohn).

Life was never this sweet in Italy, although with the benefit of hindsight it was obvious that Bergkamp was not cut out for Serie A. High-profile players at Italian clubs are seldom given the benefit of the doubt or the luxury of time. Instead, they are relentlessly hounded and denounced until they come up with the goods and for Bergkamp, who was hailed as the answer to all Inter's problems, the intense scrutiny and the ardent expectation proved too much. Perhaps it even gave him cause to regret turning down Real Madrid when the Spanish club were courting him in 1993.

At Arsenal, though, it was all so very different. Although he was championed as the great white knight on arrival (hardly surprising since his transfer fee was three times the previous club record fee of £2.5 million for Ian Wright), he was shielded from the weight of expectation by the more laid-back approach of the supporters. Summing up the contrast in approach, he said of the habit of both sets of fans to wear shirts with 'GOD' on the back in tribute to him: 'In England there's an irony behind it. In Italy they really believe it.'

Besides, he fits in at Arsenal. Highbury is no goldfish bowl and the fans want him to feel that he belongs as much as they want him to perform, so they will never pester him or hassle him for fear of upsetting his equilibrium. Crucially, however, the love and respect is mutual. Bergkamp signed a four-year contract on arrival and a two-year extension after that, and he shows no signs of wanting to renege on that agreement, which is refreshing in these mercenary times. He speaks about Arsenal as might a fan. 'Arsenal is a way of life,' he says, 'with all those funny, good, bad, strange and illogical traditions about it. Arsenal is Arsenal, and will still be Arsenal when I am dead and gone.' You can sense his contentment by listening to what he says about being 'happy at Arsenal. All I want to do is stay ... coming to Arsenal has resurrected my career.' You can see it too, in his demeanour around the place: an interested observer at Arsenal's training ground might be surprised to see Bergkamp sharing a laugh and a joke with his colleagues, or even gently ribbing the club's press officer Amanda Docherty, because that flies in the face of his introspective image. Bergkamp feels at home at Arsenal and, just as Eric Cantona and Jürgen Klinsmann perfectly fitted Manchester United and Tottenham's bills at the time, so Bergkamp's DNA matches that of Arsenal.

The relationship between Bergkamp and the fans has mirrored a real-life affair. In the early days they were blind to his shortcomings for he possessed everything they had been dreaming of in a player since Liam Brady had dumped them for Juventus – flair, grace and all that skill. (He is, ironically, one of those stars whom George Graham is said to admire: one who prioritizes the team.) As Nick Hornby puts it: 'He's come from afar to perform miracles.' Latterly, however, the first real strains have begun to show. Bergkamp pulled so few of Arsenal's strings in 1999–2000 that Stuart Preston, writing in the *Gooner*, even felt confident enough to suggest (without signing up for extra life insurance) that Arsenal might be better off selling him while he still had a year left to run on his contract. Picking up on the rumour at the time that PSV Eindhoven would like to take Bergkamp back to Holland (possibly in exchange for Ruud van Nistelrooy) Preston admitted that 'in an ideal world I would love us to sign a world-class number nine to play alongside Dennis but there are very few players of that calibre and they all end up in Italy or Spain. Dennis is thirty, van Nistelrooy is twenty-two. We need a centre-forward and we already have Kanu to play in the hole. Dennis gets to go home, PSV get a replacement for van Nistelrooy and we get some cutting edge.' He went on to note that selling Bergkamp would probably be Wenger's 'toughest decision to date'.

Most fans still believe that if Bergkamp is fit then he has to start, but that was so rarely the case in 1999–2000. The statistics show that he lasted ninety minutes just eight times in the Premiership. He scored just six League goals. He underperformed in key games: Barcelona away, Tottenham away, Galatasaray. He was less productive for the team as a whole, and displayed an increasingly unhealthy tendency to become ratty. In fact, his last truly memorable act was the goal against Argentina and that was more than two years ago. In between there was that penalty miss at Villa Park which dashed Bergkamp's hopes of playing in a Wembley FA Cup final (having been absent the previous year through injury), an ambition he had harboured since childhood. Many observers contend that he has not been the same player since, as if he has somehow been dispirited by failing to score.

Perhaps, at this stage in his career, it is asking too much of Bergkamp to expect him to live up continually to his own superlative standards. He has always been the fulcrum of hopes: at Ajax, when Johann Cruyff gave him his debut at sixteen and he had to fill Van Basten's boots; at Inter; and now at Arsenal. And although he fulfilled his golden dreams in his homeland, and subsequently at Highbury, no player can be a spellbinder for ever and it is conceivable that if Bergkamp is not yet past his peak, then he has certainly reached it. He has nearly eighty caps for Holland and a record number of goals, yet Euro 2000 represented his last chance to win silverware at international level, and his place in the national side was under threat until Ruud van Nistelrooy damaged his knee. He won the Cup-Winners' Cup with Ajax and the UEFA Cup with Ajax and Inter, and he's won the Double with Arsenal, but the European Cup continues to elude him and Arsenal must help him to put that right if he is not to remain ultimately unfulfilled.

Yet given Wenger's assessment that a player only reaches his peak in terms of 'mastering all aspects of the game between twenty-nine and thirty-two', then the manager clearly believes there is life left in those lithe legs. 'Of course I want to keep Dennis,' he stated in March 2000, 'and I really don't see any problem with talking to him about it at the end of the season. He still has a year to go [on his contract] so there is no rush. Dennis was playing with a smile on his face on Thursday [during the 5–1 UEFA Cup rout of Deportivo La Coruña] because he is happy when he feels he can perform like he knows he can.' Besides, Wenger understands the real issue. 'How do you find,' he asks rhetorically, 'a player with that level of skill?' How indeed, but Wenger has to decide whether his side can afford to carry its playmaker when he is out of form, for the balance has to be exact and the going perfect for a finely tuned racehorse to run its best. But although Bergkamp may not be the thoroughbred of old, while he still has the pedigree his manager is unlikely to put him out to grass just yet.

It is the ultimate irony, of course, that the fans who now worship the ground Bergkamp plays on could have been bad-mouthing him for getting involved with their greatest rivals. Not only did he follow Tottenham as a boy, but as a treat his parents took him to White Hart Lane where he only had eyes for Glenn Hoddle. So, in 1995, when he was looking for an escape route out of Milan, he asked his agent Rob Jansen to contact Tottenham and ask if they might be interested. Of course, the answer came back: thanks, but no thanks, and a deal was soon struck with Arsenal. But at the eleventh hour Bergkamp allegedly asked Jansen to contact Tottenham again just to make sure that the door to White Hart Lane was definitely closed. When he had finally satisfied himself that this was indeed the case, only then could he give himself whole-heartedly to Arsenal.

It is mystifying that one Tottenham manager could turn down a player of Bergkamp's calibre, just as another could marginalize a player like David Ginola. Ginola has probably done as much for Tottenham as Bergkamp has done for Arsenal, even though for the most part they are as different as chalk and *fromage*. They are both gifted individualists, blessed with the ability to illuminate their particular stage, but while Bergkamp is introverted and low-key, Ginola is extroverted and flamboyant. While you can't miss Ginola, with his flowing locks, Gallic features and infectious smile, Bergkamp is far less conspicuous. And there is one more glaring distinction: Bergkamp gets preferential treatment at Highbury, yet Ginola, the undoubted leading light at White Hart Lane, has all too often been discarded by his manager for a less accomplished understudy.

Witness Old Trafford, in Tottenham's penultimate League game of 1999–2000. Of course the result was largely academic: United had already won the Championship and Tottenham were expected just to make up the numbers, having themselves secured that clichéd position of mid-table mediocrity. But Manchester United offers visiting players the chance to perform in front of a crowd of 61,000, and on this occasion in front of the television cameras too, as this game had been singled out by Sky. You would expect any self-respecting footballer to gear themselves up for this match, let alone a player like Ginola.

So, unaware of the axe hovering over his head, Ginola makes the four-hour trip to Manchester the day before the game with the rest of the Tottenham squad. He stays at the team's hotel, and presumably sleeps well, dreaming, perhaps, of the torrid time he will give Gary Neville down United's right flank. He surfaces on the Saturday morning in his customary good mood and boards the coach to Old Trafford with his colleagues. On arrival he goes out on to the pitch to savour the atmosphere, his adrenalin starting to flow. But it is at this point that the axe finally falls; Stewart Houston, still deputizing for his indisposed boss, informs Ginola that he is not in the starting line-up. *Merde.* It is a shock, but as a substitute at least he stands a chance of playing at some stage. But no; now comes the *coup de grâce*: there is not even a place for him on the Tottenham bench.

For a proud man (Ginola fills up recounting how he was called up to the French national side while a player at unfashionable Brest, and admits that when France won the World Cup 'I thought I was the only one who wasn't happy. I could not believe I wasn't part of the best moment in French history. I should have been there, on the left side'), this was really rubbing his nose in the dirt. 'I am bitterly disappointed,' he said. 'Playing against the best teams brings out the best in me and we all know they don't come any bigger than Manchester United. I always feel I can turn a game. I have to ask myself why the management don't pick me for the big games. Why don't they want me? I am just sorry for the Spurs fans as I was not able to help the team [they lost 3–1].' His agent, Chantal Stanley (whose fiercely protective attitude towards her favourite client has deterred many journalists from bothering to approach him), predictably took up the cudgels on Ginola's behalf. 'David,' she said, 'is very frustrated and cannot understand why he was treated in such a way. Perhaps it was an indication that the club are getting ready to sell him. The simple truth is that his talent is wasted on the bench. He doesn't want to leave Tottenham but a player cannot stay at a club if he is not getting a game.'

Forget all the lame excuses that this match represented the perfect opportunity to assess youngsters in Old Trafford's pressure-cooker atmosphere. Surely, if Houston and Graham (for although absent from Old Trafford he was still ultimately responsible for team selection) had really been intent on following that policy then it would have been consistent to omit Ginola again in the final game of the season, against Sunderland at White Hart Lane the following week – which of course didn't happen because there would have been pandemonium. This, frankly, was a shameful way to treat a senior player; a player, moreover, who during his three seasons at White Hart Lane has been not just the chief creative source – invariably the *only* creative source – but the solitary joy during a particularly insipid time in Tottenham's history. As he says himself: 'When you have players who can create you have to let them do their stuff. This is what gives me the most pleasure in my game because when you look at the game now there is a lot of tactics and most of it is defensive so there are not many paths for creativity and to put pressure on opponents is the main thing for my game. There is a big expectation on my shoulders and I know I have to provide because it is this that makes the fans stand up. If you are sitting and freezing and looking, what you expect is to see something you don't see every weekend.'

Perhaps Graham felt he was justified in his action as in the days preceding the fixture the media had been filled with stories of how Ginola felt he had 'wasted my time at Tottenham'. It made provocative headlines but it simply wasn't the whole story. What Ginola actually said, when asked by Denis Campbell of the *Observer* how fulfilled he felt as a footballer, was that he felt 'frustrated', and then proceeded to explain why. 'To be honest, sometimes I think "I'm thirty-three years old" and looking back the best days are present and future, but when I look at the past – almost fifteen years now I play professional; it's a long time since I began playing in the first team when I was eighteen – and I think about my quality and my skills, what I'm capable of doing on the pitch, I really deserve maybe to play in a really top team. I will not say that Newcastle and Tottenham are not big teams, but when I talk about big teams I mean Milan, Barcelona, Manchester: teams who are playing year in, year out at the top level and playing for the best things [i.e. biggest prizes]. Because I will always have this in my mind, thinking well, if Newcastle had let me go to Barcelona a few years ago when Bobby Robson was the manager over there ... I had him on the phone one day. He called me and said: "I want you in." And the year before Johann Cruyff called me. I went to Barcelona and met him in his house. We played golf together. But we didn't have the Bosman law then so he just needed three [foreign] players to play each Saturday. But he had six. And the club president, Nuñez, and Gaspar [the general manager] told him, "If you want to buy [more] foreigners we need to sell the ones we have. So it was Hagi and Stoichkov. He wanted to get rid of them but could never find a club that would give them the same wages so he kept them and called me and said, "Unfortunately we can't do the deal because Nuñez and Gaspar will not allow me to have seven foreigners in the squad." And this is the kind of feeling I have today, because I know that if I was playing today for four or five years in Barcelona, or a club like that, I would be huge, because I know myself. If I had been in these surroundings to play football, with people who know me, they all know that I am really wasting my talent. My friends all said to me: "David, if you will be in Spain playing for clubs like Barcelona we know you and know that that is the best environment for you, and you will play at the top."'

A player with his gifts, cast out by his national side and substituted so often by his club, would not have been human if he had not felt frustrated. Yet instead of reflecting his frustrations through mediocre performances after taking a couple of months to acclimatize, he shone like a beacon in the gloom that hung over White Hart Lane – and those who claim that it's easy to shine under such circumstances might consider that in a confidence game like football it is equally easy to become extinguished by the all-pervading darkness. Paradoxically, as Tottenham got worse, Ginola got better.

His first campaign (after arriving from Newcastle in a £2 million deal) was the Gross season – Christian, that is – and Ginola carried the side almost single-handedly to the safety of fourteenth place after they had been relegation candidates from the autumn. Jürgen Klinsmann's goals were vital but it was Ginola who kept the flag fluttering, and that against a backdrop of frequent in-fighting between himself, Gross and Klinsmann over his most effective position. The following season Ginola helped Tottenham reach the semi-final of the FA Cup – along the way scoring an outstanding goal against Barnsley that evoked memories of Ricky Villa's effort in the 1981 FA Cup final – and the final of the League Cup, in which they beat Leicester (although Ginola was largely ineffectual at Wembley).

In 1999–2000 he continued on his one-man mission to create – although he stresses that 'I am not playing just to entertain the fans … the most important thing is the result and if I don't have a very good game and it's a positive result for us then it will be fine' – but it has been progressively harder for him to satisfy both the high standards he sets for himself and the fans' expectations of him. Not for Ginola the old *Mastermind* catchphrase, 'I've started, so I'll finish'. On the contrary, he failed to last almost half the games he started. The decision to remove Ginola (and replace him with teenage Matthew Etherington, not long out of the Third Division) against Derby at White Hart Lane in the penultimate home game of the season, with the visitors 1–0 to the good, was too much for one fan to bear. As Ginola trudged off, refusing to shake hands with Stewart Houston (who afterwards patronizingly claimed that 'I would have been surprised if he hadn't shown that kind of reaction, but he took it on board and accepted it. I wouldn't think the decision gives any indication of Ginola's future at Tottenham'), this fan, sitting in the lower West Stand adjacent to the press box and dug-out, was overheard lamenting that 'they take him off when we're winning and take him off when we're losing, yet he's the only person who makes us win and helps us score. Bloody f★★★★★ Gooners.' It mattered little that Stephen Clemence's last-ditch scrambled goal got Graham and Houston out of jail. The damage was already done.

Essentially, Ginola's treatment in the closing weeks of the season was the management reverting to type, although by way of explanation – there was no excuse – Graham had been suffering from chronic arthritis, which probably engendered a Pavlovian response. Of course it is the manager's job to get results and if he believes that using an individual in a particular way is in the best interests of the team he has an obligation to do so. Perhaps it was pointless to expect Graham to change his spots. However, it is a sine qua non of his methods that he has to call the shots, and his treatment of Ginola smacks of an unnecessary attempt to take the one player at White Hart Lane with genuine charisma (according to one Tottenham director the team's only other star, Sol Campbell, is, along with Ginola, the chief butt of Graham's criticism during the first half of games, which the manager invariably spends in the directors' box) down a peg or two. 'David had better get used to the idea that no one is guaranteed to start every time,' he declared. 'More and more the name of the game these days is rotation and it's one we will have to play once we have enough players, so it's unlikely that David will get as many starts next season.'

Graham's answer to those who question his policy is that Ginola started more games during the season than did either Ole Gunnar Solskjaer at Manchester United or Kanu at Arsenal, which is true. But both Alex Ferguson and Arsène Wenger have an embarrassment of riches. Graham, on the other hand, has just one. It is clearly one too many. Ginola is an artist playing among craftsmen. The role Graham wants him to carry out is akin to asking Renoir to paint your walls. Of course he would do a good job, but it would hardly be making the best use of his virtuosity.

Graham could make the counterpoint that Ginola is a liability; it is almost etched on his lips as he stands on the touchline, shaking his head and muttering under his breath every time Ginola loses the ball. 'Especially away from home, I've had to bite my tongue and pull my hair out – which I haven't got much of – and I've substituted David quite a few times, but believe me it's for the good of the team,' he claims, as if that explains everything. 'He does love the game but he still doesn't understand certain aspects of it because he expects other people to win the ball for him and let him do the business on the ball.' But surely the better option would be to give Ginola some help to minimize his defensive deficiencies, while at the same time retaining his attacking capability? If even Gerry Francis, who never prioritized creative ability over teamwork, can appreciate what Ginola can bring to a side, then surely it should not be beyond Graham? 'I think you can always afford one David Ginola type of player,' says Francis, 'who off the ball isn't going to give you a lot but who on it makes everything happen. It's not that he's not physically capable, but that his mind switches off when he loses the ball.'

Graham seems all too ready to focus on the weaker aspects of Ginola's game – he's obviously still drinking from that half-empty glass – a point that is not lost on the player himself. In response to his manager's criticism that 'for his ability David could score more goals', Ginola retorted: 'If one day I score more goals then he will find something else, so you always have to say what is wrong, and look at the weak part of my game. Obviously I should score more goals, but I assist a lot and when you spend most of your time on the side trying to get the ball into the box then you are not there to score. But for the manager you must do everything and I know he wants that from me.'

Given his treatment by the French public – 'Somewhere the people find in me the one who was killing their dream [of going to the World Cup],' he says, 'and at times I thought they wanted to kill me' – it was tantamount to a £2.5 million rescue package that Keegan put together to bring Ginola to Tyneside, where he was an instant hit in Newcastle's team of all talents. In Ginola Keegan discovered a player who embodied everything he loved about the game. Ginola, he says, 'is a unique talent. He reminds me a bit of

Peter Thompson [who played on the wing for Bill Shankly] in that you'd try to get the ball off him in training but it was impossible. He's got tremendous feet, the ability to turn people well on both sides, and can provide quality crosses.' Like Graham, Keegan was surprised by Ginola when he first arrived, but that had more to do with Ginola's gifts than his graft. 'Sometimes, when a foreign player arrives,' Keegan explains, 'they disappoint you, but with David it was the opposite. For weeks I kept pinching myself and saying to Terry McDermott [his assistant]: "Did you see what he just did?" He was even better than I thought he'd be.'

Keegan will admit that 'there are downsides to David Ginola' but he goes on to acknowledge that 'he's got to be a free spirit. I had to ask myself at times whether to play him or leave him out, particularly away from home when I knew teams would be coming at us and putting us under pressure, but I kept coming back to him. I kept seeing him beat people and cross the ball, I didn't see him not quite getting back to cover the full-back. So I tended to lean his way but maybe that's just the kind of person I am.' Keegan's cup, evidently, is full to the brim.

But not George Graham's, and neither Kenny Dalglish's. When Dalglish replaced Keegan at St James's Park Ginola described it as 'one of the worst moments in the last five years for me' (not least because just six months earlier Keegan had blocked an approach from Barcelona on the grounds that they had something good going and the fans would never forgive a parting of the ways). According to Ginola, Dalglish 'was not a sympathetic guy. He was always shouting so it was so difficult to have some kind of understanding if you are just shouting and saying bad things instead of communicating and being happy together.'

He sees football as a means of expression. 'When you feel good in your life and you don't have any worries then you can train well and look forward to games,' he explains. 'Sometimes on the pitch when I do things I look at my friends on the bench and they respond and I'm laughing, because I know this is a game at the end of the day [even an urbane Frenchman cannot avoid using the odd cliché]. It's a bloody game, even with the pressure and the money involved. You have twenty-two players and a ball and you have to fight for the ball but you also have to enjoy yourself. I will not perform on the pitch if I am not enjoying myself.' He attributes this outlook to his child-hood in the South of France. 'It is in my nature always to be smil-ing, to be positive, to arrive every day with a smile on my face. I was born with the sun and the sea, I grew up with these kind of things, so every time I opened my shutters I had a big smile on my face.'

It takes a lot to knock him off his stride and dampen his spirits for he is a naturally ebullient character who is able to appreciate that he has it better than most. That is why he has never sulked on Tottenham's sidelines or spoken out of turn when it would have been all too easy to do so given the media's appetite for pitting a rebel against authority. Instead, he has buckled down and kept on working. 'I don't say anything,' he says, 'and you can see me arriv-ing at the training ground with a big smile on my face because I don't want to affect other players arriving with this sad face every day. I will never arrive at a training ground without smiling, so that people think: "What is going on with David now?"' Like Jürgen Klinsmann before him, he has made an indelible impression at White Hart Lane at every level. 'I've worked very hard to get the love of the fans, and for everyone here,' Ginola says. I'm good to them. I arrive in the morning and I say *"Bonjour, comment ça va"*. I've even taught the cook in the canteen some French so she says *"aujourd'hui, le menu est ..."* and they all smile and that means a lot to me. You bring a positive vibe, which I like. If I can bring a smile to someone's face that's very good.'

Although his detractors will inevitably cite the modelling, the advertising (for L'Oréal and Renault), his chat show appearances and the eleven-page spread in *Hello!* as evidence of a narcissistic nature and other priorities over football, he will have none of that. Clearly riled (which is unusual for him) he says: 'I am working so hard to be an athlete and I will not accept people who come to me and say, "Oh, you are just a showman."' But the lack of appreciation from those whose support he expects, has disappointed him. He was upset when his chairman took some time to call to congratulate him on winning the Double Footballer of the Year award in 1999, not just from a personal standpoint, but because he viewed it as an honour for Tottenham. Sugar's excuse that he had been away cut no ice with Ginola, and he told his chairman so. He certainly feels that 'people don't know my true worth, and I will say when I retire that maybe I didn't get what I really deserve in football. Most of the best players are in the Champions' League and not to be too much of a big head I think that when you work hard you deserve something in life.' However, when Tottenham won the League Cup and Ginola saw how a little success could galvanize everyone connected with the club, he was pleased that he'd played his part. 'You really wish it will be like that every year,' he says.

The realization that he would not be the first talented footballer to end his career without a surfeit of silverware is probably of little consolation, but he does take comfort from being able to recognize that football is not, despite the hype that surrounds him, the be-all-and-end-all. He has his work for the Red Cross anti-landmines campaign which he takes very seriously. He is also a good sport (and it may also be true that he enjoys the show business lifestyle) hence the regular appearances on the chat show circuit and even on entertainment programmes such as *Stars in Their Eyes* (his performance in the guise of his compatriot Sasha Distel, when he attempted to croon his way through one of Distel's hits, must have persuaded him that there are some things he shouldn't repeat). But Ginola admits to a love/hate relationship with fame. On the one hand he can appreciate that he has the power to win friends and influence people, but on the other hand he craves privacy. 'Everything I do,' he acknowledges, 'I have to be careful of my image as a father, football player, husband and person with the badge of the Red Cross. It's like to be a priest. I have to be a saint everywhere I go.'

Paradoxically, he is certainly afforded more privacy in London than was ever the case in Newcastle, where he found the personal intrusions intolerable at times. 'The people are so passionate in Newcastle,' he says, 'and at one stage I was thinking that I didn't belong to myself but that I belonged to them. Even when I had my kid on my shoulders and I was holding my wife's hand they came and pushed to see me and it was hard ... you end up staying at home. But in London they come up and ask for an autograph and that's OK. Even the Arsenal fans are OK. They say, oh I'm Arsenal but I like you very much.' His agent's attempts to keep the whereabouts of his north London house secret has even meant prospective interviewers being led on a wild goose chase around N20 before the exact address is revealed at the very last minute.

For the record, Ginola lives with his wife Coraline, son Andrea and daughter Carla in a house which, were it featured in *Through the Keyhole*, would not readily reveal the occupation of its owner. There are cream leather suites and candles and numerous paintings, giving an overall sense that here is one footballer whose interests might extend beyond his colleagues' more limited horizons. But then, we know that Ginola is not your average footballer. The average footballer, for example, is not blessed with either the wit or the wisdom required to address the Oxford Union (as Ginola did on the dangers presented to English football by the influx of foreign players presumably excluding himself). Yet put his confidence and his charisma aside for a moment and another striking aspect of the out-of-hours Ginola emerges, one which concerns his reaction towards people who, as his agent puts it, are 'trying to get a bit of him'. The response of many celebrities is objectionable self-interest, but in the company of Ginola you really do get the feeling that he is not the only one who matters. He shows an interest in the people he meets, and in what they have to say. He will talk, often beyond the call of duty, to those who are granted access to him at home (his agent's rigorous vetting process keeps the numbers in check) even though he has done this kind of thing many times before, and it is late and he is keen to retire to the kitchen and share the meal that Coraline has prepared. One interviewer even recalls departing with the chant of 'Come on you Spurs' ringing in the air after both Ginola and his wife had said a courteous *au revoir*.

Unlike many of his team-mates, whose reluctance to talk to the media only distances them further from the fans who ultimately sustain them, Ginola seems to understand that he has a duty to give something back to the game that has elevated him to superstar status. At the Football Writers' Dinner at the Royal Lancaster Hotel in 1999 Ginola made a speech in which he acknowledged the importance of the relationship between the players and the press. Before that, he had sat at the top table listening to the after-dinner speaker Jack Charlton, genuinely mesmerized by Charlton's vocabulary and his hold over the audience, and afterwards spent ages chatting to the Chairman of the Football Writers' Association Christopher Davies. When asked later what they had talked about Davies revealed that the topics had ranged from gardening to cricket, which says something about the way in which Ginola has embraced life in England. He gets a huge kick, for instance, out of being able to go up to the golfing heartlands of St Andrews and Turnberry (of course celebrity status and a well-lined pocket facilitate entry to such exclusive courses) and play where immortals like Jack Nicklaus and Tom Watson have played before him. 'Over things like that,' he says, smiling, 'you know, we are big babies.' In fact, he says he's 'proud to be British, by adoption. It feels good to be adopted by another country', although he acknowledges that 'you have to work hard to prove yourself. It's not something that happens just like that.'

The extent to which he feels at home in England does not preclude frequent visits to his French villa, hewn into the rocks high above St-Maxime on the Côte d'Azur where he grew up. 'I like life here [in London] because this is a fantastic city. The opportunities, the quality of life, and on top of it, if you are able to go back to your homeland as much as you can, well there's no point to live in another country. It's not like living eight or nine or ten hours from your home.' However, the constraints placed upon Ginola – and on top-level footballers in general – by an increasingly congested fixture list has left him feeling that he has missed out on valuable family life and that is something he wants to put right, as he puts it, 'in my next life'.

It is not inconceivable that Ginola could follow his compatriot Eric Cantona onto a different kind of stage; several film scripts have come his way but he is not making any hasty decisions. Instead, he appreciates how much hard work he's put into getting where he is, and says: 'When you did a job like football all your life and it was carrying so much emotion, to find something else that's giving you the same kind of emotions is really difficult. So I will not really be able to work in an office or do something like that.'

Retirement, he admits, will be 'a sad moment for me'. But one wonders whether there will be one more stop-off on the footballing map before that moment arrives. It was only a year ago that Ginola was talking about finishing his career at Tottenham. 'I tell you something,' he said, resolutely. 'If Spurs answer me in a good way then I would like to finish my career here. I like Spurs very much, but they have to be honest with me. When you pledge your life for the club they have to answer you in a good way because that's all part of the recognition. Like, "David, we know what you have done, why don't you stay longer?" But even though I might want to stay, it's not just about me. I'm not the only person dependent on me. I've always said that a football club has short memories but there are no short memories for my boy and my daughter. So I've always said that if I cannot have this certainty then I will go straight away.'

If George Graham adheres to his assertion that Ginola can expect only a cameo role in future, then there is a distinct possibility that there will be a parting of the ways, for such a stop-start, bit-part role is surely not the 'certainty' Ginola has in mind. It seems illogical that Tottenham could even consider offloading their one truly gifted performer just at the time when the club's change of policy would appear to signal the arrival of some long overdue quality signings, but then this is not a logical game. For while Alan Sugar might be 'confident with Mr Graham's road map for the way forward', the feeling persists that this manager is driving in the wrong direction and appears unwilling to change his course. His refusal to espouse the Tottenham way smacks of a man who is too set in his ways to come to terms with the changing environment, for a successful team nowadays requires some flair and flamboyance to supplement technical acumen and tactical awareness. It is quite possible that as someone who learnt to navigate his way around football's map in a different era, Graham is unable to appreciate just how far things have moved on. He has certainly been able to steer a direct course along the straightforward boring motorways but appears less adept at deploying the skill required to negotiate the twists and turns of everyday traffic. Changing gear seems beyond him.

As someone who has worked closely with him has observed, 'a man of fifty-five does not watch the game in the same way as he did at forty-five: he does not go to as many games as he used to, nor does he look at as many players'. Frankly if Graham cannot see how much Tottenham need a player like Ginola then perhaps it is time for him to vacate this particular parking lot. Tottenham's history is littered with the memories of players who reflected the club's philosophy, people like Chris Waddle, who as a Marseille player was Ginola's idol. It is faintly ironic that the former Marseille president Bernard Tapie, on purchasing Trevor Steven from Rangers, said of Waddle: 'I'm fed up with dribbling showmen like Waddle. Now he can stay out of the way on the wing'... if only Graham had that in mind for Ginola. Yet Ginola has had more of an impact at White Hart Lane than almost all on his predecessors simply because he is a singular man in the Tottenham side of 2000.

If, or rather when, he goes, the downside – the exaggerated reaction to tackles, the reckless shooting and the drifting out of games – will fade in the memory. But shining bright will be images of the audacious backheels, the shimmies and the feints, the almost gravity-defying balance, the mazy dribbles, the near-endless supply of top-drawer crosses and the spectacular strikes. Moreover, the fans will miss the roar of anticipation that goes up every time Ginola gets on the ball, for he is the one who turns them on, as even his wife acknowledges. 'She was really surprised, and really scared. She told me: "David, the expectation of the crowd is so huge. The ball is playing on the right-hand side and suddenly it is coming to you, the people are responding, they are waiting for something. If you provide something they are cheering."'

Hopefully the cries of 'Geenola, Geenola' will once again accompany the entrance of the most popular player in a lilywhite shirt. Unfortunately, if they are heard to reflect the dismay of his departure or worse, to greet a returning hero wearing opposition colours then such cries will just serve as a reminder of how out of step the management are with the fans.

Whatever Ginola's fate, one thing remains clear: actions will have to speak a great deal louder than words if Tottenham are not merely to mark time next season with the Premiership also-rans. The rumour mill has as usual been running overtime, with one of the most interesting scenarios being based on the initials of Tottenham managers past (Gerry Francis), present (George Graham) and possibly, future (Glenn Hoddle; artistic licence allows one to discount Christian Gross for most fans would like to be able to wipe him from the club's slate). However, like always winning trophies when the year ends in a 'one', and next season ends in 2001, all that remains pure conjecture. But on a realistic level reinforcements must be forthcoming – and they are better late than never – to return the buzz to White Hart Lane.

The route is not straightforward. With Tottenham, it never is. There are many obstacles to overcome before the club can be proud again, and much depends on whether or not David Ginola remains a member of the cast. For whether George Graham likes it or not, there are some traditions, some unwritten rules, which are set in stone. For Ginola is a footballer in the true Tottenham tradition, a throwback to a more romantic age, certainly, but for Tottenham, a more successful one, too.

As far as Arsenal are concerned, well, it's more of the same please. However, with Steve Bould already gone a year and Nigel Winterburn surely on his way out after losing his place to Silvinho, it is finally the end of an era for the legendary defence. Can the survivors shake that Champions' League monkey off their back and graduate to Europe's élite? In order to 'get a winning team' (David Dein's thought for the day, every day) the ante will obviously have to be upped once again and the squad replenished, and how to juggle the needs and ambitions will be the difficult task facing Arsène Wenger et al. Oh, to have their problems, eh, Tottenham?

THE BEST IS YET TO COME?

One can picture David Pleat, the evening before he was due to take Sergei Rebrov on a guided tour of London in an attempt to convince the Ukrainian striker to sign on the dotted line, pouring over his Michelin guide book, meticulously planning his itinerary. Which of London's many tourist attractions Tottenham's director of football eventually plumped for is anyone's guess, although it can't have been too difficult to impress a young man whose previous sightings of the capital had probably been limited to the view from a coach window en route from Heathrow to Wembley.

Perhaps Pleat elected to boost the Millennium Dome's beleaguered coffers, or took Rebrov on a double-decker bus to visit the London Eye or the Tower of London? Madame Tussaud's, though, would certainly have been a home banker. For there Rebrov would have espied waxworks of three of the greatest players in Tottenham's recent history – Paul Gascoigne, Gary Lineker and Jürgen Klinsmann – and Pleat would have had an excuse to wax lyrical on the club's past, and of course the present and future too, which might have proved a little more challenging.

However, it was clearly more what Pleat said to Rebrov than where he took him that had the desired effect. The following day he signed, claiming that the fact that 'Tottenham managed to find a common language with me' had been the key factor in his decision to eschew the chance of daily chinwags over a cappuccino in a picturesque Milanese piazza with his erstwhile team-mate Andrei Shevchenko in favour of a bacon sarnie and a mug of Rosy Lee in a north London greasy spoon with Chris, Les and the lads.

The euphoria surrounding the signing was tinged with a definite sense of bewilderment. For here was a world-class striker joining a mid-table Premiership side. In fact, conjecture had for so long been the name of Tottenham's game in their quest for a new striker that the fanzine *Cock-a-Doodle-Doo* even printed a full list of forwards signed by other Premiership clubs during the two years of their club's futile search (they made it forty-six, just for the record).

Yet here was 'Super Sergei' (as the fans immediately dubbed him; in Kiev he was known as 'The Rescuer' because of his ability to score late goals) pitching up at White Hart Lane having agreed a five-year deal that made him the third-most-expensive player in British transfer history. However, as a fan of English football, the Premiership obviously had the edge over a move to Serie A, where he might run the risk of once again playing in Shevchenko's shadow. Moreover, he must have been hugely impressed with David Pleat's concerted efforts to woo him.

Rebrov's pedigree speaks for itself, but his attitude was doubtless music to his new manager's ears, for he is the personification of a George Graham star. 'I never cared at Dynamo how many goals I scored,' he admits. 'I was working all the time for the team. My philosophy is that football is a collective game, that I should serve the team.' However, just as Rebrov arrived, the club's first truly world-class signing in three years, the last player to fit that description looked set to depart.

Irving Scholar recalls Terry Venables telling him: 'The key is always to try and improve every season, even if it's only by one per cent.' However, with the potential sale of David Ginola, here Tottenham were seemingly taking one step forwards and at least one step backwards again. What's more, just as actions for once looked to be speaking louder than words, then typical Tottenham – they decided Ginola was expendable. If he goes, a replacement will have to be found who can emulate him in providing Rebrov with regular goalscoring opportunities. But surely, as every manager will tell you, all transfers are gambles, so isn't it better the devil you know?

From Tottenham's viewpoint, they were adeptly handling a potentially awkward situation. Graham made out he wanted to keep Ginola, but only for a cameo role, yet if the player refused to accept this snub the club could end up with a nice tidy £1 million profit on a thirty-three-year-old (interested parties had allegedly offered in the region of £3 million) and could then congratulate themselves on having played a good game. In modern football the power lies with the players, but only when the players concerned are highly desirable. This was one situation where the club, not the player, was calling the shots.

Graham's emphasis on the team ethic was manifest in another new signing: the Wimbledon goalkeeper Neil Sullivan, who arrived on a free transfer under the Bosman ruling. However, it was hardly a signing to return the buzz to White Hart Lane. Maybe Ian Walker's form had been variable, yet the goalkeeper is arguably the one position in a side where competition for place is not paramount. The side's other needs – most crucially, for an intelligent playmaker – were far more pressing.

Instead, Tottenham confirmed a perverse interest in Wimbledon players, the latest being full-back Ben Thatcher, which meant that there was a very real prospect of the Wimbledon defence of 1998–99 reuniting at White Hart Lane (Sullivan, Thatcher and Chris Perry). No longer just Wimbledon in disguise then.

It wasn't much of a surprise, therefore, to hear the Arsenal defender Oleg Luzhny suggesting that Rebrov had picked the wrong club, and that he wished his erstwhile team-mate had chosen to come to Highbury. However, Luzhny's chance of still being at Highbury next season appeared slim when he became one of six Arsenal players placed on the transfer list by Arsène Wenger, making a decisive attempt to streamline his squad. Stefan Malz, Nelson Vivas, Christoper Wreh, Alberto Mendez were all put up for sale as well, along with Nigel Winterburn, who was snapped up on a free transfer by West Ham (continuing in their quest to give ageing full-backs a new lease of life), so ending a 13-year association with Highbury.

Following Winterburn to Upton Park was Davor Suker, after just one season in Arsenal's colours. While Suker's sojourn was ultimately a disappointing one his attitude was exemplary. He arrived from Real Madrid as a big-time Charlie, but quickly learnt to stay on his feet and cope with the frustrations of staying on the bench all too often. A player of his calibre would be welcome in most other teams and he should prove to be an astute acquisition for West Ham.

Luzhny, evidently, was deemed surplus to requirements following the arrival of the Cameroon international midfielder Lauren, a £7 million acquisition from Real Mallorca, who had been voted the player of the tournament during the last African Nations Cup and whose versatility afforded Arsenal options in both defence and midfield. Also, to provide insurance cover for the possible departure of players like Petit and Overmars, who were perturbed with Arsenal's inability to come to terms with Champions' League requirements overtures were made to a little known twenty-two-year-old Brazilian midfielder Edu, from Corinthians (Silvinho's former club) and Robert Pires from Marseille.

Winterburn's departure, meanwhile, was no surprise given Silvinho's form during the latter half of the season. Arsenal had offered the veteran defender a one-year extension to his contract but you could hardly blame him for opting to seek the prospect of regular first-team football elsewhere, especially considering that youth team player Ashley Cole, recalled from a loan spell at Crystal Palace, would be also be pressing his claims at left-back. Cole was not the only youngster whose knock on the first-team door was anticipated next season. Striker Graham Barrett had already enjoyed a tiny taste of Premiership action in 1999–2000 and had done his prospects a power of good with his performances in the victorious Youth Cup campaign; similarly midfielder David Noble. In fact, the success of Arsenal's youngsters – as well as the Youth Cup, there was victory for the Under-17 side against Crewe in their Academy League final (although the Under-19s lost to West Ham in their corresponding final) – meant that Arsène Wenger had youthful options in almost every position. One player who would not be a candidate for promotion was the enigmatic Jay Bothroyd. His shirt-throwing after being substituted in the Under-19 final brought a harsh response from Liam Brady, who said: 'We will not tolerate that kind of behaviour at this club,' and Bothroyd was immediately put up for sale. However, his £1 million price-tag hinted that this might just be a frightener both to deter potential buyers and galvanize the player himself. There was to be no rapprochement though and Bothroyd was sent to Coventry.

Regarding the future, both sets of fans had something to get excited about as the new season hurtled into view (the term 'close season' has almost become an anomaly nowadays), even though the two clubs clearly have different priorities. Alongside the growing Wimbledon contingent at White Hart Lane, Tottenham at last had one genuine world-class player on the payroll with the arrival of Rebrov, even if they seemed intent on discarding another. Arsenal, meanwhile, had at least half-a-dozen on theirs. For once, so far as season 2000–01 was concerned, it was shaping up nicely at both ends of north London. Notwithstanding the great divide.